WITHDRAWN

RALLY 'ROUND
THE FLAG, BOYS!

BERKELEY COUNTY LIBRARY
MONCKS CORNER BOYS
CSPEX, SC 10445

RALLY 'ROUND THE FLAG, BOYS!

South Carolina and the Confederate Flag

K. Michael Prince

University of South Carolina Press

© 2004 University of South Carolina

Published in Columbia, South Carolina, by the
University of South Carolina Press

Manufactured in the United States of America

08 07 06 05 04   5 4 3 2 1

Library of Congress Cataloging-in-Publication Data

Prince, K. Michael.
   Rally 'round the flag, boys! : South Carolina and the confederate flag / K. Michael Prince.
      p. cm.
   Includes bibliographical references.
    ISBN 1-57003-527-X (cloth : alk. paper)
    1. Flags—Confederate States of America. 2. Flags—South Carolina. 3. Symbolism in poli-
tics—South Carolina. 4. Political culture—South Carolina. 5. South Carolina—Politics and
government—1951– I. Title.
    CR113.5.P75 2004
    929.9'2—dc22   2003020072

For my family, both those still living and those gone on

6-25-04   34.95   6-C

Father, what is that in the sky
beckoning to me with long finger?
And what does it say to me all the while?

Walt Whitman,
"Song of the Banner at Daybreak" (Drum-Taps)

CONTENTS

ACKNOWLEDGMENTS

Though writing is often considered the loneliest of trades, few books spring forth pure and unaided from an author's mind, like Athena from the head of Zeus. In one way or another, most are ensemble pieces, the result of collaboration, support, and cooperation in a variety of forms, both active and passive. Without the help and backing of many generous people, this book would never have come to be.

Thanks go to John Coski, of the Museum of the Confederacy in Richmond, Virginia, for the direction he graciously offered during the early phases of this project. Thanks also to Patrick McCawley, of the South Carolina Department of Archives and History, for his indispensable aid in providing orientation and advice in searching for state records. My appreciation goes out as well to Allen Roberson and Bonnie Moffat, of the Confederate Relic Room; Allen Riddick, of the Aiken County Historical Association; Edith Butler, of the Union County Historical Foundation; Karen Swager, of the McKissick Museum; and Devereaux Cannon, whose vexillological knowledge was instrumental in helping me better understand some of the finer points about the history of Confederate-era flags.

I would like to express my special gratitude to Carlos Sisco and Matthew Dever, for their thoughts and for the opportunity to bounce some of my ideas off of theirs. Special thanks also go to John Mays, whose own writing helped ignite the spark of inspiration that set my own creative machinery in motion. And an extra special note of gratitude goes to Edwina Campbell, both for her ever perceptive and thorough proofreading and for her abiding encouragement and steadfast friendship.

Finally, there is that unique category of thanks that belong to my parents, for their certain (though sometimes puzzled) support during the writing of this book—and especially to my father, whose work as unofficial lookout, gopher, and all-around go-to-guy has been a big help in handling all sorts of minor essentials crucial to the success of my work. Lastly, thanks to my family for their patient sufferance during all the days, weeks, and months that I've spent pondering, researching, and finally writing this book.

I am much obliged to you all.

MUNICH, 2003

PRELUDE

Their voices tottered up the stairs from the den below:

> "Oh, I wish I was in the land of cotton—
> Old times there are not forgotten"

Thin old-ladies' voices, shaky, cracking and fragile, singing a familiar southern tune, drained now of all its martial air and boisterous dash. Theirs was a version rendered in porcelain, dainty and tinkling like lead crystal and old jewelry. Of all the variations of this song that I had ever heard, this one seemed the most antique, like an heirloom carefully placed atop a circle of lace on a corner table—an ornament of bygone days, past all purpose or remembering. Like some grandmotherly objet d'art, this pale and dusty performance of "Dixie" seemed far removed from the bloody conflict that had made it famous. And as I stood there by the door of my rented upstairs room eavesdropping on this quaint ceremony performed by this small band of superannuated Daughters of the Confederacy, I felt sure I must be witnessing a kind of remnant, a relic of a rapidly vanishing era, soon to fade away and disappear forever.

I was wrong. But it would be several years yet before I would discover just how wrong I was.

It was 1983, and I was studying in Charlottesville, Virginia, after having returned from an extended stay abroad the year before. As with others who spend long periods removed from their native culture, my experience overseas had been as much a time of self-discovery as it was of foreign exploration—a spur to find out who I was and where I came from. No doubt homesickness and a general sense of adolescent alienation played a role in urging me to take a second look at my southern homeland. What led me to seek distant lands would also eventually lead me back home again. But that would all take time.

My journey had begun with a desire typical of many of other restless southerners: the desire to escape the South, to flee from its insularity and parochialism, its suspicious small-mindedness and its backslapping hypocrisy, from its stifling good-ol'-boy conformity, its rock-ribbed sanctimony, and its sometimes brutal intolerance. Or so I perceived it at the time. And so my youthful rebellion had led me to take flight in search of faraway alternatives.

But with distance came a turning. Once out of the South, it became easier to look back without falling into the crabbed defensiveness that distorts all it perceives. More than that, I felt a need to look back, to explore critically the place I came from, and to try and make sense of the past that lent it its special character. I rejected Somerset Maugham's notion that we are bound inescapably by our birthplace, background, and history. But I was beginning to appreciate the significance—and value—of origins.

Alongside the formal education I was receiving, I had begun an informal course of self-study. I started reading histories of the South. And I began to delve into its rich literature, everyone from Thomas Wolfe to Walker Percy, from William Faulkner and Eudora Welty to Shelby Foote, Shirley Ann Grau, Alan Gurganus, and Padgett Powell—anything either by a southerner, set in the South, or which dealt in some way with southern themes. My relationship to the South remained an ambivalent one. I couldn't revel in it or even feel fully part of it—but I nevertheless felt strangely intrigued by it, in much the same way that Mississippian Willie Morris described his own sense of "exile":

> alienated from home yet forever drawn back to it, seeking some form of personal liberty elsewhere yet obsessed with the texture and the complexity of the place from which [I] had departed as few Americans . . . could ever be.[1]

My ramblings along the road to my southern self were still mainly a sideline, however, little more than entertainment. My primary interests were directed abroad, outside and away from the South. But as a castaway, thrown together with others from all parts of America and other parts of the globe, I quickly became aware of what set me apart from others—though my appreciation of those qualities was still too vague for me to define in any detail. By the time I returned from abroad I had reached the point where I was beginning to see both the good and the bad in the South. I had even begun to sense a kind of mourning, a sadness over the disappearance of those elements of an older South that were being cast aside in the rush toward prosperity and modernity or taken under by their association with the South's darker side.

A conscious sense of southernness was settling into my evolving personal identity. At the time of my chance encounter with those elderly matrons of southern heritage, however, the Civil War was for me still largely unexplored territory. Aside from the color and drama of it, that seminal conflict had never really captivated me the way other wars had. Like many boys, I had gone through a period in which I was mesmerized by tales from war. But the war I read about was World War II. Faulkner's dictum no longer rang true for me: Those days that supposedly came for every southern youth, when it is once again that fateful third day at Gettysburg (with all options still open), had now passed. The image seemed outmoded, a remnant—it belonged to that generation of serenading

Confederate daughters. Like them, Confederate sentimentality seemed more a relic, a crumbling and fading vestige from another time.

But there were other fragments, too—other faint echoes of the Civil War. I had attended a high school named after a Confederate general. The school yearbook bore the name of his most famous engagement, and the football team was called "the Generals." A major thoroughfare in town—our main street, really—had also been named in his honor. Even the simple fact of having been born and raised in South Carolina carried with it other traces of a distinctly Confederate heritage. There were shards of family recollections, tales of Sherman's march through the state. And then there was the direct link, the ancestor who'd fought for the southern army—along with the stories (true or not, I can't say) of his long walk back from Virginia at war's end.

As a child, I'm sure I even had my own miniature version of the rebel flag. (And we *did* call it that: "rebel flag.") We weren't particularly rebellious, per se. The flag simply belonged to most kids' (boys,' that is) kit of playthings. It was a useful device for marking territory and playing army. I don't know if this is still the case, but I suspect it isn't. For one thing, the kind of low-end trinket shops that commonly sold rebel flags are not as easy to find as they once were. They have been replaced by perfumed upscale boutiques that market "taste" in the form of mass-produced "collectibles" sold to an upward-striving generation of New Southerners (and similar wanna-bes) afloat on a rising tide of recently attained affluence. Rebel flags find no place in their collections.

Then again, Confederate flags are simply not as innocent as they once seemed to be. Now they are loaded with meaning. To display one is to make a statement (though there is considerable disagreement over precisely what that statement might be). To us children, the rebel flag was little more than a colorful piece of cloth. It held few associations. Sure, we were aware of the flag's special and intrinsic association with the South. We knew about its origins in the Civil War, though our understanding of that conflict was vague at best. But the Civil War lacked appeal. We were growing up in the "Space Age." A foot- and horse-powered nineteenth-century army was just too slow-moving and lacking in firepower to keep up with our warp-speed, phasor-armed imaginations. The coonskin caps of our predecessors had long since been traded in for space helmets and astronaut gear. Our heroes were in the stars, not on the battlefields.

The South had always looked back selectively, but we hardly looked back at all. The last vestiges of an older, traditional South were crumbling away—and to the extent we were aware of it at all, we were wholly indifferent to its passing. The past was a foreign country to most of us. The future was our realm, and we were in a hurry to get to it. So, if our knowledge of the Civil War was muddy, our comprehension of slavery and its legacies was dimmer and hazier still. Perhaps we detected and absorbed our elders' unease with the subject. And there's no doubt their discomfiture was reflected in our school curriculum—especially in our scant exposure to the topic of human slavery. But even if we had been offered more, I doubt we would have been interested. The passive, mostly economic nature of the institution had little in it that could appeal to our bustling, exuberant minds. The mundane images of slavery, of men and women working the fields or even those of people in chains bought and sold on an auction block, were simply not sufficiently compelling to cause us to want to take a closer look. And as for the suffering, the terror, or the moral denigration inherent to the institution of slavery, our sense of compassion and our powers of imagination were too immature and underdeveloped for us to grasp the enormity of it. Slavery was dead and gone, as distant and incomprehensible as the Dark Ages. It had no direct bearing on our lives, as far as we could determine.

But even though our ability to understand the legacies of slavery and the Civil War were limited, those legacies bore down on our lives with ever increasing intensity. For in addition to being children of the "Space Age," we were also children of the Civil Rights Era, and, more importantly, of integration. Battles were being fought around us, over us, and with us of which we were only partially aware. Most of us who were the objects of integration did not come to understand the greater meaning of it until years later. But it is unlikely we would have ever understood the larger significance of integration—the history that had led to it—had we never gone through it at all.

For many of us, integration became both the new norm—and an ideal. My own attitude toward race sprang from a kind of revulsion over the violation of basic notions of justice and fairness—of right and wrong—that played themselves out on the southern stage. That revulsion was not born of either ideological principles or historical insights, however, as may have been the case elsewhere, but was instead a byproduct of a moral sense formed by a very southern religious sensibility. There was perhaps something of youthful rebellion in it, too—though by then "rebellion" was a pretty safe affair, since most of the major events of the Civil Rights Era had already passed into history and most of its leaders had already entered the pantheon of American heroes. So there was nothing in my biography that you could rightfully call a racial or moral "conversion." It just sort of happened *for* me. I, like many others, was pulled along by the tide of the times.

The concept of integration that we gleaned from the lessons of recent southern history was, however, not the only valid interpretation from which to choose. Ideas about what integration meant differed from the start and changed over time. The interpretation of integration that formed in the Civil Rights Era was still bound up with notions about the American "melting pot," with the belief that blacks simply needed to be granted full entry into the white world for all to be made right again. Intuitively we all understood that blacks were not merely "white men in black skins" (one only need read W. J. Cash to see that). But we were nevertheless disappointed when it became clear that most blacks were not going to be satisfied with living "in a world," as W. E. B. Dubois put it, "which yields [the Black] no true self-consciousness, but only lets him see himself through the revelation of the other [White] world." It was only after a lot of hard and sometimes difficult reflection—and through much careful listening—that we began to understand that we still had some distance to travel.

This is, in large measure, what the Confederate flag debate in South Carolina was all about: coming to terms with newer forms of integration. The conflict was only superficially about the flag itself, though the flag was certainly the central symbol at contention. And the conflict could be considered the "last battle of the Civil War" only in the sense in which the Civil War itself was a symbol for America's broader struggle over race. The "new integrationism" (as you might call it: the next phase of integration) involves finding commonalities—locating mutual interests where possible and agreeing to disagree where necessary. The process of working through this was what occupied South Carolina for over a decade.

In February 1997, more than three years before passage of the compromise that brought the Confederate flag down from the dome of the State House, an editorial writer for *The State* newspaper in Columbia addressed the crux of the matter: "The victory for all South Carolinians," he wrote, "would not lie in the physical act of moving the banner itself but rather in the process of agreeing to do so."[2] In this case, agreement equaled integration: the integration of differing perspectives into a commonly accepted whole. That process was long and arduous. And in the end, the flag compromise plan that passed the South Carolina legislature was as much an agreement to disagree as it was an attempt at mutual accommodation (or a new condominium). The process could have been conducted more constructively and purposefully perhaps, but the exercise lacked neither purpose nor worth. The racial battles of the past were undoubtedly more momentous. By contrast, many of our moral struggles nowadays are really little more than moralistic campaigns conducted on virtual battlefields of mere symbolic significance. But that does not mean that the flag debate was devoid of function or meaning—though more could have been (and may yet be) achieved. No new consensus was attained—certainly nothing of any depth. But there were hopeful hints of a slowly developing understanding.

As in the past, it was the white population that had the most to learn, the farthest distance to go. There was little, if anything, new that most blacks could have learned from the debate—just the same old patterns of white resistance. Whites, on the other hand, had the opportunity to take another look at their history, to examine their collective past, and to try and come to grips with the distinction between heritage and history. In the end, it was our appreciation and interpretations of the past that stood at issue.

In his 1938 novel, *The Fathers,* native Kentuckian and southern agrarian Allen Tate made the following observation about the problematical relationship of memory and history to the objects and symbols we choose to embody them:

... there is not an old man living who can recover the emotions of the past; he can only bring back the objects around which ... the emotions have ordered themselves in memory, and that memory is not what happened in the year 1860 but is rather a few symbols, a voice, a tree, a gun shining on the wall—symbols that will preserve only so much of the old life as they may, in their own mysterious history, consent to bear.[3]

Memory is a strangely transmutable substance. It has no perfect state. We are not simply vessels conveying purest memory untainted to the next generation. Our mere touch alters the inner structure of historical memory, sometimes mellowing it, like oak casks to the refinement of wine, at other times souring it like vinegar. History is a repository of hard facts, standing coldly apart from us. But heritage is intimate, personal—and, as such, is infinitely malleable and bends to our innermost ardent wishes. How we remember the past—how we memorialize it—reflects how we see ourselves and what we wish to be. What we recall we do for our own sakes, not for those already gone. The dead are past caring. The Confederate flag flew (and continues to fly, in places) because there is something in it we think we need—for good or ill. To many the flag brings to mind our Thermopylae, what we have come to think of as our almost mythic defining moment. We relish both the roaring spectacle and the grand tragedy of it. Sometimes we may find ourselves falling too much in love with it. It would do us well to try and determine why that is.

Although this book is focused exclusively on South Carolina's long battle over the Confederate flag, the issues it raises are more general in nature. While South Carolina was the only remaining state where the Confederate flag flew in such a singularly conspicuous fashion, it is by no means the only place where the dispute over Confederate symbols has ignited. The Confederate flag atop the South Carolina State House became a cause célèbre because it represented a kind of first among equals: It was the preeminent display of a flag that flew in numerous other locales and settings around the country, many of which were themselves objects of controversies large and small. The rebel banner in South Carolina led them all. It served as the principal element in a broad color guard of Confederate symbols, a high watermark of the South's Confederate heritage, and a restatement in cloth of John C. Calhoun's strategy of defense at the outermost margins of principle.

The South has been called a "history-haunted" landscape. It is still a place, as Abram Joseph Ryan put it in his poem "The South," "where the battles' red blast / Has flashed on the future / The form of the past," a land "That hath legends and lays / That tell of the memories / Of long-vanished days." In the South, the past still intrudes on the present in uncanny and sometimes fantastic ways. Some of this is fading now. And, to a degree, that is regrettable. But it is good that we not allow ourselves to be ruled by nostalgia, that we not "set up the grave in the house," as Tate warned—"the ravenous grave" that has devoured so many southern futures in vainglorious pursuit of a chimerical past.

Dixieland refuses to just look away. But when it looks at itself, it should do more than simply bathe in the glow of its own self-reflection. It should, instead, seek to bear witness to the simple wisdom and grace contained in the words,

> *Was blind,*
> *But now I see.*

One

DIXIE'S CONQUERED BANNERS

Our Dixie forever, she's never at a loss,
Down with the Eagle and up with the Cross,
And we'll rally 'round the flag, boys,
We'll rally once again,
Shouting the battle cry of freedom

Henry H. Barnes,
"Southern Battle Cry of Freedom"

It fell . . . but stainless as it rose,
Martyred, like Stephen, in the strife—
Passing, like him, girded with foes
From death to Life.

Henry Lyndon Flack,
"The Confederate Flag"

Flags. What is it about them that captivates us so? Essentially a flag is nothing but a piece of cloth, dyed in various colors to form a specific pattern or design. It may be attached to a pole, hoisted on a mast, hung from a window or rail, or carried by hand. Flags are displayed on public buildings, in private homes, at businesses, in churches, from towers and rooftops, in public parks and alongside monuments. They may adorn clothing, vehicles, and various types of accessories and other equipment. Flags are carried in parades—and into battle. They fly over cemeteries and sometimes drape a casket. Perhaps there is something in this last—in the association between flags and human mortality—that might help us better understand our peculiar affection for these symbols—and our keen devotion to particular ones of them.

Unlike any other symbolic object, flags seem to have a life of their own. More precisely, it sometimes appears as if flags were themselves living entities. No other abstract emblem, no other symbol of human design, moves the way a flag does. They are animated by the wind. They are said to "wave" in the breeze. They "fly" like birds on the air. They "rustle" like grain in a field. They "flutter" like leaves and "furl" like flowers. In a brisk wind, they snap at the pole with the cord binding them to it, as if demonstrating a will of their own, protesting the shackle that holds them captive. In so doing flags display almost human traits, reflecting our own basic desire for independence and freedom. It is no wonder, then, that we feel a special bond to them. Whether made of organic or inorganic materials, they seem almost alive. And it is this illusion of life that sets them apart.

Flags become infused with deeper meaning through their close association with human experience. Our affinity for flags speaks to their ancient use as a tool of war. Their relationship to men living in close proximity to death undoubtedly reinforces the lifelike quality of flags. They have accompanied us into battle. They have been there with us in those moments when, as Civil War veteran Oliver Wendell Holmes put it, "we have felt the passion of life to its top."[1] The preciousness of life, as magnified by the nearness and the intensity of a battle-field encounter with death, may seek out a symbol on which to attach itself, to forestall forgetting by encapsulating memory in symbolic form. Thus flags become a means of expressing the inexpressible, of communicating "the incommunicable experience of war."[2] Flags continue to bear witness even when those who bore them have long since passed on. A flag once carried into combat may show signs of mending done by those who bore it, of bullets that pierced it, of blood that stained it. In this way, a flag is "given voice." These token reminders lend it a special power to "speak" to us across the generations. Flags and monuments both serve the same purpose: they memorialize and represent. But there is something in the impermanent nature of a flag—in both its susceptibility to injury and its fragile ephemerality—that makes it more like us, sealing the bond between flags and men.

Historically, a flag's primary function has been to serve as a military instrument, a means of facilitating identification, control, and maneuver. The Spanish American War at the end of the nineteenth century appears to have been the last occasion when flags were put to this use. The advent of reliable means of electric (later wireless) communication brought an end to the flag's traditional and time-honored purpose as a tool of war. They were, in that sense at least, outmoded. But by then flags had already been endowed with broader meanings that lent them an almost implacable vitality and an abiding loyalty among men. It is said that in war soldiers fight for just two things: their own survival and the lives of their fellow soldiers. All ideological, national, patriotic, or other abstract motivations dissolve in the heat of battle, leaving only the personal and collegial behind. But in retrospect, after the smoke has cleared away, the battle ended, the wounded borne away, and the dead buried, a veteran might say "That's the flag I fought for" or "That's the flag men died to defend." Flags become, for many soldiers (and civilians too), like comrades, buddies of a sort, invested with a life all their own— they represent all the lives cut short and the causes and principles those deaths supposedly served to protect. Brazed to our emotions by the heat of war and the pressure of commonly held memories, flags become symbols of our collective experience, of our journey through history, encapsulating our sense of unity as a people, of our principles and values.

Flags are uniquely evocative symbols, a strangely powerful mixture of ill-defined abstraction and precise reference—they are, to quote Whitman again, "out of reach, an idea only, yet furiously fought for . . . loved by me."[3] Through the profound and all-consuming experience of war flags have come to represent entire territories, whole peoples. Though the specific design of any one flag may have been the choice of a relative few—reflecting a time in which flags represented royal lineage, ecclesiastical rule, or aristocratic and economic dominion—the crucible of war has since emblazoned them onto the consciousness of entire nations. A flag ceased to be a statement of elite privilege or military caste and became instead the common emblem of whole societies. It became a *standard:* a declaration of commonality—and a convenient mark of national (as well as political and cultural) identity. But it also served as an expression of exclusivity and demarcation, a way of differentiating "us" from "them."

While distinguishing us without, flags are meant to serve as a source of unity within—ideally, at least. This is often not the case, however. Differing historical experiences and perspectives may lead to different attitudes toward what are supposedly our collective national symbols. The relationship between Native Americans and the American flag, for example, remains ambivalent, owing to their particular encounter with it in history. The same thing applies to other ethnic or minority groups within any given country. A distinctive (yet vaguely defined) symbol like a flag will have different meanings applied to it, depending on how this or that person or group of persons views it.

But it is the odd mix of the abstract and concrete, of the general with the specific, that makes a flag inherently difficult to define with any measure of fixed finality. And there is perhaps no better example of this than the Confederate flag. Unlike other symbols of the Confederacy, the Confederate flag is both a relic of that era *and* an abstract design still in use today. It is different in nature from the monuments that were erected long after the events they commemorate occurred, because the Confederate flag springs directly out of the war itself. And unlike a battlefield or fortress, a building, or any other object that bears a direct and limited connection to the era that produced it, and which are forever tied to a specific function, the Confederate flag possesses a kind of intellectual portability—it is stuck in time, and yet liberated from it, bound to a certain role yet loosed from the bonds of its historical origins. The Confederate flag is both concrete, history-bound symbol and an unbound, free-floating symbol. It is a genuine relic and a figurative replica, simultaneously definite and abstract. The Confederate flag may not be unique in this respect, but it does stand out as a premier example of the dual nature of historical symbols. And herein lies a source of our troubles with the flag today: the flag's dual nature seems almost to invite conflict. Our different interpretations about what it symbolizes and how we should handle its display in public places (especially on public property) have made of the Confederate flag an object of intense and often rancorous debate.[4]

A people's relationship to the flag that represents it is often thought of as being permanent and immutable, as if existing since time immemorial and forever fixed and unchanging. But flags and other national symbols are actually more variable than we sometimes think. Few remember, for example, that "The Star-Spangled Banner" was not declared the national anthem of the United States until the middle of the twentieth century; or that many of our national holidays were not celebrated until well after the founding of the Republic; or even that the Stars and Stripes bore only forty-eight stars as recently as 1959. Earlier periods of our own history are later perceived as tales of the inevitable, with an arrow-straight line leading inexorably from past to present. We often overlook the arbitrary or improvisational element in our own past and assume that many of the fundamentals of our national life have always been much as they are now. We lose sight of the unsettled and fluctuating association between a people and its symbols.

The history of South Carolina offers a good example of this—both in terms of its state flag and in the interrelationship between that flag and the Confederate flag itself. Many South Carolinians are no doubt aware that their state flag (the so-called Palmetto Flag, which bears a palmetto tree in the center of blue field with a waxing quarter moon in the upper-left corner) had its origins in the American Revolutionary War. What often gets lost is the fact that the Palmetto Flag was the symbol neither of the colony of South Carolina nor of the sovereign state that emerged from the War of Independence. A blue banner with crescent existed and was in use as a signal flag as early as 1776. And a flag bearing the palmetto tree made its first appearance as a consequence of the war and gained acceptance as a symbol of South Carolina identity over the ensuing decades. But the two were not married together into a single flag until almost a half-century after the American Revolution. More importantly, the flag we know today did not become the officially recognized state flag until early 1861, just prior to the outbreak of the Civil War—at a point in time (following South Carolina's secession from the Union in late 1860) when the state had become an independent country (if only in its own perceptions).[5]

In effect, the South Carolina state flag was itself the premier symbol of the state's separatist leanings, of its insistence on what it considered were its sovereign rights. No other flag was needed to fill that particular role. The Palmetto Flag had already gained a reputation as a statement of a peculiar Carolina cussedness during the Nullification Crisis of the early 1830s. And South Carolina's participation in the 1846 war with Mexico helped set the bond between the Palmetto Flag and the soldiers who served under it.

By 1860, the Palmetto Flag had become the primary symbol of South Carolina identity (though not of state authority). Significantly, the flag's imagery also symbolized coastal Carolina's dominant role in state affairs and its controlling influence throughout much of the state's early political history. Palmetto trees do not flourish in the higher elevations and cooler climes of the South Carolina inland. Thus, the state flag speaks indirectly of the geographic and legislative division within the state. For a long time the South Carolina Upstate had to make do with whatever the Lowcountry gave it—including the state flag.

The state flag was not the only one set on the secessionist winds of early 1860, however. South Carolina reveled in a riot of newly minted banners during the heady days leading up to and immediately following its break with the Union. The so-called Sovereignty Flag of South Carolina was one of the more popular designs hoisted aloft. Somewhat reminiscent of the Confederate battle flag yet to be born, it bore star-studded bars on a field of red—except that, in contrast to the battle flag, those bars ran horizontally and vertically across the field rather than diagonally, and it contained the familiar tree and crescent in the upper left-hand corner. "Big Red" (basically a red version of the Palmetto Flag design, and the emblem of Charleston's Citadel cadets) was another flag on display at the time. Citadel cadets are credited with firing the first shots of the Civil War, when they opened fire on the *Star of the West,* a ship attempting to resupply federal forces in Charleston Harbor in January 1861.

Many of the new flags bore the familiar palmetto—some green on a white background, others yellow on a red background. In addition, there seemed to be a veritable galaxy of stars and crescents, in various shapes and colors, alongside an assortment of mottoes and slogans, from "Semper Parati" (Always Prepared) and "Dieu et Mon Droit" (God and My Right) to the declaratory "Cotton is King" and the straightforward "Now or Never!" Even more obscure (to us today, at any rate, though not to those living at the time) was the South Carolina Secession Flag. This pennant-shaped flag had a forked fly-end and bore a large white star on a field of red, along with the familiar white crescent. There was also an eighteen-by-twelve-foot monstrosity that sported a regular hodgepodge of images, everything from cotton bales and locomotives to the obligatory palmetto tree (this one wrapped around by a rattlesnake sporting twenty-four rattles!). Everyone, it seems, wanted to display a banner of his own: the local newspaper, the train depot, the fire company, the packet wharf, and even the hay-and-grain store, just to name a few.[6]

Debate about which design would be recognized as the official emblem of the state (now an "independent country") began almost immediately following passage of the Ordinance of Secession. Debate over the question was lengthy, extending into the following year and consuming the South Carolina legislature for almost a full week during that hectic time just prior to the outbreak of war. It seems as if South Carolina has always been rife with debate when it comes to the symbols that represent it.

By deciding in favor of the Palmetto Flag, secession lawmakers chose a symbol that had already established itself as an intimate part of state life and made it South Carolina's statement of sovereign independence. Through the bond forged by the state's ensuing fate, the Palmetto Flag became in effect the state's Civil War banner. More than any other emblem, this flag represented the state and its citizens during that conflict. In 1869 a resolution calling for the display of both an American and a South Carolina banner atop the State House passed the state legislature, but only over the objections of several black state senators. For them, the state flag remained a symbol of the state's defiance against federal authority and of the treachery that had led to war. In their eyes, it still represented a social and political order that had denied them their freedom.[7]

South Carolina's relationship to the various flags of the Confederacy is in some ways less intimate than that between the state and its Palmetto Flag. There is no evidence, for example, that a Confederate battle flag ever flew either atop or near the State House during the Civil War. It is entirely possible that a Confederate First National flag (the so-called Stars and Bars flag, not the more familiar battle flag) flew, along with the state flag, on top of the original State House at some time during the war—but, again, there is no documentary evidence to that effect. However, a large state flag *was* draped over the front of the still-incomplete new State House in mid-1865, perhaps as a kind of last-minute gesture of spite directed against the arriving federal troops. But as far as can be determined, no Confederate battle flags remained to proclaim defiance in the face of Sherman's advancing legions. The Confederate army units that may have carried them had by then already skedaddled out of town.[8]

The Confederate battle flag has been the object of some considerable mythmaking—though perhaps we should call it "historical mis-remembering."* And some of that confusion has made its way into the flag story in South Carolina. First of all, to speak of *the* Confederate battle flag, as if there were only one, is misleading. There were in fact a plethora of different Confederate battle flags, some of them containing a number of similar design elements, but others not. The most

---

*This is where we enter the sometimes trivial realm of flag minutia. The general reader is urged to bear the following with patience and understanding, while flag aficionados must forgive the omission of no doubt interesting but nevertheless nonessential detail.

famous of these was the "Southern Cross" (not the rectangular Rebel flag we all knew as children, however, but rather a square version of the same design). This flag may have been primus inter pares among its brethren banners, but it was by no means the only design vying for the hearts of the men on the battlefield. There were a great many other designs around, each with its own band of adherents. Flag scholar Richard Rollins puts it this way.

> The Southern Cross was not the first flag carried into battle by Confederate troops, nor was it the banner most widely flown during the war. It was rarely seen west of the Appalachian mountains. Some southern men fought and died without ever seeing or walking under it.[9]

The battlegrounds of the Civil War sported numerous battle flags, a fact that reflected the hodgepodge character of the southern Confederacy itself.

Though the Civil War was fought across half a country, it was in essence a local, even an intimate conflict. To many of the characters in Alan Tate's novel *The Fathers,* for example, everything beyond the local is an incomprehensible abstraction: "For papa . . . all that territory from below the James [River] to the Rio Grande was a map, and the 'war' was about to be fought between the 'government' and the sons of his neighbors and kin in the old Northern Neck of Virginia."[10] It was local in the sense that most, if not all, of the men who entered into Confederate military service were mustered in at the local level. The men often came from the same area within a state (at least at the outset of the war), and many knew each other personally. These men fought together as a unit and remained together for the duration of the war, for the period of their enlistment, or at least during the life of the unit. Thus, the Civil War was a conflict of local and regional loyalties. The southern soldier felt a bond first to his local community; second, to his state; third, to the larger military grouping to which his unit was attached (regiment, division, corps); and only lastly (if at all) to the Confederacy as a whole. It is understandable, then, that the emblems with which they chose to identify themselves often reflected a regionalism and an individualism characteristic of their particular origins. Indeed, it would have been oddly contradictory to the states' rights nature of the Confederacy if all of its military units had campaigned under a single, standardized banner.

The Confederacy was, by its own definition, a loose association of states. There is at least a measure of truth in the frequent charge that the Confederacy died of its own internal divisions, that is to say, from its chronic provincialism. It had little power to impose its will on its constituent parts—and when it tried, the effort was often met with stubborn opposition. It is appropriate, then, that the Confederacy's flags reflected its diversity and local color. Many flags were homespun, put together by the mother, wife, or lady-friend of a recruit being mustered into Confederate service or presented to an entire unit as they departed for the war. The unique qualities of these flags gave tangible expression to the local origins of the war's participants. The variety of designs and variations on designs reinforced the bonds both within the unit and between the unit and the loved ones at home.[11]

The diverse origins contained within the Confederate ranks were reflected in the different banners its armies chose to identify themselves by. There were red flags spattered with a field of white stars (Van Dorn's regiments); red St. George's crosses on fields of blue (Polk's Corps); white crosses on blue fields (East Tennessee units); white Christian crosses on red-bordered blue backgrounds (Missouri units); blue-and-white bars and white stars on red fields (North Carolina troops); blue flags with white ovals, circles, or squares (Hardee and Cleburne Divisions); and even a few with exploding stars at the center (some South Carolina units). Certain variations within a pattern, in particular the inclusion of eleven, twelve, or thirteen stars (depending on the flag in question), spoke to the Confederacy's eternal hopefulness—or, as some might say, its stubborn self-delusion—that others would yet join the fight. And then there was the "Bonnie Blue Flag," with its single white star in the middle of a blue field, the flag that inspired the song of the same name (which quickly became a kind of unofficial southern national anthem during the early war years). There were also blue-colored variations on the Southern Cross design. State flags were carried into battle quite often as well. And of course there were the better-known Confederate national flags: the First National (Stars and Bars), the Second National (or "Stainless Banner"), and the Third National—along with the red Southern Cross (or "battle") flag (which also occasionally appeared in a blue-colored variation). All these and more were carried by southern soldiers. They were fought over, surrendered, recaptured, cherished, and even loved by those who bore them. There was no single "Confederate battle flag," but rather a multitude of different flags, each with its own unique character and story.

Time and fading memory, however, have a way of erasing distinctions that once seemed important and dear. In time, even the most famous of Confederate symbols, the Southern Cross, proved not to be immune to the ravages of the passing years. At some point, the square version of the Southern Cross battle flag, the flag of the Army of Northern Virginia under the command of Robert E. Lee, was replaced as the primary Confederate symbol by a rectangular version of the same pattern. This became the "rebel flag" we all know from childhood—the one that entered into popular culture as the symbol for all things southern, the "redneck bandana," an emblem of undifferentiated regionalism and sectional pride. It is this flag that made its way around the globe, becoming a kind of generic symbol of rebelliousness and individualism. It was the same flag that the true believers in "segregation-forever" bore during the Civil Rights Era, and it is still the banner associated primarily with the Ku Klux Klan. This is the flag that flew above and within the South Carolina State House for more than a quarter century.

Whether referred to as the Confederate Naval Jack or the Banner of the Army of Tennessee, this rectangular version of the Southern Cross pattern would have been encountered by few of the soldiers engaged in campaigns east of the Appalachians, since it was used almost exclusively by units further to the west. Whenever we attempt to fit the messy details of history into a neat package, suitable for handy illustration, we often end up reshaping the history we are trying to depict. This is especially true when the issue in question becomes a bone of political contention, as it did in the case of the Confederate flag in South Carolina. One of the selling points, for instance, of the compromise removing the flag from the dome of the South Carolina State House and replacing it with a different one at the Confederate Soldier's Monument on the capitol grounds was that it would replace an "inaccurate" (or "unhistorical") flag—the rectangular Army of Tennessee flag, which ostensibly no South Carolinians marched under—with a "historically accurate" one—namely, the square Army of Northern Virginia design, which South Carolinians had actually borne into battle. The truth of the matter is, South Carolinians served in both theaters of war, both east and west of the Appalachians—and may well have marched under both the square and the rectangular versions of the flag. By censuring one version and holding high the other (in effect "surrendering" one to the Klan), flag defenders inadvertently cast aspersions on both—and in the process did an injustice to history. Interestingly, both flags remained relatively obscure until World War II, their use up until then being confined mainly to Confederate veterans' organizations. It is only during our latter-day civil wars that they have become sources of controversy and conflict.

During the Civil War itself, the Southern Cross flag was something of a Johnny-come-lately, born of military necessity. It did not appear in large numbers until almost the middle of the war. And it never lacked for competition. Many southern troops had marched into early battles of the war carrying the First National flag, the Stars and Bars, adopted as the official flag of the Confederate States of America in March 1861. During those first engagements, however, and most notably during the Battle of Manassas, the Stars and Bars was occasionally mistaken for the Union flag, the Stars and Stripes, causing confusion and disarray, and leading at times to tragic exchanges of what would later be called "friendly fire."

In order to try and prevent further instances of mistaken identity, Confederate General P. G. T. Beauregard, working together with Congressman William Miles (of South Carolina) and General Joseph E. Johnston, arrived at a design they believed would solve the problem and offer the Confederate forces a distinctive standard by which to identify themselves. This new battle flag was quickly adopted by the Army of Northern Virginia. But supply problems prevented broader distribution of the flag until the latter half of 1862 and into 1863. Even as late as the Battle of Gettysburg, in July 1863, Lee's headquarters flag remained the Confederate First National pattern—and eventually would be replaced not with the new Southern Cross pattern but rather by the Stainless Banner, which incorporated the Southern Cross into a white field.

Some units resisted the switch from the First National to the Southern Cross flags. By this time many men had already been engaged in numerous battles and campaigns under the Stars and Bars. They had suffered with it and seen friends die alongside it. The bonds forged between these men and their flag could not be easily broken. They cherished their flags as mementos, both of home and war. It was not until late 1863 (more than two years after the war had begun and less than two years before its end) that the new battle flags finally attained general distribution—at least in the eastern theater. (It took even longer west of the Appalachians.) And even then it still was by no means the only banner in the field—nor was it uniform in design (as the flag of the Army of Tennessee attests).[12]

Toward the end of the war, the Stars and Bars even made something of a comeback. As Southern Cross flags were captured or succumbed to wear and tear (and with material shortages making the manufacture of replacements increasingly difficult), Confederate units in the field once again unfurled their original battle flags, the Stars and Bars, which they had stored away for safekeeping. First National flags were returned to service during Lee's retreat from Richmond to Appomattox, for example, and in numerous other venues. Some units had stuck with this flag throughout—while others had clung instead to any number of different state or unit banners. Just as the Confederacy never managed to march to the beat of one drum, its armies never marched all under a single banner.

Richard Rollins sums up the role played by the different flags as follows:

> More First National patterns would be surrendered in 1865 than either of the two later official designs. If there was one, single "Confederate flag" that was most widely recognized, most widely flown across the South from 1861 to 1865, and under which the majority or a plurality of Southern troops marched, it was the First National flag, the "Stars-and-Bars."[13]

Admittedly, the Southern Cross pattern was the only flag developed specifically as a general-service battle flag for use by all Confederate forces. But it was neither the only battle flag taken onto the field, nor was it the only flag that flew in battle. As we have seen, there were many other battle flags in use, especially early in the war. And others, like the Stars and Bars, though not created specifically for battlefield use, nevertheless served as *the* battle flag for many Confederate units. More importantly, "of the types of Confederate flags created, either for political, battle use, or both, the [Stars and Bars] pattern is the only one that saw service from the beginning of the war until the very end."[14]

The question arises, then: How long does it take for a symbol, a flag, to become the cherished emblem of a time, a place, a people—or a cause? By which route does it nestle itself into the hearts of a community or a nation? How is it that a late entry into the competition for the favor of the Confederate soldier became the preeminent symbol not only of the southern soldier, but of the southern cause and of the South in general? How did the Southern Cross so thoroughly sweep aside all comers in the bout for southern sympathies, emerging as the champion of the "southern civil religion," of the southern way of life? The flag was distinctive, to be sure. And yes, it eventually enjoyed the advantage of a wide distribution among the Confederate armies. But there must have been more to it than that. Was the flag's preeminence perhaps partly a result of the cold mathematics of wartime attrition? Is it possible that wartime losses left (relatively) few to recall the banners with which the war had begun while comparatively more were left who had entered the war later and under a different flag? Moreover, why were later generations so eager to cast aside the once beloved Stars and Bars in favor of the Southern Cross? Was it a tacit admission of the taint of slavery that clung to the First National flag—a taint they believed the Southern Cross to be free of?

Or was there something in the experience of defeat that endeared the Southern Cross flag to generations of southerners, both those living and those yet to be born? It was long said that the South savored the wound of its own defeat, that it reveled in a vainglorious and backward-looking mystification of its past. One of the main characters in Charles Frazier's 1997 Civil War novel, *Cold Mountain*, observes that "the man that whips generally feels better than the man that takes the whipping, no matter who's in the wrong of the matter."[15] The "man that whips" may look back fondly on his victory from time to time, draw strength from it perhaps, and then move on. The victor is comfortable with his past; it flows easily into the present, confirming his present station and justifying his future course, lending him confidence and certainty. In time, he may well become complacent and forgetful of the past as it settles in and is slowly covered over by new layers of experience and memory.

The defeated cannot rest so easily. The past sticks in his craw (even—and perhaps more so—if he never talks of it). He can neither live contentedly with it, nor can he be completely satisfied without it. It may provide a kind of sad solace, but it does not encourage restful ease. With the defeated, the past does not automatically meld into the whole of experience, becoming part of a continuous progression toward an inevitable present; it no longer flows straight and steady into the present, nourishing and fortifying it with encouraging reassurances. Instead, the past is broken off, shattered, the links with it damaged or severed by violence and ill fortune. And yet, the past does not sink into the depths of the memory hole. Ironically, the defeated often cling to the past (or at least to certain aspects of it) in a way that the victorious seldom do. The connections to the past must be forged anew, and in the process are often refashioned according to present needs or desires, based on models drawn with a quill pen. The result may be a distortion of history or the imposition of a past that no longer serves present circumstances.

Defeat scourges the mind like a brand (though it may in no way contribute to a clarity of vision or ensure an accuracy of reflection). Vanquished peoples are often desperate to "wrest some elevating meaning from the destruction of their highest dreams"—they engage in "the ancient, sociable alchemy of mythmaking . . . the process of gradual exaltation by unlegislated consensus and assent of historical fact into transcendental example, as a way to ease and dignify the pain of remembering."[16] This is not necessarily an unworthy enterprise. Indeed, it may be essential at times in order for a society to hold itself together through periods of calamity and change. Defeat places in question all that once was taken for granted. The established order stands in the dock of the accused and must find a way of reestablishing its legitimacy, or else abdicate whatever sovereignty it holds over the hearts of men.

In 1865, many southerners saw the political and social order of the South hanging in precarious balance. The changes they had hoped to forestall through secession flooded in with redoubled strength and swiftness. The military debacle unleashed at Fort Sumter and the social upheaval brought about through emancipation sent the South on a desperate search for a means of stemming, or at least ameliorating, the tide of change sweeping in upon it. The specific mechanism it chose was the "Lost Cause." It provided a sense of consolation—but it also signaled defiance on the part of a South that had been militarily subdued but that remained unwilling to accept what it felt was a form of political subjugation. The South said to the victors, "Our armies have been defeated, but the ideals and principles they fought for were not nullified by capitulation; they are superior to the enemy's and live on." And in that sense, the cause was not really even lost—it had merely been transformed. By enshrining the past as the model, the ideal, the Lost Cause served to check and control the onrush of modernity.

The book that gave the movement its name, Edward Pollard's *The Lost Cause* (which appeared in 1866), declared war on what was perceived as the North's campaign of cultural imperialism against the South. But the religion of the Lost Cause did not spring forth instantaneously whole and complete following Appomattox. The ingredients that made up the South's postwar civil religion merged and gained momentum over time. The Lost Cause was largely a postwar invention, created as much (and perhaps more) in response to the disruptions caused by Reconstruction—both real and imagined—as it was a genuine expression of wartime experience. "The Southern civil religion emerged because the experience of defeat . . . had created a spiritual and psychological need for Southerners to reaffirm their identity"—and in the process "Southerners made a religion out of their history," employing their new creed to "symbolically . . . overcome history."[17]

In the wake of Appomattox, the South faced a period of dislocation, disorientation, and gradual reconstitution. For a time, southerners' reflections on the Confederacy were shrouded in grief. It was an era characterized less by celebratory ancestor worship than by a sense of loss and mourning. The glorious remembering to come was still in the making. "Between 1865 and 1885, southerners placed approximately 70 percent of their Confederate monuments in cemeteries," says historian Gaines Foster, not in city parks or town squares.[18] Almost all were funereal in design—obelisks of loss and bereavement, not of glorification or once-and-future triumphalism. This was the era of the doleful, dirgelike elegies of Abram Joseph Ryan, whose poem "The Conquered Banner" captures the tenor of that time:

> Furl that banner, softly, slowly!
> Treat it gently—it is holy—
> For it droops above the dead.
> Touch it not—unfold it never,
> Let it droop there, furled forever,
> For its peoples' hopes are dead!

And not only their hopes. Many southern men lay dead. Mourning their loss and coming to terms with their absence would occupy the South for many years to come.

And yet, even in this furling one can hear other, less fatalistic tones. For this was also an era of wounded bitterness, of battered pride and smoldering resentment. Many southerners undoubtedly stood with Confederate Major Innes Rudolph's "Good Old Rebel": Displaying a defiant pride, spiteful and begrudging, he remains unbending ("I won't be reconstructed") but at bottom is cynically scornful and detached ("And I don't care a damn!").[19] Others perhaps shared the sentiments expressed by Sir Henry Houghton in his poem "A Reply to the Conquered Banner."[20] Although English-born, Houghton no doubt expressed a lingering recalcitrance felt by many southerners when he wrote:

> Gallant nation, foiled by numbers!
> Say not that your hopes are fled;
> Keep that glorious flag which slumbers,
> One day to avenge your dead.
> Keep it, widowed, sonless mothers!

Keep it, sisters, mourning brothers!
Furl it now, but keep it still—
Think not that its work is done.[21]

Most former Confederates, however, returned from the war with their minds set to the more mundane matters of daily existence. Rather than seek retribution or rally for resistance, most southerners focused their efforts on reestablishing their pre-war lives—or some semblance of the same. They set about repairing the damage of war, rebuilding their farms and reconstructing their businesses and factories. They were in large measure too occupied with concerns of daily life to be bothered with refighting old battles or seeking new conflicts. But too many southerners fooled themselves with the mistaken assumption that clinging to the familiar and established patterns of the pre-war order could mitigate the pain and disruption of war and defeat. Salvaging as much as possible of the antebellum status quo was the South's response to defeat, despite the fact that one of the primary pillars upholding the Old Order—slavery—had been swept away in the war the southern states had unleashed. The South sought to minimize the effects of the manumission of the South's black population through ever-tightening enforcement of traditional social relationships based on patterns of racial subordination that had been established in antebellum society.

The battle of Reconstruction was a direct consequence of the Civil War. But it was not simply a continuation of that war. It was a new kind of conflict—fought out on territory where the forces of southern traditionalism enjoyed the advantage. The South felt no need to defiantly hoist the banners of war or organize armies for battle (though some of the battles of Reconstruction would be fought with muskets and rifles). The battle banners of the southern Confederacy remained furled through most of the latter half of the nineteenth century, relegated almost exclusively to the Confederate veterans groups scattered across the South. Though there were undoubtedly echoes of the Civil War in the struggle over the postwar political order in the South, the symbols and imagery of the Confederacy were put aside, left behind for a time as relics of defeat.

During the period in the South's history when, by many accounts, southerners felt their culture and identity—"southern civilization," as they called it—to be under siege and in dire threat of extinction, no Confederate battle flags were raised in defiant reaffirmation of southern ways. Southerners had no need of them—they found more effective means of defending their heritage, some of which—such as the Ku Klux Klan—served only to further smear the legacy they professed to defend. Throughout the 1860s, 1870s, and into the early 1880s, Confederate regalia remained largely absent from the southern landscape.

Interestingly, it was not until well past the final demise of Reconstruction, in 1877—during a period of rising southern self-confidence encouraged by the ascension of the "southern Bourbons"and in an era of growing goodwill and mutual respect between North and South—that "the bereavement of the early memorial movement gave way to greater celebration and eventually to a kind of reverential glorification of the Confederacy."[22] The United Confederate Veterans (UCV)—the only region-wide organization of former Confederate soldiers—was not organized until 1889. The Sons of Confederate Veterans (SCV) did not emerge until near the end of the century, in 1896. This coming together marked a new phase in the South's awareness of its Confederate past and coincided with a coalescence around the Southern Cross as the symbol of the region's Confederate-era identity. Even so, war nostalgia was hardly all the rage. Recalling his own youth in South Carolina in the early twentieth century, journalist James McBride Dabbs wrote that "by 1900, the war had faded into the past . . . almost as much as the First World War has now faded into mine." Civil War veterans "seldom spoke of it to little boys unless the little boys bothered them too much."[23]

With the South's newfound self-assurance to support it, and with the aging—and slow passing—of the wartime generation, veterans' reunions became grand celebratory affairs during the 1890s and into the new century. But even then, they often were held jointly with Union veterans and thus were living symbols of regional reconciliation rather than unadulterated statements of southern distinction. The winnowing of Confederate symbols marched in step with the gradual winnowing in the ranks of the Confederate veterans—and the fading memories of the war. The multitude of flags that had flown during the war were gradually reduced to one, just as the multitudes who had once fought under them were being decimated by the passage of time. An era of grand monument-building and large-scale public commemoration now dawned. It brought with it the sort of gallant and heroic style of equestrian sculpture that seems now almost standard issue for the nineteenth century, but which to those then living was a source of great pride and jubilation, as demonstrated by their placement of those monuments at prominent public locations—locations which would, in our own day, become a source of acute racial and political conflict.

Two

A LAND PRIMED FOR FATALITY

*"In this state . . . mystique is honored almost
as much as history. . . ."*

Greenville News *editorial,*
7 November 1999

South Carolina was in no way remiss in its own efforts to memorialize either its Confederate-era dead or the Confederate cause. It had, for example, the distinction of possessing the oldest Confederate monument in the United States, erected in Cheraw in 1867. And like a lot of other southern states, it quickly adopted the practice of decorating the graves of the Confederate dead on Confederate Memorial Day, 10 May. But in a state where one of the longest battles of Reconstruction had been fought, South Carolina's Confederate memorials also took on a distinctively political significance. They became implicit statements of defiance, even in an era still characterized primarily by loss and bereavement. It was nearly impossible to parse out the anguish and grief from the bitterness and contempt.

The Confederate Soldier's Monument on the State House grounds—which would later become the final destination of the Confederate flag—became a kind of football in the political rugby match fought out in the state during Reconstruction. In 1873, when planning for the Confederate memorial began, the State House was still occupied (though not necessarily controlled) by what many disparagingly referred to as "carpetbaggers and Africans," and the state government in the hands of what some termed a "band of rabble." Consequently, many in the state considered the State House grounds an unsuitable and inappropriate location for a memorial to Confederate soldiers. Delays and money problems kept the project from being completed until after the downfall of the state's Reconstruction regime in 1876. Then, with "alien rule . . . overthrown" and the State House grounds restored to their "pristine" state under a "rightful" (i.e., white) sovereign, the State House once again became the one-and-only suitable site for the new Confederate monument. A prominent location was set aside, and in 1879 the completed statue was unveiled there before a crowd of some fifteen thousand spectators.[1]

The current monument is not the one erected in 1879, however. The original 1879 monument was struck by lightening in 1882, destroying the soldierly figure atop the pedestal, leaving only his boots behind. There was a time when South Carolinians might have taken an event like this as a divine commentary on the state of the southern soul. But this time, whether because of their newfound worldly self-confidence or as a consequence of the Gilded Age desire to get on with things, South Carolina quickly ordered a replacement, one somewhat taller than its predecessor, and, in 1884, placed it at the location where it stands today.[2]

For many years after, the statue was thought sufficient memorial to the state's Confederate foot soldiers. Later on, in 1907, a statue of South Carolina's Confederate general (and postwar governor) Wade Hampton was added to the collection. And later still, the so-called Women's Memorial, honoring the sacrifices of South Carolina's female wartime generation, joined the others. But there it stopped. No flags or other decorations were considered necessary to honor the exploits and sacrifices of the state's Civil War–era citizens.

Nevertheless, a proposal was introduced in the state legislature in 1899 to change the color of the state flag from blue to purple. The alteration was meant to serve as a visual reminder of the state's losses in the war, to symbolize, as the proposal's authors put it, the "very life-blood of her sons, which ensanguined its folds from 1861 to 1865."[3] Significantly, the primary sponsor of the measure, Thomas Wright Bacot of Charleston, was too young to have served in the Civil War himself. On the other hand, Rep. J. Harvey Wilson of Sumter, the proposal's main opponent, was a Confederate veteran. It was as if the postwar generation was struggling mightily to find some way of participating—however vicariously —in the glory of past conflict, while the wartime generation held up a warning hand, as if to say, "Stop, no more." The Confederate veterans passionately admonished the proposal's authors not to forget that many of "the gallant dead . . . fell beneath the [state flag's] folds."[4] Changing it would, in effect, eliminate the very flag they had fought to defend. By keeping it unchanged, South Carolina demonstrated that its state flag was as much a memorial to the Confederate Era, and to the soldiers who served it, as any marker, monument, or flag that the state might erect. South Carolina's flag was left unaltered even as other states (Georgia, in 1879; Mississippi, in 1894; and Alabama, in 1895) incorporated more-explicit references to the Confederacy into their state flags in an expression of fealty to the Confederate past.

——•••••——

Things remained pretty much the same on the grounds around the State House during the forty years that followed—while the complexion (though not the skin color) of those inside the State House underwent a kind of radical reconstruction that would set the stage for the flag fight to come. The old-style patronizing attitudes about race practiced by many of the Bourbon-era politicians in South Carolina had, by the 1890s, given way to the race-based politics of "Pitchfork" Ben Tillman. These would in turn degenerate into the even baser politics of race endorsed and encouraged by the likes of Governor (later Senator) Cole Blease and Ellison D. "Cotton Ed" Smith, who served as South Carolina's U.S. senator from 1908 to 1944 (foreshadowing the political longevity of Strom Thurmond). Gradually, South Carolina spun down into ever-deeper levels of the Jim Crow hell that the South was creating for itself.

This is not to say that Blease and Smith were the only variety of political fruit produced for the South Carolina electoral market during this period in the state's history. On the contrary, neither the Progressive Era nor the New Deal went by entirely unnoticed; each had its adherents in the state. The New Deal in particular enjoyed broad public support in South Carolina—especially since the state government seemed either incapable or unwilling to do anything to mitigate the effects the Great Depression was having on the state and its residents. The textile strike of 1934 proved that the state's working people were ready, when necessary, to join unions and organize industrial action.

South Carolina's politics ran on two tracks—but those tracks often ran parallel to one another. There was certainly a progressive element present in the state, though most of its effort was directed at improving the lives of the state's white, not its black, citizens. But the mainline of state politics throughout much of the twentieth century was forged from race-based populism. For almost two-thirds of a century, even the more worldly and progressive-minded of Carolina politicians, men like Richard Manning, Olin Johnston, and James F. Byrnes, had to at least give a nod to the prevailing racial prejudices and predilections within the state. And most did more than just nod—they bowed down and worshiped them, egging on popular bigotries and exploiting them for their own political gain. South Carolina's political culture was what some have called a "Herrenvolk democracy."[5] Similar to W. J. Cash's "savage ideal," it was built on the notion that all white men within the state were political equals by virtue of their superiority to blacks. White solidarity reinforced the illusion of white equality and was nurtured through a system aimed at keeping the state's blacks "in their place."

Governor Tillman had virtually eliminated black political participation in South Carolina by means of the new state constitution he shepherded through to passage in 1895 (a constitution that remained largely in effect into the 1960s). But social order (and white solidarity) required constant vigilance—which racial populists, such as Blease and Smith, were more than willing to provide. Blease openly promoted lynching as the most effective means of controlling black insolence, proclaiming "when mobs are no longer possible, liberty will be dead."[6] He also opposed spending public monies on black education, since schooling, he said, would only serve to "ruin a good field hand, and make a bad convict."[7]

While Blease represented the sort of standard-issue racial puritan of the early twentieth century, Smith signaled the full flowering of race politics. He belonged to that set of classic southern demagogues, like James Vardaman and Theodore Bilbo of Mississippi, Eugene Talmadge of Georgia, or, later, George Wallace of Alabama, who became the stars of the showmanship school of southern populism. And, like most of them, Smith's vision was nothing if not backward-looking. Rather than embrace diversified crop production (let alone a diversified state economy), "Cotton Ed" proclaimed cotton king both now and forever. He wore a cotton boll on his lapel, appeared at campaign rallies atop a wagon loaded with cotton bales, and serenaded his audiences with his rendition of "Cotton, Cotton, My Sweet." A self-described "born-aginner," Smith opposed most every manifestation of modernity, including organized labor, social-welfare programs, progressive taxation, and all forms of federal intervention. He was also most definitely "agin" anything that even sounded like a threat to racial segregation. As scholar Bryant Simon put it, Smith

> dredged up the imagined horrors of Reconstruction—black voting, corruption, and sexual assaults on white women. This is what would happen if Washington once again told southern men what to do. As he defined it, the job of a southern senator was to defend states' rights and to make sure that the federal government stayed out of southern affairs.

For all this and more, *Time* magazine awarded "Cotton Ed" the title of "conscientious objector to the 20th Century."[8]

Smith's antics may have been off-putting to some, but his foot-stomping fulminations undoubtedly spoke to the prejudices and phobias of many one-gal

used white South Carolinians. Trends were afoot in the country that left a great many South Carolinians unsure about their state's place in the nation. Once again, as in their grandfathers' time, it seemed as if much of the rest of the country (and the North in particular) was taking entirely too much pleasure in bad-mouthing the South. Many southerners were increasingly put out by it, and Smith, like others of his ilk, wasted no time picking up and running with their resentment:

> By 1934, Smith was developing a sense of regional victimization. In his mind, southern control of the Democratic Party was ebbing as northern liberals, foreign-born big-city bosses, and African-Americans increasingly held positions of authority. At the same time, an overbearing federal government, acting under the New Deal's reformist guise, oppressed the South, disrespecting its traditions and customs. Southerners, in other words, not African-Americans or the poor, were the real victims in the 1930s.[9]

With blacks abandoning the Party of Lincoln for Franklin Roosevelt's Democrats, the solidly Democratic white South suddenly found itself sharing a party with the very people it had struggled to eliminate from the political process. This, combined with the growing self-assertion of an increasingly organized and mobilized black populace, led many South Carolinians to fear that control over their own fate was, once again, slipping from their hands.

A good taste of Smith's style of rhetoric can be found in the tale he endlessly told and retold of his famous walkout at the 1936 Democratic National Convention, held in Philadelphia. "Cotton Ed" was clearly in his element as he described the scene to his eager listeners:

> When I came out onto the floor of that great hall, bless God, it looked like a checker-board—a spot of white here, and a spot of black there. But I kept going, down that long aisle, and finally I found the great standard of South Carolina—and, praise God, it was a spot of white! I had no sooner taken my seat when a newspaper man came down . . . and said, "Senator, did you know a nigger is going to come up yonder in a minute and offer the invocation?" I told him, I said, "Now don't be joking me, I'm upset enough the way it is." But then, Bless God, out on that platform walked a slew-footed, blue-gummed, kinky-headed Senegambian!
>
> And he started praying and I started walking. And as I pushed through those great doors, and walked across that vast rotunda, it seemed to me that Old John Calhoun leaned down from his mansion in the sky and whispered, "You did right, Ed."[10]

"Cotton Ed" marched out of the convention, grousing "this mongrel meetin' ain't no place for a white man."[11] But he was back the next day. Smith knew how to put on a good show, sure enough. But he also knew that the South was not ready for full-scale party secession of the kind Thurmond would demonstrate twelve years later. And for that matter, southern Democrats did not yet need to take drastic measures, since they still held the upper hand. By the time Thurmond staged his own walkout of the Democratic Party in 1948, to form the breakaway Southern, or "Dixiecrat," Party, the South was on the run and in full revolt.

The South may have been in no mood for secession. But it *was* prepared to resist. Over the course of the 1930s, South Carolina became increasingly discontent with the New Deal, and Smith was one of its most vocal detractors. Though his knee-slapping shenanigans had pretty much eliminated him as an effective force in Washington, he was not alone in opposing Washington's "intrusions" into southern affairs. Other, less flamboyant southern political leaders were also growing restive over those aspects of the Roosevelt program aimed at promoting racial fairness. By 1937 Senators Harry F. Byrd and Carter Glass of Virginia, Walter George of Georgia, Josiah Bailey of North Carolina, and Millard Tydings of Maryland had all grown increasingly critical of what they considered to be the more "radical" outgrowths of the Roosevelt reforms.[12] Even an otherwise staunch supporter of the Roosevelt Administration such as South Carolina native James F. Byrnes balked at proposals such as the Fair Labor Act or the anti-lynching bill.[13]

The Fair Labor Standards Act, proposed in 1937, was a particularly hard bone of contention. The measure would have set minimum wages and a maximum workweek. That reason alone would have prompted the low-wage South to view the measure as a threat to the region's economic viability. More importantly, however, its equal-treatment features would have mandated that black laborers receive equal pay for equal work—a dagger aimed at the heart of the South's segregated and unequal labor system.

The dispute seemed to come to a head in 1938, an election year. The battle lines between South Carolina and the Roosevelt Administration were clearly drawn. Roosevelt had decided to make a concerted effort to try and rid Congress of his loud-mouthed opponents, like Smith, who had joined with Republicans to stymie the administration's proposals. Moderate New Dealer Olin D. Johnston entered the race as Smith's challenger, anxious to oblige the president by attempting to take the long-serving senator's seat away from him. "Cotton Ed," meanwhile, was engaged with a whole swarm of fellow southern senators in an effort to block passage of the anti-lynching legislation that had been drafted by the NAACP and sponsored by Senators Robert F. Wagner (New York) and Frederick Van Nuys (Indiana). "Cotton Ed" compared the measure to the Force Bill of 1890* and assisted in the southern filibuster against it that occupied several weeks of the 1937 session. Opponents of the anti-lynching legislation hoped that they could tie up other congressional business and thereby compel the Roosevelt Administration to order the offending measure withdrawn. Meanwhile, down in South Carolina, *The State* newspaper was running anti-Roosevelt editorials, calling for the dismantling of various New Deal programs. Judging from all the vociferation, South Carolinians were clearly rankled by outside interference in their state's internal affairs and were bound and determined to bring it to a halt.[14]

In the end, both South Carolina and the South won. "Cotton Ed" beat off his Roosevelt-backed challenger to win reelection, with 56 percent of the vote. And the anti-lynching bill was withdrawn from consideration in the face of the onslaught by the South's "durable talkers." *The State* paper was quick to clarify what the South had been fighting for in this legislative battle: not the right to lynch, it pointed out, but the principle of local control over local affairs. "This conflict [has been] waged to maintain an ancient and wholesome Southern concept of democracy," the paper's editorial concluded.[15] Just as it had in 1860, South

---

*The so-called Force Bill had consisted of legislation introduced by Representative Henry Cabot Lodge of Massachusetts that called for federal oversight of congressional elections, especially in the South. The bill failed to pass both houses of Congress.

Carolina stood firm in the conviction that it was fighting for fundamental "American principles." But just as in 1860, the principles it fought for were inextricably bound together with race.

The world in general seemed a rather threatening place in early 1938. In a pictorial overview of the preceding year, *The State* newspaper had described 1937 as "a violent year." The German luxury airship *Hindenburg* had exploded and burned at Lakehurst, New Jersey. Workers and strikers had fought pitched battles during the steel strike in Hershey, Pennsylvania. The Japanese invasion of China had culminated in the destruction of the city of Shanghai. There had been bombings in Madrid and floods in the American heartland. A gas explosion had leveled a public school in New London, Texas. Even fun took on a violent tinge as the new craze, the "Big Apple Dance," ushered in an era of unusually aggressive footwork. In a sign that some were eager to escape all the hubbub and bother, the paper also noted that "front porches" were now being built on the sides or backs of new homes, as people sought quiet and privacy away from the street. To most living at the time, the word "rebels" conjured up thoughts of the anti-Franco forces fighting in the Spanish (not the American) Civil War. But there were still some reminders of the South's "late great unpleasantness"—alongside reports foreshadowing a greater unpleasantness in the making. In February 1938, a Confederate flag was hoisted out the window of the Georgia Confederate Pension Division. And in March, Adolf Hitler announced the annexation of Austria.

One other thing happened that eventful year of 1938. Compared to other events, it was a rather minor affair—but significant nonetheless. A Confederate flag appeared in the South Carolina State House—the first of three that would become the focus of debate and eventually be removed sixty-two years later. The bill that placed the "battle flag of the Southern Confederacy" behind the Speaker's desk in the state House of Representatives was introduced by a young state representative from Union County in the north-central part of South Carolina, a man named John D. Long. The resolution (H. 1954) that Long sponsored was simple and straightforward. It merely called on the clerk of the House of Representatives to secure a federal flag, a state flag, and a Confederate battle flag for display in the house chambers. Nothing in the resolution spoke of defiance against national policies or federal interference; nowhere does it mention segregation or southern traditions.[16]

But there is something about the timing of it that raises suspicions, that taints any notion that the gesture was meant to do nothing other than honor southern heritage. The Long resolution was introduced on 2 March 1938, shortly after the anti-lynching debate had ended. It came about against the backdrop of a senate reelection campaign in which President Roosevelt had "intruded" into state affairs by advocating Smith's reelection defeat. And it passed in the face of increasing worry over black political assertiveness and, more importantly, indignation over growing (northern) white support for southern black demands—along with the susceptibility of the federal government to (and Eleanor Roosevelt's open championing of) black causes.

Moreover, there are also Long's own statements, made several years later, in which he condemned northern agitators who were "seeking the amalgamation of the White and Negro races by a co-mingling of the races upon the basis of equality."[17] That was in 1942. Two years later he urged his colleagues in the state legislature to pass another resolution, this one declaring "our allegiance to established White Supremacy as now prevailing in the South and pledging our lives and our sacred honor to maintain it, whatever the cost, in war and in peace."[18]

The evidence that the Confederate flag went up in the state House chamber as a statement against federal interference in state racial affairs is only circumstantial. But for most southerners at the time, everything seemed somehow bound up together—in much the same way as it had been back in 1860. Federal interference posed a threat to the state's control over its own affairs—in particular its control over the state's racially segregated social order. Defending that order meant fending off federal challenges to it. Every intrusion was perceived as a potential threat to the core of southern life. Raising the Confederate flag was a signal that the southern cause, the "southern way of life," was still very much alive, and that South Carolina was prepared to defend it. No one needed to put it more explicitly—everyone understood the underlying meaning.

In 1944, at the same time that Long was reaffirming the state's allegiance to white supremacy, the state legislature, or General Assembly, had been busy adopting the so-called South Carolina Plan. This particular form of massive resistance attempted to forestall black participation in state party primaries (which, in a solidly one-party state such as South Carolina, were tantamount to general elections) by declaring those primaries private events organized by private organizations and thus exempt from federal jurisdiction. In order to lend greater credence to its effort, the General Assembly, meeting in special session that year, set about eliminating all state statutes relating to primaries—passing 147 bills during six days of feverish activity in order to do so. All the effort was in vain, however, after a ruling by Judge Waties Waring (a native Charlestonian) in 1948 effectively eliminated the white primary. So the state switched to another front. In 1951, in a signal that the state was prepared to throw the baby out with the bathwater in its fight against desegregation, the legislature passed a referendum deleting the constitutional requirement that the state provide for public schools.[19]

By 1956, challenges to the "southern way of life" seemed more imminent than ever before. Despite its best efforts to the contrary, the state was slowly being forced to back up into the future. The *Brown v. Board of Education* school desegregation ruling of 1954 (the core of which had grown out of a case originating in South

Carolina) had come down like a nine-pound hammer, shaking the state to its foundations and sending it scrambling to throw in supports to prop up the state's system of legal segregation. South Carolina was still following the old Calhoun strategy, meeting the opposition at the outermost edges of resistance. But to segregationists, however, it seemed as if those edges were creeping ever closer to the core.

The national Democratic Party, meanwhile, had moved further toward embracing the cause of black equality, with President Harry Truman offering new initiatives aimed at moving things forward. Unwilling to be "crucified on the cross of civil rights," several southern delegations had split from the Democrats in 1948, forming the States' Rights Democratic (or "Dixiecrat") Party, with South Carolina Governor Strom Thurmond running as the party's presidential candidate (a campaign in which the Confederate flag played a prominent role). Thurmond lost the race, but his defeat by no means marked the end of his crusade for the southern cause. In 1956 he authored the so-called Declaration of Southern Principles (or "Southern Manifesto"), setting down the case against the Supreme Court's *Brown* decision and restating southern resistance to integration. Thurmond's renowned physical hardiness came in handy a year later, during the senator's single-most energetic (not to say athletic) effort on behalf of the cause of states' rights, when he set the record for the longest filibuster in U.S. Senate history by talking almost ceaselessly for 24 hours and 18 minutes. The senator's Herculean verbosity failed to halt the offending bill, however, as the Civil Rights movement continued its advance.[20]

Meanwhile, back in South Carolina, the General Assembly was so furiously caught up in efforts to bolster segregation that one local journalist labeled 1956 the "Segregation Session." Describing the legislative year just concluded, R. E. Grier of *The State* wrote in his "Around the State House" column, on 11 April 1956, that "the 91st General Assembly . . . was largely dominated by one note—maintain at all costs segregation in the public schools of South Carolina. That note was echoed in bill after bill. . . ." In a show of resistance, students at the all-black South Carolina State College organized a strike to protest the dismissal of several members of the faculty, forced out by Governor George Bell Timmerman for advocating desegregation. The governor ordered state and local police to keep a check on "subversive elements" who might seek to incite demonstrations on campus.[21] Timmerman would be offered as the South's alternative to the liberal Stevenson/Kefauver presidential ticket at the Democratic National Convention in 1956.

John D. Long had been hard at work that year as well—now over in the state senate, to which he had been elected in 1955 and where he would remain until 1966. On 10 April, the last day of the 1956 legislative session, Long introduced a resolution (S.749) calling for the addition of a Confederate flag to the (state and

U.S.) flags already on display in the senate chamber. In his resolution, Long said that the Confederate flag represents "the divine cause of human freedom," adding that it "inspires our dedication to the resurrection of truth with glorious and eternal vindication." The record concludes tersely, saying merely that "On immediate consideration, the Resolution was adopted."[22] The front page of Columbia's *State* that day ran a story about President Eisenhower's proposal to create a federal civil rights commission.[23]

Early the following year, Senator Long delivered a brief address to his fellow legislators on the subject of the Confederate flag. The senator began his comments jauntily, almost jokingly, pointing out that the flag is the "symbol of the only nation known to history whose soldiers wore themselves out whipping and chasing the armies of the enemy and thus lost a war by utter exhaustion and collapse." He then offered a detailed account of the birth of the Southern Cross flag, reminding his fellow lawmakers that it was a South Carolinian (William Porcher Miles) who had "the honor of designing the famous Confederate battle flag." And for that reason, he continued, "there is unique and added appropriateness to the hanging of this famous and beloved banner in the legislative halls of the General Assembly of the State of South Carolina, the first state to secede from the Union. . . ." Then, speaking in a fashion more reminiscent of 1866 than of 1956, Long concluded by saying that though the battle flag is often referred to as the symbol of the Lost Cause, "there are those who believe . . . that no cause is lost whose principle is right."[24]

Now there were two Confederate flags in the South Carolina State House, within the very chambers where the arbiters of the peoples' sovereignty make the laws that govern all the people in the state. One *could* say that this was the act of a single man—a man whose actions on behalf of the Confederate flag were not necessarily linked to his views on segregation. One *could* say that the placement of those two flags in the chambers of the state legislature was an act of memorialization, done in commemoration of the sacrifices of southern soldiers and of southern families during the Civil War, or that it served as a rededication to more-general principles encompassed by the "Lost Cause," to the doctrine of States' Rights. One could claim all this—and one might well be correct. But that claim would be incomplete, insufficient to capture the picture whole and unedited.

Of course it was the act of a single man. But it was taken and made manifest with the consent of the majority of the peoples' representatives in the state. Long's segregationist views might very well have had nothing to do with his affections for the Confederate flag. But his views were consistent with a majority of public opinion in the state at that time. Being southern meant being segregated. Legal discrimination was part of southern self-identity, part of the "southern way of life." And for many the Confederate flag had come to represent not only the

Civil War era and the Lost Cause, but the contemporary southern cause of seg-regation in the battle over civil rights. It was part of a larger whole.

Similarly, although it is altogether possible that the installation of the Confed-erate flags in the state legislature was merely coincidental with the civil-rights struggle and aimed at nothing more than honoring the Confederate dead, it seems at least a bit strange that no Civil War or Confederate anniversary was being celebrated each time a flag was added. The state could have chosen to raise the Confederate banner in 1877, at the end of Reconstruction. But it did not. It could have hoisted one in 1906, when a joint resolution authorized the secretary of state to procure both a state and a U.S. flag for display over the capitol dome. Or it could have added a Confederate flag in 1910, when state law made flying the state flag mandatory. But it did not do so in any of these instances. Instead, each Confederate flag went up at a time when the state felt itself besieged by "outside" forces of change, with established patterns of social order and tradi-tional ways of life under challenge from within. For those in the state who viewed things the same way as Long did, it was but a small step from the battles of the Civil War to the battles of the Civil Rights Era. For them, the two were inextrica-bly linked. They would become even more so in the immediate years to come.

In the early 1960s, *The State* newspaper was still running a cartoon called *Ham-bone,* prominently placed near the top of the page and toward the front of Sec-tion A. Hambone was a black character of the Amos 'n' Andy variety—a simple soul who delivered humorous one-lined bits of "folk wisdom" in his daily appearances in the South Carolina state capital's chief newspaper. As race car-toons go, *Hambone* was a fairly innocuous affair. (A sample strip from 1961 has Hambone out working in the garden with a hoe as he says, "Kun'l Bob say wid all de millions a-cookin' ev'y day, hit's cur'ous how few evuh larns how!!" Back in 1938, when the first Confederate flag had gone up, Hambone uttered things such as "Miss Lucy says she wuscht I cud git things *in* mah haid quick ez I gits 'em outen it!!") To us today Hambone seems like a relic of a long-ago age. And even in the early 1960s, it was clear (at least to some) that his time was quickly passing—just as the era of Jim Crow would soon be passing.

By the early 1960s, many (especially many of the state's black citizens) felt that it was time for South Carolina to finally and fully rejoin the Union. But before it could take that final step, South Carolina first had to take a moment to commem-orate the last time it left the Union. The national Civil War centennial ran paral-lel with the struggle over civil rights, which some were calling the nation's "Second Reconstruction." But the civil rights struggle so overshadowed the commemoration of the South's glorious past as to nearly obliterate it. Most folks appeared too caught up in the problems of the day to worry themselves with memorials of events a hundred years gone. Others disliked the very idea of commemorating a time of national division and were concerned that nothing undermine the sense of national unity in the face of the threat posed by international communism. As one South Carolinian put it, "I don't believe in talking about all this Confederate business—this is America."[25] But the Civil War centennial would offer a small demonstration of just how intricately intertwined history and contemporary affairs still were.

Preparations nationwide for the Civil War centennial had been under way for several years—but South Carolina was rather slow to start organizing its own participation in the event. There seemed to be no burning interest in such observances at the time, certainly not in the state legislature. And except for the Sons of Confederate Veterans and United Daughters of the Confederacy, the sort of southern heritage organizations and reenactment groups we are familiar with today did not yet exist. Most of the early support for the establishment of a state centennial committee came from historians—as well as some state officials, such as Dr. J. H. Easterby of the South Carolina Archives Department. A national committee already had been established, at a time when South Carolina's own state committee was still nothing more than a piece of draft legislation. The state senate passed a bill (introduced by Senator Long) in 1958 authorizing the creation of a state centennial committee, but the House of Representatives failed to vote on the issue, so it had to be reintroduced in the 1959 session.

By the time the state General Assembly finally passed legislation creating a state centennial commission, twenty-one other states already had their own centennial commissions up and running. And even then there remained some confusion over exactly what South Carolina's commission should call itself (confusion that contained undertones of lingering historical contention). The joint resolution creating the state commission referred to it as the "South Carolina War Between the States Centennial Commission," a real mouthful. By contrast, correspondence coming from the national Civil War Centennial Committee was addressed to the "South Carolina *Civil War* Centennial Commission." By April 1959, the state organization had begun printing its own stationery, with a letterhead that bore the title "South Carolina *Confederate* Centennial Commission." But even that did not seem altogether satisfactory. By late 1960, as preparations for centennial events gained momentum, the group made one small addition to its name, now calling itself the "*Confederate War* Centennial Commission." (By contrast, South Carolina's neighbor to the south chose to keep in step with most of the rest of the country, naming its centennial organization the Georgia Civil War Centennial Commission.) It is also interesting to note that whereas the original stationery bore only a version of the South Carolina state seal in its letterhead, the Confederate War Commission soon adopted a letterhead that bore not only the state flag but also the rectangular version of the Southern Cross flag. It was a kind of flag-raising in miniature that foreshadowed the flag-raising over the capitol that soon followed.[26]

This southern name game also reflected the more general problem of what to call the conflict that had run its course between 1861 and 1865. The official term coined by the federal union was "War of the Rebellion." That, of course, did not sit well with most southerners, who insisted that they had not been engaged in an armed rebellion *against* U.S. civil authority, but rather in a political separation from the United States. Interestingly, the South had for a time following the war settled on the term "Civil War" as an acceptable alternative to the War of the Rebellion. Having won this small victory, however, the South later turned around and attacked its own invention (perhaps at the insistence of the Daughters of the Confederacy or the SCV), and now demanded that the erstwhile hostilities be referred to as "the War Between the States" (thereby emphasizing the states' rights aspect of the conflict). Newspapers—even southern ones—were reluctant to use such a clunky and cumbersome term and settled on a compromise of sorts. As Georgia-born journalist John Temple Graves put it, "newspaper people [were] afraid of the Daughters [and so] hit on [the idea of] calling it 'The Confederate War.'"[27] Thus was yet another term born.

Whatever disagreement there may have been about what to call the war, South Carolina left no doubt as to what it thought the war had been about. The joint resolution establishing the state centennial commission spoke of the "American War Between the Confederate States of America, South, and the Federal Union of the United States of America, North," then went on to describe

> the hardships borne by the people of South Carolina . . . the awful sacrifice . . . and the indignities thrust upon and suffered by the helpless people of our ravaged and plundered state, ground into the dust under the ruthless and relentless heels of overpowering military might, spanned by a bestial ferocity unmatched by savages, that laid waste our land and homes by death, destruction, fire, pillage, plunder, pestilence, famine, loot, poverty, and vandalism, invoking upon the defenseless women and little children of Columbia and of South Carolina a holocaust of horrors by an ordeal that even language failed its Chief Executioner, by having no word that could describe adequately the conditions of terror, and the Chief Executioner was compelled to resort to the nether regions and Holy Writ for the infamous slogan that "War is Hell," and so it was wherever he went. . . .[28]

Yes, South Carolina had accepted the results of Appomattox and had reentered the Union with the Constitution as the "supreme law of the land." But its 1960s legislators were keen to point out that the U.S. Constitution reserved certain rights "to the people and to the several states respectively," adding, in distinctly pugnacious terms, that the "liberty loving people [of South Carolina] ... are prepared in mind and resources to defend their state and land." In purple words wafted by the smoke of recent battle, it was as if the war had only just ended.[29]

Despite their late start, South Carolina officials expressed a wish to move up the date on which the centennial events would commence. The state commission sought to have the opening ceremonies set back to 20 December 1960 in commemoration of the hundredth anniversary of the state's signing of the Ordinance of Secession. By defining when the conflict began, the commission hoped also to define what it was about. Placing the start of the conflict in December 1860 rather than in January or April 1861 accorded better with the southern view that the Civil War was a fight over constitutional principles, such as states' rights, rather than a mere rebellion against federal authority. The national centennial organization, chaired by Gen. Ulysses S. Grant III (grandson of the Union commander), politely refused to participate in such an observance while wishing South Carolina well in any ceremony it might conduct in commemoration of the occasion.[30] The national Civil War Centennial Commission insisted on beginning the centennial observance with the *Star of the West* episode (the first hostilities of the war) in Charleston, in January 1961.

Chairman of the South Carolina commission was John A. May, a state representative from the south-central South Carolina town of Aiken (just down the road from Edgefield, Thurmond's hometown). May, who sometimes sported the honorary title "Colonel," had participated as a prosecuting attorney in Nazi war crimes trials following World War II, then returned to practice law and pursue a political career in South Carolina. After being named head of the state centennial commission in 1960, May put aside his law practice in order to devote his full effort to planning centennial events. Aside from his responsibilities in the state, May was also vice chairman and later chairman of the Southern States Centennial Commission, charged with organizing and coordinating centennial activities across the South. He was also a member of the Sons of Confederate Veterans and assumed various leadership roles within the group, including that of national commander-in-chief and commander of the South Carolina state division.

John May was a Civil War buff who avidly collected Civil War relics and other Americana, which he kept in a small museum at his estate, Mayfields, near Aiken. He was quite proud of his family's connections to the Civil War and had erected a memorial on the grounds of his estate to a great-great-uncle, John Amasa May, who had been killed at the Battle of Second Manassas and in whose honor May had been named. At one point, May chided the national commission for failing to include the middle "A" of his name when addressing correspondence to him; he insisted that they do so in proper recognition of his Confederate-era ancestor. May was sometimes jovially referred to as "Mr. Confederate" because of his interest in the Confederate era and because he occasionally appeared in public (including at the State House) dressed in Confederate uniform. During the centennial opening ceremonies in Charleston in 1961, however, May chose instead to don a flashy vest bearing a Confederate battle-flag pattern—which spread rather ostentatiously across his short, stout form.[31]

Also named to the state commission (following the death of state archivist J. H. Easterby in early 1961) was Senator Long, the man who had been instrumental in creating the commission in the first place. In recognition of his efforts in that regard, Chairman May presented Long with a reproduction of the South Carolina Ordinance of Secession just prior to the commencement of the centennial festivities in April 1961. During the presentation, May said that Long represented the "'true spirit' of the 'Old South.'"[32] It is unclear whether Representative May had in mind comments that Senator Long had made on the floor of the state senate in 1959, when, noting newspaper reports of the first black students admitted to the Virginia public schools, Long had said that it appeared "Virginia needed another Stonewall [Jackson]," and added: "South Carolina has segregation in the public schools and South Carolina intends to keep it."[33]

Against the backdrop of simmering sectional and racial tensions, centennial organizers knew they were treading on thin ice. They were at pains to "keep the . . . program on a high plane and always on a non-sectional, non-partisan, non-political level."[34] The southern organizers were especially keen to make sure that any speaker who might be invited to official centennial events be "a national figure who will *not* give an antagonistic speech," and they were constantly vigilant for any signs of "animosity and any hint of 'opening old wounds.'"[35]

There seemed little real cause for concern, though. The spirit of the Compromise of 1877 was still alive and well. The chairman of the National Civil War Centennial Commission, Ulysses S. Grant III, was described as "sharing the determination of his grandfather in striving to keep the nation's observance of the Civil War centennial on a neutral course.[36] Grant was eager to accommodate southern preferences and willing to give the South what it felt was its due during centennial observances. Grant offered an example of the gentle (though precarious) balance he sought when he said, "Southerners . . . cannot be expected to ask forgiveness for 'the heroism and self-sacrifice their forefathers displayed, even if fighting for a cause some of us feel was in error.'"[37]

The main problem facing centennial organizers in South Carolina, however, lay in how to generate more public interest in centennial events—and to sustain that interest over time. Commission chairman May wrote in late 1959 that he "had visited Charleston and Ft. Sumter twice during the summer and did not find the people there too enthusiastic."[38] But aside from organizing the debut events in Charleston and publishing several informational pamphlets and a guide with suggestions on how to mark the occasion, the state commission appears to have left the bulk of the work to local groups and organizations or to county and

city centennial committees, where they existed. These would take on the responsibilities of coordinating parades, inviting speakers, establishing displays and
exhibits, putting on plays, and creating school programs. Many of the events
would cluster around Confederate Memorial Day and would concentrate on
larger towns and cities, especially Charleston and other coastal areas. For many
South Carolinians, however, the events would leave little lasting impression.
With some, the only recollection associated with the centennial had to do with a
personal form of commemoration practiced by a small band of southern men.
Dubbing themselves "The Brothers of the Brush," these fellows decided the best
way to mark the occasion would be by letting their whiskers grow long in imitation of their Confederate-era ancestors. In the clean-shaven, buzz-cut South of
the early 1960s, it was the kind of display that was bound to attract attention.

It might not have been the kind of attention the state commission sought,
however. State organizers made it clear that they encouraged only events that
were dignified, that avoided any display of bad taste. They were especially anxious to discourage the sale of tasteless souvenirs, in particular those making
unflattering or disrespectful use of the Confederate flag. In *South Carolina Commemorates the Confederate War Centennial, 1961–1965: A Manual for Observance
in the Counties and Cities of the State of South Carolina,* the centennial commission said (in italics) that "the use of the Confederate flag as a design on jackets,
underwear, handkerchiefs, paper plates, napkins, and receptacles is generally to
be deplored."[39] The overall character of the centennial was of great concern to
both national and state commissions, though they may have differed over details
and interpretations. All of the participants were of one mind that "the 100th
anniversary is not a celebration, it is a commemoration."[40] South Carolina echoed
the goals set down by the national commission, that "observances be a new study
of American patriotism," in accordance with the "sentiments of Robert E. Lee,"
who, at the end of the war, had admonished his fellow southerners to "'abandon
all local animosities and make your sons Americans.'"[41] *The State* newspaper said
that this new study of American patriotism "must be based on a broad knowledge of the underlying facts," pointing out that "we are not preparing to commemorate a romantic myth. . . . we are preparing for a searching look at a chapter
from our own history." "Where fables and legends have obscured the facts," the
paper declared, "the truth must be made clear."[42]

But it was unclear exactly *whose* "fables and legends" should be targeted, and
which truths were to be made clear—or even, for that matter, just how willing
the South would be to take a "searching look" at its own "romantic myths."
Southerners were intent on making sure that the character of the centennial
adhered to their interpretation of history. South Carolina's centennial planners
were determined to see that the South's viewpoint be defended, and that it not be
deprived its proper place in centennial celebrations. It saw its duty not only in

honoring its Civil War veterans, but in telling the "true story of South Carolina's people" during the war—"their leadership in a cause they believed to be right, their willingness to fight for principle . . . the great ideas that are the basis of our freedom." "Hold[ing] dear their sovereignty [and] oppos[ing] all-powerful government, . . . they fought for freedom [and] suffered perhaps more than other states in the aftermath of war."[43] While willingly acknowledging that "Americans from every section produced the divisions that led to war," the South remained far too defensive to fully accept its own culpability in the calamity, implying in hardly veiled terms that the North must admit that it was at least equally to blame for the war. And most notably: the South failed to make any mention of slavery as a cause of the conflict. The South was in no mood to have its solemn commemoration inconvenienced by any discussion of the region's erstwhile peculiar institution. It was well aware that by permitting any consideration of slavery, it would be opening itself up to a general discussion of contemporary racial affairs—a prospect most southerners were unwilling to face.

But the legacy of slavery lay smoldering just beneath the surface. And despite the best efforts of organizers, both North and South, the emotional and political ice they were treading over was—even a hundred years on—still far too thin and fragile to avoid cracking. The legacies of history rushed in through the portal of civil rights, threatening to swamp the grand festivities that marked the start of centennial. South Carolina's policy of segregating public accommodations was the impediment to the demonstration of national unity that centennial organizers claimed they were trying to promote.

The National Civil War Centennial Commission had scheduled its fourth national assembly, to be held in Charleston, to coincide with the events centered around the 1861 firing on Fort Sumter. Numerous other state commissions were invited to attend as well, among them the state commission from New Jersey. The New Jersey delegation included a black member, however, who, by the laws of South Carolina, would be prohibited from staying (or even attending meetings) in any of Charleston's racially segregated hotels. New Jersey protested South Carolina's policies and threatened to boycott the Charleston events. A geographic schism appeared unavoidable. President John F. Kennedy intervened in the "verbal civil war" that ensued by asking that South Carolina put aside its segregation practices for the duration of the centennial ceremonies. When the state rejected his proposal, he called for the national assembly to be moved to the Charleston Naval Base, a federal installation where South Carolina's segregation laws would not apply.

An event designed to demonstrate regional reconciliation and national unity instead reflected something of the same sentiments that had led to the sectional conflict it was commemorating. The official opening of the Civil War Centennial became a divided event, with dual headquarters and dual programs. Except for a few luncheon speeches and the events held at Fort Sumter, centennial functions followed separate (but equal) tracks. The southern delegations stayed and conducted their affairs at the Francis Marion Hotel in downtown Charleston, while several other delegations were quartered in the more spartan setting of the Charleston Naval Base. A spokesman for the naval base said that "most guests [would] be housed in enlisted men's quarters—cubicles with six to eight double-decker beds." The guests would not be charged for their accommodations, he announced, but they *would* have to pay a fifty-cent laundry fee.[44]

Passing almost unnoticed against this noisy backdrop, another Confederate flag was raised at the state capitol in Columbia. Like the two that had preceded it, this latest Confederate flag was hoisted without any special fanfare or public declaration. The chairman of the South Carolina Centennial Commission, John "Mr. Confederate" May, acting in his capacity as state representative, simply requested that the state agency responsible for State House maintenance add a Confederate flag to those already flying atop the state capitol, in observance of the Civil War centennial.[45] The new flag was not hoisted above the dome right away, however. The dome flagpole (which was really nothing more than a piece of plumbing) had not been used for more than five years, after it had been determined that a ladder leading up to the dome was unsafe. State law, however, mandated that the state flag fly above the State House daily. And so a second flagpole had been erected on a lower part of the building, visible only from the front, where the federal and state flags could be flown. At the beginning of the centennial week, a Confederate flag was purchased for nine dollars and hoisted beneath the other two. Some suggested that it be placed on top, above the other two. But "non-legal minds," *The State* newspaper reported, "said there [was] probably something on the books preventing that."[46] It is unclear whether or not Representative May intended that the Confederate flag continue to fly beyond the centennial week. But continue to fly it did. It remained atop the front of the State House for a year, until it was eventually raised above the dome itself.

The world over which this newest Confederate flag rose was a world of diverse tensions and diversions, a world different from our own, yet not altogether dissimilar. As Civil War centennial ceremonies got underway in Charleston, the trial of Holocaust organizer Adolf Eichmann began in Jerusalem—while, back in Germany, Chancellor Konrad Adenauer proudly (though perhaps somewhat prematurely) declared that "no trace of Nazism remains in the German people."[47] That same day, the United Nations in New York approved a plan for an economic and diplomatic boycott of the Republic of South Africa, in protest against its system of white supremacy and racial apartheid. Two days earlier, Greenwich Village in New York City had been the scene of violent rioting, the result, according to some sources, of "Beatnik racial mixing."[48] Speaking before the newly established Committee for Equal Employment Opportunity, President Kennedy "launched a drive to remove 'every trace of discrimination' from the filling of federal jobs or hiring by contractors who do business with the government."[49] A day later the president issued an executive order to this effect, which (South Carolina papers duly noted) would have the effect of "forcing the mixing of races in South Carolina textile plants." The entertainment page of those same newspapers carried ads announcing that *Gone With the Wind* would begin a special return engagement in state theaters to mark the Civil War centennial.

Events in the state capital took a backseat, however, to those getting underway down along the coast, where a cheeky prankster had painted one of the Confederate soldier monuments along Charleston's famous harborside battery with a coat of Union blue, adding to the inscription at its base the words "The Yankees have landed."[50] The honorary guests at the Charleston commemoration included not only General Grant of the National Civil War Centennial Commission, but also P. G. T. Beauregard III, grandson of Confederate General Pierre Beauregard, as well as Robert E. Lee IV, descendant of the Confederacy's most celebrated military commander. Upon his arrival in the port city, Grant graciously accepted the gift of a Confederate flag from South Carolina's "Miss Confederacy," who was decked out in period costume for the occasion. But neither Grant's benevolent indulgences of southern predilections nor the historical heft that a Lee or a Beauregard lent to the event could patch over the divisions that had cleft the centennial ceremonies in two.

The South was on edge and in no mood to have anyone picking at its sore spots, neither historical nor contemporary. "Please don't start another Civil War while you're here," the editor of Charleston's newspaper, the *Post and Courier*, enjoined half-jokingly as the centennial guests arrived. Anxious to avoid a row, most of the attendees were careful about what they said.

But some were less guarded in their remarks. Speaking at a luncheon hosted by the South Carolina Confederate War Centennial Commission, former South Carolina governor and one-time U.S. Supreme Court justice James F. Byrnes said that he felt the creation of a national Civil War centennial commission had been a mistake. Too little time had passed, he believed, to allow for a fitting and dispassionate commemoration of the war and its aftermath—a war that had been preceded by what former U.S. Secretary of State Byrnes termed a "cold war, diligently conducted by the political extremists of the North." Moreover, it was a war that was still continuing. "For our sins we are still being punished," he said. Slavery was the cross that southerners were forced to bear. "It prevents us from giving to many subjects the unbiased consideration of which we are capable." Refusing to go into what he termed the "nightmare" and the "crimes" of Reconstruction, Byrnes nevertheless blamed most of the disruptions of that era on northern "carpetbaggers" and their southern "scalawag" compatriots. Only with the end of Reconstruction had the South been able to return to a state of "normalcy," the former governor said. "When governmental control returned to white hands, whites and Negroes together, without a Marshall Plan or aid of any kind from the federal government, brought the South from poverty to prosperity." Byrnes concluded his speech by declaring that "the Negro has made greater progress in the South than in any other place on earth . . . and, certainly in this state, their schools are as good and in many instances are superior to the schools for white children."[51]

Later that same evening it was (then still Democratic) Senator Strom Thurmond's turn to speak to the all-white group of southern state commissions assembled in the Francis Marion Hotel. Thurmond made a plea for national unity based on toleration of sectional peculiarities and peaceful coexistence between the country's distinctive regions. The country should "capitalize on our differences," he said, rather than crucify ourselves with diverse ideas, problems, and conditions. Referring to the South's segregationist policy of "separate-but-equal," the senator "contested the notion" that in order for anything to be equal it must be the same, that "anything that is separate must of necessity be unequal." In words strangely (though inadvertently) reminiscent of former Governor Cole Blease, Thurmond said that "inequality will exist as long as liberty exists." Those calling for desegregation, he believed, were "equalitarians who cry out for equality beyond reason." Due to the threat posed by the Soviet Union and China, it was quite common at that time to suggest a nefarious association between the advocacy of desegregation and Communist subversion. And so Thurmond did not neglect to add that advocacy by Communists of "social equality among diverse races . . . is the surest method for the destruction of free governments. . . ." Senator Thurmond went on to proclaim the South "the biggest and most persecuted minority in this country today," the target of "idealists who are willing to preach idealism for others but who are unwilling to put their idealistic ideas to a personal practical application." He called on "over-zealous radicals . . . to restrain themselves in their fervor to impose their views on others who have to live with the problems the radicals would conjure up in their caldron of integrationist idealism." Then, hearkening back to John C. Calhoun's doctrine of concurrent majorities, Thurmond urged that each section of the country be left to deal with its own problems as it saw fit.[52]

Meanwhile, over at the Charleston Naval Base, the racially integrated Fourth National Assembly of the National Civil War Centennial Commission was having its own banquet, with its own set of speakers. Most of the attendees there came from northern state commissions. But there were also a number of southerners on hand as well, including South Carolina Governor Ernest Hollings and Julian Metz of the Charleston Chamber of Commerce. Most of these southern representatives kept their remarks noncontroversial. But one among them did not flinch from taking the fight to the enemy, returning fire on those who had criticized the South for imposing its segregation laws on the centennial observance. The fighting words did not come from either General Beauregard or General Lee, however, but from Ashley Halsey, the Charleston-born editor of the *Saturday Evening Post.*

Speaking to the banquet the evening of 11 April, Halsey said that "no real problem of human relations has yet been solved by the bayonet . . . yet we have seen bayonets again in Little Rock and we may see them perhaps tomorrow in New Orleans." This was more than the New Jersey delegation could stomach, having already been angered by an earlier speech in which Halsey had criticized New Jersey for hypocrisy, calling it a "state of racial bigotry" and charging that "racial prejudice and discrimination in New Jersey are such that it takes amazing effrontery for its politicians to rebuke any other state or community upon any circumstance or pretext." At General Grant's request, Halsey had agreed to eliminate several portions of his address thought objectionable to the New Jersey delegation (including his suggestion that states be allowed to vote on the question of whether or not to maintain segregation laws). Despite these excisions, however (which Halsey later called "a sad capitulation of free speech," likening the experience to Lee's surrender at Appomattox), the New Jersey delegation protested the editor's comments and demanded that Grant permit them fifteen minutes for rebuttal. Grant turned down the request, and the Jersey delegation walked out of the banquet in protest. Most of the delegation left town before the reenactment of the firing on Fort Sumter, though three among their number chose to stay and attend a rally sponsored by the local NAACP instead. Following the fireworks at the fort, the remaining centennial guests packed their bags and left town, most of them probably at least a little dissatisfied at the outcome.[53]

The State paper shared in this sense of disappointment, agreeing with James Byrnes that organizing a centennial observance like this one had been a mistake. Suggesting that a "minimized commemoration" might have better avoided opening up "old sores," it went on to say that

> In a sense the War Between the Sections of 1961 is worse than that of 1861–1865. Frightful as was the original conflict, it was an honest war. It was fought on the basis of sincerity.
>
> More good blood was shed in the original war than in any in modern times. More bad blood has been shown in the commemoration than in almost any such supposedly mutual event aimed at being an expression of national unity.

Instead of what its organizers had intended it be, the centennial commemoration had become an occasion for "deceit," "effrontery," for "intersectional charges of prejudice," for the "low tactics of bickering," and for "charges and counter-charges that make the commemoration a mockery."[54] The lingering legacies of war and the pressing demands of contemporary social change had combined to defeat attempts at a commemorative demonstration of national accord.

John May remained vigilant in defense of southern honor and equal treatment of the Confederate memory. During the Sixth National Assembly in Baton Rouge in 1963, the same black New Jersey Commission delegate who had been at the center of the Charleston controversy complained about a "ceremony held at Fort Warren by the United Daughters of the Confederacy, where a Confederate flag was displayed on the same level as the national colors." May shot off a letter to the national commission, asking if reports were correct that they intended on "rectifying" the situation during the next assembly, in Atlanta in 1964. National commission director James I. Robertson wrote back denying any knowledge of the complaint and pointing out that he intended on treating any aspect of the Confederacy—including the display of the Confederate flag—on equal terms. And there the issue rested.[55]

In 1961 the Civil War centennial still had four more years to run. And with the Civil Rights movement gaining momentum there would be plenty more opportunities for the country to demonstrate its continuing disunity over both history and race. During the centennial observances in Charleston, South Carolina Commission Chairman May had tried to avoid controversy, limiting his own public comments to an inventory of historical events and a hortatory adulation of the Confederate-era generation. His only openly contentious assertion, if it can be called that, came when he claimed that the "war of the South" had not been "fought for property interest in slaves," and that "the war was not . . . waged by the South in defense of slavery." May's interpretation of history was, of course, perfectly in tune with the general opinions in the South at the time. But his claim that "the world is surely coming to the conclusion that the cause of the Confederacy was right" could only apply to those who accepted May's (and the South's) reading of history.[56]

While May played the role of the old-fashioned southern gentleman, anxious to avoid any unpleasant public bickering, John Long was less concerned with the p's and q's of protocol, preferring undiluted directness over decorum. By choice, compulsion, or mere circumstance, Long did not address any of the official centennial gatherings in Charleston. He instead chose to direct his commemorative comments to those assembled in the chambers of the state senate, during the closing days of the legislative session in early May 1961. In an address he delivered while introducing a resolution (S.411) calling on the state legislature to officially recognize 10 May as Confederate Memorial Day, Long once again telescoped the past into the present, casting contemporary conflicts in Civil War terms. While calling for national unity in the face of the Communist threat, Long blamed the North for creating the kind of divisiveness within the country that directly imperiled national security. While others lay the burden of guilt on the South's refusal to forget the Civil War, "the truth," Long said, "is that try as hard as we may, we have never been allowed to forget." Ever "since that fateful day when we laid down our arms at Appomattox," Long continued, "the North has never ceased to carry on and wage unrelenting Black War against the South and the white people of the South, seeking to destroy our way of life. . . ."[57]

In his appeal for national solidarity, Long called on the North to put an end to its intrusions into southern affairs, which could only serve to weaken the country's resolve, and turn its attention instead to the threat from abroad. "This nation was founded by a race of people who have never been conquered," Long said. And "the only way that we can be conquered," he added, "is by disunity and by the enemy from within. . . ." Complaining that "the North unceasingly insults and prods the South at every opportunity," Long warned that "the North should remember—should never forget—that this . . . nation is founded upon integrity"— first and foremost "racial integrity." With images that once again recalled the Civil War, Long went on to inveigh against efforts he felt had been wasted on behalf of civil rights, efforts that could have better been spent in meeting the Communist challenge:

> The seasoned and battle-trained paratroopers who were dropped from the skies upon the unfortified and defenseless city of Little Rock, capturing and occupying the city like enemy territory, could have been far more fittingly dropped on Havana to far better account. . . .

Long then jokingly suggested that some ammunition be set aside for "shoot[ing] at the sit-inners," before adding in a similarly colorful vein:

> If all the time, effort, money, and brains that have been wasted to carry on the futile Black War of the North against the South and the Southern white people were piled up in one heap to use against communism it could provide enough thrust to blast Khruschev's head through the moon and ram the whole of Russia into orbit where space doesn't count.

Long's interpretation of southern historical experience since the Civil War inclined him to view the Confederate cause as one and the same with the South's (and the nation's) struggle for freedom—though it remained unclear which he considered the greater threat to the cause of liberty: that posed by international Communism, or the one posed by the crusading North. To him, it was apparently all one and the same.[58]

The battles over the meanings of history and the proper commemoration of historical events continued to nag at the centennial observance. In late 1961 May read a newspaper story indicating that the National Civil War Commission would "place great emphasis in 1962 and 1963 on the Emancipation Proclamation and that an attempt would be made to get European and African speakers for this observance." May immediately fired off a letter to the national commission asking if it were "true that the Commission is going to use the Emancipation Proclamation as a vehicle to promote so-called Civil Rights." He then pointed out in no uncertain terms that "we in the South vigorously oppose any effort to turn our commemoration of the Civil War into a political issue of any kind"—moreover, he did "not know what anyone from Africa could add to this." In early 1962 May sponsored a resolution of the Southern States Centennial Conference reiterating their concerns about this matter along with their wish that the commemoration be conducted "in fairness to both sides." There was little real reason to worry, however. The national organization proved quite accommodating to southern sensibilities, leaving the celebration of the Emancipation Proclamation up to the individual states to decide.[59]

The year 1962 was an unsettling time for the South. The Civil Rights movement was in full blossom and on the advance. More so than in the recent past, many in the region appeared to adopt a more fatalistic view of events. Acting like a society besieged, they waited to see where the next bombshell would land. South Carolina's *State* newspaper wrote, in an editorial on New Year's Day, that "the year 1962 may be that in which ultimate pressures, initiated or supported by the federal government, may be applied in the Civil Rights field" and encouraged South Carolinians to "maintain their customary composure, without the surrender of personal principle."[60] There was a sense of things ending, of a turning in the road, of old affiliations broken and traditional patterns dying.

In his State of the Union address in January of that same year, President Kennedy called on Congress to pass legislation aimed at eliminating literacy tests and poll taxes as a requirement for voting. Some in the South were surprised by Kennedy's move, expecting him to avoid civil-rights issues, as he had the year before. Instead, his administration quickly followed up with a bill giving concrete form to his initiative.[61]

The South struck back, denouncing the proposals as "politically motivated and unconstitutional." They found Kennedy's "New Frontier" of "increasingly questionable character" and declared that southerners might well assign themselves the role of "watchmen [over] the trend toward . . . a genuflection to minorities so ostentatious as to blur the fact that majorities even exist." *The State* editorialized that it had not "been established that the elimination of [the poll tax] has produced better government or cleaner or more responsible government." And it declared the elimination of literacy tests an "evil act," saying that "a republic such as ours cannot successfully exist without an intelligent electorate. . . ."

By early 1962, the southern social and political order was under attack along several fronts. In late February the U.S. Supreme Court ruled against all forms of segregation in public transportation. Vice President Lyndon Johnson took on the southern working world, telling the NAACP that the administration intended to make every effort to "end racial discrimination by unions and important southern industries." *The State* lamented that "our civil liberties are being lost . . . in the fight for civil rights."[62]

Meanwhile, in the midst of all this, the Confederate flag at the state capitol in Columbia was quietly moved from its perch on one side of the State House up to the dome to join the federal and state flags already flying there, following renovations to the flagpole earlier in the year. The move was accomplished by means of a concurrent resolution, a simple legislative device normally dispensed with in an almost pro forma fashion, with little or no discussion or debate. Concurrent resolutions are often associated with matters of no significant legal weight, such as declarations of appreciation, condolence, or congratulation. They do not prompt the same level of scrutiny or consideration that a regular legislative bill would—which, in contrast to a resolution, requires three readings (and three votes) for passage. The measure (H.2261) was short and to the point, unadorned by rhetorical flourishes, much like the two that preceded it. It simply directed that the Confederate battle flag be flown on top of the State House. The resolution moving the flag was introduced by "Mr. Confederate," Representative May, in mid-February 1962 and concurred to by the senate a month later. The flag was hoisted atop the dome for the first time in early April of that same year.

The legislature could have elected to place the flag somewhere on the State House grounds, perhaps alongside one of the many memorials that grace the capitol's lawns. During the debate that preceded the vote to remove the flag from the dome in the year 2000, one pro-flag senator even admitted that the flag probably should have gone to the grounds to begin with. But back in 1962, placing the flag on top of the dome may have simply been the easiest, most convenient solution available. A decision to put it anywhere else would have required an additional appropriation—for a flagpole and other equipment. Using a concurrent resolution to move the Confederate flag to the newly installed pole on the dome was simply the most hassle-free option available.

Was all this flag-waving a sign of defiance, a way of staking out territory in the battle over civil rights? Perhaps. Then again, maybe it was just the obsession of a self-proclaimed Civil War buff and Confederate enthusiast. In June 1964, May, in his capacity as head of the S.C. Centennial Commission, had sent a request (endorsed by a resolution of the U.S. Centennial Commission) to the U.S. Park Service asking that the state commission be allowed to erect a flagpole at Fort Sumter, from which the Confederate flag would be flown. The Park Service turned down the request, "with every possible sympathy," saying that "only the United States flag is to be flown over a federal establishment as a symbol of the United States sovereignty, and to indicate federal ownership."[63] It would have been ironic to say the least—a kind of belated and symbolic victory in defeat—had the South succeeded in re-raising a Confederate banner above the very "federal establishment" where the Civil War had begun and which the federal Union had fought so long to recapture. The federal government (in the guise of the National Park Service) was unwilling to surrender the fort so easily the second time around.*

"Colonel" May's enthusiasm for things Confederate was boundless and expressed itself not only in his eagerness to erect Confederate flags wherever and whenever an opportunity presented itself. He also sought to establish what he called the "Southern Heritage Foundation," which would continue the work of the Southern States Centennial Commission after the centennial period ended. The organization quickly faded away, but it served nevertheless as a prototype for the kind of southern heritage groups that began spreading across the landscape during the 1980s and 1990s. May also stipulated that after his death, his estate, Mayfields, should become a museum and exhibition center for his collection of Civil War relics and other memorabilia. Like the Southern Heritage Foundation, however, this plan was also never realized. Rather than become the permanent home of his collection, Mayfields was instead demolished, sometime during the 1970s. May's collection ended up at the South Carolina State Museum and includes books, furniture, silverware, guns, cooking items, and even a cannon— along with a full-sized replica of the Confederate submarine, the CSS *Hunley*. This is May's most lasting (and least controversial) bequest to South Carolina's Civil War heritage.[64]

The flag May had hoisted atop the State House (and, even more clearly, those erected by John Long) bore a more mixed legacy, bound together as they were with the attitudes and circumstances of a time in which the South was still struggling with the meanings and consequences of its own history. The Civil War centennial ended in 1965—but the Confederate flag continued to fly over South Carolina's capitol for many years thereafter. It remained in place while time moved on, circumstances shifted, and attitudes changed. A new generation came of age that had been altered by the experience of a more racially integrated life. Integration changed the political constellation in South Carolina, too. The political culture of mid-1990s South Carolina differed in many ways from that of the early 1960s. Political, social, and economic change gave the state a new complexion.

But the changes and challenges that modernity posed to this newest "New South" came upon a region still contemplating the lingering implications (and

---

*Fort Sumter does, however, now fly both the Stars and Bars as well as the Stainless Banner, for historical reasons—but not the Southern Cross flag.

lasting values) of its past. For much of its history, South Carolina had seemed, to borrow Faulkner's phrase, like "a land primed for fatality," in which considerations of race had often overwhelmed reason and respect. The battles fought out on the South's behalf by May and Long would resonate in the fight over the flag's display thirty years later, as the issues of history and race became subsumed into a debate about the proper interpretation of southern history and the inherent meanings of the Confederate flag. The heritage battles of the 1990s were a mix of myth and fact, past and present, politics and principle, in the latest round of the seemingly never-ending struggle to define southern identity.

Three

STANDING GUARD AT THE GATES
OF SOUTHERN HISTORY

*The river that does not know its own source
will dry up.*
                              Yoruba saying

*. . . to remember too much is, indeed,
a form of madness.*

              Caryl Philips, The Nature of Blood

"The Night They Drove Old Dixie Down," by The Band, is a song about a pros-trate South, a South lying "in defeat." And for a good portion of its history, that is how the South perceived of itself: defeated, bitter, and anxious. The South had felt put upon even prior to the Civil War, hard pressed by forces at work beyond its borders and largely outside its control. Then the war came and made things worse. The postwar South, burdened with the consequences of military and moral defeat, remained ever wary against future challenges, anxious about the capitulations it believed were certain to follow if it failed to practice constant vigilance. Prior to the war, the South had been perpetually on guard. After the war, it fell into a state of nearly constant defensiveness. Most of its wounds were self-inflicted—and most of its anxieties were chimeras. But for the South, they seemed palpably real—and for many southerners, they became marks of proud distinction. Like someone suffering from a chronic (though not incurable) con-dition, the South became accustomed to its injuries, and in a sense even grew fond of them. It coddled and doted over its wounds, alternately hiding them away and then holding them out, Amfortas-like, for all to see and venerate. The South held onto its wounded past like the corpse of a favorite child, unwilling to accept the undeniable and surrender the body to the tomb. The South stood for-ever mourning at the graveside of its former self.

We often say that history teaches lessons. And we like to think that we can avoid future mistakes by learning from past error. But as often as not we become habituated to error, accustomed as we are to the patterns of thought and action that have led us to err in the past—we elect simply to repeat our mistakes rather than commit ourselves to the fundamental changes necessary to avoid making the same mistakes in the future. We commit the same errors, perhaps because we have drawn the wrong lesson from history or because we stubbornly refuse to see the past for what it is. The trauma of defeat left the South defensive, distrustful, and apprehensive—and obstinately resistant to elemental change. Its resistance to change committed the South to a pattern of perpetual "lost causes"—which may help explain the perennial "New Souths" that emerged almost once a generation: The South continually found it necessary to reinvent itself, to replace the "old" with "new." But it always seemed to reinvent itself according to familiar designs.

The pattern began even before the Civil War. Just as there have been numerous "New Souths," there was more than one "Old South"—though each was, or became, something both less and more than real, a myth. Even the "Old South" we think of today, the South of magnificent plantations built from the wealth generated by the unholy amalgamation of cotton and slaves, had its own, even older, "Old South," to which it hearkened back with longing and wonder—the kind of longing only mythmaking can satisfy. *Their* "Old South," was the pre-cotton, tobacco South, located, as Edmund Wilson puts it, "in the eighteenth century . . . in eastern Virginia, colonial and post-Revolutionary. . . ."[1] It was there, in nostalgic reminiscence, that the antebellum South found its sense of sustenance.

The pattern continued (and even intensified) after the Civil War. In contrast to the forward-looking momentum in the rest of America, the postwar South preferred to keep its eyes focused rearward. Through much of its history, the region was held in tension between those who would move the South surely (albeit slowly) into the future and those who rejected the present for an improved version of the past. The novels of Thomas Nelson Page and Kate Chopin provided the literary harmony to the sentimental melodies of southern tradition. They, like Joel Chandler Harris, Ellen Glasgow, and others, rejected the "New South" promotionalism and commercial materialism of Henry Grady for a more graceful and bucolic model drawn from an idealized southern past. Later on, the same conflict would be fought out between the Southern Agrarians and representatives of southern progressivism, such as Howard Odum. The Agrarians' classic 1930 manifesto, *I'll Take My Stand: The South and the Agrarian Tradition*, was a paean to traditional southern culture and a declaration of opposition to modern capitalist industrialism and to the kind of scientific social criticism offered by Odum and others.

Southern traditionalism was so strong that even progressive and reform-minded southerners—people such as Grady and Odum, along with writers George Washington Cable and Walter Hines Page—felt compelled to pay it obeisance by couching their own ideas in terms that did not directly challenge the established social order. They, too, remained fundamentally conservative in their attitudes toward change, preferring to keep as much of the traditional South as possible, though reshaping it to fit contemporary needs. "The future was to be the past repeated," wrote southern journalist James McBride Dabbs, "though improved in detail."[2] Henry Grady, for one, employed the "Lost Cause" as a tool in his efforts to bring about a diversification of the southern economy. Rather than denounce the past, Grady and other "New South" promoters sought instead a blend of progress and tradition that would bring the South more into line with developments elsewhere while preserving enough of the old order as was necessary to ease the process of transition.[3] For many southern traditionalists, however, even this small step went too far.

So the South stepped backwards into the future, its movements slow, its advance often tentative and reluctant. And because of its awkwardly inverted approach to progress, the region was ever eager to find secure handholds along the way, handles that through habit became dependencies. Jim Crow was one of those handles; it became a habit of mind, an addiction. The "Old South" (the one we know best, the one from the first half of the nineteenth century) had fallen into a deep dependency on cotton—and on the slave-based economic and social order that cultivated it. After the destruction of the old order in the war, the South managed to take only a minuscule step away from its single-minded dependency on one-crop agriculture—and on the race-based social order that went with it. In the process of industrialization, the South soon fell into an equally deep dependency on textiles, a dependency that would last into the second half of the twentieth century. Each step along the way, each successive dependency, was thought to hold the key to perpetual satisfaction and unperturbable stability, to be just the thing to check the onrush of modernity. But each new phase became, in turn, yet another "Lost Cause," another kind of dead-end.

Even in the latter half of the twentieth century the region was still unable to shake its habit of dependency. This time it was cut-rate labor and an anti-union culture of civic boosterism, a pattern of cheap land and low taxes coupled with a laissez-faire, low-service attitude in state and local government. It was a success, of sorts. But in the process, the modern South, the South of the new consumer age, has become dependent on shopping malls and golf resorts, on chain restaurants and chain stores and all the other neo-colonialist elements of suburban sprawl that are rapidly eating up the last of the South's remaining natural resources, its land. It seems as if the South has merely reached the latest in a long series of one-crop economies that denude, erode, and exhaust the southern landscape.

Critics of contemporary trends have accompanied the South through its history, right up to the present. There is a straight line leading from Thomas Nelson Page (or William Grayson of South Carolina, or George Fitzhugh of Virginia before

him), through the Southern Agrarians and the representatives of southern conservatism (such as Richard Weaver and M. E. Bradford), right up to the southern
heritage promoters and the neo-Confederate groups of today. Like their predecessors, these modern-day southern traditionalists view many contemporary
trends with a jaundiced and disapproving eye.

For many of the southern traditionalists,* the homogenization of southern
culture, of American culture in the South, is itself a kind of defeat, a surrendering of particularity and uniqueness, a capitulation to uniformity. "You can go to
Ashley Phosphate [Road, in Charleston], or to Harbison [Road, in Columbia], or
Haywood Road in Greenville, spin around three times and open your eyes, and
you couldn't tell which city you're in," says Chris Sullivan, one of these contemporary southern traditionalists. "And that's just like some road in Charlotte,
which is just like some road in Raleigh which is just like . . ."[4] The South has
become like every place, and like no place in particular: Xerox, U.S.A.

Sullivan is one the defenders of the faith, one of many in the southern heritage movement standing guard at the gates of southern history and identity. Sullivan is a native South Carolinian, who, like many in the movement, can claim
Confederate ancestors on both sides of his family. And like many of his fellow
southern traditionalists, he was "knighted" to the cause through the good graces
of the protectors of the faith, the United Daughters of the Confederacy—the
keepers of the grail of southern heritage. The UDC, more than any other group,
has kept the candle lit at the altar of southern conviction. From the time that a
young Sarah Morgan wrapped herself in a Confederate flag (a "Bonnie Blue
Flag," that is) in a show of defiance against federal troops occupying her native
Baton Rouge in 1861, southern women have taken a prominent role as the un-
armed wing of the southern cause. It is their unfailing constancy that did much
to keep the Confederacy alive through some rough patches And it was southern
women who almost single-handedly preserved the memory of the Confederacy
long after the Confederacy itself had passed away.

Ensconced in an office displaying portraits of Robert E. Lee and Strom Thurmond, along with thick stacks of *Civil War Times* magazines, Sullivan recalled his
own initiation at the knee of these gentlewomen Confederate evangelists. "When
I was growing up in downtown Greenville, there were two old-maid sisters, the
Jennon sisters, living nearby. Both of them were in the UDC. And I'd ride my
bike up there to see them from time to time when I was a little boy and they
would give me books and we talked about all aspects of South Carolina history.
One day I went up there—I guess I was in my early twenties—and Catherine

*The term "southern traditionalist" serves here as a catch-all for the various groups
(neo-Confederate, flag defenders, heritage enthusiasts, etc.) that have been involved in one
way or another in the debate over southern heritage and southern history.

Jennon asked me why I wasn't a member of the Sons of Confederate Veterans. And I said, well, I didn't even know anything about 'em. And so she signed me up."[5]

The sisters would not be disappointed with Sullivan's subsequent service to the Confederate cause. Sullivan not only joined the SCV, he later became the organization's state commander—at a time, in 1994, when the Confederate flag was becoming a hot topic of political debate. As a consequence of his position in the SCV, Sullivan became one of the leading pro-flag spokesmen in the state. From there, he would go on to serve as associate publisher and acting editor of *Southern Partisan* magazine, based in Columbia, South Carolina.

Founded in 1979, *Southern Partisan* is perhaps the oldest continuously running, and certainly the foremost, southern heritage/neo-Confederate publication today. The editor-in-chief is Richard M. Quinn, a Republican campaign consultant whose clients have included Ronald Reagan and Strom Thurmond. Quinn's son, also named Richard, is a Columbia attorney and leader of the Republican majority in the state House of Representatives. The younger Quinn was a strong supporter of the Confederate flag display during the battle over the flag's fate in the state legislature—though he eventually chose to support the decision to move the flag to its new location on the State House grounds. Interestingly, the flagpole at the offices housing Richard Quinn and Associates flies both the U.S. and S.C. flags, but not a Confederate one. *Southern Partisan* has been joined by an ever-expanding group of similarly oriented periodicals, including *Chronicles,* put out by the devoutly conservative Rockford Institute; the *Edgefield Journal,* another South Carolina heritage publication; the *Citizen Informer,* from the Council of Conservative Citizens; and *Southern Patriot,* published by the League of the South—along with a seemingly endless collection of websites devoted to the Confederate cause, with names such as "The Confederate American," "All Things Southern," "The Land of Cotton," "Southern Commentary," "The Southern Traditionalist," "The Confederate Lady," "The Virginia Gentleman," "Dixie Rising," "The Closet Rebel," "Children of the Confederacy," "Johnny Reb's Home Page," and "Confederate States of America—Past, Present, and Future," just to name a few.

Although they may differ somewhat in terms of their emphasis and political involvement, these sources do have a certain outlook in common. Many of the websites are nonpolitical, directing their attention almost exclusively to the Confederacy and to Civil War military history. Others are aimed toward the minutiae of period reenacting. And some are simply interested in making a buck. Of those that take political positions, the spectrum of opinion generally ranges from conservative to very conservative, with (as one might expect) a heavy emphasis on matters such as states' rights and federal government interference in local affairs, opposition to affirmative action and abortion, promotion of home-schooling and school vouchers, support for caps on immigration, a disapproval of foreign entanglements, and an emphasis on a more unilateral approach to the promotion of America's interests in the world.

Southern heritage groups often seek to distinguish themselves from their neo-Confederate brothers in arms. And to an extent, the distinction is a useful one. While heritage defenders tend to concentrate on contemporary battles over Confederate history, Confederate monuments, and the display of the Confederate flag, neo-Confederate organizations, such as the Southern Party or the League of the South, focus their attention on constitutional questions about the roles of government, interpretations of American history, and the "cultural oppression" of the South. Neo-Confederates view themselves as political separatists and southern nationalists and tend to take the idea of southern secession more seriously than heritage groups do. While neo-Confederates tend to be more concerned with political theory and fundamental questions of statecraft, southern heritage folks devote their energies mainly to defending southern (particularly Confederate) symbols and observances.

But at some point, the distinction tends to break down, with influences, positions, and even personnel flowing back and forth between the two movements. The neo-Confederates' concern for the survival of southern culture often contracts into a defense of the Confederate flag. And the heritage groups' efforts to organize a defense of the Confederate flag often turns into a general criticism of political correctness, liberal bias in government and the media, the decline of standards in society, and the ongoing oppression of the South. It all eventually turns into a rather heady stew of resentment, cultural criticism, and political stridency.

Any distinction between political advocacy and political abstinence dissolves as well. In one issue of *Southern Partisan*, for example, articles on southern culture, southern lifestyle, and southern history are mixed together with reports on contemporary battles over the Confederate flag, Confederate monuments, and other "heritage" issues, as well as opinion pieces on presidential candidates, rulings by federal courts, and school prayer. Alongside a full-page advertisement for classic "heritage" literature (James Ronald Kennedy and Walter Donald Kennedy's *The South Was Right!*, for example, or Michael Andrew Grissom's *Southern by the Grace of God*) and another soliciting donations in support of a lawsuit to return the Confederate flag to the top of the Alabama capitol, there is also an ad drumming up support (and contributions) for the "Southern Military Institute," a private, all-male academy "steeped in Southern tradition" and "emphasizing the foundations of Christian faith and morality," the goal of which is to "train young men to be strong moral leaders who are devoted to God, dedicated to constitutional government . . . and who are able to serve their church, community, or State" (though, notably, not country).[6]

The primary concern of *Southern Partisan* is "southern heritage," and its tone alternates between stentorian adamancy and resentful defensiveness. It misses no opportunity to state a southern point of view. All subjects, no matter how innocuous or mundane, stand in service to a general defense of southern ways of life. Even a simple travel piece—a tour of the Jack Daniel's distillery in Tennessee— provides an opportunity to remark on the hard-pressed South, victimized by Yankee crusaders (in this case, by New England prohibitionists): "If we line up the abolitionists, the prohibitionists and those who are engaging in the current attack upon the South's tobacco industry, we can see a long history of organized societal hatred towards Southern culture."[7] Not surprisingly, then, an editorial in the same issue refers to the fight over the Confederate flag as "nothing less than a skirmish in the on-going struggle to define the meaning of southern history."[8]

For heritage defenders the stakes are high—and the South is forever on the defensive. But from the South's point of view, the stakes have *always* been high and survival perpetually imperiled. This was certainly the case during the period leading up to the Civil War. And it was equally true—some might say more so— after the war was over. Southern defensiveness quickly reignited and spared no effort to explain and justify southern actions and attitudes. The effort began right away, in 1866, with the publication of such books as *Is Davis a Traitor?* by Albert Taylor Bledsoe (the answer: of course not) and *A Defense of Virginia*, by Robert Dabney; and in magazines such as *The Southern Review* and *The Land We Love*. Former Confederate President Jefferson Davis did his part with his two-volume *Rise and Fall of the Confederate Government* (1881)—an "unrelenting, and seemingly unending, defense of the South," quipped one observer.[9]

The erstwhile vice president of the Confederacy, Alexander Stephens, certainly did his part to promote and defend the southern cause. Even the title of his 1868–1870 work speaks volumes: *A Constitutional View of the Late War between the States; Its Causes, Character, Conduct and Results: Presented in a Series of Colloquies at Liberty Hall*. Judged by weight alone, Stephens's two-volume defense of the Confederacy would have tipped the scales in favor of the South. Not counting its appendices or indices, the work came to a total of 1,455 pages of mercilessly unabating explication and argumentation.[10] And Stephens's defense of the Confederacy did not stand alone. The cause was carried forward by means of enterprises such as the *Southern Historical Society Papers* (an effort originally headed up by former Confederate General Jubal Early) and through publications such as the *Confederate Veteran*. These, along with the activities of the UDC and SCV, formed the foundations of the original Confederate heritage movement.

The southern heritage groups and neo-Confederates of today are direct descendants of that earlier movement—but their lineage is not an unbroken one. The links between the two are emotional and philosophical, not institutional. The gradual reconciliation between North and South, which had begun during the Spanish-American War at the end of the nineteenth century and which reached its fruition during World War I, helped to reintegrate the South into the fabric of national life, soothing its fears of northern cultural domination, diminishing its need for historical exculpation, and reducing its defensive dependency on Confederate hagiography. A new sense of self-assurance curtailed the South's urge to lean on its Confederate crutch.

But if the original Confederate movement did not beget these latter-day rebels, what did? Was it perhaps H. L. Mencken's biting 1917 essay "The Sahara of the Bozart" or the embarrassing portrait offered in James Agee's book *Let Us Now Praise Famous Men* (1941)? Was it the scathing novels of Erskine Caldwell or Lillian Smith, or any number of similarly unflattering portraits of what was called the "benighted southland," portraits that were perceived by many in the South as assaults on southern dignity and self-respect? No doubt Franklin Roosevelt's comment that the South constituted the nation's number-one economic problem also played its part (even if many south of the Mason-Dixon Line agreed with his diagnosis). And surely *I'll Take My Stand* played a role in this too, as did, perhaps, in its own way, W. J. Cash's *The Mind of the South* (1941) and C. Vann Woodward's "The Search for Southern Identity" (1958). And of course we should not underestimate the influence *Gone with the Wind* had in reinvigorating the romantic view of the South, hearkening back, as it did, to the moonlit and magnolia-draped school of southern literature founded in the previous century.

The increasing strength and activism of the nation's blacks and the growing criticism of southern segregationism also played a key role in inflaming southern defensiveness, spurring the southern reaction that stimulated a renewed sense of southern sectionalism. As we have seen, agitation for progress toward black equality and black participation in all aspects of national life had, by the 1930s, prompted the South to redouble its guard and signal its disapproval of those trends by, quite literally, sending a flag of alarm up the flagpole. The placement of the Confederate battle flag within and atop the South Carolina State House was just one example of a more general reawakening of southern consciousness.

Even as early as World War II—a war that supposedly united the country to a degree and with an intensity that melted all lingering divisions—something was clearly already afoot in the South. There were some, such as members of Prof. Clyde Wilson's family, whose wartime experiences—their coming together with men from other parts of the country—made them suddenly more aware of their own "southernness," a sense of difference due solely to their origins. "When they came back from World War II," Wilson recalls, "their southern identity had heightened, basically because of the reaction of others. Other people had made an issue of their speech and their customs." It was childhood memories of those returning southern soldiers, he says, that spurred his interest in southern history and led to his involvement in the crusade in defense of southern culture. Wilson went on to become professor of history at the University of South Carolina, a Calhoun scholar (and enthusiast), and a founding member of the League of the South, one of the premier organizations in the southern heritage movement.

Wilson and his colleagues established the League of the South in order to organize those "who want to keep something different" about the South. As Wilson puts it: "A lot of people were coming together with the feeling that southern identity was in peril and that we needed to do something to *actively* preserve and celebrate it. Our distinctive identity was being attacked from all sides. But also, it was simply being forgotten by a lot of our own people. We had a feeling that there was something valuable there and we wanted to consciously preserve it. That was the negative side. On the positive side, there was a considerable movement toward devolution working in the advanced world. There was a strong feeling that government is too centralized and that there was a need for a reassertion of traditional culture, instead of allowing everything to be homogenized. And certainly the South represents the most genuine subculture in the United States—the longest, and the most historic." But according to Wilson, the South was (and still is) threatened with "ethnic cleansing," its cultural patrimony on the verge of being wiped out.

League members tend to be "educated and affluent, middle-aged men who work professional jobs and live in the suburbs."[11] Unlike some of their fellow southern traditionalists, Leaguers (as they call themselves) tend not to get directly involved in political activism or demonstrations (though they may engage in such things under a different guise). Its members prefer to think of themselves as a cultural vanguard, whose purpose is to promote southern cultural awareness and distinctiveness. They are not populists, however. While sharing the same ideological disposition with the rest of the movement, Leaguers are a well-spoken set whose writings are, for the most part (and in contrast to many other heritage defenders), well-formulated, coherent, and clearly stated. All take an interest in history and some are (like Wilson) professional historians or other academics. Since their viewpoints reside somewhere outside the mainstream of academic life, however ("non-politically correct," as they say), these renegade pro-southern scholars often find themselves at odds with the bulk of the intellectual and scholarly community.

The League of the South sees itself as a cultural bulwark against outside influences that threaten to undermine the South's sense of itself. As a cultural elite, they aim to bring about a South capable of defending itself from those outside influences by reinvigorating the region's sense of its own cultural distinctiveness. The League of the South is modeled after a pattern established by nationalistic cultural movements of the nineteenth century (most prominently in central and eastern Europe), and by contemporary sub-national groups such as Italy's Lega Nord or the Quebecois separatists in Canada. Like these, they see their task in first developing a sense of separate cultural unity within the South in preparation for the eventual establishment of a southern "nation" separate from the United States—or, barring that, to create a South that is at least culturally independent of the rest of America and coequal to it in political sovereignty.

All of this may sound rather far-fetched, but the Leaguers take it quite seriously —and they underpin it all with a specific plan of action. In the spring of 2000, the organization issued its "Declaration of Southern Cultural Independence," stating that the "sovereign states of the South . . . are a separate and distinct people with an honorable heritage and culture worthy of protection and preservation." It called on southerners to "abjure the realm of the American Empire that now threatens the liberties of our families and communities, and the corrupt and sterile national culture that pervades this land." It urged them to "decline to participate in this alien, national culture" and instead "attempt to preserve southern language, speech, manners, music, literature, tradition, thought, custom, and faith." Contrasting the ethos embodied in the two "cultures," the declaration continued:

> Our cultural inheritance is not based upon the abstract slogans, armed doctrines, and sanctified greed that characterizes the present American regime. Instead, it is based on the permanent things that order and sustain life: faith, family, tradition, community, and private property; loyalty, courage, and honor. Cut off from these permanent things, the South will become only a point on the compass. . . .[12]

To promote southern cultural independence, the League supports the establishment of so-called Hedge Schools. These southern cultural academies are modeled after Irish institutions of the same name set up to preserve "the Irish . . . language and culture [at a time] when [Ireland] was under British occupation and the English were trying to wipe out their language and customs."[13] The League also has proposed sponsoring "Southern Culture Clubs" in public schools, which would be directed toward encouraging and promoting "the study and appreciation of our Southern history and culture" and "counter-attack[ing] the current mindless, man-centered egalitarianism" prevalent in American culture. In its "Proposed Cultural Mandate for South Carolina" the League recommends that southerners develop a separate "Southern Scouts" program (as an alternative to the Cub and Boy Scouts of America, which "strayed" when it began "accepting alternative lifestyles"). Southerners should strive to "use traditional orthography" based on the British Oxford standard; and they "should invoke

Southern . . . ways of communicating that bespeaks of locale." The League also hopes to encourage local restaurants "emphasizing southern cuisine," and declares that all "non-southern foods shall be referred to as foreign. NY bagels [and] fast foods, like McDonalds and Subway, should . . . be considered as foreign 'restaurants,'" the League declares.[14] The League's program of cultural independence is aimed at encouraging the development of a southern consciousness that will be strong enough to, at the very least, fend off "foreign" influences, and, at best, one day culminate in the South's political independence.

The worldview and political philosophy of the League runs in direct line from the old-line conservatism of Edmund and John Randolph through John C. Calhoun and on to contemporary thinkers such as Russell Kirk and William F. Buckley. Although they may sound like conservative Republicans, "hard-core" Leaguers consider the Republican Party to be as much a part of the problem as the Democrats, since both parties function indistinguishably as coequals in the ruling regime. As Wilson puts it, the Republicans "only propose to capture the decent conservative instincts of the people and make sure they don't go anywhere." After all, he points out, "the Republican Party came into existence for the purpose of conquering and exploiting the South."[15] In Leaguers' eyes, the Republican Party once again proved its cupidity when a majority of its members in the state legislature voted in favor of removing the Confederate flag from atop the S.C. State House. Southern nationalists (or "paleo-federalists," as they sometimes call themselves), such as the League of the South, define the southern conservative tradition as a movement in opposition to the "gradual drift toward Leviathan" that began with the Confederate surrender at Appomattox. It is embodied in a southern culture that preserves the legacy of traditional virtues, "a country in which people are sober, honorable, jealous of their liberty and, most importantly, God-fearing." It is based on "social-bond individualism," which "emphasizes both the rights of the individual and the pivotal role that social institutions have played in sustaining these rights." And it rejects "much of the intellectual legacy of the Enlightenment, which has tended to emphasize the immediate gratification of human needs over transcendent values such as faith, honor, and patriotism." Adieux, Thomas Jefferson—and most of the rest of the nation's Founders, Enlightenment thinkers all![16]

In spite of its growth over the past decade, however, the League of the South remains a marginal outfit with hardly measurable influence in southern affairs. These modern-day Calhouns keep largely to themselves (as befits a cultural vanguard), issuing their proclamations and dispersing their creed to like-minded members within the confines of their own limited congregation. Most South Carolina flag defenders are not attracted to the kind of secessionist bluster and wordy philosophizing that Leaguers enjoy. Southern secession hasn't the remotest appeal to them, even as a joke. The League only gets their ear (when it does at all) by linking the battle over Confederate symbolism to the broader struggle for southern identity.

To League members and others like them, the Confederate flag is a center-piece in the campaign for southern awakening. As Wilson puts it, the flag is "part of the cultural struggle [aimed at] keeping the South alive. It is a very strong symbol, an unusual symbol. It is one of the few things that really exhibits a deep current of brotherhood in the South right now." And perhaps as importantly, he adds, "southern symbols are some of the most trenchant symbols of non-politically-correct thinking in the country."

A trenchant symbol it is indeed—and not only in the United States. The Con-federate flag is like no other symbol of its kind. It has become an internationally recognized brand name, the standard currency of rebelliousness across the globe. And in the process it has been ripped from its cultural roots. It has become just another trendy accessory, a truck-driver's necessity, an essential accouter-ment of country-music fandom, a "cool" adornment for an international set of pseudo-individualists and short-cut iconoclasts. For many it is just a curiously appealing splash of flamboyant color, an eye-catching design with a certain inde-finable panache, but with no more intrinsic meaning than, say, the national ban-ners of Monaco or the Central African Republic. The commercialization and internationalization of the Confederate flag may have refashioned the connota-tions associated with it, but it has not altered its essential historical meaning. It has not redefined what the flag means in the South or as a part of southern history.

And what about South Carolina's League of the South? What does this neo-Confederate cadre of contemporary southern rebels have to say about the flag? What does it mean to them? As one might expect, the League makes no bones about either the flag or who they consider its enemies to be:

> We assert that the Confederate battle flag is a symbol of the conservative Christian culture of the South. That culture is diametrically opposed to the leftist culture that has destroyed the foundations of numerous countries (including the United States) in the 20th Century. . . .
>
> The Flag . . . is more than a mere piece of cloth. Not only does it represent the blood sacrifice of our Christian Confederate ancestors, but our future as well. Wherever that flag waves, there exists a commitment to the principles of States' Rights and local self-government. The starry St. Andrews Cross waves in opposition to the illicit and immoral concentration of power in Washing-ton, D.C. . . .[17]

For the League, the flag is much more than a mere historical relic, more than a memento of a bygone era. To them it is the embodiment of ideals whose validity have not been diminished by time, altering circumstances, or changing attitudes.

For the League, the political (and social) philosophy that underpinned the Confederacy remains as credible and legitimate today as it was over a century ago. And so, for them, the flag is not merely a symbol of a glorious southern past, peopled with characters whose values and conduct remain worthy of emulation today. It is the outer regalia of an ongoing campaign aimed at cultural preservation and regeneration. Leaguers do not see themselves as mere caretakers of the Confederate legacy. To neo-Confederates, the Confederate flag is a means of rallying contemporary southerners to the cause of a South yet to come, to a South (whether independent of or merely distinct from the United States) that does not simply hearken back to the past but attempts to reconstruct that past in the present.

This is rather heady stuff for most folks in the broader southern heritage movement. And again, most of them are not attracted to the ideas and ideals of groups like the League of the South. Most define the struggle more narrowly: They just want the symbols of their heritage safeguarded. While they may share certain attitudes and outlooks in common with the neo-Confederates—and most do adhere to a conservative political philosophy and an orthodox worldview—they are not out to erect a new southern republic based on an antebellum model. For the bulk of heritage defenders, the struggle is over the past: its defense in the face of critical interpretations by detractors and its preservation in the face of negligence and indifference on the part of its inheritors. They seek to preserve the past from the oblivion of forgetfulness and to prevent the memory of their ancestors from being tarnished by what they see as the distortions of contemporary political correctness and racial politics.

This is where folks such as Chris Sullivan believe their task lies. And so, in addition to his role as past commander of the South Carolina Sons of Confederate Veterans, and alongside his work at *Southern Partisan,* Sullivan has also headed up the Southern Heritage Association (SHA), a political action group specifically devoted to the flag debate in South Carolina. The Southern Heritage Association was set up by the folks at *Southern Partisan* to rally support behind the continued display of the Confederate flag at the State House. As its head, Sullivan served as a leading spokesman for the cause and participated in numerous mediation sessions with flag opponents. The SHA was part of a loosely confederated group of pro-flag forces in South Carolina—some of which, such as the South Carolina Heritage Coalition or the Heritage Preservation Association, were established specifically because of the flag controversy; while others, such as the Council of Conservative Citizens, got into the fray as an extension of their broader (right-wing) political agenda.

In the eyes of the SHA and the S.C. Heritage Coalition, the Confederate battle flag flying over the State House was nothing more, or less, than a "war memorial." It had been placed there in 1962, they said, "in memory of the centennial celebration of the War . . . to memorialize [South Carolina's] more than 18,000 known war dead—as well as thousands of additional unknowns." While admitting that "the Civil Rights movement was certainly a major issue during the sixties," they unblushingly denied that "the raising of the Confederate flag over the capitol is any more relevant to the Civil Rights movement than it is to the Cold War, the Vietnam War, Beatlemania, or the moon landings." They somewhat audaciously claimed that the Confederate flag's "placement underneath both the U.S. and the South Carolina flags puts it in a position of submission to the sovereign flags of the federal and state governments." As such, they said, the flag "should properly be viewed as a *unifying symbol* [emphasis added]— one that recognizes the reunification of South Carolina with the United States, and yet honors the common soldier who gave his life when his state called, without regard to the political correctness or incorrectness of that cause." To them, then, the flag is irreplaceable. "This simple symbol of blood-stained cloth carries more emotional impact than any sterile sculpture of bricks and brass could ever hope to do."[18] As a war memorial, the flag display was sacrosanct. To those standing in its defense, it was as deserving of protection and reverence as the Vietnam Memorial or the Grave of the Unknowns at Arlington National Cemetery.

The flag is sacrosanct not only because of its function as a war memorial, but also because of the past it embodies—because of what the flag represents. The first order of business for heritage defenders lies in making certain that the existing memorials to the past remain intact and in place. But along with that—and indeed, of even greater importance in the long run—is to make sure that the past itself also be kept intact and unaltered, that it not be lost through negligent forgetfulness nor obliterated by organized assault.

Keeping alive the public memory of the past is probably the easier of the two tasks. But even that is a challenge. Sullivan sees the fight against historical amnesia as a battle for public memory. He finds ample evidence of the way in which public memory can be lost in our civic commemorations of the Revolutionary War. "In South Carolina, prior to the Civil War, and even after," he points out, "June 28th was a big day. That was the day that we won the victory over the British at Fort Moultrie. June 28th, 'Carolina Day,' was a bigger day than the Fourth of July. But now, nobody other than the South Carolina Historical Society, which has made an effort to try and restore that commemoration, knows the significance of June the 28th."

The loss of cultural memory—or, more importantly, the disappearance of the mechanisms for commemorating the past—goes deeper still, Sullivan adds. "There was a time in South Carolina when the Revolutionary War was venerated; when Washington's birthday was solemnly observed. Now we have 'Presidents' Day.' We've taken all the presidents and put 'em into one day for commemoration.

Well, to me, none of the presidents—no matter what you think of them, Abraham Lincoln or Ronald Reagan—in my opinion, none of them compare to George Washington. So, to combine 'em all and say one president's no different than another is practically . . . well, to me it's disappointing. Despite the significance of the American Revolution to the founding of this country, a good bit of it is now receding in public memory. Now, Presidents' Day is an opportunity for Sears to have a tool sale. And the Fourth of July is a day to have a stock-car race."

Wilson takes a coolly Machiavellian view of all this. For him, the past we choose to celebrate, the ways in which we honor it, and the symbols we choose to represent it are decided on the basis of power relationships: Whoever has the power in a society determines what is celebrated and what is not. "What is it President Clinton says?," Wilson remarks. "In 2000 or 2050, the majority of the American people will be recent immigrants. The Founding people will be a minority. Not only the Confederate flag but George Washington and everything else you might want to think of as traditional will be irrelevant to people whose ancestors came from China or Latin America. That's certainly part of the cultural struggle going on in this country right now. Multiculturalism. Most of the history that Americans have traditionally honored will be seen as arrogant, evil, and aggressive." For Wilson, it's a struggle—perhaps a losing struggle—for political hegemony and cultural self-determination. One wonders, however, whether this sort of zero-sum game might bring about precisely the result that heritage groups aim to prevent. Maybe it simply promotes the same kind of uncompromising cultural impasse that brought about the South's first "Lost Cause."

Sullivan, Wilson, and other heritage promoters echo the sentiments expressed by proto-heritage defenders such as Robert Lewis Dabney, who said after the war: "If the generation that is to come ever learns to be ashamed of those men [i.e., the Confederate veterans] because they were overpowered by fate, that will be the moral defeat of Virginia, a death in which there will await no resurrection."[19] Sullivan also can foresee a time when the battle for southern heritage may be finally, and irretrievably, lost. "The demographics are changing in South Carolina so much," he points out, "that twenty-five years from now, we may have a Hispanic majority, or at least Hispanics may be a dominant factor in South Carolina. The way things are going down on the coast, around Hilton Head, we could have a situation where blacks, Hispanics, Yankees, and transplants from other parts of the country are in almost equal proportions to native South Carolinians. And, in regards to things Confederate, the other three may outvote native South Carolinians. So, at some point, twenty-five, fifty, a hundred years from now, maybe South Carolina will forget its heritage, its history. And at that point, the flag ought to come down. South Carolina won't deserve that flag any more, because it will have, in effect, sold its birthright. South Carolinians won't deserve to keep the emblem of their ancestors. I hope that day never comes, but I can certainly read enough about population trends to know that it's possible."

Wilson views the conflict in even more fundamental terms—with serious implications for cultural identity and, more importantly, for social cohesion. To him, the idea of a multicultural society is simply anathema. A true society, he believes, cannot be built on an ever-changing identity formed from the mixing of "old" and "newly arriving" cultural strains. Society's goal should instead be directed toward subsuming new arrivals into the primary culture. In other words, we should aim for fixed stability rather than fluid flexibility. But that is only possible, Wilson believes, if the existing culture retains its integrity, a cohesive sense of itself based on a collective appreciation of a common history and traditions. "To me," he says, "that's the symbol of a real civilization: You can absorb people . . . without altering your own culture. That is not true of America, of American civilization at large." It is only true of the South, the only section of the country that preserves an organic cultural identity.

Wilson then illustrates what he means. "A friend of mine, from South Carolina, went to Rockford, the second biggest city in Illinois. It's a hodgepodge of Italians, Swedes—but there's no culture, except in a very superficial way. There's no real society there at all. This is not true in the South." For Wilson, the consequences are obvious: "There's no way that a Rockford is going to produce a great novelist or a great songwriter or anything. There's no cultural family there," he says. A place such as Rockford, he believes, will not possess the cultural creativity or intellectual innovation necessary to make that society flourish—or, at the very least, it will not provide the sense of belonging essential to make life purposeful or rewarding. Only a society like that found in the traditional South— one that possesses social cohesion and a strong cultural identity—can provide a social structure that is whole, organic, and capable of continuous regeneration. Only it is capable of absorbing the new, the foreign, while keeping intact a specific and distinct sense of itself.

"Of course, in our terms," Wilson continues, "Yankees are foreign, too. My next door neighbor came to South Carolina from Iowa. But their children were raised in South Carolina . . . and they have become acculturated. You can do that if you have a real society," a society like that in South Carolina. Unlike Illinois, or Iowa, or most any other place in the United States, he says, "South Carolinians, possibly more than any other group of Americans, are people whose families have been here for a long time, who have specific personal memories of their family's experience in the war and Reconstruction and other things that are meaningful to them—it's part of their being. It's not just an abstraction, the way it is to most Americans. Most Americans do not have a depth of personal history. They believe in abstract things . . . it's not a tradition that's built over time. But we have that in South Carolina."

For the southern traditionalists, the social bond that holds a community together rests on a foundation of cultural integrity, which in turn depends, in large measure, upon a general consensus about the past, on a reading of history that dignifies cultural heritage. A proper respect for the past requires that the past be inherently worthy of respect, that it be exemplary, deserving of veneration, the object of civic reverence. And as far as the South's heritage defenders are concerned, that is only possible so long as history itself remains pristine and intact, undefiled by critical interpretations.

To them, history is inviolate. As the League of the South puts it: "History books change, but the past does not." History simply *is*. It exists in an unambiguous and pristine state not subject to challenge or reinterpretation. Heritage defenders carry their historical "facts" before them like monstrances, employing them to cast out falsehoods and to imbue their traditional view of southern history with unshakable and impervious legitimacy. Since truth is indivisible, there can be no competing claims to veracity, no two equally valid versions on what is or was. The heritage faithful claim to themselves sole possession of historical truth. Everything that differs from that is, to them, mere perception, opinion, or even willful misinterpretation and outright lie (born of the whims of politically motivated agendas).

The Confederate battle flag may mean a lot of different things to heritage defenders: southern honor, battlefield valor, wartime sacrifice, states' rights, southern identity, and pure individualism. But the one thing it *cannot* mean is what its detractors say it means: slavery, treason, and racism. To the flag's defenders, these interpretations have been applied to the flag solely for the purpose of robbing it of its respectability and undermining its cultural legitimacy. Take away a culture's symbols, its cherished icons, they say, and you destroy that culture. Reinterpretations that undermine the "purity" of history, that tarnish or denigrate it, do as much to destroy cultural cohesion as does the physical elimination of a culture's historical icons.

And so, at the bottom of it all, the wrangle over the Confederate battle flag is really a debate about history, about the history that the flag supposedly embodies, about what the past *means*. It is a battle over our understanding of the past, over our sometimes differing perspectives on history and the lessons we are to draw from them. Each side in the debate arrays its forces in a contest for possession of the past. History becomes the prize—capturing it the key. To heritage activists, it is a crusade for southern essentials. To their opponents, it is a struggle for equal recognition and a proper respect they feel is their due—a respect they consider long overdue.

The southern traditionalists rallying in defense of the battle flag (neo-Confederates and heritage enthusiasts alike) form their line of battle across a wide front of history. They throw up breastworks along the rough ridges that delineate the causes of secession and civil war. They set up defensive positions among the thickly wooded, rocky ravines of Reconstruction. They dig deep trenches and stout earthworks across the broad and treeless plains of American slavery and racism. Their line of attack is always the same: the adversaries are ignorant of history; they are misled victims of the mendacious, dupes of politically motivated historical relativists and other falsifiers of history; they are the hirelings of big-business boosterism, spineless scalawags who conveniently and thoughtlessly abandon the cause, selling off their birthright to the highest bidder; they are the soft-minded, self-deluded followers of multicultural fabrication and academic faddishness or the purveyors of hateful and malicious fakery, dealers in bogus sham. Their opponents are arrogant in their historical illiteracy and consumed with a matchless and unappeasable resolve to drive truth from the field. For the soldiers of southern tradition it is always the third day at Gettysburg. Everything hangs in the balance. Every hand is required and ready. The final assault is imminent. The Confederacy stands on the cusp of its greatest victory—or on the brink of impending collapse, rout, and defeat.

This may seem overly dramatic. But then again, southerners often have demonstrated an overripe passion for the drama of history. They take romping delight in the vicarious re-creation of the southern past—a predilection shared by non-southerners, however, as demonstrated by the general preference, among Civil War reenactors, for portraying rebel rather than federal soldiers. Heritage activists spare no effort—especially when it comes to rhetoric—in defending their cause. Words are their primary means of defense; and their supply of verbal ammunition seems inexhaustible. Perhaps even more than their love for the pageantry of history, southerners are known for their love (and liberal use) of strident and swaggering oratory. Many of the neo-Cons and other southern traditionalists write as if the ghost of Calhoun moved their pens, loading up their rhetorical broadsides with a measure of grandiloquence, verbosity, and orotund bluster not heard since 1860.

————◆◆◆◆◆————

It would burst the bounds of this book to try to deal with the whole range of arguments that southern traditionalists muster in defense of their view of history. But since history is their primary field of battle, as well as their weapon of choice, it might nevertheless be useful to take a brief look at a couple of cases, to examine, for example, how the southern traditionalists deal with slavery and its role in bringing about the Civil War, how they work their way around, over, and through the South's slaveholding and racist past. In the process it will hopefully become clear that heritage and history, though linked, are not identical or interchangeable concepts. It should also help to demonstrate that many of the "facts" that the heritage defenders wheel out as "proofs" of their readings of history are, in truth, the same kind of selective interpretations of the past they accuse their opponents of employing.

So just what does the historical record have to offer to help us better understand the causes of the conflict between North and South? If we are to take the principal actors at their word, on the face of it at least, slavery certainly was foremost in many a southern mind at the time—and on the tip of many a southern tongue. Here is what the father of southern traditionalism and the original defender of southern honor, John C. Calhoun, had to say about the matter (as captured in the diary of slavery opponent John Quincy Adams):

> I can scarcely conceive of a cause sufficient to divide the Union . . . *unless* a belief arose in the slaveholding states that it was the interest of the Northern states to conspire gradually against their property in slaves, and that disunion is the only means to avoid the evil.[20]

Calhoun understood the depths of the regional divide, the widening emotional chasm that increasingly separated North from South. He was certainly no novice in the struggle. He had served as the South's leading defender for more than a quarter of a century. And during that service he had done much to contribute to the growing tensions that divided the country—even though he saw himself as merely the desperate champion of an increasingly beleaguered South, a believer in national unity and a bulwark against the hotter heads that would seek to tear it asunder. The author does not wish to imply here that Calhoun alone spoke for the South. There were many other voices being raised at the time in the region—some of whom differed with Calhoun on the issues of the day. But Calhoun was a preeminent spokesman for southern interests and a principal defender of "southern rights." He was, and certainly has since, become an archetype in the pantheon of southern traditionalists. Moreover, he is viewed by many contemporary heritage enthusiasts as a premier symbol of a vital, self-confident, and self-sufficient South.

Calhoun stood ever vigilant to defend southern interests on the national stage. Historian William Lee Miller's exquisitely intricate recounting of the political battles over slavery fought out during the 1830s in the U.S. Congress reveals that Calhoun's strategy was aimed at preventing every congressional challenge to slavery—even to the point of squelching the mere discussion of the issue. Calhoun meant to stop the South's enemies "at the frontier," as Miller puts it.[21] Efforts to introduce into congressional debate public petitions calling for the abolition of slavery in the nation's capital, the District of Columbia, met with massive resistance from the South. Southern legislators responded to the initiatives by instituting a "gag rule" that smothered all discussion of the matter, at least for a time. Measures such as this were essential, Calhoun believed, since

> Any treatment of the petitions other than outright rejection might be taken implicitly to concede, however minimally and with however little likelihood of practical result, the legitimacy of congressional consideration of slavery.

Calhoun denied that legitimacy; that was the outpost not to be yielded, the threshold not to allow the fiends to cross. Even answering no was giving an answer, was acknowledging the question. And if the answer today is no—tomorrow or some future day it might be yes. So do not admit that the question can properly be asked.[22]

In Calhoun's view, the South stood on a precipitous slippery slope: to yield was to begin the descent to surrender—an attitude that would find similar expression in the debate over the Confederate flag more than a century later: If we surrender the flag, heritage defenders said, we will eventually lose everything. Calhoun believed that "even the least reproachable, best established institutions can be rendered suspect . . . by constant criticism and attack."[23] And like his flag-defending descendants of the late twentieth century, Calhoun sought to fend off what he and other southerners felt were "malicious" and "slanderous" insults to southern honor that came wrapped up in the anti-slavery (later anti-flag) arguments of opponents. Resentment over abolitionist attacks on southern character found expression in a kind of southern self-pity, echoes of which could be heard in the plaintive laments of the Confederate flag defenders. Like Calhoun, they, too, felt that "We must rise like culprits to defend ourselves." "We must ultimately be . . . degraded in our own estimation and that of the world."[24]

According to Calhoun, of course, the conflict involved more than merely the struggle over slavery. For an "intellectual force" such as Calhoun, a man with "a capacity to think down to first principles," the conflict between North and South contained broader implications about the proper relationships of power within the country and its political institutions.[25] In short, it was also a conflict over constitutional principles. This is a point that southern heritage defenders are fond of making: that the South fought the Civil War over constitutional principles, not for slavery; that it sought to defend the original constitutional order of 1789 against the "consolidationist" tendencies of an overbearing federal government intent on monopolizing all power to itself while riding roughshod over the rights reserved to the states.

But at its core, slavery was the force driving the debate over constitutional principles, not the other way around. Only by elevating slavery to a constitutional issue could Calhoun, could the South, lend their cause the legitimacy required to make it more than just a struggle for sectarian interests. As Calhoun put it in 1837:

> . . . domestic slavery, as it exists in the Southern and Western States of the Union, comprises an important part of their domestic institutions, inherited from their ancestors, and existing at the adoption of the Constitution, by which it is recognized as constituting an *essential* element in the distribution of its powers among the States, and . . . the passage of any act or measure of

Congress [to abolish slavery] would be a direct and dangerous attack on the institutions of all the slaveholding States [emphasis added].[26]

Calhoun stood on principle—the principle that slavery was a recognized and accepted element of the original constitutional order. Calhoun made it clear that the South considered the protection of slavery a vital interest to the South, open to no compromise:

> . . . the constitution is a rock. On it we can stand. . . . It is a firm and stable ground, on which we can better stand in opposition to fanaticism, than on the shifting sands of compromise.
>
>   If we do not stand up as we ought, in my humble opinion, the condition of Ireland is prosperous and happy—the condition of Hindustan is prosperous and happy—the condition of Jamaica is prosperous and happy, compared with what must be that of the Southern States.[27]

Speaking on the Compromise of 1850 (allowing California to enter the Union as a "free state"), Calhoun once again repeated the South's unyielding stand on the issue:

> The South . . . has no compromise to offer . . . and no concession or surrender to make. She has already surrendered so much that she has little left to surrender.[28]

Calhoun was certain that there was little the South could do "honorably and safely" to simultaneously promote national unity *and* defend its own interests. The only effective remedies to the nation's dilemma, he said, would have to come from the North; it would have to "conced[e] to the South an equal right in the acquired territory" (for the expansion of slavery) and "cease the agitation of the slave question. . . ."[29]

The South reacted with increasing irritation and growing unease to "agitation on the slave question." And it had good reason to be uneasy. Faced with, in some areas, a majority black population and intricately dependent on a slave-based economy, it should come as little surprise that the South would take offense at abolitionist agitation. It believed that, as Calhoun said, "to destroy the existing relation between free and servile races [in] the South would lead to consequences unparalleled in history"[30] It feared those consequences, and its reaction grew out of that fear. The notion that the institution of slavery was in decline, on its way out, and would have eventually faded away if given the opportunity to do so is mere speculation. The argument is undercut by the eagerness with which the slaveholding states sought to open up the new territories to slavery. Had the institution been in decline, it seems unlikely that the South would have invested such effort in defending it and ensuring its expansion. To attempt to downplay or dismiss, as southern heritage defenders do, the role that the struggle over slavery played in the conflict between North and South, in the secession of the southern states, and in the creation of the southern Confederacy is to argue ahistorically; it is an attempt to try and talk a way around history.[31]*

Southern heritage defenders have become increasingly adept at distracting attention from the main issue. They pursue a highly selective reading of history that attempts to shift blame and thus avoid the central concern. It is a well-worn southern path they've taken.[32] As South Carolina historian Lewis Jones has written:

> After the old order began to pass in the 1820s, population began drifting away. Cotton prices did not rise as did cotton production. Charleston lost its foremost place as a port. . . . It was easy for South Carolinians to blame the tariff, or to counterattack against the outside critics of the slavery system— but neither exercise coped with their real problems.
>
> South Carolinians are like that. Their response seems to be a haughty reflex: to embrace a Horatio-at-the-bridge stance, confess nothing, seek to appear righteous and shout loudly . . . all the time vociferously blaming "outside forces," such as the tariff, the abolitionists, the federal government. . . .[33]

Perhaps not *all* "South Carolinians are like that"—but many southern heritage traditionalists certainly appear to be.

Few southern traditionalists and heritage defenders entirely dismiss slavery's role in the Civil War. But even the more reasonable among them are nevertheless intent on minimizing the significance of slavery as a catalyst in bringing about the war. They prefer instead to place the Civil War–era into a much larger context. To them, the struggles of the twenty-first Century are the same as those fought out between North and South a century and more earlier. It is a struggle against a growing centralization (or "consolidation," in Calhoun's terminology) of governmental power.

For Chris Sullivan, the true nature of the "Lost Cause" encompasses virtually the entire history of the United States, from 1776 right into our own time. "By 1861," he says, "the North had begun to trample on the rights [established in the

---

*The South's attachment to its "peculiar institution" was so great that it proudly featured images of slave life on its paper currency. Most were simple cameos, showing slaves picking or carrying cotton (Corporation of Columbia [S.C.] 5 cent note, issued 28 June 1861). Others were more elaborate, such as the Farmers and Exchange Bank of Charleston $20 note (issued 13 April 1861), which featured a slave driving an oxcart loaded with bales of cotton, while, in the background, other slaves worked the fields. The right-hand corner of the same note bore a cameo of John C. Calhoun. The South's fondness for slavery scenes held firm over time. Notes featuring them are extant from at least 1857 (Bank of South Carolina $20 note) through 1872 (State of South Carolina $1 note).

Constitution] in progress toward the situation that we have now, with an all-powerful, omnipresent, central Federal government. The South wanted to uphold the ideas that the Founders had in 1776. And so they separated themselves from the compact that was the Union. The result was: the North invaded, we lost, and the Hamiltonian wing has proceeded pretty much unchecked to this day."

"Slavery," Sullivan continues, "was one of the symptoms of the conflict, but it was not the disease. I mean, certainly, you can't remove slavery from the debate. But if slavery had never existed, I still think there eventually would have been a separation. And just to add one more thing: I think the causes that led to the outbreak of the Civil War have not disappeared from the nation's headlines today. That's why I say that even if slavery could be classified as *a* cause, it certainly was nowhere near *the* cause of the war."

Clyde Wilson agrees, both in terms of the causes of the war and in the broader interpretation of the ongoing conflict: "The Civil War was a very large event. That's one of the first things that a historian understands, that you can't put something that complex and that vast, you can't put that down as being caused by slavery. That's simply absurd. There's no doubt that the southern states were precipitated in part to secede by the feeling that people were interfering, or intended to interfere, with the slavery system. The war, however, consisted of the North invading the South. Was slavery the cause of that? No. The cause of that was the desire of the North to preserve the Union, which meant, basically, to preserve an economic empire controlled by them. Now it's certainly true that South Carolina stipulated that the interference with slavery was one of the reasons for secession. But were all those people fighting and dying simply to defend slavery? I don't think so."

Slavery was undeniably a constitutional affair. The South *did* view slavery as an inherent component of the Constitution, an element in the original compact of 1789 (codified, for example, in the three-fifths clause on representation). The southern leaders of the era were not merely cloaking their pro-slavery arguments in constitutional garb. But the South did not exit the Union over constitutional principles in which slavery played only an *incidental* part; it departed because it believed the constitutional order no longer allowed a place for the proper maintenance of a slave-based economy. Even the South's own definition of the contesting parties—as the "slaveholding" and the "non-slaveholding" states—shows that southerners themselves viewed this as the central issue distinguishing and dividing the South from the rest of the nation:

> We affirm that these ends for which the Government was instituted have been defeated, and the Government itself has been made destructive of them by the action of the non-slaveholding States. Those States have assumed the right of deciding upon the propriety of our domestic institutions; and have denied

the rights of property established in fifteen of the States and recognized in the Constitution; they have denounced as sinful the institution of slavery; they have permitted open establishment among them of societies, whose avowed object is to disturb the peace and to eloign the property of other States. They have encouraged and assisted thousands of our slaves to leave their homes; and those who remain, have been incited by emissaries, books and pictures to servile insurrection.

For twenty-five years this agitation has been steadily increasing, until now it has secured to its aid the power of the common Government. Observing the forms of the Constitution, a sectional party has formed within the Article establishing the Executive Department, the means of subverting the Constitution itself. A geographical line has been drawn across the Union, and all the States north of that line have united in the election of a man to the High Office of the President of the United States, whose opinion and progress are hostile to slavery. He is to be entrusted with the administration of the common Government, because he has declared that "Government cannot endure permanently half slave, half free," and that the public must rest in the belief that slavery is in the course of ultimate extinction.[34]

Present-day neo-Confederates and heritage defenders are disingenuous (or are deluding themselves) when they claim that slavery was, at best, only a contributing factor in the South's secession and that the primary impetus lay in the South's concern with abstract constitutional doctrine distinct from all particular concerns.

Even ten years prior to secession, during debate over the Compromise of 1850, the South—and South Carolina in particular—was already stating in clear and certain terms what it felt was at issue: "We must give up the Union or give up slavery," said the *Charleston Mercury;* while another Carolina paper, the *Winyah Observer,* declared that "slavery is indispensably necessary to our very existence."[35] In 1856, South Carolina's pro-slavery radicalism even spilled onto the floor of the U.S. Senate. In mid-May of that year Massachusetts Senator Charles Sumner, something of a firebrand in his own right (as a leading abolitionist), verbally attacked his Senate colleague, A. P. Butler of South Carolina, for choosing as his "mistress . . . the harlot slavery."[36] Edgefield (S.C.) Congressman Preston Brooks, incensed by this insult to his fellow Carolinian and to his home state, stormed into the Senate a day later and, in a scene that foreboded the greater bloodshed soon to come, beat Sumner with a walking cane until he lay bloody and nearly lifeless on the floor of the chamber. "We of the South have no politics but the Negro," Brooks declared.[37] And, apparently, many southerners agreed—with both his sentiments and his deed. He was showered with trophies and other tokens of praise and celebration—including several decorative canes meant to replace the one Brooks had shattered over Sumner's back. With their tokens of solidarity, it was as if Brooks's supporters were saying, "Here, go and finish the job!"[38]

By 1860, many southerners were ready and willing to take the cudgel into their own hands. And they were quick to point out why: As one member of the South Carolina Secession Convention (which had voted 169 to 0 in favor of secession) said in a letter to President James Buchanan, "Slavery with us is no abstraction—it is a great and vital fact. Without it our every comfort would be taken from us. . . . Nothing short of separation from the Union can save us."[39] Meanwhile, over in Georgia, pro-slavery sentiment was so strong that even the remaining Unionists in the state did not question the legitimacy of the institution: ". . . our people not only see the justice of slavery, but its providence too," said Georgia state legislator Benjamin Hill in a speech to his fellow legislators in mid-November 1860, adding, in no uncertain terms: "The world can never give up slavery until it is ready to give up clothing and food."[40]

Another Georgian, soon-to-be Confederate Vice President Alexander Stephens, though not one of the staunchest secessionists in 1860, was nevertheless no shrinking violet when it came to defending slavery. Far from threatened with extinction, Stephens saw slavery as an institution of continuing vibrancy and durability—if given the proper framework in which to flourish. What's more, his reading of constitutional history had led him to conclude that, though the Constitution did contain certain guarantees for slavery, it was not the sure foundation that many of his fellow secessionists believed it to be. He warned that any guarantees contained in the Constitution had been created under the assumption that slavery "would be evanescent and pass away." The United States constitutional order, Stephens said in his "Cornerstone Speech" of 1861, rested upon the assumption of racial equality—an assumption that had led to the misguided attempt "to make things equal which the Creator had made unequal." A secure defense of the institution of slavery, he declared, could not rely on such a "sandy foundation." That is why, he continued, "our new government is founded upon exactly the opposite idea; its foundations are laid, its cornerstone rests, upon the great truth that the negro is not equal to the white man; that slavery, subordination to superior race, is his natural and moral condition. Thus, our newer Government is the first, in the history of the world, based upon this great physical, philosophical, and moral truth." Slavery was the fundamental principle underlying the secessionist impulse; and it was the foundation on which the new Confederate States of America were to be built.[41]

Others across the South were not satisfied with the rhetorical niceties and intricate legal arguments like those in South Carolina's Declaration of Immediate Causes. Mississippi put the matter rather more bluntly when it stated, in its own declaration, that "our position is thoroughly identified with the institution of slavery."[42] And by the time Texas issued its Declaration of Causes, in February 1861, the time for rigorous constitutional exactitude had long since given way to the kind of matter-of-fact straight talk that finds in candid directness the greater virtue. In words that echoed 1776, Texas declared that

> We hold as undeniable truths that the governments of the various States, and the confederacy itself, were established exclusively by the white race, for themselves and their posterity; that the African race . . . [is] rightfully held and regarded as an inferior and dependent race, and in that condition only could their existence in this country be rendered beneficial or tolerable.[43]

One scarcely could have put it any plainer.

Even after the war, the fundamental racial nature of the conflict remained conspicuously present. In a sense, the war never had ended—it continued, though employing different methods than before. Edward A. Pollard, in 1868 his book *The Lost Cause Regained,* argued that slavery had served "as a bastion against . . . contention" and race war, and as such was a guarantor of social peace and proper order. More importantly, the southern cause was not yet lost. The South might still prevail, he believed, even without the benefit of the slavery system, so long as it managed to retain "the Negro as laborer, and [keep] him in a condition where his political influence is as indifferent as when he was a slave." To the extent the South succeeds in "securing the supremacy of the White man . . . she . . . triumphs in the true cause of the war."[44] This became the South's Lost Cause, the principle it struggled to uphold, the battle it sought to win, over the course of the century to come.

The purpose of this short excursion into Confederate history has been to demonstrate and reinforce the undeniable link between slavery as a cause of secession and war—the very linkage that southern heritage defenders deny or obfuscate through their selective rendering of history. The Civil War brought with it sweeping changes in the South, to be sure. But the war transformed the whole of America as well. "With the war," wrote southern poet and novelist Robert Penn Warren, "the old America . . . was dead. With the war the new America, with its promise of realizing the vision intended from the old America, was born."[45] The war brought about a redefinition of American purpose, the "new birth of freedom," that Abraham Lincoln codified in his address at Gettysburg, and which historian Garry Wills, in his exquisite explication of that address, has described as a "new founding of the nation, to correct things felt to be imperfect in the Founders' own achievement."[46] Not just the South but America itself had been freed from slavery, freed to fulfill its own creed, to give greater substance to the legacy of its own democratic origins.

Southern traditionalists will have none of this. Though acknowledging that the Civil War marked a turning point in U.S. history, as far as they are concerned, it was a turn for the worse. To them, the Confederate defeat brought an end to the only force within the United States that acted to counter the growing power of the federal state—and the only alternative model to the culture of industrialized modernity embodied by the North. From the southern traditionalist point of view, the original struggle for a balance of power was played out not between the United States and the Communist Bloc, but within the United States itself, between North and South, between the so-called powers of consolidation and those of regional and local distinctiveness, between industrial consumerism and agrarian paternalism, between the slaveholding and the non-slaveholding sections of the country. And as with the end of the Cold War, the titanic struggle of nineteenth-century America left only one power, one means of production, and one way of life as the supreme hegemonic power with respect to the nation's fate. For the southern traditionalists, the South's fall meant that the forces of governmental centralism and industrial capitalism were allowed to dominate and eventually control the course of the nation, as the only guiding authority remaining in the country.

Moreover, the southern heritage defenders reject the notion that the Union fought the Civil War in order to end slavery. At most, they say, actions directed against slavery and slaveholders were merely wartime measures aimed at undermining the South's ability to conduct war. And, again, to an extent, they are correct—but only to a point. Certainly, at the beginning of the war, the North's main concern was the preservation of the Union. But as Civil War historian James McPherson has pointed out, many Union soldiers not otherwise motivated by abolitionist sympathies nevertheless "became convinced that this goal [i.e., restoration of the Union] was unattainable without striking against slavery."[47] Over time, abolitionism gradually ceased to be merely a means of persecuting the war and became a goal in and of itself: "By the summer of 1862, antislavery pragmatism and principle fused into a growing commitment to emancipation as both a means and a goal of Union victory."[48]

Even if one rejects the idea that the North was fighting to end slavery, it is difficult to reject the notion that the South was fighting to preserve it. It would stand to reason that if the South went out of the Union over the issue of slavery, and if they formed the Confederacy over the issue of slavery, then the war that followed surely must have been about slavery, too. But just as some Confederate soldiers felt no "inconsistency in fighting for their own liberty while holding other people in slavery," southern heritage defenders find no inconsistency in denying that the Confederate soldier fought a war to preserve a slave-based socioeconomic order.[49] And even if they are prepared to accept the proposition that the Confederacy did come about as a means of defending slavery, they still insist that the war itself was not about slavery and that the southern soldier was not fighting in defense of it.

Soldiers fight in wars for various reasons. They may be motivated by the lust for adventure or by the chance to escape the confines and conventions of home; they may be seeking glory or some other form of personal aggrandizement; they may, through their participation, seek to explore their own limits, to develop maturity, or to gain the approval of others; or they may be in it for altruistic, idealistic, ideological, or patriotic reasons. McPherson writes that soldiers have different motivations for their actions at different stages and under different circumstances, that there may be one set of reasons motivating them to go to war, another that keeps them from deserting, and still others that propel them into battle, in spite of the threat to life and limb.[50]

For many southern soldiers, no doubt, the "Southern Cause" became merely the "cause" of Shiloh, or of Wilson's Creek, of Bull's Run and Culp's Hill, of Sharpsburg or Rivers Bridge—or any number of the named and unnamed battles and skirmishes fought out across the country during the course of the war. On the battlefield, the "issues" of the war were reduced to their most elemental, most essential aspects: to win the fight, to survive, nothing more. Everything else faded away for the moment—perhaps for good. Seen from that level, however, all wars are alike, all causes equal, with nothing distinguishing one from the other. All battles are equally good or bad or indifferent, revealing nothing about the what-for of war.

While the search for adventure, glory, or personal gain may have sustained some for the duration and others for a time, many, perhaps most, of the soldiers who fought in the Civil War must have had some greater purpose that kept them going, that kept them fighting through all the deprivation, danger, disease, and death that four long years of war threw at them. A vague but abiding and strongly felt sense of duty and honor played its part, no doubt.[51] But some sort of conviction about the reason for it all must have played a role as well. And for the South, slavery and a slave-based economic and social order remained an elemental part of the cause.

The Confederate soldier, regardless of rank or station, must have been at least vaguely aware that defeat would bring with it major changes in the slave-based order of the antebellum South. Since the vast majority owned no slaves, emancipation would not necessarily have any direct material consequences for them. But in the "slaveocracy" regime of the prewar South, which rested on a foundation made by slave labor, the disruptions that would result from the demise of the plantation system would reverberate throughout the economy, with rippling repercussions that also would be felt by those only indirectly associated with it. More importantly, the freeing of the slaves would have an even greater effect on the social order of southern life. As revealed in their letters, the fighting spirit of the common southern soldier was not motivated by any great concern for states' rights, or any other constitutional principle. Instead, as historian Bell Irvin Wiley points out,

> The threat to slavery was resented rather widely, not so much as an unwarranted deprivation of property rights, but as a wedge for "nigger equality."[52]

Facing the potential threat posed by the liberation of blacks from their bottom-rung status, many whites (and in particular those on the lower end of the socio-economic ladder, who owned no slaves themselves) feared they would eventually find themselves in direct competition with the same former slaves who, under the old regime, would have been perpetually condemned to be their social and economic inferiors. This is what forced all strata of white southern society into a community of common interest. This is what forged the bonds of the southern "savage ideal."

In a broader sense, however, the reasons that motivate individual soldiers to join up and fight are secondary to the reasons that cause a state or regime to engage in war in the first place—the goals that a state is pursuing by sending men off to fight. Soldiers who fought in the Gulf War of 1991, for instance, may have gone off to war motivated by a desire to overthrow tyranny and to liberate Kuwait from Iraqi aggression. But that does not alter the fact that the underlying purpose of the war was to reestablish strategic and political stability in a region of the world of vital interest to the United States and others (in large part because it possesses a raw material, oil, essential to the economic well-being of most of the industrialized world). Soldiers who fought in the war against Iraq were, in a limited sense, fighting for oil. But that fact does not detract from the necessity of the action. By the same token, Confederate soldiers may have been motivated to fight for a thousand different reasons—many of them honorable and fully deserving of recognition and even emulation. But none of these should obscure the fact that the underlying purpose of the conflict, from the Confederacy's point of view, was to establish a regime separate from but in most every respect similar to the United States—excepting that it would ensure legal and constitutional protections for the perpetuation of the practice of human bondage. Regardless of what motivated each individual Confederate soldier, this was the cause he served. There is an interesting parallel here to the German experience of the twentieth century. The common German soldier of World War II may not have gone off to battle with the intent of serving Adolf Hitler's expansionist or genocidal goals—indeed, the evidence seems to indicate that most did not. And yet, the reputation of those common soldiers remains forever tainted by their service of those ends.

In one last effort to, as they see it, rescue the Confederate flag (and thus the honor of the Confederate soldier) from the moral condemnation that ensues from the Confederacy's entanglement in slavery, the southern heritage defenders have advanced the argument that the Confederate battle (Southern Cross) flag is purely a "soldier's flag" and should be distinguished from the "political" flags that served as the official symbols of the Confederacy (i.e., the Stars and Bars, the Stainless Banner, and the Third National flag). This argument says, in effect, that the Confederate battle flag was adopted and used solely by soldiers in the field and never graced any official Confederate building or served in any way to represent the government of the Confederacy. The implication is that no matter what one may think of the Confederate government or its policies, the valor of the Confederate fighting man remains untarnished—and so does "his" flag.

To heritage defenders, the Confederate flag displayed atop the South Carolina State House was a "war memorial," equally deserving of the same kind of respect that any other public memorial would receive. The flag made no political statement, they claimed, it sent no political signals of any kind—indeed, it contained no overt political content whatsoever.

This easy but artificial divorce of flag from cause reflects both the attempt to separate the Confederate soldier from the Confederate regime and, more importantly, to remove the flag from the historical context in which it was born. Such neat distinctions do not hold up well under closer scrutiny. As we have seen, many of the so-called political flags, like the Stars and Bars, served as unit banners for many elements in the Confederate army. Perhaps more importantly, two of the later official flags of the Confederacy, the Second and Third National flags (adopted in May 1863 and in early March 1865, respectively), both incorporated into their design the Southern Cross pattern. Rather than diverge, the "flag of battle" converged and eventually merged with the "political" banner of the Confederacy, until the two were more or less interchangeable. As the Confederacy shrunk down eventually to become identified almost exclusively by its armies in the field, so too did those armies become the main means of expressing the southern cause. In accordance with Carl von Clausewitz's dictum, war was politics by other means. And once war had been enjoined, the Confederate army was invested with the defense of a prospective southern republic that would rest on a racially defined social order and a slave-based economic system. Whether on the battlefields at Antietam or in the halls of the Confederate government in Richmond, the overarching and fundamental purpose was the same. Soldier and cause were forged together in the bloody cauldron of war.

———•◦••◦•———

Of course, none of this will satisfy the die-hard southern traditionalists, neo-Confederates, and southern heritage defenders. Any associations drawn between the flag and slavery are simply unacceptable. For them, the Confederate flag is the primary vehicle in the campaign against those who would besmirch their ancestors' good names. It offers the best means of rallying troops in defense of their interpretation of southern history, an interpretation largely free of the "contamination" of contemporary scholarship and "politically correct" thinking. In the end, the southern traditionalists' primary goal lies in tying history to the cart of cultural integrity, to use history to promote their specific brand of southern identity.

Heritage is not hate, the pro-flag people are fond of saying. Perhaps. But heritage is also not history. The two may intersect at certain points—one may draw on the other from time to time—but they are not identical. In his book *The Heritage Crusade and the Spoils of History* (1998), historian David Lowenthal has provided a masterful study of heritage movements around the world and across time. Lowenthal describes these movements as quasi-religious cults, whose views of the past are based primarily on faith rather than fact. He writes:

> Sacredness secures fealty, enhances community, and exalts purpose as long as heritage is a creed not to be queried. But to bolster heritage faith with historical scholarship, as is now the fashion, smudges the line between faith and fact. It deprives adherents of rational scrutiny and choice, mires them in fatalism, and leaves them at the mercy of simplistic chauvinists. To embrace heritage *as history,* disguising authority as authenticity, cedes it a credence it neither asks for nor deserves.[53]

This, in and of itself, would go a long way toward explaining the southern heritage defenders' devotion to the Confederate flag. To them the flag has become a pseudo-religious icon, a holy relic not unlike the saintly bones and fragments of the "true cross" housed in holy places throughout Christendom. It is an object of reverence, a symbol manifesting their faith in conservative virtues and a traditional interpretation of the southern past. For them, the past is something one believes in, not something one studies (except for the purpose of strengthening one's faith and solidifying one's convictions). For heritage true believers, examining the past is a kind of celebration of affirmation; it serves to reinforce a sense of security, the feeling that though the past may not be a story of unceasing virtue, it is at least a repository of stories of inspiration. It is more akin to the sermon than the lecture.

Lowenthal is not a historical literalist; he recognizes that the study of history can never be absolutely free of personal or cultural bias: "the actual past is beyond retrieval; all we have left are much-eroded traces and partial records filtered through diverse eyes and minds."[54] "Above all," he continues, "history departs from the past in being an interpretation rather than a replica; it is a view, not a copy, of what happened."[55] He adds,

> History is *more* than the past because it deals not only with what took place back then, but with myriad consequences of events that go on unfolding

beyond their participants' lifetimes. History is not just what happened at the time, but the thoughts and feelings, hunches and hypotheses about that time generated by later hindsight.[56]

But having said that, Lowenthal then points out that historians nevertheless do make an effort to provide a better understanding of the past:

> Knowing they cannot be objective, they feel duty-bound to be at least impartial. . . . Save for a post-modern solipsist fringe that fancies all history fatally flawed, Historians trust that research enlarges what is known of the actual past.

And he goes on to define what it is that distinguishes history from heritage:

> History differs from heritage not, as people generally suppose, in *telling* the truth, but in trying to do so despite being aware that truth is a chameleon and its chroniclers fallible beings. The most crucial distinction is that truth in heritage commits us to some present creed; truth in history is a flawed effort to understand the past on its own terms.[57]

Unlike other critics of the heritage movement, Lowenthal finds some redeeming value to the heritage crusade: its promotion of a sense of cultural cohesiveness and social harmony, for example. And he appears to assume that there is little in any case that can be done to eliminate it. But he opposes the kind of historical counterfeiting that occurs when heritage is mistaken for history, when historical fact is commingled with heritage faith.

Given their general preference for the past over the present, southern traditionalists, as one might expect, practice what is, in effect, an old-fashioned type of history. It is a concept of history that can trace its lineage back at least as far as Plato's *Republic*. In Plato's design for a perfect society, poets (and historians) are thought of generally as useless and even dangerous—except as the inventors of songs of praise and adulation meant to glorify the ruling regime. These state-supported (and -controlled) myths were meant to promote civic virtue and social order by reinforcing a sense of solidarity both within the community and between the populace and its rulers. This concept of history shaped historical writing for centuries to come. Well into the nineteenth century, history was still conceived of as a means of promoting communal identity, in particular among the numerous nationalist movements across Europe. Rulers around the globe made use of self-serving, perhaps fact-based but largely fictionalized versions of history as instruments of power and social harmony. These civic myths served to legitimize the rule of a particular person or dynasty and glorify his achievements, while also denigrating or obliterating the achievements of rivals or predecessors.

Gradually, there were advances toward what we might call "objective" history, but they were long in coming and often sidetracked by contemporary needs and preferences.

> Medieval and early modern Europeans set the facts of history against the fictions of poetry. But the facts sought were eternal verities of character; it was the historian's task to chronicle deeds and to illustrate motives and processes that faith and moral experience had already established as timeless truths.[58]

Rulers were portrayed in such a manner that their personal character reflected and provided exemplary moral behavior. They were honorable, gentle, and generous, yet forceful of intellect and decisive in action, piously faithful, incorruptible, just, possessing fortitude and greatness of spirit—virtuous in most every way. An echo of this can be found in the portrayals of some of the Confederate leaders: most notably in the "gallant" Lee, the pious "Stonewall" Jackson, or the Christlike Jeff Davis, suffering for our sins in his prison cell at Fort Monroe.

History as science did not really begin to take shape until the Enlightenment. But even after that, there were still traces of an earlier understanding of the role that history should play in society. American public education, for example, conceived of history largely as a means of inculcating civic pride, of promoting patriotism and national identity, the basis of our civil religion. Southern traditionalists, on the other hand, practice a kind of alternative civil religion, substituting southern figures, southern (mainly Confederate) themes, and southern points of view for the generally accepted American story. They have fashioned a southern creation myth that is exclusively theirs, one that sets them apart and provides a sense of historical and cultural depth that many of them feel is increasingly lacking in modern American life. It offers them a comforting feeling of rootedness, historical continuity, and cultural integrity.

Many southern traditionalists—and, more specifically, those who honor Confederate-era veterans—seem to be searching for something that stands in sharp contrast to the cynicism, archness, and pervasive lack of seriousness, commitment, and authenticity they feel characterizes our own age. They yearn for the simple, the straightforward, for the "eternal truths" they believe veterans of that era held to and died for. They revere what they see as the honesty and uncalculating belief, the clarified bonds of trust and faith, that ring out of that bygone era. Everything they say and write seems drawn in primary colors—clear, crisp, undaunted, and often unvarnished; there are no grays, no ambiguities, no hindering uncertainties—and few, if any, real complications. Their portrait of the past stands out in brilliant relief against the drab entanglements and compromises of modern life.

Not everything the southern defenders say is historically incorrect, of course. Their views and arguments are based on historical facts. But their views are too often marred by a highly selective reading of those facts, by a tendentious interpretation of the historical record, and by a purposeful disregard for the broader historical context. Moreover, their rhetoric is aimed as much at serving contemporary political needs as it is in correcting what they see as historical inaccuracies. History is not considered on its own merits. Instead, it serves as a means of filling out current creeds or advancing contemporary political agendas. As Lowenthal puts it: "heritage clarifies pasts so as to infuse them with present purposes."[59] In the most extreme instance, that purpose may be to declare the South a "white man's country." Or it may be to provide a sense of cultural coherence. The two are linked, though they are obviously not the same.

The views and arguments of the southern heritage movement have about them something distinctly artificial, something oddly antique and anachronistic. Many in the movement still focus on the "threat" posed by "northern aggression"— though now in a cultural rather than military sense. The arguments in favor of the Confederate flag often sound suspiciously like the pro-slavery arguments of the nineteenth century. Both contain a preference for the status quo, along with an underlying assumption that what *is* is unalterable. This is the essence of conservative traditionalism: the sense that the past holds the key to dealing with current problems and future challenges; the desire to hold on to the way things are, both because it is easier and because change brings with it so many uncertainties.

In the era leading up to the Civil War, as Margaret Coit puts it in her 1950 biography of John C. Calhoun, the South had chosen

> Not progress toward the unknown, but a rebuilding of the known. Not industrialism, but agrarianism. Not the future, but the past.[60]

So, too, it seems with many southern traditionalists today. The question, however, is: How seriously should we take them? Do these southern Galahads possess real political substance, are they a kind of symptom of deeper cultural trends, or are they merely elaborate game players, a sort of southern society for the creative anachronism? The answer appears to be a mixed one.

Just as reenactors portray Civil War–era soldiers, today's neo-Confederate is a sort of political reenactor, faithfully playing the roles of his southern predecessors (though filtered through the neo-conservative renewal of the past few decades). Do these contemporary Calhouns in any way measure up to their philosophical ancestors?

As misguided as the late-nineteenth-century Lost Cause "religionists" may have been, they did at least live fully within their own time. They were a vital part of their society and were serious in their convictions. Their modern-day counterparts, by contrast, appear to engage in little more than a kind of escapist ancestor worship, a reductive sort of idolatry that begins and ends with the adoration of the Confederate-era veteran. It is a faith become dogma, largely denuded of content and substance. Though they claim to be defending fundamental principles, the battles they fight are waged over trivialities. Rather than deal with the grand themes of history, their effort quickly dissolves into a fight over a flag. My impression is that many of those involved in Confederate heritage organizations see their activities as, at most, pseudo-political in nature—as a kind of intense, oddball hobby. Theirs may be a somewhat unusual hobby, but it is still largely just a hobby, not unlike golfing, gardening, stamp collecting, or weightlifting. Any hobby can, when pursued with exceptional intensity, become an obsession. And the most committed of the heritage defenders and neo-Confederates are undoubtedly obsessed with their pastime. Still, though the neo-Confederates and southern heritage folks may have learned their lines well, there appears to be little behind the rhetoric.

Contemporary southern traditionalists are as much children of the age of mass consumerism as everybody else. They may suffer twinges of conscience about it, they may (like a lot of people) find it empty and unfulfilling. They may oppose many elements of political and social modernism. But they offer little if any criticism of finance capitalism or of individualistic consumer culture, though each of these has done as much or more to undermine the region's distinctive cultural identity as have the political and social changes that the southern traditionalists bemoan. To Calhoun, finance capitalism and (northern) industrial interests were as much a threat to the American political system as any concentration of centralized government power. Both worked to the detriment of states' rights and the southern way of life. But capitalist industrialism posed an even greater threat than political consolidation, because it was the combined interests of capital and industry that were driving the concentration of power in Washington in the first place.

Although the modern-day southern traditionalists see themselves as the spiritual and philosophical heirs to the southern apologists of the nineteenth century, it is unlikely you would ever hear them rail against the dangers of "mammon," as their predecessors once did. Their defense of heritage is hobbled by its one-sidedness. Like Chris Sullivan, they may mourn the growing homogenization of the southern landscape, but their sentiments differ in no significant or substantive way from the vague and general feeling of ennui and loss of meaning that many people share. They may bluster about the past and decry the loss of distinctiveness and authenticity, but, for the most part, their cultural critique quickly merges with mainstream contemporary conservatism.

Politics is more often than not a battle over perspectives, a conflict of perception. The memory war over southern history served as a catalyst to set in motion the machinery of political combat. Each side in the conflict—the heritage movement and black leadership—fed off of the other. South Carolina's battle over the battle flag demonstrated how efforts to seek equitable solutions—especially when they become entangled in partisan politics—can become misguided exercises in moral equivalency and historical relativism, resulting in a kind of semiotic jumble that leaves both sides dissatisfied.

What made the situation in South Carolina oddly ironic, almost comical, was the extent to which many white flag supporters and the whole of the southern heritage movement came to ape the attitudes and even the language of their black nationalist/separatist counterparts. Tamar Jacoby has described contemporary black separatism as "more an attitude than an ideology or political program; it is part pride, part disappointment in whites, part diffidence, part defensiveness and part resentful defiance."[61] These are all terms that might equally apply to the "southern separatists" in the heritage movement. Like their black counterparts, southern heritage champions also display an ostentatious pride—in this case, a pride in "all things southern"—meant as an in-your-face act of defiance aimed at compensating for what they feel are cultural biases against southern life and history. Heritage defenders express a certain disappointment, too, both with the course of cultural modernization in the South and with their fellow southerners' abandonment of many of their region's distinguishing characteristics. They have become suspicious of the tone of black demands and are dubious about the character of black/white relations. They distrust and resent the media's portrayal of the South and academia's explications of its history. They are defensive about their own interpretation of the southern past and their vision for a southern future. They are embittered over the treatment of their movement, aggressive in their promotion of a separate southern identity, and defiant in their defense of the symbols and memorials their movement reveres.

Like the black man forced to make concessions to the larger society in which he lives, modern southern traditionalists feel that they also are being forced to shed a good portion of their birthright. As a consequence, the most committed of them call for a rededication, a hearkening back to southern traditions distinct from the rest of contemporary American culture. It's the same sort of cultural self-sufficiency preached by many black nationalists and Afrocentrists.

Speaking in terms that closely resemble those of the black identity movement, the League of the South's titular head, Michael Hill, says that "We must rebuild communities that are economically and culturally independent"—in preparation for the political independence the South might one day wish to seek (should developments not go in its favor). He and others complain of a double standard that works to the South's detriment, pointing out that in a country where "ethnic slurs are punishable as hate crimes, it is still acceptable to describe Southerners as 'rednecks' and 'crackers.'"[62] Some, including South Carolina State Senator Glenn McConnell, have even gone so far as to describe the "campaign against the

South" as a form of "cultural genocide." The ease with which terms like these are bandied about shows how popular a weapon the "cult of victimhood" has become on the battlefields of contemporary American politics. But even though their political agenda may seem as silly as childhood sandbox games, the very existence of groups such as the League of the South or the Southern Party, along with the multitude of other southern and Confederate heritage organizations, is a significant symptom of burbling sentiments and important divergences in American life.

Most southern traditionalists might prefer that we deal with the disruptions in American cultural and political life by turning back the clock to a time in which we were all, allegedly, just one big happy national family. To blacks, for whom the past conjures up recollections far less fondly held than those their white counterparts cling to, this hearkening back seems less a benign form of nostalgia than an act of conscious and deliberate disrespect—a barely veiled assertion that times were better when blacks and other minorities "knew their place." Of course, blacks may be hearing things that aren't there, that aren't even implied. But one wonders whether the southern traditionalists have a proper appreciation for the connotations their comments conjure up—or if they even care. As sworn enemies of "political correctness," they seem almost proud of the racial tone-deafness they practice.

There is yet one other thing about the southern heritage movement that lends it a tinge of artificiality, and it has to do with its exclusivity, with its clannishly narrow interpretation of just exactly what "being southern" means. The movement takes an almost proprietary view of southern history and culture, circumscribing and restricting our definition of southern identity. Perhaps in an effort to lend greater substance and historical depth to what they describe as "southern ethnicity," some in the movement claim that the South traces its cultural roots back to Celtic origins. One might easily come to suspect that such an exclusive emphasis on the South's "European heritage" arises as a result of an embarrassment over (and indifference about, or even a rejection of) the region's equally important African heritage. Reasonable people might even conclude that it is a half-cloaked way of saying that the South is, at its core, a white man's country.

Admittedly, relatively few in the southern heritage movement share such views. Even those most committed to the cause, such as Clyde Wilson, are hesitant to embrace wholeheartedly the notion of the South's Celtic roots. Even so, there is something cramped and stingy in the way in which southern heritage defenders view the South. And ironically, their push for southern consciousness comes at a time of ever-deeper cultural mixing. Indeed, the southern identity movement is, in large part, fueled by the trend toward cultural amalgamation and homogenization, by a fear of cultural encroachment from outsiders, and by the decay of cultural memory from within, each of which contributes in its own way to the decline of southern distinctiveness. This is what lies behind the movement's call for a "defense of southern culture . . . before it fades away." And it places contemporary neo-Confederate and other southern traditionalists squarely in what Charles Reagan Wilson has called the "Church of the Lost Cause," in a direct line of descent from the likes of William James, the "evangelist of the Lost Cause," and other purveyors of southern civil religion. James believed that

> By affirming the tenets of the southern creed and evoking the memory of past sacrifices, Southerners could be made to realize their place in a distinctive culture, and to understand the need for continual commitment to it.[63]

Southern distinctiveness, according to this view, should not be sought in the creativity that sprang from the region's unique cultural mix, but rather in an exclusive historical experience that spanned a brief four years.

But the source of the American South's grander cultural identity lies in its amalgamation of two great world cultures: the European and the African. Through their "continual commitment" to a crimped view of southern heritage, many southern traditionalists are blind to the rich culture they inherit. By worshiping at the altar of the Confederate past, they are prevented from acknowledging and embracing the broader patterns of southern history. They may say, in a "to-each-his-own" fashion, that the black man and the white man should each be proud of and equally free to celebrate his own culture, separately. But this attempts to segregate what cannot be segregated and reveals a reluctance to recognize the intricate links that bind all the strands of southern culture together.

Southern heritage enthusiasts seek an exclusivity about their past that, in an odd way, greatly resembles—and, to an extent, is a response to—the black identity movement that predated it and that still represents a kind of counterpart to it. The black identity movement was itself, in large measure, a reaction to the exclusionary views about southern (and American) history that predominated prior to its advent. Together, these two identity movements—the black and the southern—have become two poles in a kind of Hegelian dialogue of the deaf. Rather than promote greater understanding, their interaction has instead brought about a greater sense of exclusivity, on both sides.

"Heritage exclusivity," David Lowenthal reminds us, "is rooted in tribal needs for cohesion with like-minded kith and kin and for solidarity against outsiders." And, as he goes on to say, "true insight is seen to need native upbringing."[64] In other words, only an insider, one who *belongs*, who is both born to and identifies with the larger group, can fully appreciate the group he is part of. "It's a (Black/White) Thing—You wouldn't understand," so the saying goes. It is an attitude that rests on our failure to recognize the "otherness" in what we think of as exclusively our own. It is born of and festers in the shy or hateful unwillingness to cross tricky ground, to prefer the easier route of indifference and resignation over the risky venture involved in crossing the unprotected, open spaces that still divide us. Southern culture—southern identity—is made of many parts; its cultural tapestry is deep and rich. There is no great evil involved in our deriving sustenance from any one of the strands that form its pattern. But our undue attention to a single strand may prevent us from seeing that larger pattern; it may keep us from appreciating the grander design within it. There are other Souths besides the Confederacy, other wells to draw from, other legacies to explore.

Four

THE OTHER SOUTH CAROLINA

". . . they see only my surroundings, them-
selves, or figments of their imagination—
indeed everything and anything except me."

Ralph Ellison, Invisible Man

Most travelers "see" South Carolina from the highway, while hurtling down I-95 to Florida or I-85 to Atlanta: concrete roadways with numbered exits in the middle of nowhere, roads that disappear into piney woodlands or the sandy-bottomed remains of antediluvian dunescapes. Rushing on, we soar past white-on-green road signs, mute attempts to better acquaint us with the state's towns and hamlets, places that lend it character and distinctiveness. Their names are spread along the highways like wares at a roadside market, enticing us to stop and look. Some of those names hint at a remote, tribal past: Socastee, Taxahaw, Ashepoo, Catawba, Daufuskie, or just Indiantown. Others speak of places left behind: Bath, Lancaster, Switzer, Blenheim, Rimini, Georgetown, Bonneau, or DeBordieu —names packed up and brought along to lend a sense of familiarity to a strange new land. Still others proudly herald figures from state history: Pickens, Tillman, Pelzer, Laurens, Huger, Lowndesville, or Calhoun Falls—memorials to past fame indelibly printed onto the landscape. Some are whimsically idiosyncratic or seemingly indefinable: Round O, Nine Times, Pumpkintown, Outland. While others are too plain and simple to be anything other than token reminders of the vast, anonymous common folk: Trio, Red Bank, Smoaks, Little River, Jordan, Cave, Plain Branch, and Fork. A glance to the left—a glance to the right. Yet most of it stays well out of sight, hidden away by the impatient disregard of our own hectic pace. A vulture banks toward the highway for a moment, but finding nothing there of interest or significance, gracefully (and with an air of indifference) slides out of view, returning to the world we are rapidly passing through but never touching.

The state is a place of contrasts, home to the sacred and profane. Our hurried traveler—motoring down from Gastonia, or up from Lavonia, swinging into the state past Savannah or wheeling down by way of Fayetteville—might be startled, as he tops the first rise past the state line, to find himself suddenly confronted by a blaring billboard demanding that he choose (without delay) either "Heaven or Hell?" Entering the state another way, he might instead come upon a squalid little tourist encampment known as South of the Border, whose seedy garishness and soulless vulgarity serve as a compact monument to our crude covetousness and predatory callousness. Just a little further on, though, he might find promise of salvation in a snippet of Bible verse attached to a passing taxi—John 3:16: "whoever believes . . . shall not perish, but have eternal life."

South Carolina is full of belief; it loves belief. It believes in God—and it believes in itself. Its ever-expanding suburbs are temples to the belief in the latter—just as the state's success is taken as testament to the former. If our traveler stops at all, he will more than likely choose one of the state's anchor cities: Greenville, Columbia, or Charleston—each of which assumes its position in the hierarchy of southern go-getters. As Greenville hustles to become South Carolina's Charlotte (which itself strives to become North Carolina's Atlanta, and Atlanta the New York City of the South), Columbia toddles along in imitation, while Charleston stands to one side, hugging the coast and trying to remain aloof—as aloof as it can afford to be—while becoming ever more like the rest. The three cities shine like polished brass buttons on the state's fine new vest of progress.

South Carolina—the South in general—is ultramodern Christian fundamentalism and good-ol'-fashioned commercial boosterism, humming along in splendidly incongruent coexistence. Lancelot, the main character in Walker Percy's 1977 novel of the same name, has this to say about the bizarre contradictions in modern southern life:

> the Southerner started out a skeptical Jeffersonian and became a crooked Christian. That is to say, he is approaching and has almost reached his essence, which is to be more crooked and Christian than ever before.[1]

The judgment is a tad harsh. But then, Percy's Lancelot *is* a madman, after all. The South is not so much crooked as it is deluded—or just plain confused. Still, there is something in Lancelot's angry condemnation that nevertheless rings true, something about the nature of the South's (and America's) schizophrenic state of mind. Our visitor may be excused if he, too, comes away somewhat confused by the jumbled spectacle of it all.

Our traveler may be a tourist, come to visit the packaged sands of Myrtle Beach or the rationed charm of Charleston. He may be a businessman, flying in for a week or two to help the Upstate grasp for a bigger piece of the pie. He may find himself heading down the Calhoun Memorial Highway or up the Jefferson Davis Memorial Highway, seeking out those fine and graceful southern mansions of a century or more gone by, the carefully preserved myths and memories of Boone Hall, Hampton Plantation, Ashtabula, or Middleton Place. Or he might be heading up to visit friends at one of the fine (though less gracious and more ostentatious) modern-day mansions that line the shores of Lake Keowee or cling to the slopes along the Upstate Escarpment, mansions that are themselves monuments to the success and prosperity of the latest New South (or else retirement retreats for the comfortable classes from colder northern climes). The South has it all (now that it's air-conditioned). And what it doesn't yet have, it's eager and determined to get (though it might be satisfied with a reasonable facsimile). The South has always been a strange mix of black and white, gallant and plain, old and up-to-date. It perches, sometimes uncomfortably, somewhere between the past and the present, gazing hungrily yet warily at its future prospects, like a red-tailed hawk atop a rotting fencepost alongside a freshly blacktopped back road.

If our visitor goes to Columbia, the state capital, he'll find a city sitting astride its own history, just as it straddles the Congaree River. Whether you zoom in from the North, down the multilane runway known as Interstate 26, or take the western approach through a strip-mall- and fast-food-infested stretch of state route one—either way you'll find it surprising how swiftly you're dropped into downtown. Most of the capital's New South shell lies far out, beyond the super-highway ring that encircles the city like a moat. After you've penetrated that outer zone of late-twentieth-century prosperity, it's a mere hop into Columbia's old core. And once there, you're quickly struck by how much of a small-town character the city still possesses.

Just across the river from the business and governmental quarter at Columbia's heart, you'll find homes that could have been lifted out of any southern cotton-mill village—modest, functional but comfortable places, the kind of houses where elderly aunts and grandparents live. Most of the old downtown is like this: low-key, simple and well-worn, even a bit homely. Only a few blocks from the State House you might pull into a dog-eared quickstop—its low-slung cinder-block form squatting alongside gas pumps on an oversized spread of cracked concrete, giving the establishment a semi-abandoned look. Down the street, past the abandoned warehouses that hug the riverbanks, you might cross a set of rail-road tracks, fixtures of every southern town and reminders of the city's small-town past, of a time when creaking freight trains hauled their cargoes right through the middle of downtown. Here and there are token echoes of the state's famous: Rutledge Street, Longstreet Theater, the Wade Hampton Hotel. And yet, amid all this, there is a smattering of renewal: long-empty buildings and store-fronts now converted into chi-chi restaurants and boutiques, or made over into office space for consultants and attorneys. The city is a southern plain-Jane, doing what it can to spruce itself up, trying to keep in step with the current fashion by adding on some rouge here or a string of flashy baubles there. But strive as it might, the city never quite gets it right—and maybe it doesn't really even want to. So it lives betwixt and between, a mishmash of store-bought and homespun, comfortable in its maturing dowdiness.

Much of the South is like this: a hodgepodge of irreconcilables jumbled up together in odd and sometimes shaky coexistence. And yet there are some southerners whose own biographies successfully encompass all the clashing currents of southern history. Tom Turnipseed is a case in point. Though most lives contain elements of self-contradiction, few house the kind of diametrical oppositions wherein each half stands as a rejection of the other, the way they do in Turnipseed's life. From "genteel segregationist" and political strategist for one-time presidential candidate George Wallace to evangelist of racial reconciliation and friend of progressive causes one and all, Turnipseed's career encapsulates, in miniature, the span of the southern experience in the second half of the twentieth century. Once instrumental in establishing thirty-five all-white private schools in South Carolina (in an effort to thwart the U.S. Supreme Court's 1954 desegregation decision), he now heads up Turnipseed and Associates, his Columbia-based law firm—an enterprise that is, to all appearances, a model of racial integration and diversity. And as a sideline, the man who was once a true believer in the myths of the gallant South now presides over a local drive-time AM radio program that he half-jokingly calls "Radio Free Dixie."

Although a native Alabamian, Turnipseed has been a fixture of South Carolina state politics and an activist in the state Democratic Party since the mid-1970s. He served as a state senator (from Aiken, same as "Mr. Confederate," John A. May) from 1976 to 1980 and has campaigned, unsuccessfully, for state attorney general and the U.S. Congress. Although his association with Wallace means that he once worked hand in hand with members of the Ku Klux Klan and other racial hate groups, Turnipseed is proud of the fact that he now serves as the first white elected president of the Center for Democratic Renewal, an organization formerly known as the National Anti-Klan Network. He is equally proud of the role his law firm played as co-counsel in the case brought by Morris Dees of the Southern Poverty Law Center against members of the South Carolina Klan who had conspired to burn down the Macedonia Baptist Church in June 1995. The case resulted not only in the conviction of several Klan members, it brought the largest judgment ever awarded against a hate group in the United States, nearly $38 million—a financial penalty that broke the back of the South Carolina chapter of the Christian Knights of the Ku Klux Klan.[2]

"Let me introduce my son," Turnipseed says with a slight wink as a young man enters his office. "This is Jefferson Davis Turnipseed—one of my last Confederate acts." What now seems like an implausible exercise in sly and mocking tomfoolery was, some thirty years earlier, an uncontrived statement of conviction and allegiance. "I was totally deluded by Dixie—totally seduced by it," Turnipseed says, describing his former self. It all goes back to upbringing and unreflected acceptance, he says. "Y'see, I think one of the things we're taught to do—one of our heritages—in the South is to admire and emulate our fathers and our grandfathers. But even though we're part of them, part of their flesh and blood, we don't have to adopt their wrong thinking about race and the like."

"My daddy used to tell me," Turnipseed goes on to say, "Hitler did a lotta good. He helped the people, he got 'em all together, got 'em out of the depression, and all that. And my daddy wasn't a mean guy. He was what you call a genteel southern segregationist—a nice guy, a kind of country boy. One day I got to talking to him about my grandfather, who was a very interesting guy. He died the year I was born. His name was 'Big Daddy'—that's all they ever called him, just like in Tennessee Williams. And my dad said, 'You know, the Klan's got a lotta trash in it nowadays, Tom, but, y'know, Big Daddy was in it—and he did a lotta good.'"

Although most southerners, even of that place and time, were not members of the Klan, the education of Turnipseed at the school of southern segregation was not significantly different from that of most southerners of his generation. "I was taught not to even think of black people as real people. Don't factor them in. Don't even think of slavery. It was probably best for them anyway; they became Christians by coming over here. And they're doing well now, so just don't worry about them. And the stereotype I was taught was Uncle Remus and Old Black Joe—you know, Uncle Remus was a happy guy, and Old Black Joe wanted to come back to the plantation. *Gone with the Wind,* and all that—a land of knights and gallantry. As Rodgers and Hammerstein put it: 'It was drummed into my little head—you have to be carefully taught.' And even today—just two years ago, Strom Thurmond said we'd treated our slaves well! Now how do you do that? Isn't that an oxymoron? And he's a United States Senator! Anyway, that was the kind of thinking that, as a kid, I know helped to shape me into finally becoming George Wallace's national campaign director."

"I don't have any real excuse, though," he continues, talking about the way he thought back then. "I should've changed a lot earlier. But I didn't take the Golden Rule and apply it to African Americans—didn't try and walk in their shoes, share their history, and empathize with them. But what finally did happen, I got nervous, because I didn't like the violence that Wallace precipitated. I got afraid, particularly, to be honest, up North, with some of the ethnic groups in Milwaukee and Massachusetts. They were having riots—and these groups, the immigrants, they wanted to kill black people—and I didn't. I've sat around and heard people say things like, 'somebody ought to kill Martin Luther King'—and laughed about it. And it's hard for me sometimes, because, I swear, it's almost like I helped kill him."

Even though there was no sudden awakening, it was at this point that Turnipseed's life took a turning, and a period of atonement began. "It wasn't like a conversion on the road to Damascus or anything like that, because it had been building up in me for a long time anyway." In 1972 Turnipseed resigned as head of George Wallace's second presidential campaign. The break with Wallace happened after Turnipseed had, as he puts it, "begun to liberalize my thinkin.'" He had an idea for a broad-based third party, "kind of like Jesse Ventura [and the Reform Party] now." Odd as it may seem, Turnipseed was trying to persuade the Wallace campaign to consider having Ralph Nader join the ticket the next time Wallace ran. "That worried some people," Turnipseed recalls, "because they knew that Nader had black friends, that he was too much of a liberal." Klan leaders in particular made it clear that Turnipseed would be none too welcome in the campaign if he continued to promote ideas like this. Turnipseed had also grown increasingly disgusted with Wallace's brother Gerald's crooked financial dealings. He came to South Carolina, where he became involved in utility reform, organizing the South Carolina Rate-Payers Association. "We raised hell about the disproportionate amount poor people were having to pay—some five-and-a-half times what the large industrial users were being charged. And for the first time in my life, in 1973, I went out and met with African American people—because African Americans made up a large part of the lowest-volume residential users."

As part of his efforts toward utility reform, Turnipseed was asked to speak at an NAACP meeting in Greenwood. "Another lawyer was there," Turnipseed recalls, "a guy named Harold Boulware—who was the first black to become a family court judge in the state. He gave the keynote address. He told about the time, back in the late '40s or early '50s, when he had served as defense lawyer with the NAACP in a case involving a black man falsely accused of raping and killing a white woman, and about how he had to slip out of town in the trunk of a car because of the threats against his life—just for taking the case. Since he and I were both lawyers, it made me empathize. I thought, what if I was a black guy, and there were people out there who were gonna kill my ass just for representing a guy who was innocent. It hit me like a ton of bricks. And I made up my mind then, about 1973—I told my wife, if I don't do anything else in my life, I'm gonna fight racism. And so, ever since then, I've been doing everything I can. There's nothing wrong with people changing and admitting they're wrong. But that's the problem we face. What we've done is so wrong, and we've done it so long, that it's hard to own up to it."

The Confederate flag is one of the stumbling blocks on the road to recognition and reconciliation, Turnipseed says, a symbol of our unwillingness to own up to our past and to seek atonement for that past. "It's a symbol of human bondage. That's what it was then, that's what it is now. Southerners fought and died in vain! Folks nowadays need to face up to that. It's a *lost* cause. It was the dumbest, the biggest mistake in the history of this country, and we made it! We can't own up to making the biggest mistake ever made. And we're still making it. Now maybe I'm a little extreme in what I say—and I understand where they're coming from, the heritage supporters and the others—'cause I was there. Ain't nobody been duped by Dixie more'n I was!"

The University of South Carolina football team serves as a convenient example of the extent of the problem, Turnipseed offers. "People around here talk about the 'chicken curse' and how the Gamecocks can't win football games. And the coach over there wonders why these black athletes are leaving the state and going off to play for other teams? I'll tell you why, buddy. When they get down there at practice—and it's hard playing football—I played in college—you knock the shit outta one another, and its summertime, and you're hot and sweating and the coach is pushing ya—and you got an African American kid there, who understands things, who appreciates what's going on—and most folks *do* understand what the Confederate flag is. And he looks up there, and there it is, flyin' overhead, right on top of the seat of government. It's the Lost Cause, man! It's the *ultimate* lost cause! So I say, if y'all really want to know what the curse is, it's the damned flag!"

"People here say, 'Oh, but there's nothing you can do about the flag. Damn if you can't! If I'd been elected attorney general, I was going to take that flag down myself." Symbols can send important signals, Turnipseed continues. And moving the flag, he says, is a "big admission, it's an admission that there's something wrong with everything that the flag stands for."

But removing the flag is just a first step. "Just because the flag comes down doesn't mean you stop teaching. You keep working on hearts and minds—keep seeking atonement. Sure, you can't make people like one another. We're all a little different—even within the same race, there are totally different perceptions of things. But, if you put yourself in another person's shoes and really listen to that person, you realize that we're absolutely so much more alike in things that really count."

"I mean, it's just like I told Morris Dees, during the trial of the Klansmen in the Macedonia church-burning case. I said, these folks have exactly the same socioeconomic problems that poor black people do. They're poor too: one's the son of a sharecropper; the other's the son of a cotton-mill worker. I told him, I feel sorry for them, I really do, even though I know they're eat up with hatred. But that stuff has been handed down through the generations. The schism has been kept alive ever since the slave days: 'You might be a poor-off white guy,' it says, 'but you're better off than they are.' We've kept this division, we've let it go on. Our leaders have never really taken it on. Instead, they've done too much like George Wallace and kept the schism going, manipulating it for political power."

"One of the good things about this whole flag debate," Turnipseed believes, "is that we finally got the newspapers to write about the history of racial oppression and the struggle for racial justice in South Carolina, to tell what the Confederate flag has really meant and what racism has meant for this state. And I think that's really good—to get that kind of dialogue out there. We gotta keep trying to educate people and get people to understand that we're all so much more alike than we are different, and that there's strength in cultural diversity. When people live and work in close proximity to one another, that gives them a better opportunity to see that those *other* people are just like they are—and that what daddy and great-granddaddy might've said about them is bullshit. As people work together, go to school together, and become friends, then integration becomes . . . well, it *can* become a spiritual thing."

But the road to integration has been rougher than we once imagined it would be. What at one time seemed like a fairly simple matter of racial desegregation has since become a much more complex affair involving a careful balancing of interests and perspectives. Back in the days of Freedom Rides and freedom marches, of White Citizens' Councils and church bombings, back in the time when the rebel yell was reborn and politicians such as George Wallace sported Confederate flags in their campaigns, back then it was still possible for both those who sought it and for those who fought it to agree on what integration meant—or so it seemed, at least. As we peeled the onion of racial mistrust, however, we found still more layers underneath—and at some point the stinging pungency of it caused us to turn our heads and look away.

Integration now seems almost passé, a seldom-used term, dismissed by some, thoroughly disliked or discounted by others—just another expression gathering rust in the junk heap of American idiom. Many Americans—especially many whites—look back on the heyday of the Civil Rights movement with a sense of longing and remorse, disappointed that achieving the dream has turned out to be more difficult and frustrating than we thought, troubled by the unforeseen complications that flowed from the discovery that black men are not merely "white men with black skins" (to use Kenneth Stampp's now infamous phrase), confused, and even embittered, as the uncorrupted clarity of integration has been replaced by the disjointed jumble of multiculturalism. For many, the "dream deferred" became the dream unsought.

So commitment gave way to disappointment and indifference, to resentment and even opposition. Out of disillusionment grew a hard-edged struggle for ethnic hegemony, a competition of tightly held group identities. As a result, new misunderstandings cropped up almost as fast as the old ones could be cleared away. And these new irritations, not cushioned by any sense of common purpose across racial lines, quickly erupted in fresh antagonisms that fed a cycle of incensed and indignant reaction. This tightening circle of charge and counter-charge seemed to confirm a pattern of unbending continuity: Just as the old guard saw in racial integration a threat to social order, those who absorbed and embraced the goal of an integrated society now feared the challenge to social cohesion posed by multiculturalism. And as they shrank from it, those on the other side of the racial divide could only shake their heads and feel confirmed in their belief that people never really change.

But multiculturalism itself had been warped by the temper of the times, deformed by the demands of competing interests and zero-sum politics. What began as an attempt to embrace the experiences of those long excluded from the story of American national life—"America is woven of many strands," wrote Ralph Ellison, "I would recognize them and let it so remain"—eventually turned into an instrument of political activism and control, a means of cementing exclusivity and promoting self-segregation.[3] As old identities eroded, we cast out for new ones, looking to the (sometimes mythic) past for our models and moorings.

"Whatever became of integration?," asks Tamar Jacoby, a fellow at the Manhattan Institute and author of *Someone Else's House: America's Unfinished Struggle for Integration,* in the *Washington Post* on 28 June 1998. The tone of her query betrays the disappointment and apprehension many of her generation feel over the apparent abandonment of the ideal they were raised on. "Like many whites who grew up in the 1960s and 1970s," she writes,

> I had always thought the ultimate goal of better race relations was integration. I came of age politically in the years when the very word had a kind of magic to it—a vague but shining dream of social equality and fairness to all. But if integration is still most Americans' idea of the goal, few of us talk about it any more. The word has a quaint ring today—a relic of another era . . . and the ideal, under any name, has just about fallen out of most discussions of race.
>
> We reflexively honor Martin Luther King, Jr., but not many still pursue his vision of what he called "the beloved community": a more or less race-neutral America in which both blacks and whites would feel they belong. Today, the word "community" means not one integrated nation, but a minority enclave, as in "the black community." The word "brother" evokes not the brotherhood of man but the solidarity of color.
>
> Only a tiny minority, black or white, have repudiated integration outright. But increasingly, there is a contrary mood on both sides. Some whites, tired of the issue and the emotion that comes with it, have grown indifferent to the problems that blacks face. Other people, black and white, think of integration as more or less irrelevant to the real problems of race in America—black poverty, black joblessness, lack of black advancement. Still others, particularly blacks embittered by a long history of exclusion, view the old color-blind dream as a pernicious concept. Willingly or not, we as a nation are turning our backs on integration.[4]

Jacoby believes that the separatist doctrine of Malcolm X has undermined the more hopeful prospects set forth in King's integrationist dream. Color-coded hiring, voting, and school admissions are symptoms, she says, of a nation slipping into ethnic separatism and cultural disarray. Not even the expansion of the black middle class gives her reason to be optimistic, because the new separatism "often co-exists with functional integrationism" (among black professionals, for example).[5] Our original commitment to "integration" must be revitalized, she believes, as an antidote to the separatism that is "poisoning America."[6] But for Jacoby (as for many whites), true integration implies a process of black "acculturation"— the amalgamation into a middle class based upon the prevailing white model. It is a concept of integration that places the burden disproportionately on one side of the racial divide, feeding the kinds of suspicions among blacks that in turn fuel the very separatist tendencies Jacoby decries. Until black America alters its basic attitudes toward education, family, law, and work, she seems to say, the dream of a united nation will never become reality.

This is what gives rise to the "invisible man syndrome" that Ralph Ellison describes so well in his novel of the same name: the feeling that one cannot be wholly oneself and also be a fully accepted part of the larger society, that one must abandon part of one's identity in order to be counted. "That was all anyone wanted of us," Ellison's main character says, "that we should be heard and not seen, and heard only in one optimistic chorus of yassuh, yassuh, yassuh!"[7] It is a resentment at not being given one's full due, of being overlooked, ignored, and disapproved of, the ambivalence inherent in feeling a part of and yet apart and the suspicion that one's difference is somehow still an embarrassment to the rest of society.

A friend once put it this way: "I have to live with the fact that the society that I must assimilate into views me differently. It does not make concessions to me. I have to make concessions to it. I must make adjustments in walk, talk, intellect, and culture. I must be mainstream. Who makes concessions for my existence, my culture, my viewpoint? It's like being a vegetarian at a dinner party given by someone who knows my eating habits but still serves a meal of mainly meat. This is the special predicament of a so-called minority." This has certainly been the predicament of South Carolina's black citizens, whose presence in the state was acknowledged only grudgingly and often only in negative terms. Whites were aware of blacks in the same way one is aware of a hole in the road: as something largely to be avoided.

South Carolina's century-long attempt to circumnavigate the racial crater at the center of its political and social soul began in 1877, with the compromise that settled the disputed presidential election of the previous year and simultaneously ended the Reconstruction regimes in South Carolina and several other former Confederate states. "Gilded Age" America had lost its stomach for passionate crusades on behalf of the country's new black citizens. Those passions had burned themselves out in the war and in the political struggles over Reconstruction that followed. So the fate of the South's blacks was sealed in a condominium reached without either their consent or participation. Southern blacks paid the price of North/South reconciliation. The Compromise of 1877 helped usher in the system of Jim Crow segregation that would attend South Carolina into the modern age. It was this system of segregation and legalized discrimination that sent South Carolina's black population on its long journey through invisibility. The "reform" of the South Carolina state constitution in 1895, under Governor Ben Tillman, virtually eliminated black political participation in the state. Although blacks still constituted some 60 percent of South Carolina's population, they were reduced to less than 5 percent of the state's voters.

Black South Carolina's nearly century-long seen-but-unseen existence was framed by two outstanding fits of violence. The first, the so-called Hamburg Massacre (or "Riot," depending on your perspective), occurred in 1876 and signaled the end of the Reconstruction era in the state. The Hamburg incident involved a clash between a white paramilitary group aligned with the state Democratic Party and a local (black) unit of the state's Reconstruction (Republican) militia based in a predominantly black area of the state. After being disarmed, five of the black militiamen were summarily executed by their white captors. The latter, the Orangeburg Massacre, took place in 1968, a year that marked the end of the decade of civil-rights activism that had begun in the mid-1950s. The Orangeburg incident occurred on the campus of the (predominantly black) South Carolina State College, when members of the state highway patrol opened fire on a group of protesting students, killing three and wounding twenty-eight others. The protest action had begun after several black students were refused entry to a local bowling alley, one of the remaining bastions of segregation in the area.

But violent incidents of this kind were not commonplace in South Carolina. That is not to say that violence was unheard of. The ritual of social murder—lynching—bloodied South Carolina's landscape far too often over the years, especially during the period leading up to the restoration of white control following Reconstruction. But South Carolina was by no means the worst offender in this regard: Of the eleven former states of the Confederacy, North and South Carolina recorded the lowest number of lynchings between 1882 and 1968—though, with a total of 156 murdered during that period, one could hardly call the number "low."[8]

Besides lynching, other, nonlethal forms of coercion and intimidation were also routinely employed. The Reverend Joseph Albert Delaine, a Clarendon County native and a leading figure in the school desegregation efforts that culminated in the 1956 Supreme Court decisions, was rewarded for his civil-rights activism by having first his home and then his church burned to the ground by incensed whites. Churches, the organizational centerpieces of black community life, often became targets in the campaign against black equality. And it was no coincidence that the wave of church burnings and other acts of racial violence that hit the state during the early 1990s eventually would help provoke the first serious efforts to remove the Confederate flag from the top of the State House.

By and large, however, the struggle for civil rights in South Carolina was distinguished by a lack of the kind of mob violence that occurred elsewhere across the South. Some even claimed that "it was South Carolina that showed the South the way toward racial integration with dignity" during the 1960s and 1970s.[9] This is lavish praise indeed, but not altogether undeserved. And to an extent, the calmness with which South Carolina entered into desegregation came about because of the state's image of itself. South Carolina has traditionally considered itself as somehow a cut above the rest, possessing a staid (though slightly homely) propriety, conservative and reserved, not radical or rabid (once it got past the rabble-rousing phase that landed it in the Civil War). It is significant to note, for example, that presidential candidate George Wallace never carried South Carolina and, in fact, it was the only "Deep South" state that did not join the Alabamian's ranks. Similarly, South Carolina also turned away right-wing candidates David Duke, during the 1992 presidential primary, and Patrick Buchanan, in the 1996 campaign. A mischievous observer once compared South Carolinians to the West's stereotype of the Chinese: absorbed in worshiping their ancestors, eating rice, and saving face.[10] They abjure extremes and hew to the mean, ever concerned to avoid the kinds of embarrassing situations that might put the state in a bad light.

South Carolina's political ethos tempered, and was tempered by, the state's political and business leadership. By the 1960s (the Confederate flag notwithstanding), the patented race-baiting southern demagogue of the Cole Blease and "Cotton Ed" Smith variety had faded from view, replaced by a set of more practical-minded political leaders—many of whom, though they may have remained staunchly convinced segregationists at heart, were nevertheless determined that things not be permitted to get out of control. An old-style paternalistic authoritarianism was still at work in state affairs: "Even segregationists . . . were offended by extreme activities such as bus dumping, preferring to run things with a surface grace, but with enormous emphasis on control—like a plantation or cotton mill."[11] And besides, money was at stake. Atlanta called itself the "city too busy to hate"—too busy making money and getting ahead, that is. South Carolina, too, was ready to move on, eager for its chance to grab for the golden apple dangling just within its grasp.

The new tone was set by businessmen such as Greenville construction executive Charles Daniel, who, in a surprisingly candid 1961 speech, made it clear that
in order for South Carolina to move ahead, it would have to come to terms with
the problem of segregation and see to it that its black citizens were granted equal
opportunities in education and employment. The integration of South Carolina's institutions of higher learning came about through the behind-the-scenes
efforts of the state's business, political, education, and media elites. While state
leaders elsewhere were blocking doorways and obstructing access, South Carolina's leadership was slowly shifting the state away from segregation and toward
greater inclusiveness. Although he had originally campaigned for office on a traditional segregationist platform, Governor Fritz Hollings (who later became the
state's other long-serving U.S. senator) would urge the state to recognize its obligations to its black population and seek accommodation with them in a dignified manner, in accordance with the rule of law. Other southerners may have
wondered what South Carolina was up to. Wallace, for one, ridiculed Governor
Hollings' easy acceptance of the court-ordered integration of the state's colleges
and universities.[12] But Hollings recognized that the state's legal options were
limited. Hollings' successor, Donald Russell, understood the new realities, too,
and sent his own signal by inviting all of the state's citizens—both black and
white—to an inaugural barbecue on the grounds of the governor's mansion in
Columbia in 1963. It was the state's "first integrated public social gathering since
Reconstruction."[13]

It helped, of course, that South Carolina's black leaders did not urge a strategy of direct confrontation. As one of the state's longtime civil rights leaders,
Reverend I. DeQuincey Newman (who, in 1983, would become the first black
elected state senator since the late 1800s) said, "The courts were a kind of flank
attack on the problems of segregation and discrimination. Frontal attacks would
just not have paid off."[14] There were a number of marches, demonstrations, boycotts, and lunch-counter sit-ins across the state (though they appear to have
begun somewhat later than elsewhere in the South). But the primary course of
attack was by means of the judicial system, not the streets. "While NAACP
lawyers moved methodically in the courts, carefully unhinging each plank of segregation in the state, local black leaders worked within the community to exploit
the potential of their new-found rights."[15] Serious challenges to discriminatory
practices had began as early as the 1930s, with efforts to equalize school salaries
for black teachers. The next target, taken up during the 1940s, was the white primary. After that came the separate-but-equal system of public education. In this
way, whites were able to acclimate themselves to the new circumstances (albeit
with considerable reluctance and resistance) as South Carolina's blacks slowly
emerged from invisibility.

History has a way of sometimes taking remarkable (and unintended) twists and turns on its way to its final destination. Not all the paths to desegregation were straight and narrow. Back in the 1940s and early 1950s, school desegregation was not yet even a distant goal. "All they wanted was a bus," recalls South Carolina NAACP attorney James Felder of one black community's struggle for equal treatment. "So they filed a petition asking the school board for a bus. The school board denied the petition. So then they filed a lawsuit in Charleston, in the federal district court, asking for separate facilities, but equal. Just give us some more books, and some more science equipment, and a bus."[16] Integration was not part of the mix, at least not at the start. Ironically, it was a white man, Charleston native and federal court judge Waties Waring, who would add the integrationist element into the challenge. He made the case to black leaders that court challenges that failed to attack the separate-but-equal order would never eliminate the root of discrimination, because, as Waring put it, "as long as you have separate you will never have equal."[17]

The progress made in school desegregation cases was then applied to public transportation and accommodations, forcing state parks and other recreation facilities to open their gates to blacks. Demands for an end to the various forms of legal segregation in South Carolina—and the strategies used to attack it— were often so effective that elements of the Jim Crow system sometimes crumbled quietly, without a lot of clamor, while elsewhere in the South they fell only under the greatest of pressure and commotion. The Sarah Mae Flemming case, for example, brought about the peaceful desegregation of the state capital's buses, several years prior to Rosa Parks's act of defiance in Montgomery, Alabama. But the Parks case gained national attention, because it was the one that ended up at the U.S. Supreme Court.[18]

Still, there was a pattern of tightfistedness in the way the old system was dismantled. What one might call the "South Carolina style" was really just South Carolina's version of the good-ol'-boy system.* It was the state's own way of applying elite control over the process of social and political change. The ways in which this control was applied changed from one era to another—but the control was ever present. The Hamburg Massacre inaugurated an era in which every aspect of black life, and of black/white interactions, were closely regulated by state law or public custom. The Orangeburg Massacre served as an alarm bell to state authorities, forcing the pace of progress in the state. Each event, in its own fashion, spurred public authority to step in to direct and impose solutions where none could be achieved through the goodwill and common efforts of average

---

*South Carolina journalist and historian Jack Bass traces the state's special concern for stability back to its origins as a chartered royal colony. (See Bass and Jack Nelson, *The Orangeburg Massacre.* New York: World, 1970.)

citizens. Much the same applied in the compromise solution that brought down the Confederate flag. The matter was not resolved until state elites decided it was time to resolve it.

The Jim Crow regime was wide and deep. Successive South Carolina legislatures had made it so, establishing an order in which "almost every aspect of daily life [was] segregated, including such things as separate pay windows, stairs, exits, water fountains, and lavatories. And where there were no laws, there were customs."[19] Such an elaborate and entrenched system obviously could not be dismantled overnight. And even when the superstructure was gone, the ruined mental foundation remained.

———◆•◆•◆———

Reverend Joseph Darby, pastor at the Morris Brown African American Episcopal (AME) Church in Charleston, recalls growing up in Columbia in the 1950s and early 1960s: "That was a time when I still had to ride in the back of the bus, could not go to the restrooms at the State House, could not go to the restaurants in Columbia. As kids, we had to get one of our classmates, who could pass for white, to go see Disney movies for us. He would come back and tell us about them, because the theater that showed Disney movies didn't let black folk in." This was the day-to-day face of discrimination—the division of everyday affairs that whites took for granted over several lifetimes.

Things changed—even if sometimes you had to look back in order to see just how much they had changed. State Senator Maggie Glover, for example, compares her experiences growing up in Florence with those of her daughter: "I started to school in the very same house where I live now. And when my daughter started to school, she went to the very same Carver School where I'd gone. But the two were *worlds* apart. Mine was a totally *segregated* world. To be honest, I had no one-on-one contact with white people until 1970, not until I went to Pittsburgh, into an integrated teaching environment. That was the first contact I had, because there weren't any white kids in my schools here. And whites didn't come into this community either. There wasn't any reason for them to come here. The only white people I saw as a kid were the policemen, the firemen, along with the people who came through in the morning to pick up the ladies here who worked for them. That was it. We didn't know any white people personally—and that includes those people who worked for white folks. That was as white as my world was. Even when I went to college—Fayetteville State was an all-black college. For my daughter, things were altogether different. She, your child, any child growing up today has no idea what South Carolina was like in 1962, when the Confederate flag went up."

Still, despite all the progress, disappointment creeps in at the edges, along with the feeling among many blacks that they are still not full-fledged members of society, that their history and their perceptions are not given equal weight or equal treatment. For them, the Confederate flag represents more than just old-fashioned racist attitudes. It also, and perhaps more importantly, has come to represent a lack of respect, a feeling of second-class status. It sends the signal that society is still not ready to award them the equal regard they feel is their due. "South Carolina is a *monument* to southern history," exclaims Reverend Darby— "the whole state is!" By that he means: The state is a monument to *white* southern history, in which the black experience has largely been removed or ignored. This helps explain why the display of the Confederate flag remained an issue even after the flag was taken from the dome and moved to the State House grounds. "Altitude does not affect attitude," was the rallying cry. Whether atop the State House dome or down on the grounds in front, for many of South Carolina's blacks the display of the Confederate flag continued to express the same lack of respect it always had, no matter where it flew.

Reverend Darby and Senator Glover are both longtime veterans in the campaign against the Confederate flag in South Carolina—Darby, in part, as he says, because "I have a notoriously big mouth that gets me involved in all sorts of community activities," including his role as one of the leaders of the state NAACP. Both suffer no illusions about the state of black/white relations. And while neither is overly pessimistic about the state of those relations, each expresses discouragement and dissatisfaction over the way things have gone over the past thirty years or so. "More and more, as people of color get away from the '60s," Darby says, "there is a shift in perception and in understanding. The civil rights bills of the late '60s were causes for great jubilation, because we had 'overcome,' as they say. But, twenty, thirty years later, there's an interesting fallout that has occurred—and it speaks to the African American side of southern identity. There's an understanding now that we did not achieve integration. We achieved legalized *desegregation*—and, to a degree, assimilation. Doors were opened, but not a lot of hearts were changed in the process."

"We integrated the schools," Glover says, "but we let it end with that. We didn't even really *try* to get beyond the schoolhouse. Here in Florence, our neighborhoods are just as segregated as they were prior to the '70s. The churches definitely are. And we have not done anything in terms of integrating culture or anything of that nature." Both miss the give-and-take of real compromise. For them, the process of integration was too one-sided. Whites gave up only that which was not rightly theirs to begin with—their privileged position relative to blacks— while blacks were forced to blend in and conform to majority white culture. This perception—of a loss of cultural and historical identity—caused many blacks to dig in their heels in the debate over the Confederate flag in the same way that flag defenders dug in their heels when they felt their identity was threatened.

"Unfortunately," Senator Glover says, "for white people, integration was more about assimilation than anything else. We always say that America is a 'melting pot.' Whenever I heard that term, it always bothered me, because, really, that's what integration was all about, that's what white folks expect of us—either you blend in, you melt down all your culture and your distinctive attributes and assume the attributes of the majority, or you're gonna find yourself kicked out of the pot. But if you take the 'salad-bowl approach'—which is the kind of integration that Martin Luther King Jr. was talking about—well, for most white folks, there's something militant about that. But I'm not interested in assimilation. I'm not interested in the melting pot. I want to be salad," she says with a chuckle—"which is good for all of us, but yet, I can easily tell that that's a radish, and that's a tomato, that's an onion, and that's lettuce. I know everything that's in there, and it all works together to be healthy for all who take part."

Darby points out how the push for homogenization and assimilation calls to mind an earlier era, when black was not beautiful—and how those attitudes changed as blacks gained a sense of self-assurance. "A lot of what was positive in the African American community was forsaken in a desire to melt into the majority. It affected schools, it affected families, a lot of institutions. And now there is a turning back to the kind of self-sufficiency and self-reliance that black folk practiced back in the '50s and '60s—*had* to practice, because they had no choice."

"Even while Dr. King was living," he says, "by the late 1960s, there was a growing affection on the part of black folk for being black. And that sort of affection was not there when I was a child. All you had to do was look at black beauty products, when I was a kid. Most of them had to do with lightening skin or straightening hair, to do away with distinctive racial characteristics. If your hair was exceptionally straight, that was called 'good hair.' If it was kinky, that was 'bad hair.' Black organizations that were considered to be upper-middle-class, like the 'Jack and Jills,' used to have something called the 'paper-bag-test': if you were darker than a grocery-store bag, you couldn't be in Jack and Jills. There was a whole system that denied the idea that African culture was a worthy culture. I think what you've seen since then is a total reversal of that, an awareness about blackness, and the sense that it's likeable and positive. I don't think people are just going to lay that aside."

The new sense of black self-assurance also meant that blacks were not ready to "lay aside" their resentment over the display of the Confederate flag any longer, either. "At what point in history," exclaims Glover, "have we ever known the *losing* side in a war to display their banner?! If someone put up a swastika, on top of a building or in the chambers of government, what do you think would happen? Oh, there would be all *kinds* of outrage. No one would tolerate that. No one would be allowed to simply claim it as part of their heritage. And yet, on the other hand, nobody gives a tinker's damn that I feel the *exact same way* about the Confederate flag. What's wrong with the Confederate flag being placed in the *state-supported* Confederate Relic Room? Taxpayers of all hues, nationalities, and origins contribute to the maintenance of the state's Confederate Relic Room, a whole museum dedicated to that period in history. The Confederate Relic Room is an automatic offense to 30 percent of this state's population [i.e., the proportion of South Carolina's population who are black]—but we still pay for it. Why can't the Confederate flag be taken to a place where it would be more appropriate: a state-supported library and museum *just* for the Confederacy?" The Confederate Relic Room, a museum dedicated to the care and display of various artefacts relating to South Carolina during the Confederate and Reconstruction eras, was first established in 1895 and originally resided within the State House itself. It later moved to the nearby War Memorial Building (dedicated to those South Carolinians who had served in World War I), built in 1935. It has since been moved to larger quarters in the South Carolina State Museum, also in downtown Columbia.

In South Carolina's dialogue of the deaf over the Confederate flag, a certain white refrain rankled the nerves and grated the ears of many of the flag's black opponents. "I wince," says Darby, "every time I hear one of the pro-flag folks say, 'Well, if we *give* you this, what's next?.' As I reminded one of the pro-flag senators once: I am not your child, and I am not your pet. You don't have to *give* me anything. I'm an American. You're an American. Both our ancestors built this country. You cannot *give* me what I am entitled to. A lot of the South still tends to view African Americans as children. If they're nice, you can be nice to them. But if they get out of line, then you have to be firm with them."

Glover concurs: "The folks on the other side say, 'If we give 'em that, then next year they'll want the Confederate monuments removed. After that, they'll wanna have Confederate names taken off streets and buildings.' Yeah, I've heard all that. But have we asked for any of that? You know, white folks have always taken the position that black people always wanted the *whole* pie. Now, it's alright for *them* to keep the whole pie—that's fine. But if I should say, can I have at least a slice? Uh-uhn, no. The Confederate flag is no different. All we ask is that there be something for me and mine, something for 30 percent of South Carolina's people. When black children come to the State House, there is *nothing* that says, you are welcome here, or that even recognizes that blacks live in this state. Nothing. Not until the monument. In this whole flag debate, that's been the one and only thing that we can point to and say, well, because of this debate at least we now have the African American Monument."

The African-American History Monument—unveiled on the grounds of the State House in late 2000—is meant to serve as a memorial to the black experience in South Carolina, its panels depicting scenes from black life over the course of the state's history. Although many in the state deny it, it seems apparent that the proposal for an African American monument was offered as a kind of quid pro quo in lieu of removing the flag. In other words, to many blacks in the state, it seemed as if white support for the African American monument was contingent on black acquiescence on the Confederate flag. For many blacks, it was a just another case of the same old same old: a symbolic bone meant to throw the dogs off the chase. But this time, the dogs weren't biting.

"The monument is a nice gesture," says Darby. "But it's an extremely *late* gesture." It's a gesture that strives to avoid political controversy, almost to the point of avoiding the very issue it is meant to address: the role of racial oppression in state history. "They've tried to keep it generic rather than specific," Darby adds, "not to rankle any feathers. There are no black Confederate soldiers portrayed on the monument. But, by the same token, there's no Denmark Vesey portrayed on it, either. They sought to keep it kind of neutral."

The only political controversy sparked by the African American monument arose over the fact that the legislative committee set up to oversee the design and construction of the monument was chaired by a white man—and not just any white man, but one of the leading pro-flag spokesmen in the entire legislative body, Senator Glenn McConnell of Charleston. His senate colleague, Maggie Glover, says she understands the reason for the choice—but does not like what it has to say about South Carolina or the status of blacks in the state. "Certainly I would have preferred to have an African American chair that committee. But the choice for chairman had to do with the fact that the gentleman who is in charge of raising the money to pay for the monument—since it cannot be paid for with state funds—is himself a white man. Folks felt that it would take that in order to get South Carolinians to put up the kinds of resources needed to pay for it—that white folk could get white money quicker and easier than if black folk went and asked for those same dollars."

Though pleased about the monument, Glover can't help but feel a little disappointed with the way it came about. "Yes, it's disappointing—but real," she adds stoically. "That's South Carolina for ya. That's my state," she says with a chuckle of resignation.

———◆·◆·◆———

Efforts to get the South (and the whole of the country) to seek a fuller appreciation of its collective history—both the light and the dark of it—have been slow to bear fruit. Most of the remnants—the physical reminders—of the slave past have been wiped away by time, neglect, or what might be termed a concerted effort in purposeful indifference. The slave quarters that once appended every plantation have crumbled into dust—with a few rare exceptions, like those at Boone Hall Plantation, near Charleston. And black shantytowns—disdainfully referred to as "Niggertowns" by their white neighbors—made way for new sub-divisions or were "gentrified" to attract new residents, often white. The Old Slave Market Museum in downtown Charleston was, for a long time, the exception that proved the rule—its creation and continued operation the result of private efforts and private resources, not of state endorsement or support.

On the other hand, the South (like much of the nation) has not necessarily been altogether selective in its neglect of the past. Americans are famous for their indifference to history. They have been a future-possessed people, their efforts directed at forward movement and progress, toward attainment and the material comforts that accompany prosperity. They generally have not been inclined to dwell on the past, believing perhaps that too many backward-looking reveries could hinder the drive forward. Recent increased interest in our collective (as opposed to personal or family) histories has arisen alongside (and as a conse-quence) of our increasing prosperity and education. Our very success has led to a renewed desire for rootedness, born of a nagging sense that, in our rush for-ward, we may be losing track of the path by which we came.

Our understanding and appreciation of the past has improved markedly over the last twenty years or so. But that progress has been sluggish and uneven, ham-pered by deep-seated habits of mind and by the South's customary reluctance to deal with unpleasantness—its desire to avoid dredging up embarrassing episodes out of its past and its tendency to opt for rose-colored spectacles whenever it rummages through the attic of its collective history.

Some, like Reverend Darby, can well understand what makes these impulses so strong, and how they affect our take on the past. "I really have a great deal of sympathy for those who cherish Confederate history," he says, "because I see it as a matter of human nature. I've seen how it works in my own family. Everybody's family has had its eccentric. An eccentric within his own time is considered to be crazy or even dangerous. A generation or so later, he's quaint. And another gen-eration after that, he's 'dear beloved,' who just had some interesting habits. Nobody wants crazy folk in the family—or at least they don't want to admit it. And so I understand why white folks don't want to face the fact that their ances-tors raped, murdered, and committed horrible atrocities on people."

Many southern blacks view history as a continuum, characterized not by watersheds or fundamental shifts but by the momentum of certain essential con-sistencies. And, ironically, this makes them not all that different from their southern traditionalist counterparts. For Darby, the links between past and pres-ent are clear: "I think the real problem in the South is that it never realized that it lost the war. And in the broader sense, I don't think the South really *did* lose the war. They viewed Appomattox as nothing more than a military surrender. As soon as that was done—and as soon as possible after Reconstruction—they went about reconstructing what was basically a *new* Confederacy, through Jim Crow laws and such. That's what they were fighting for, again, in the 1960s. And I think that the same fight ebbs and flows and spills over into issues today. That's why, when people ask, why does a symbol like the Confederate flag even matter, I say: If you look at the folks in the legislature who are most adamant in defending the flag, by and large (and with just a couple of exceptions), those are the same folk who are most adamant about welfare reform, or school vouchers and school choice —things which, in many peoples' minds, conjure up images of separate-but-equal. The majority of those who love that banner are people who still have a desire for a white south. And I really believe that they are afraid that removing that banner would mean that the idea of the white South would be lost. It would be an admission that the war was actually lost."

It used to be that history was lived, rather than re-created, as it is now. There was a sense of being part of something larger, with roots stretching deep into the soil of the past. Much of that has been lost—with good and bad consequences. And sometimes the good and bad are inextricably linked. The heritage of slavery is a case in point. That heritage—the legacy of slavery—lived on for a long time in a very real and palpable way: in the form of Jim Crowism and all its patterns of legal and social segregation. Once those structures were eliminated, however, the explicit ties to that part of our past dissolved, the links were lost, reminders dimmed—and with them our firsthand appreciation of the ways in which the past can impinge on the present. It's a phenomenon that the journalist David Shipler has written about, in his 1997 book *A Country of Strangers:*

A diminished sense of history diminishes the sense of responsibility for racial ills. If Americans do not tune into the reverberations of the past, a gulf is opened between the present and its origins. To Steve Suitts [head of the Southern Regional Council, a civil-rights organization based in Atlanta] that gap has only recently developed, at least in the South. "There clearly is no way in which the . . . younger generations . . . can understand how their relations and how the relations of others are profoundly shaped by . . . the . . . past. And that is new. You did understand [once], you always understood. It was the most facile explanation for why segregation could exist: because it's always been. . . . And that whole appreciation for how what *is* is built upon what *was* has been obliterated by the new references by which people come to shape their own race relations."

If a young white person can choose friends without regard to race, Suitts explains, and can choose to admire black entertainers and put posters of black athletes up in his room, he somehow transcends the past. "That pretty well means that I have no personal responsibility for the fact that 60 percent of the black kids in this country, or in my state, are poor," Suitts says. "That's their problem, not my problem. That seems to me the ultimate result of this lack of personal responsibility. Whether you liked it or not, when I was growing up and became old enough to analyze it, you understood that if you weren't responsible for something, your papa was, or your grandpapa. The obvious nature of segregation required compliance; it required complicity. It required everybody to say, 'We ain't gonna do anything about it.' It was in the laws, and we knew we could change them if we wanted to. So there was always this sense that there was a personal responsibility there. And I think that sense of personal responsibility has quickly disappeared.'"[20]

We have no cause to mourn the passing of segregation, of course. But it may have been easier, in a sense, to understand the evils of racism while its manifestations were still so palpably near. Having lost the instructive element that link to a yet-deeper past contained, all we have left is education and dialogue. The history book and the history lesson must substitute for history lived in, for the lessons of experience. They are, at best, ersatz, several steps removed from the real thing.* But they do offer hope, because our distance from segregationist orthodoxy allows us a chance to escape what W. J. Cash called the "savage ideal," to get past the strictures of social custom and an unquestioning acceptance of tradition. Our options are more open now. We can, in a sense, chose our own identity and shape it as we see fit.

This new situation poses its own dangers, too, however. Cut loose as we are from the past, a certain arbitrariness may creep in, obliterating meaning and further isolating us from any source of substance and sustenance. We are threatened with becoming like free-floating monads, full of particularity yet lacking an essential integrity, adrift on a sea of relativity and subject to the manipulations of historical fallacy, faithlessness, or outright fraudulence. Oddly enough, both sides in the flag debate—both the pro-flag southern traditionalists and the flag opponents—recognize the hazards posed by the new individualism, though their efforts to counter it may often work at cross-purposes, canceling each other out. The only antidote to arbitrariness and indifference lies in learning, in seeking a firmer foundation grounded on a deeper appreciation of how, as Steve Suitts put it, what *is* grew out of what *was*.

As a teacher, Senator Glover appreciates the crucial role that education plays. But judged against the backdrop of the Confederate flag fight, neither she nor Reverend Darby is optimistic that children will get the kind of history they need. "We have done such a piecemeal, whitewashed version that none of our children have any real sense of history," Glover says. "Race relations in this state won't get

---

*The desire to get back to the "real thing" helps explain the appeal of historical reenacting—though it is debatable just how well reenacting improves our understanding of the times in which our ancestors lived.

any better until our educational system tells the truth and gives our children a foundation on which they can start to work. I'm willing to bet that you could go to the average elementary, middle, or high school, and ask somebody, anybody there about the Confederate flag or whatever, and they wouldn't be able to tell you much about it. Our children have no *real* knowledge, and therefore they have no real concern. White children: I don't think they have any knowledge of the Confederate flag, or the War Between the States—and certainly not of 1962 and that whole period. They don't know anything—they don't know what we're talking about."

Even Black History Month has been a sometimes troubled affair in the state. The program became a source of contention throughout the 1980s and into the 1990s, as white students at several public schools around the state resisted what they felt was a privileged set-aside for a protected minority. Some resented being required to participate against their will. Rather than promote better understanding and mutual respect, Black History Month instead appeared to increase racial tensions. "'The racial confrontations that occur during the month of February,'" one Upstate high school principal reported in 1991, 'usually extend into the spring months. In 1990, racial tensions reached the point where local law enforcement agencies were summoned to the school to patrol certain hallways.'"[21]

"It's still a subject of regular debate as to whether or not kids ought to be compelled to observe Black History Month," says Darby. "My real preference would be to deal with history as a whole. It would be a history that would involve scholars of a diverse nature, a history that enables us to sit down, talk, battle, and reach points of common agreement, so that what comes out is as close to what really happened as we can get. But if there were no way to do that—and I don't think that it's ever been done in South Carolina—then I think there has to be some kind of a treatment of the African American experience in the American South, and in America generally for that matter. I don't think kids ought to be compelled to celebrate Black History Month. But I think it ought to be preserved in schools, because it's the only touch of black history that some kids get."

Whether or not one believes that black history should be relegated to a certain month or integrated into the entire school year, a more equitable treatment of the political, social, and cultural aspects of race in America is essential. Reaching a proper balance can be a difficult and tricky matter, however, especially in the politically loaded nexus where history and identity meet. For southern heritage defenders, a fairer treatment of history lay in the creation of a Confederate History Month (a proposal offered in numerous states across the South). The suggestion immediately raised the suspicion, however, that a month dedicated to the study of the Confederacy would serve as an equal-opportunity counterpart (even as a kind of "antidote") to Black History Month. While its proponents claim that Confederate History Month should be devoted to an objective study of all aspects of the Confederate-era South, suspicions remain nevertheless. After all, for many, objectivity lies in the eyes of the beholder.

Reverend Darby is not optimistic about the chances for balance or harmony. For him, black heritage appears condemned to an "also-ran" status, especially in a state where historical identity is so permeated by Confederate heritage. "*Every month in South Carolina is Confederate History Month*," he says. "I don't see how you can get away from that. My fear about the proposals for a Confederate Heritage Month is that it would be a sanitized and glorified version of Confederate History, filled with mint juleps and gallant men walking off to war—without talking about the causes of that war or the pains that resulted from that war."

For Darby and others, proposals for a Confederate History Month pose the same perils to a deeper understanding of the past as Civil War reenactments do: they tend to substitute quaint antiquarianism and spectacle for analysis and fact. They often oversimplify, elevating the trivial and secondary over the central and primary. And they pose the danger of trading in authenticity for mere "realism." "My general opinion of reenactments is, if you want to be realistic, *be realistic!*," Darby insists. "Add a couple of slaves in. Have a couple of people who would've been the body-servants, who would've been compelled to go with the master into battle. And if you can't find many black folks who're willing to do that, then that tells you something about how your history is perceived."

Like many on the anti-flag side, Reverend Darby's understanding of the Civil War—of the link between the Confederacy and slavery (and, by implication, the link between slavery and the Confederate battle flag) is clear and concise: "You cannot sort out the fact that the Civil War was about slavery. Sure, it was about states' rights. But the Articles of Secession indicate that the primary concern on everybody's mind was the right to own people. It was an inherent part of the Civil War. The Vice President of the Confederacy, Alexander Stephens, said that the war was based on the great truth that the Negro is not the equal of the white man. When they talked about conscripting black troops in the Confederate army, Governor Brown of Georgia said that you can't make soldiers of slaves—that if you can, then our cause is wrong. During the war a lot of Confederate troops made a policy of capturing white Union troops but summarily executing black Union troops. Nathan Bedford Forrest became the first Grand Dragon of the Klan, surrounded by former Confederate officers. Race and slavery are woven throughout the fabric of the Civil War."

"And," he adds, "even though there were acts of gallantry during the Civil War, as there are in every war—there was gallantry even on the part of some soldiers fighting for Nazi Germany—that gallantry does not need to be celebrated if it was for an odious cause. And to me, the Confederacy fought for an odious cause. And so I think those who consider it to be their heritage need to cherish that heritage in an appropriate context: at home, on their bumpers, in pictures, plaques, or in museum pieces. What I'd really love to see is for them to fly the flag in front of their businesses. But nobody seems to want to do that.* If their heritage is so precious, then they ought to cherish it in those venues, too. And if their heritage is such that it has to be celebrated by force of law, then perhaps they need to examine the value of their heritage."

One interesting, and often overlooked, aspect of the conflict over Confederate heritage lies in the implication of a moral equivalency between those blacks who suffered through slavery and segregation and the white southerners (both soldiers and civilians) who suffered in the war for the Confederacy. Pools of sentiment have attached themselves to each in this contest in competitive suffering. Each side feels that its forebears are deserving of equal treatment, of equal memorialization, of equal measures of respect in the temple of collective memory. And while there is an impossible artificiality in any attempt to weigh the wounds suffered in battle against the wounds inflicted by chains and whips, not *all* wounds are created equal. There is an undeniable hierarchy in historical cause and effect—as Reverend Darby explains.

"The sufferings of southern soldiers in the Civil War," Darby says with firm conviction, "is in no way equivalent to those who bore the brunt of slavery, who bore the brunt of Jim Crow. Those soldiers suffered privations and death because they were fighting for a cause. That cause happened to be the right to own slaves. In the process of prosecuting that cause, in addition to suffering, they did things that brought suffering upon my ancestors—in order to keep pursuing what they believed in. When Lee marched north to Gettysburg, one of the things that the Army of Northern Virginia did was to kidnap free black folk and send them back into slavery—whether they had originally been slaves or not. Those who lived through segregation—those, to me, are stories of inspiration, of how people can survive when they are put upon, when they are excluded, when they are marginalized and demeaned. Those are stories of courage in the face of oppression. The other stories are about soldiers who happen to do courageous things in the process of committing an atrocity. The two are not equivalent."

The fight over the flag has now become another chapter in the history of the contemporary South. But the broader story of the development of southern culture is one involving more give-and-take than the flag debate exemplified. The grand irony of southern history lies in the way in which the region's black and white

---

*Nobody, that is, except for Maurice Bessinger, the "barbecue king of Columbia." Bessinger, a Columbia-based barbecue magnate and inveterate racist, caused a small ruckus, in the wake of the flag debate, when he hoisted large rebel flags at his chain of restaurants in the state capital. Under protest, several grocery-store chains in the state stopped carrying Bessinger's own special brand of barbecue sauce.

strands intertwined to form a new cultural amalgam. The outcome is ironic be-cause it came about within a society whose white inhabitants fought to maintain racial purity and whose black inhabitants led lives largely separate from the rest. The two mixed nevertheless—and the region became all the richer as a result.

Sometimes the mixing came about on the basis of a mutuality of interests. But just as often it came about in circumstances in which black and white were locked in innate opposition, like two cocks on the killing floor. This is where the irony inherent in southern culture can be its sharpest, its most surprising. This is where making quick and pat conclusions about the South can be dangerous, where unexpected twists of plot can upset well-established assumptions and comfortable preconceptions. Even when opposition remains intractable, where give-and-take is not in the cards, even then there may be something that speaks to the deeper ironies of southern history and culture. The story of the Redneck Shop is a case in point.

Opened in 1996 in the small Upstate town of Laurens, the Redneck Shop took up residence in an old movie theater just off the central town square and just out of sight of the county courthouse with its Confederate soldier still standing at the ready. In the lobby up front, where Saturday-night filmgoers once bought bags of buttered popcorn and boxes of Raisinettes, visitors now could browse the shop's collection of unique merchandise, much of it sporting rebel flags and proclaiming white-pride, pro-southern, or anti-government sentiments. Along-side a wide assortment of slogan-bearing baseball caps, bumper stickers, belt buckles, and other miscellany, the shopper could also find a small quantity of Klan paraphernalia—and, neatly segregated from the rest, a collection of pick-aninny refrigerator magnets.

Just beyond this one-of-a-kind shopping experience lay what the Redneck Shop claimed (on the old theater marquee out front) was the "world's only Klan museum," a compact hodgepodge of letters, posters, flyers, banners, photo-graphs, pamphlets, and other mementos—some of it historical in nature, much of it merely curious. At the center of the museum stood an odd assemblage of department-store mannequins, each outfitted with its own unique Klan hood and robe. These female dummies, decked out in their satiny-shiny polyester cos-tumes, gave all the appearance of preparing for nocturnal activities—albeit of a kind more domestic in nature than that usually ascribed to the Klan.

Behind the museum with its ladies of the night lay a part of the shop not usu-ally included in the public tour. At the heart of the old building, where audiences once watched yesterday's blockbusters, is an active Klan assembly hall, its high back wall where the screen used to be now decorated with a large mural depict-ing a hooded Klansman mounted on a rearing horse. A Christian cross made of large lightbulbs stands on a stage next to a lectern. In this empty meeting place, the deranged and unsettling blend of kitsch and menace that has always characterized the Klan takes on a kind of inert mass. It is immediately obvious that the other parts of the "shop" are merely satellites in orbit around this, its center of gravity.

The Redneck Shop's proprietor, John Howard, enters, plants himself in a worn La-Z-Boy recliner and begins regaling his visitors with his own version of Klan history. Mr. Howard is friendly but suspicious. Perhaps all Klansmen are mistrustful—in a sense it's their stock-in-trade. But a high-profile Klansman such as Howard has his own special reasons for being wary. His shop has not been a welcome presence in downtown Laurens. It became the target of brick-throwers and was once rammed by an incensed out-of-towner wielding a Chevy van. The city council passed a resolution against the shop and local citizens initiated a black-and-white ribbon campaign as a way of publicly demonstrating their disapproval. A black minister, David Kennedy, became the most prominent leader in organizing opposition to the shop and in leading demonstrations against it—earning him Howard's special enmity.[22]

But the fate of this one-of-a-kind outpost of old-order thinking served as a reminder of the odd twists that race relations can sometimes take in the paradoxical South.

The original cofounder of the Redneck Shop, a man named Mike Burden, was a local boy down on his luck when he first met Howard back in late 1989. Howard took Burden under his wing, gave him a job, and, more importantly, a sense of belonging and purpose as a new recruit in Howard's local Klan group. Burden felt a new sense of power as he swiftly rose within the organization—something that filled an inner emptiness, at least for a time. Five years after their first meeting and two years before the Redneck Shop was born, Burden bought the old movie theater from Howard, on the condition that Howard retain full use of the building until his death. Burden and Howard then joined together to create the Redneck Shop, originally Burden's idea. The men's relationship soon soured, however, and Burden left the Klan—while retaining ownership of the old theater building. Finding religion, Burden underwent a change of heart, a conversion of sorts that altered his views on both the Klan and blacks. In an act of atonement, Burden sold the building he owned to the church ministered by David Kennedy, Howard's arch-nemesis. Kennedy then became, in effect, Howard's new landlord. The proviso granting Howard lifetime use of the building remained in force, preventing Kennedy from evicting Howard from his property. But he was willing to wait.

The ironic black/white entanglements of the Redneck Shop symbolically illustrate the intricate pattern of racial ties typical of the South. Southern history has been the scene of an oddly symbiotic relationship between blacks and whites—a relationship that, as Reverend Darby says, "sometimes makes for some convoluted lines and interesting stories." It also has led many whites to the belief (taken almost as a matter of faith) that whites and blacks enjoy a "special relationship" in the South, a certain feeling and understanding for one another that cannot be found anywhere else in the country. In the South, as the old saying goes, "We can get to know each other well just so long as we don't have to sit at the same table together—while in the North, we can sit at the same table, so long as we don't have to bother getting to know each other." It may indeed be true that the long historical proximity of blacks and whites in the South has lent an element of "genuineness" to racial relations there that is absent elsewhere.

But this same sense of "kinship" has also made for a certain smugness about black/white relations. There is a feeling among many southerners that in transcending its segregationist self, the South has finally gotten past all that and need not be bothered with race matters any longer. The white sense of having a privileged relationship with black southerners, combined with the notion that racial conflict is (or should be) a thing of the past, causes many white southerners to throw a blanket over the problems that remain, to assume that the "special understanding" that supposedly exists between the races in the South will serve to smooth over any rough spots still remaining. Southern whites too easily forget that good relations do not grow of themselves but must be constantly nurtured and tended. Whites often talk past the racial issues still outstanding, believing that a friendly gesture, a warm smile, a joke, or a slap on the back will do to overcome the divisions that remain.[23]

Eliminating the longstanding injustices of legalized segregation in the South, as difficult as it seemed at the time, was perhaps the easiest part of the problem. The bald-faced character of the southern segregationist system made it easy to identify what needed to be done. Once that layer had been stripped away, however, there was still another, deeper layer left to contend with—one which existed in both the South and the North:

> As Jim Crow laws were overturned, less tractable problems were revealed, and they frustrated King toward the end of his life as he tried to being his campaign to cities in the North. There, villainy was less identified. Rooted in the prejudices, the poverty, the poor education, and the culture of hopelessness that divided blacks and whites, the racial predicament proved too deeply embedded in the society to be pried out by mere personal contact and legal equality.[24]

North and South had become more alike. Both now faced the more general, underlying problems associated with race in America. Warm personal relationships between blacks and whites were well and good, and may have helped to prevent the kind of violence that erupted in Watts, Detroit, and other places around the country during the 1960s and 1970s. But, as David Shipler notes, "In the South, bigotry often coexisted with friendship, challenging the assumption that association tempered prejudice." Here he again quotes Steve Suitts: "The paradox was that southern whites loved blacks as individuals and hated them as a group."[25] Even today, Shipler adds, "many whites in the South sugarcoat their hostile views and exaggerate their region's tolerance in a kind of gauzy self-congratulation."[26] Self-congratulation leads to self-satisfaction—the feeling that all is right with the world (or would be if the professional complainers and activists would just keep their noses out and not stir things up)—and to a sense of aggrieved resentment when reminded that there is still unfinished business to attend to.

The preferred approach to race encounters—in the North or the South—is what Reverend Darby calls "Kumbaya race relations." "It's when we get together once a year, we agree that we're all one, we sing 'Kumbaya,' and then everybody goes back to doing what they were doing before. When we talk about race in America, nobody wants to insult anybody. So everybody's very, very careful. And sometimes we're so careful that we don't say anything." What has to happen, Darby says hopefully, is we have to try and get past this "thin-skinned" attitude on matters of race. "People ought to be able to sit and talk, and, if necessary, argue, until we get to know each other. The more opportunities we have to talk to each other, the better off we will be." But he doesn't believe that the Confederate flag itself can serve as a vehicle for productive debate or discussion, "because that's a battle that by its very nature is going to be divisive."

There are others in South Carolina who disagree, who believe that the flag *can* be used, or at least transformed, into a symbol that promotes discussion, racial reconciliation, and a new shared identity. In fact, some have even staked their financial futures on the idea.

The name of the venture is NuSouth, based in Charleston. The company's emblem—and, if you believe the company's young founders, the symbol of a cause—is a redesigned Confederate flag with a rectangular shape. It probably would be more accurate to say that the flag has been merely recolored rather than redesigned, since the familiar pattern of stars on an x-shaped cross remains unchanged. Only the colors are different. Rather than the red, white, and blue of the original battle flag, the NuSouth emblem employs various combinations of red, black, and green—the colors of Black Nationalism and black liberation (most often associated with the Black Liberation Flag of Marcus Garvey). The color pattern can vary: in some cases the emblem sports green stars and black crosses over a red field; in others, red stars on a green cross on a black field; and in still others, black stars on a red cross overtop a green field—a variability meant to reinforce the message of diversity and change.

The story of how the NuSouth emblem came about (along with the creed that goes with it) is a mix of entrepreneurial creativity, fortuitous (not to say opportunistic) timing, and skillful Zeitgeist merchandising. It also marked probably the most creative and imaginative response to the flag debate in South Carolina.

Neither of NuSouth's founders is a native South Carolinian. Sherman Evans, who projects a Spike Lee–like pointy pugnaciousness, grew up in Ohio, though both his parents originally came from the South. Angel Quintero, who, in contrast to Evans, is possessed of a Buddha-like calmness that nevertheless contains within it a passion equal to his partner's, was born in Cuba, but his family "migrated" to Miami in 1967. Both men did stints in the U.S. military, each serving a turn in Charleston, and eventually returned to settle there. Quintero started an auto customizing business called Buff-It and later a small recording studio. Evans and his wife went into the apparel trade, opening a shop called Utopia. The two men eventually hooked up to form a recording company, Vertical Records, along with a concert and event promotion agency they dubbed Free at Last Entertainment (evidence of their cheeky sense of humor). Quintero was managing several local music groups at the time, and Evans joined in "to try to create specific identities for the groups—through fashion design."

One of the groups they had taken on was a South Carolina hip-hop act called DaPhlayva. By 1992 the group had an album ready and were trying to come up with a concept for the cover. Given the regional rivalries that were playing themselves out in the hip-hop scene at the time—the East Coast versus West Coast sound—Evans and Quintero thought it might be a good idea to have DaPhlayva represent its own region of the country. "These guys were from South Carolina," Evans recalls saying, "so why not have them represent the South? And so we started talking about southern symbols. And the most recognized symbol of the South is, of course, the Confederate flag. At first, we were like, wow, we can't do that, because that doesn't really say 'us.' But then we said, well, maybe we can do something with it, maybe we can change it somehow. And so Angel started playing around with some ideas, throwing colors around. At one point we had what we called the 'rainbow stars'—we were gonna represent every group that we felt were oppressed. But that was really skirting around what we were truly saying. So what we ended up with was the red-black-and-green design."

Quintero jumps in: "We kept saying, 'Keep it simple, keep it simple.' Because if you make it too complicated, nobody would understand it. Just change the colors, make it represent unity. The group didn't like it—they didn't understand how we saw it. And we told them, this thing makes a statement about the South. So we incorporated it anyhow—we were the executive producers, after all. We made up promotional t-shirts for a live show here in town. The back of the shirt read, 'The past is the past,' and the front said, 'The future is DaPhlayva.'—and we put the flag on the front, with the integration colors. During the show, we threw these out to the audience, and a local black schoolgirl, Shellmira Green, grabbed one."

As it turned out, Shellmira Green was the bridge that would take the new flag from being a mere marketing device for a local rap group and turn it into a political statement that attempted to redefine a central icon of southern heritage—and with it, the meaning of southern identity itself.

Green and other black students began wearing the DaPhlayva t-shirts to their high school beginning in late February and early March 1994 (at the end of Black History Month) and encouraged their friends to get their own and do the same. As Green and the others saw it, wearing the shirts was an act of black pride. "I wanted to wear the shirt to school because it stands for black people in the South," she said. "White people aren't the only people living in the South. That's why I liked it."[27] But the shirt was also a form of protest. By wearing it, Green and the others were reacting to another crop of t-shirts that had appeared around school, shirts worn by white students that bore slogans such as "One Hundred Percent Cotton—And You Picked It," or "The Original Boyz in the Hood" (alongside a picture of hooded Klansmen). White students protested the DaPhlayva campaign, and rather than have the t-shirt wars escalate into the kind of racial disruption that had plagued other schools, the school's principal imposed an across-the-board ban on "any symbol that depicted heritage or race, such as the Confederate flag or the Malcolm X logo."[28] Most students agreed to fold their shirts and put them away. Everyone except for Shellmira Green. She refused, saying the ban violated her right to freedom of expression, and charged her school with practicing a double standard by the way it had cast a blind eye on displays of the original battle flag but found its "Africanized" alternative an intolerable source of disruption. Green was suspended, and her case ended up in court—while Evans and Quintero were borne off on a wave of publicity.[29]

A couple of weeks prior to the Shellmira Green episode, Evans and Quintero had unveiled their new flag at an event staged on the steps of the State House in Columbia. They offered their flag as a way out of the quickly deepening morass over the Confederate flag—a rapidly worsening wrangle that would turn 1994 into the year that brought on the first full-scale battle over the flag. The two entrepreneurs unfurled their new banner and proposed that it replace the Confederate battle flag on the State House dome for one year. Its display, they declared, would signal a change in perspective, a transition to a new, more integrated era. After a year, it, too, would be removed, leaving only the state and national flags atop the state legislature. Drawing attention to the fact that there were no southern symbols that blacks could "share in and take pride in," Evans said that their new emblem proclaimed "I am proud to be an African-American and I am proud to live in the South. We transformed the symbol that oppressed us, we took away the power it had over us and eliminated the hatred it represented."[30]

Their proposal had the life span of a mayfly. It was quickly washed away in a rising tide of competing proposals over what to do about the Confederate flag on the dome. Evans and Quintero say they weren't terribly interested in the politics of the Confederate flag debate, anyway. They were after something bigger. "We had evolved beyond that," Evans says. "We realized that getting our flag up there was not going to be the solution to the problem, at least not for us. This needed to be a grass-roots kind of thing. We were truly going to put the past in the past."

And besides, they wanted to make some money.

By now, the rap group that had set it all in motion had fizzled—but the symbol lived on. So Evans and Quintero (with some help from Quintero's mother, an old hand in the garment industry) set to work embroidering the emblem "on everything we owned." They were encouraged by the reaction they had been getting and were eager to see just how far their idea would carry them. The next step in their campaign took them to the Million Man March in Washington, D.C., in the autumn of 1995. "We wanted to see if folks there would 'get it.'" Could people "see what we were saying" with this new symbol—would it be accepted? "We were surprised to find out," Quintero says, "that a lot of people really did get it. People started requesting the t-shirts. In fact, we used to say it was almost like selling crack, because we couldn't make enough t-shirts to keep up with demand. So we said, wow, we gotta come out with a full line of clothing."

It was at this point that they decided to give their new line of clothing a name—a brand name that would express the same idea that the symbol embodied. "Hey, it's a new South we're living in," Evans recalls saying, "so why not just call it that: *New South*? And since we came out of the music business, out of the hip-hop scene," Quintero adds, "we took the spelling from there, and turned it into *N-U-South*—which was also a little easier to trademark."

The trendy spelling was meant to bear a message. It declared that the change had to come *N-U*—"in you"—in personal attitudes about race and how we judge one another based on preconceptions and inherited biases.

"Because the true oppressor is oneself," Evans announces.

"Now we had the *big picture*," Quintero adds with bravado.

Opening up their first boutique in downtown Charleston was meant to bring home the message as well—in a very literal sense: "Everything started here," they said. "So let's bring it back home and end it here." Coming into the heart of downtown was part of the plan, part of the image they sought to project. It was another act of in-your-face bravado. And it just so happened to be a good marketing strategy, too. "We put it down here because we wanted to break all the boundaries," Evans proclaims. "NuSouth steps outside those boundaries." "We knew we had to come down here," Quintero adds, "because, if you notice, there are no black shops down here. None—not black-owned, at least." Had they taken their shop to another part of town, they point out—to a predominantly black section (not too many blocks away)—their image would have been blurred, even fundamentally altered. Their merchandise would have been labeled an "urban line," Quintero says. "It wouldn't have been acceptable" to the white mainstream. "It would have made it a polarized product," Evans quickly adds. "And NuSouth is not a polarized product. NuSouth is all-inclusive, not exclusive."

Never shy about self-promotion, NuSouth's youthful impresarios had a large billboard erected at a strategic location along one of the interstate highways that feed into downtown Charleston. In a cheeky paraphrase of Martin Luther King Jr., the sign read, "For the sons and daughters of former slaves. For the sons and daughters of former slave-owners. Threads that connect us—words that free us: NuSouth."

"Words that free us: NuSouth." Quintero repeats the phrase for emphasis, in a tone of almost messianic reverence. To its founders, NuSouth was more than just a business—it was a mission. They didn't just sell clothes. They sold attitude. For them, it was almost a spiritual thing—a call to reexamine, to "go inside and process," as Evans puts it. Just by wearing NuSouth, they believed, a person would be making a statement: about his relationships with others, about his way of viewing and dealing with race and history. But, more importantly, it would be a statement of the wearer's attitude about himself, and how he views himself in relationship to diversity. Liberation comes from within, not without, they proclaimed. NuSouth aimed to change mentalities and the way we view each other. It wasn't a political campaign as such. It didn't seek short-term fixes or political compromises. It looked toward the long term, the long haul. Grassroots.

The name itself was a kind of incantation—the clothes merely the outer expression of an inner feeling. "*NuSouth*," Quintero intones—"that word right there frees you from all the oppressive things that have dogged you. And just like that—you shouldn't have to be haunted anymore. If you pass somebody with a Confederate flag—so be it. It's part of history. Just keep going—keep liberating yourself. Like we say: It's *N-U*."

Start with *today*, not with the past. Make a new beginning. Judge people as individuals, not as part of a group. "You know that incident where that guy got dragged in Texas?" Quintero continues. "There are a lot of people who see something like that and say, 'Those damn white people!' But no, that's wrong. It's those damn *three guys* who did it! When a black man carjacks, or does a drive-by—then it's, 'those damn black people!' Naw! Don't judge a generation because of an incident. That's what we need to start doing. Stop stereotyping."

"You gotta go within," says Evans. "All your oppressions, all your fears, that you hold within—those are yours. Those are your choices. You have to go inside and process, and let go of a lot of stuff, let go of all that programming you got through the boob-tube. All those stereotypes. I've had 'em too. Is everyone who owns a Confederate flag a racist? I don't think so."

That's what NuSouth means, Quintero says: learning to see differently. "If you knew nothing about NuSouth when you first saw this," he says, "you might just see the Confederate flag. But then you look at the colors and ask, 'Hey, who is behind this?' It catches your attention and all of a sudden you start asking what it means. That's exactly how you should look at people."

"I truly believe," Evans adds, "that people who embrace NuSouth are people who want to make a difference. They want to make a positive statement about where we're going, about respect for our fellow man. They're looking for a united front. And I believe that through the vehicle of NuSouth, they're opening themselves up to healing and moving forward."

"The Confederate flag has never been a symbol of unity," Quintero says, continuing the thought. "A lot of people have been oppressed by it—both black and white, right down to this very day! But that's not what we're focusing on. We knew that the Confederate flag is part of history. But with NuSouth, we will *make* history. One of the things we stay away from in this country is race. Why? Because we don't know how to talk comfortably about it without somebody getting offended. So we said, hey, if this symbol, the NuSouth flag, causes somebody to come up and ask, what does that mean? That just opens the door up so easily— and nobody gets offended! All we have to do is talk."

"Ignorance plus fear breeds racism," Evans adds. "So I'm glad that there's a NuSouth, because it gives everyone an opportunity to become educated, to become conscious. We're living in a new thirteen states [of the former Confederacy]. And NuSouth is definitely going to have a voice in those new thirteen states."

For Angel Quintero, it's become a way of life. "I'm always talking about it," he says. "And I live it. My kids live it. I went to the grocery store one day with my daughter, who's six years old. She was wearing a NuSouth shirt. And the cashier there asked her, 'Do you know what that flag means?' And she said, 'Yeah, my daddy and Sherman.' That's cute, I thought. But then the lady says, 'No, do you know what that *really* means?' And my daughter said, 'Yeah, it means when black people and white people can come together.' And I thought, Wow!, if *she* can learn that, then you can teach the whole world the same thing!"

"The past is the past." History starts today. That's the NuSouth mantra.

But others are not so sure it's as easy as that. While white reaction to NuSouth was largely positive—and most of NuSouth's clientele are white—reaction in parts of the black community was considerably more tepid and skeptical. "That was not an idea I particularly cared for," Senator Maggie Glover says of the NuSouth flag. "I commended them for at least caring enough to try to come up with something that brings the races together. But no, I wouldn't buy that one myself."

Reverend Darby dismisses it as just another commercial come-on. "I don't know the brothers," he says, "so I can't pass judgement. But it's like somebody once said: If it's a pig, you can put lipstick and a wig on it, but it's still a pig—and I wouldn't wanna date it. So, you know, you can change the colors on the flag, but it's still recognizable as the Confederate flag. If it were something that was giving fits to those people who love the flag, then I would see it as something effective. But it's not giving those folks fits. You can give it chartreuse and purple stars and bars and call it 'our' version—but as long as those folks can keep *their* version, it won't change a thing. I think it's a nice way to make a few bucks. And I wouldn't begrudge anybody the chance to make a livin.'"

To the brash, young go-getters at NuSouth, however, the whole approach of black leadership to the Confederate flag has been wrongheaded. To them, the Confederate flag was a pseudo-issue, a distraction from the real problems. "The flag is a scab," Evans says impatiently. "Deal with the wound. If you want to make a real difference, deal with what's *inside* the capitol."

"I think you should focus on real issues," Evans continues. "I think that's what's wrong with our country today. We're stuck. The people we appoint as leaders don't lead. And I think that the African American leadership structure is afraid of having their position challenged, they're afraid that they're about to be replaced. Because the only thing they continue to do is bring along baggage. They keep dragging the same old baggage forward. They didn't win with it before— and they're not going to win with it now."

Evans then expands on his theory about contemporary black leadership: "You know, there's a theory about animals. If you cage an animal—and if you put them in a cage long enough—when you open the cage door, they won't even try to leave, because in his mind that animal truly believes that freedom is just a dream. These folks couldn't see freedom if you gave it to them. They don't even know they're free. That's why they keep fighting the same old war. They're look- ing for someone else to acknowledge their pain and suffering. They're looking for someone else to free them. It just doesn't happen that way. Freedom is within."

And as far as black attitudes toward NuSouth are concerned, "It's just a crab- in-the-barrel kind of thing," Evans believes. "It's better to pull 'em down, don't let 'em succeed, because then all those other efforts will be put in question. But I laugh at it, because, you know, what happens if all of a sudden I don't have someone to blame, and I have to be responsible for myself? It's a lot easier to blame someone, to be a victim, than it is to really take responsibility for yourself. It's a new millennium in the South," he says with firm insistence. "Time to *act* like it is."

Quintero echoes the same impatience and self-reliance, reflecting a self- empowerment tradition that has its own deep roots in the black American ex- perience. "There are some people who're stuck in their old ways. They're not gonna change. Well, gimme a solution! I mean, you have all these rights, bitches, whatever—but you have no solutions. We can't keep pointing a finger at something that happened so long ago. That war was more than 140 years ago—and we're still fighting it! That's crazy!"

"They say the best way to stop progress is to get stuck debating one period in your life," Evans adds. "So the truth is, we haven't advanced one iota if we're still sitting here talking about who won that war."

"Empower yourself today!" Quintero declares. "Stop blaming. That's what our parents do. They say the white man this and the white man that—the system is keeping us down. No—hell no! The Confederate flag is not stopping us from achieving anything. Bringing down the flag—what did we really gain? Can I walk into the bank and get a loan a little easier? When they talk about history in school, do they talk about slavery? What did we gain? Respect? No—respect I gain for myself. I gain respect when I walk out that door and people say, 'Damn, those guys are doing some shit down here that I didn't think anybody could do! Look at them. They're doing it—and doing it in a positive way.'"

"The past is the past." Evans intones the NuSouth mantra once more—this time with the sound of determined finality. "We're gonna *make* the past the past. By putting on a NuSouth shirt and walking out the door, the past *becomes* the past—because I am now working on the future. Freedom means: what am I gonna do today? I think the whole debate about history is good. But what are we gonna do *to-day*? I'm not afraid of the past. What scares the hell out of me is, what's going to happen to our future?"

"What are we gonna do today?" he asks again.

Then he answers, confidently: "NuSouth—we're gonna work together."

It was a hopeful, optimistic campaign, that much is sure—all about perception and change. It's about changing habits of mind and of behavior. Nothing is fixed, NuSouth's confident founders claim. Everything can be altered. History, the past—none of that need play a role. In fact, focusing too much on the past can hinder us from getting where we need to be. NuSouth is a thoroughly American project. It emanates a spirit of messianism and eternal new beginnings, together with the can-do optimism of do-it-yourself entrepreneurship. But NuSouth is also a thoroughly postmodern project, combining semiotic experimentalism with textual deconstructionism. It has taken a potent historical symbol—one of the most trenchant symbols America has produced, as Clyde Wilson would say—and attempted to recast it in such a way that it serves a contemporary purpose different from (indeed, in direct opposition to) that which gave it birth. As Sherman Evans says, "It's the strategy of going right into the fear and claiming it—you embrace it and make it mean something else."

NuSouth is, at heart, just a clothier—albeit one that combines consumer commercialism with not-so-subtle political symbolism. Evans and Quintero seamlessly combine the evangelist's belief in his mission with the salesman's faith in his wares (and in his talents at selling them). With them, it is impossible to separate one motivation from the other. The two are so intricately entwined that is not clear whether even Evans and Quintero know where conviction ends and marketing begins. And perhaps they don't really care.

NuSouth is one of an ever-expanding group of merchandisers who use increasingly subtle and sophisticated means to market identity, image, and self-perception. But at what point does image replace substance? Can we willy-nilly rip out pieces of the historical mosaic and reassemble them in any fashion we like? In its NuSouth rendition, does one of the most weighted of southern symbols become just another deracinated object floating free in historical limbo, a kind of whirligig in a playhouse of postmodern relativism and arbitrariness?

As Evans and Quintero point out, the cultural and fashion industries have made a bundle marketing black styles to deep-pocketed suburban whites. The NuSouth twist on this theme is to "hijack" a white cultural symbol, run it through a "blackwash," and then sell the result back to their predominantly white clientele. A good joke? A shrewd marketing strategy? Or a substantive prod to social consciousness and intercourse? Does it spur debate or is it just another form of the same old thing: a way for whites to play at being black—in this case by allowing progressive-minded whites the opportunity vicariously to "be" black by "standing with" blacks in mocking a central symbol of white culture—without doing anything to promote black advancement or racial understanding? Just don a hat, pull on a shirt, or slip into a pair of slacks—and leave it at that?

We have moved away from a time in which symbols—including styles and fashions—made or reinforced political statements. Now, styles and symbols *are* the statement. Counterculture and mainstream culture have merged into a bland porridge of self-selected "identities." Political movements have ceased to exercise much influence—and any coherence that once existed has since splintered into a patchwork of group demands and vague generalities. The "anything goes" openness and playfulness of American culture (and the tendency of everything eventually to become part of popular consumer culture) makes it difficult for any symbol to maintain its meaning over time. Symbols become unmoored from their point of embarkation—a phenomenon that applies to the original Confederate flag as well.

There was a time when images of Che Guevara or Huey Newton were powerful political statements. But once they became products of the mass market, they lost much of their previous punch. They degenerated into just another way to "be different," devoid of any deeper political content. The same applies to "X" caps and other clothing displaying that particular symbol. While Malcolm X embodied an important and sophisticated political movement in America, the "X" that appeared in the 1990s was just another example of vague sloganeering, at most a kind of in-your-face assertion of cultural difference. It was largely devoid of political meaning—and ceased to have any meaning whatsoever once it entered the (white) mainstream.

But there is still something more that NuSouth hints at. It marks an attempt to find something worthy of celebrating about the South that goes beyond the familiar clichés about manners, magnolias, and the Lost Cause—the pastoral scenes of a gallant South. More importantly, it aims to get past the confined and confining view that many southerners have of their own history, that perspective that still forces too many southerners into tired old attitudes of backward-looking defensiveness and reactionism. NuSouth aims toward a southern heritage that can be cherished equally by blacks and whites alike. Within this there is an implied question: Why have we for so long failed to take into consideration the full story of our regional past? Why has it been so difficult for so many of us to see more of the southern past than just the Old South and the Confederacy—and to bind ourselves to an incomplete picture of even that? Why hasn't it been possible for us to embrace the full panoply of the southern past, including its evils and misdeeds? Why have we failed to see the South whole: the writing, the music, the art, the entire folk culture that it has produced, as well as the powerfully dramatic story of its history—in *all* its detail? NuSouth's very existence implies that we are now headed in that direction. The NuSouth flag serves as a marker on the road toward a more integrated society—one that takes in all the stories that make up our collective memory.

Impatient declarations that "the past is the past," however, may not point us down a path that we should follow. Future-focused youth is often indifferent to the past. It is often frustrated by the ways in which their elders remain fixated on it, by their weary insistence that the present remains in many ways a captive of what preceded it. In its eagerness and impatience to move on, youth is unable to fully understand why history should matter any longer. But today is a starting point only in a limited sense. With the South, it is precisely in the past that the source of our contemporary discontent lies. By focusing exclusively on today, saying that the here and now is all that matters and that history starts in the present moment merely swings us around that crater in our soul once again. It becomes another way of avoiding the central concern of southern history.

———❖———

The Redneck Shop and NuSouth have since passed into history. Both closed their doors within a couple of years after the Confederate flag came off the dome of the South Carolina State House. Both were echoes of the southern past, both reminded us of the unusual resonance that history has in the South. In a sense, though, it seems odd that we should even need reminding, since the repercussions of the past surround us daily. Its importance is evident, for example, in the ways in which historical experience colors black perception. As David Shipler reminds us,

> black America generally lives with a different memory, one that feels the reverberations of slavery. . . . Present events occur in context, not in isolation, so they are interpreted according to what has gone before. Hence, in the eyes of many blacks, elements of the complex relationships of slavery are constantly being reenacted—between bosses and workers, between blacks and whites sexually, between African-Americans of lighter and darker skin, among blacks who suppress dissent within their ranks. Slavery is a permanent metaphor.[31]

It is a form of memory that cannot be wiped away with a catchy slogan—nor should it be. Ignoring the specific circumstances and continuing legacies of history will not bring us further along, neither black nor white.

Heritage *is* important, memory *does* matter—just as the southern traditionalists claim. And, in their own way, their black opponents would no doubt agree. Heritage is important as a means of creating a sense of identity, a safe harbor from the gales that can tear at solitary souls. History in the South involves a fundamental human relationship to our collective past. Both black and white southerners find special significance in origins, family bonds, ties to place and people, a love of stories. And there, in a sense, lies the source of the trouble. For despite their commonalities, the division brought about by historical experience remains. While blacks and whites in the South both hold deep cultural memories, and though those memories grew from roots that shared a common soil, they have matured in a state of antipathy and competition, like two trees whose proximity to one another bred in each an inexorable antagonism toward the other. History has made us this way—not our intrinsic natures. And if it is to do more than divide us further, heritage must be refashioned to give proper recognition to this fact. If it is a just society we seek, then the identity we shape for ourselves must be inclusive, not exclusive.

No one can say it will be easy. We may not be able to wear our identity with the ease and comfort we might like. The identity we derive from our collective past may be as much a hair shirt as it is a cozy sweater—it might not always offer the full measure of contentment we wish of it. But if it is to be honest and real, our identity will likely be an ambivalent one—reflecting the very contradictory nature of human existence, a mixture of good and bad. At least in a negative sense, the old Confederate flag itself represents as well as anything this sense of ambivalence over our cultural legacy:

The [Confederate battle] flag is simultaneously an effort to remember what many Americans honor as a cherished past and to forget or to otherwise gloss over what many other Americans consider to be the single-most important aspect of that past.[32]

The flag is, in its very essence, irresolute and contradictory. Wiping it out, eliminating it from view, would be just as wrong as hoisting it atop the highest flagpole in the center of town—if only because it serves as a useful reminder of a past that failed and of an alternate future not taken.

History does not often proffer us the neat lessons we demand of it. The lessons we pull from it are frequently merely caricatures created out of current needs. Our perspective on the past may be as much clouded by hindsight as those who inhabited that past were hampered by their inability to see clearly what lay ahead of them. It would be wise, then, not to judge them too harshly—lest we be judged ourselves by a similar measure. Our uses of the past should be tempered by a healthy doubt about clear and easy certainty. It would do us well to recall the closing words of Ralph Ellison's Invisible Man, for whom ambivalence becomes the clearest stance he can take:

So it is that now I denounce and defend, or feel prepared to defend. I condemn and affirm, say no and yes, say yes and say no. I denounce because though implicated and partially responsible, I have been hurt to the point of abysmal pain, hurt to the point of invisibility. And I defend because in spite of all I find that I love. In order to get some of it down I *have* to love. I sell you no phony forgiveness, I'm a desperate man—but too much of your life will be lost, its meaning lost, unless you approach it as much through love as through hate. So I approach it through division. So I denounce and I defend and I hate and I love.[33]

A truly integrated culture of the kind the NuSouth flag was meant to represent could only be achieved, Martin Luther King believed, "by true neighbors who are willingly obedient to unenforceable obligations."[34] To achieve that, says Maggie Glover, "we're going to have to have that kind of integration in our minds." And in our hearts, too. Only then will integration become the "kind of spiritual thing" that Tom Turnipseed dreams of.

Five

TAKING THEIR STANDS

This War ain't over. Hit just started good.

William Faulkner,
The Unvanquished *(1938)*

Brett Bursey jokingly refers to himself as "the oldest living Confederate prisoner of war." His encounter with Confederate heritage came early and was long-lasting. Back in 1969 Bursey was a twenty-year-old student at the University of South Carolina in Columbia and an activist with the Southern Student Organizing Committee and Students for a Democratic Society (SDS). He and others had been trying, unsuccessfully, to find someone in the all-white state legislature who would agree to promote the removal of the Confederate flag from the State House dome. And in February 1969 he helped organize a workshop on racism at the USC campus to commemorate the killing of three black students at South Carolina State the year before, during the Orangeburg Massacre.

At the end of the week-long seminar, Bursey and a group of around thirty-five fellow student activists gathered in front of the university president's residence to, as Bursey puts it, "agitate on the issue" of race—to engage in what today might be called "consciousness raising." As part of that protest, the students burned a Confederate battle flag. Bursey, as organizer of the action, was arrested and charged with violating a state law (16-17-220) that made it illegal to, among other things, "publicly mutilate, deface, defile, defy, jeer at, trample upon or cast contempt, either by word or act, upon" the U.S., state, or Confederate flags. He was never brought to trial for his offense, however, and the relevant portions of the statute were later dropped from the books after the U.S. Supreme Court ruled in favor of protecting flag burning as a form of political speech. The Supreme Court's decision was apparently sufficiently worrisome to prompt several members of the state legislature to introduce bills, in 1975 and 1977, in the House of Representatives aimed at replacing the offending segments of the state code with a new ban—one directed at making it unlawful to *prohibit* the display of the Confederate flag. In other words, it sought to ban the banning of the Confederate banner. The concern was not great enough at the time, however, and the measure was left to die in committee.[1] But Bursey, who continues to be involved in progressive political activities in South Carolina, says he is still waiting for justice to be served in his case. The state, he says, still owes him the $200 bond he paid over thirty years ago.

Bursey's story may contain the longest personal postscript to his encounter with the Confederate flag, but he was probably not the first to protest against it. As near as can be determined, that distinction appears to go to Robert Ford, now a state senator from Charleston County. Back in 1967, the Louisiana-born Ford was a seventeen-year-old student volunteer with the Southern Christian Leadership Conference on his way to a strategy meeting on the South Carolina coast. On the way there, he and three other SCLC staff members stopped off in the state capital for a two-hour demonstration against racism in the state—and against the Confederate flag displayed over the capitol dome. It was a small event by any measure, made even smaller by the weight of more-fundamental civil-rights issues that lay still unresolved in many parts of the South. The Confederate flag was an important symbol of the old southern way of life and an expression of defiance in the face of changing times, but it was hardly the most pressing issue facing the Civil Rights movement at that time. Ford later asked Martin Luther King whether or not to tackle South Carolina's Confederate flag display. King, Ford recalls, told him that the flag "is an issue for another time; the issue of basic civil rights and human rights takes precedence over anything that we can do right now."[2]

It would be quite a while before the flag's time finally came. Except for sporadic and brief flashes of disapproval, things stayed fairly quiet around the Confederate flag throughout much of the 1970s and into the 1980s. The flag display was taken for granted almost as if it had always been there, distinctive but hardly any more unusual than the cross atop a church or the Stars and Stripes in front of the local post office. By the 1970s the flag had already become part of the visual landscape, a source neither of conscious pride nor concern—to whites, at least. Early complaints met with a mixture of irritated bemusement and dismissive amusement. The flag displays* did not become the focus of public attention, let alone of legislative activity, until the election of the first black state representatives during the early and mid-1970s. Even then, most white South Carolinians failed to take these early protests very seriously. They were nothing more than stunts, most folks believed. Whites chuckled when one black state lawmaker angrily declared, in the late 1970s or early 1980s, that he would scale the State

---

*There were, at that time, not three but five Confederate flags on display within the state legislature. In addition to the one atop the dome and in each of the legislative chambers, one also hung on display in the building's rotunda and another was located outside the governor's legislative offices. The latter two were removed, without fanfare or folderol, during the general renovation of the State House in the mid-1990s.

House roof and rip the flag off the pole himself if it could not be removed any other way. "Those black folks are up to it again," whites would say with a grin and a shake of the head. Blacks were not quite ready to scale that pole just yet, though. Unlike their fellow black parliamentarians in Alabama, who, in 1988, actually did attempt to ascend their state assembly building to remove the Confederate flag flying there (and were arrested for their effort), no one in South Carolina followed through on the threat. So the matter rested yet a while longer.

The first state lawmaker to take on the flag in any serious, continuous fashion, making it into a personal crusade of sorts, was Kay Patterson, a young black representative from the Columbia area who had entered office as part of the first group of black legislators elected in the wake of the civil-rights electoral reforms of the 1960s. Patterson, who was later elected to the state senate, gained notoriety both for his early legislative actions against the Confederate flag as well as for his colorful, combative style and his sometimes salty tongue. As legislator, Patterson demanded attention be paid to the new black presence in state government and sought the respect he felt was its proper due.

Patterson, who had once written an occasional newspaper column titled "'Spressin' Myself," was nothing if not outspoken. Over the years few have been spared his verbal barrages. Once, reacting to racist stereotypes about "lazy" black welfare mothers, Patterson angrily asked his white colleagues who they thought it was that had "cleaned up that damn nasty pigpen you called home?! Who washed your dirty stink-clothes?! Who raised your children from little damn house-ape heathens into decent God-fearing citizens?!"[3] Language like this led some whites to label Patterson a black racist. It also helped set in place a pattern of mutual distrust and sniping that would echo through the debate over the Confederate flag. Whatever one may think about his tactics or his style, however, it was clear that Patterson was unwilling to allow certain elements of long-held white conventional wisdom to stand unquestioned or unchallenged any longer.

The same applied to his struggle against the Confederate flag. His attacks on the flags were Patterson's means of insisting that the state demonstrate equal consideration of and proper respect for the dignity of its black citizens. This is evident in the language used in a bill Patterson cosponsored and helped introduce in the state House of Representatives in early 1980. The measure, which called on the body to create a study committee to develop a policy concerning the "furnishings, memorabilia and trappings which may be placed in the House chamber," specifically referred to the changes in the "composition of the membership in the House of Representatives" brought about by reapportionment (meaning: the election of blacks) and reminded the institution that "goodwill and consideration of the feelings and emotions of everyone are essential" to the proper functioning of the body.[4] The bill assigned the committee the task of appraising the appointment of the house chamber "so that symbolisms which are distasteful to a number of the members of the House may be determined and thus removed or not permitted."[5]

The legislation Patterson introduced approached the issue in an indirect fashion, using general (even courteous) terms, never mentioning the Confederate flag by name. It should be noted that a similar proposal had been introduced in the house a week earlier, which made express reference to the Confederate flag as the source of contention. The measure was voted down almost as quickly as it was introduced—which might perhaps explain the more careful choice of language in the second attempt. But the intent was clear, and those on the other side stated in plain and certain language that they would have none of it. "I am here because my great-grandfather was a Confederate soldier," Representative John Bradley declared as he rose to speak against the resolution. "The Confederates," he said, "fought rather than compromise their principles of self-government. . . . And in their defeat they left a heritage to every succeeding Southern generation. . . . I am tired of the slanders made against our southern history and its defenders. A careful and unbiased study of that history establishes beyond doubt that the government and the soldiers of the Confederacy were not fighting for slaves and slavery, but for the right to self-government." He insisted that "the part the South has played in our nation's history is forever glorious" and closed his comments by reaffirming his faith in his ancestors: "We owe them not only respect and gratitude . . . we own them justice and pride. We owe them honesty and truth in history. We must never, never be ashamed to accept our ancestry and its gifts to us. Until the last soldier in gray passed away from among us it could well be said that there was no prouder boast an American could make than to say, 'I was a Confederate soldier.'"[6]

To fellow Representative Pat Harris, the Confederate flag represented love, devotion, and bravery, not slavery. Devoting a paragraph to each of these virtues, Harris said, "The flag is not a symbol of slavery and never was. . . . Love of their land and pride of ownership brought [southerners together] under this flag to repel any invader from their lands. . . . Devotion, not slavery, sent those men off to battle under this flag. . . . Bravery, not slavery, is what this flag symbolizes." And, as if the point had not already been made plain enough, he repeated, "This flag is a symbol of free men—not slavery."[7]

Representative Patterson would return to the issue again in 1983, when he attempted to insert an amendment into the state budget stating that "$100 of the amount appropriated" for the operations of the Confederate Relic Room would be "used to permanently remove the Confederate flags from the dome of the State House and the House chambers, thereafter displaying them in the Confederate Relic Room, in a place of honor."[8] Support for the flags remained solid, however, and the amendment was comfortably defeated (through procedural means that avoided any direct vote on the substance of the proposal). It was the last time the House of Representatives would address the flag question in a vote of any kind until the final adoption of the compromise plan that removed the flag from the dome seventeen years later.

This brief legislative episode would have a coda over a decade later, however, during the gubernatorial campaign of 1993. The matter concerned that trio of procedural votes (a common practice in legislative maneuver) and whether or not then-Democratic Representative David Beasley's stance back in 1983 placed him in cahoots with the anti-flag forces. During the primary season of 1993, now-Republican gubernatorial candidate Beasley came under fire from heritage groups for his apparent "softness" in defense of the flag. He defended himself, in a letter to *The State* newspaper, by pointing out, correctly, that his votes in 1983 had not touched on the question of whether or not to remove the flag and instead merely expressed a willingness to permit discussion of the issue to continue. He then affirmed his "preference for leaving the flag where it is"—but flag supporters remained suspicious. The votes would surface once more during (by then) Governor Beasley's abortive campaign to bring the flag down from the dome in late 1996—further proof, as far as the heritage defenders were concerned, that Beasley was an inviolate "turncoat" who could not be trusted on this or indeed *any* issue.[9]

The Confederate flag resisted the winds of change for many different reasons, not all of them having to do with lingering racism, political insensitivity, or moral indifference—though they were certainly part of the mix. It wasn't even so much the passions over heritage that kept the flag in place for so long. A strong dose of Carolina cussedness also played its part in keeping the flag flying over the dome of the State House right into the first months of the third millennium. The flag display was the last of its kind. Alabama had removed the Confederate flag from atop its state legislature in the spring of 1993, increasing the pressure on South Carolina to do the same. But that pressure also made South Carolina's flag defenders, and heritage activists across the South, more resolved than ever to see that the flag stayed put. Other states—Georgia and Mississippi—had incorporated the battle-flag pattern into their own state flags. But only South Carolina kept one flapping over its seat of government. And perhaps there was something fitting in that—a kind of historical consistency: The first state to dissolve the bands that tied it to the Union became the last to remove the symbol of that schism.

For many South Carolinians, the flag display was no doubt an embarrassment. But many others found in it something exhilarating and energizing. The greater the pressure to remove it, the prouder they became that South Carolina stood out, defiantly holding up the flag as a symbol of headstrong obstinacy and mulish, unyielding resistance. The object of the resistance was not the primary concern. Resistance would suffice—it was, after all, the essence of being a "rebel." "Being called obstinate—I don't see that as an insult," Chris Sullivan said. "It was South Carolina's obstinacy that gave us America, in places like Cowpens, Kings Mountain, and in the swamps of the Pee Dee. If obstinacy is the opposite of being weak-minded and irresolute, I'd much prefer to be obstinate."

But it was more than a perverse obduracy that kept the flag up. South Carolina's political culture—the "South Carolina style" of elite-directed democracy—played a role as well. The same political inclinations that had ushered the state through the Civil Rights Era—the same preference for slow, deliberate change (when change appeared inevitable), directed and controlled from above and from the center, not from outside and below—came into play in the battle over the Confederate flag as well. Clearly, the state's political culture had undergone change over the years, albeit reluctantly. During the 1970s and 1980s, the old guard that had made South Carolina a politically "fossilized" state began to leave power. Still, many old habits and ways of doing things lived on. Despite signs of an increasing openness and a growing readiness to embrace progress and popular reform, South Carolina did not suddenly transform itself into a "peoples' democracy." The state talked long and hard about putting the flag question to the voters to decide. But public referenda are not entirely kosher in a state like South Carolina. They cut against the grain of the state's essential conservatism. They are too messy, too much of a disturbance to the state's preference for long, leisurely deliberation, gradualism, and polite orderliness.

South Carolina has a long history of this sort of thing. Best known, of course, is the role that the state's cantankerous and diffident attitude toward change played in helping bring about the Civil War. But it had resisted change in other ways, too. South Carolina was, for example, the last of the original parties to the Constitution to allow for popular election of state presidential electors, leaving that power with the legislature until 1860. It was one of the last states to permit the direct election of its U.S. senators. And it did not ratify the Nineteenth Amendment to the Constitution (granting women the right to vote) until 1969.* The tenures of its elected officials also provide evidence of the state's preference for conservative continuity and an almost immutably static status quo. Next to the longtime control exercised by the Tillman machine during the latter part of the nineteenth century, and alongside the lengthy terms served by Senators "Cotton Ed" Smith and, later, Ernest Hollings, there is of course the fantastic political longevity of Strom Thurmond, who, in addition to his years as governor of the

*Of course, women were allowed to vote prior to ratification—the state passed its *own* law to that effect after the Nineteenth Amendment became law—but they were nevertheless banned from serving as jurors.

state also set two records in the U.S. Senate: one for longest-serving and the other for oldest living member. Like a hound snoozing in the shade of a poplar tree on a hot and humid southern afternoon, once South Carolina settles itself in a comfortable spot, it can only grudgingly be compelled to move off it.

The baton of power in South Carolina has passed through very few pairs of hands during the course of the twentieth century—and the governor's were not among them. The state legislature has jealously guarded its lock on power, purposely leaving the governor's office one of the weakest in the country. Originally granted only a two-year term, the legislature later expanded it to four years but did not permit the governor to succeed himself until 1980. Moreover,

> Until the cabinet form of government was adopted in 1993, it was the legislature, not the governor, which controlled the budget process, made a majority of the appointments to the many boards and commissions which ran state agencies, and elected judges and university boards, functions performed by governors in many other states.[10]

Budget and appointment powers are the most important functions of any government. Lacking them, and the mutual dependencies and patterns of influence they bring with them, a state executive is largely reduced to a bit player, dependent upon his powers of persuasion and a good relationship with the state legislature to sway the minds of the state's lawmakers. As a result, South Carolina's governor held a weak hand in the state's political poker game over the Confederate flag.

The governor cannot depend on party discipline to help him coordinate political affairs, either, since there is little of that to be had. The South Carolina legislature has (traditionally, at least) been divided less by party affiliation than by other internal divisions and diverging interests: by the competition between Upstate and Lowcountry, for example, or, more importantly, between the metropolitan and rural areas of the state. There are Democratic and Republican caucuses, of course, and a black caucus, too. And the rise of a fully functioning two-party system in the state has meant that partisanship has come to play an ever-increasing role in state affairs. But the division of state interests still break along multiple fault lines, prompting the formation of various caucuses in the state legislature: the textile caucus, the tourism caucus, and the tobacco caucus, for example—along with a rural caucus, which grew out of the state's agricultural past. These multiple divisions have made it easier to block than to initiate or pass legislation, giving the status quo a distinct advantage over change. Moreover, until the advent of single-member districts in 1974, the dominance of the rural areas in state affairs went largely unchecked. In fact, the conflict between urban and rural interests played itself out in the battle over the Confederate flag as well, with rural areas in the state being generally more pro-flag than the cities.

These sentiments were represented accordingly in the General Assembly. Single-member districts came about as the result of a U.S. Supreme Court civil-rights decision, handed down in 1964, that declared South Carolina's at-large election districts a violation of the principle of "one man, one vote." The old at-large districts had been drawn without proper regard for population, in effect giving the rural areas a disproportionate share of seats in the state legislature. The South Carolina senate did not come into complete compliance with this court ruling, through the creation of its own set of single-member districts, until 1984, a full twenty years after the original ruling.

Businesses in the state—dominated for a long time by the textile manufacturers and agricultural producers, and, later, by the burgeoning tourist industry, state utilities, and the nuclear-waste industry—also have exercised great influence in state politics, forming an informal fourth branch of government (which at times further undercuts the already limited powers and independence of the governor's office). In more recent times, the growing influence of the State Chamber of Commerce has given business groups added clout—power amplified through the support given to such interests by conservative, business-friendly Republican politicians in the legislature.[11] The chamber's influence would show itself quite prominently during the flag fight. In fact, the growing discomfort state business leaders felt over the unflattering (and unprofitable) publicity flowing out of the flag impasse was one of the deciding factors in bringing about the compromise that eventually moved the flag off the State House dome. Although they were not among the very first to join the chorus calling for an end to the flag display (that honor goes to churches and church-related organizations within the state), the state's businesses would eventually join in the campaign as it became apparent that the flag controversy was becoming an embarrassing drag on the state's image.

The governor's powers were further undercut by the creation of the State Budget and Control Board, an institution established in the 1950s and unique to South Carolina. The Control Board was set up as a means of centralizing a broad array of the administrative and regulatory functions of state government (such as procurement, property services, personnel affairs, information services, and financial and budgetary planning). The maintenance and operation of the Confederate Relic Room and Museum are also part of its responsibilities. Although the governor himself sits on this five-member board, he shares responsibility (and power) with two legislative members as well as the heads of two state agencies (the state treasurer and comptroller general)—whose budgets, it should be noted, are controlled by the state legislature. Back in 1961, a simple request from Representative John "Mr. Confederate" May to Walter Brown (the head of the Budget and Control Board's General Services Division) was all it took to have the

Confederate flag hoisted above the State House. The governor was not a party to the decision. More than twenty-five years later, the governor would still not be the deciding actor in the drama played out over the Confederate flag. The state legislature made sure that only it would have the final say on what happened to the flag. Cotton may have been king in the South for a time—but in South Carolina, the state legislature remains the only abiding sovereign.

Control over state affairs was not only focused in the state legislature, it was for many years concentrated in the hands of a comparative few within that body. House Speaker Solomon Blatt and Senate President Edgar Brown formed what became known as the "Barnwell Ring" (named after the county that Brown represented, which borders May's Aiken County to the north and is bounded by the Savannah River border with Georgia to the South). These two (along with their senate colleague Marion Gressette) kept an iron grip on legislative business across a broad swath of the twentieth century. Like Senators Smith and Thurmond, they also set records for political longevity. Blatt's thirty-three years as Speaker of the House of Representatives is believed to be unsurpassed anywhere in the United States. Altogether, these three men—Blatt, Brown, and Gressette—sat in the State House for total of 155 years. "These men and their allies," wrote South Carolina historian Walter Edgar, "mostly from rural lowcountry counties, controlled state government until the 1960s and, without much difficulty, were able to preserve the status quo."[12]

The old guard's power had begun to wane by the early 1970s, but the seniority system that had underpinned their power lived on. The persistence of old-order, business-as-usual attitudes led Harriet Keyserling (then a Democratic state representative from the Carolina coast) to conclude, that, even in the late 1970s and early 1980s, "we [still] had a good-ol'-boy system which protected the status quo and vested interests at the expense of the public interest and open government."[13] The system is something of a holdover from an older era: it reflects the hierarchical character of the state's political culture and the cultural preference that control over state affairs remain in the hands of an established elite. As long as the state legislature's senior leadership opposed an issue, it had no chance of passage (perhaps even of consideration). Once that leadership comes together behind something, however, then the matter is as good as settled—as the compromise over the Confederate flag would demonstrate.

For a long time, South Carolina was the kind of place that "holds the world in such high regard that it objects to any change unless the change goes unrecognized until after it has occurred and taken its place in the pattern," wrote Carolina native James McBride Dabbs in his book *The Southern Heritage* (1958). South Carolina liked the kind of change that didn't disturb the peace, that didn't ruffle feathers, and that promised nothing but advantages. It wanted the kind of change that made itself useful around the house and didn't make many demands. "The South changes, like any society, in recent years even rapidly," Dabbs went on— "but . . . it doesn't like to admit it's changing, and it objects hotly to being told it must change."[14]

South Carolina has gradually ceased to be the wholly traditionalist culture it once was. Economic development has spurred change, helping break down entrenched elite structures and the established social order. Outsiders began settling in the state, long an insular society, in ever-larger numbers during the 1970s, further upsetting existing mentalities and patterns of behavior. Television performed its own special brand of magic, too, absorbing provincial South Carolina into a national pop-media culture while simultaneously transforming elements of southern culture into products for the national and international market. Gradually, it seemed, the South was merging into the larger world.

The fossilized internal order of the South Carolina legislature began to be reshaped and reshuffled during the last quarter of the twentieth century. South Carolina politics started to appear almost multifaceted as blacks, women, progressive Democrats, and the newly invigorated GOP slowly gained influence in state affairs. Reapportionment bought new blood (and new perspectives) into a governing apparatus long controlled by the status quo predilections of one-party politics. Still, the new did not entirely replace the old. New and old coexisted side by side. It was only when they got in each other's way that one (or both) suffered.

The opening shot in the ambitious campaign aimed at the South's premier symbol—which would eventually decide the fate not only of South Carolina's Confederate flag display, but also reshape the Georgia state flag and lead to a rethinking of numerous other Confederate memorials all across the South—was contained in a March 1987 resolution passed by the Southeast Region of the National Association for the Advancement of Colored People (NAACP). It said, in part, that

> the delegates . . . consider the Confederate battle flag to be a symbol of divisiveness, racial animosity, and an insult to black people through the region; and . . . requests the states of South Carolina and Alabama to take necessary action to remove the Confederate battle flag from the domes of their capitol buildings; and . . . requests the state of Georgia to return to its standard state flag of pre-1956; and . . . the state of Mississippi to return to its standard state flag of pre-1894.[15]

It was an across-the-board effort, directed not only at South Carolina, but at all states that employed the Confederate battle flag as part of an official state symbol or display. It is worth noting, however, that the resolution was not aimed broadly at all Confederate symbols or at every display of the Confederate flag. It was directed solely against ostentatious and laudatory exhibitions of the battle flag in official settings.

It promised to be a hard-fought campaign. And at first, at least, few relished the prospect of more conflict over the Confederate flag. Even an old warhorse like Patterson seemed reluctant to reenter the fray. Saying that he had matured while in office, he indicated that he was not inclined to go after the flag during the 1988 legislative session. "I've come to believe in the smoke-filled room," he said half jokingly. But if quiet negotiations failed to bring about movement on the flag, he added, "then as a last resort [I] might fight the battle flag again."[16]

Patterson's moderate tone was not simply the result of age. It was also a consequence of his entry into the state senate, a body that generally disdains the kind of hot rhetoric and boisterous free-for-all common to the House of Representatives, preferring instead sedate (and sequestered) consensus building. Then again, it might have been the prosaic power of cold numbers that helped cool the senator's ardor about the flag. Polls in early 1988 indicated that 58 percent of South Carolinians wanted to leave the Confederate flag where it was—and only about a third, 34 percent, preferred that it be "relegated to museum status."[17] Senator Patterson would continue to be a part of the campaign to remove the flag—but he would no longer play the leading role he once had. The baton had been passed to a new generation.

Pastors, church organizations, and other religious leaders began to speak out on the issue and would become increasingly active in the flag debate as time went on. One of the first to take a stand after the 1987 NAACP resolution was Reverend Bill Bouknight, a Columbia-area Methodist minister. Building on a proposal offered several years earlier in *The State* newspaper, Reverend Bouknight suggested moving the flag to a prominent place in front of the newly constructed state history museum—including it in a semicircle with other flags that had flown in South Carolina at various times during the state's history.[18] Bouknight's suggestion would be just one of many proposals that would follow during the course of the decade of debate that followed.

Taken together, the multiple variations on this idea might be lumped together under the term "dilution solution." The goal of all these plans was not merely the removal of the flag from its prominent place on top of the State House dome, but to diminish its presence—and dilute its effect—by surrounding it with numerous other flags. It would become just one of several flags that had flown over the state, placing it in a "historical context" that lent proportionality to its place in the state's history, a sense of its relative weight in the continuum of the Carolina saga.

Bouknight's proposal, like all the others to come, quickly passed into the archives of noble intentions. Neither side of the General Assembly was prepared to do anything about the flag—neither Republican nor Democrat. Then Democratic House Speaker Robert Sheheen (who would later join those calling for the flag to come down) said that "misuse of the flag by the Ku Klux Klan is not a reason for removing it," adding: "It would be just as much an insult to some people to remove the flag as it is an insult to people letting it fly over the State House"—a statement which revealed whose insult counted for more and whose for less. For Sheheen it was an either-or dilemma: "If I had a choice," he said, "between implementing programs to help black people and not removing the flag or removing the flag and not implementing programs, I would leave the flag and enact the programs." Removing the flag *and* enacting programs was apparently not yet a viable option. Political expediency was already working to prevent a quick and early resolution to the flag controversy.[19]

———————◆◈◆———————

While the legislature stood pat, other rumblings around the state served to keep folk entertained and focused on the "Confederate" issue. In the fall of 1989, prior to the football face-off between the two schools, students at the predominantly black South Carolina State College called on South Carolina's premier military academy, The Citadel, to put an end to its tradition of waving the Confederate flag and playing the song "Dixie" during football games. The protest did not go unnoticed. It set in motion an internal review of race relations at the Citadel. In early 1992, the commission established to conduct that review concluded that "Dixie" should no longer be used as the school fight song and that uniformed cadets should not be allowed to wave the Confederate flag at football games. The panel not only found the Confederate flag to be "one of the most sensitive and divisive issues related to race relations at the college," it also determined that there was "no legitimate tie" between the school and the Confederate battle flag, noting that "the flag never was flown during any engagements cadets fought during the Civil War."[20] After considering the recommendations for half a year, however, the school's president came down in favor of tradition and decided not to end either practice, saying that the school needed to "strike a balance," based on "common decency," between heritage and current needs. The president said he was certain that "Dixie" could be played "in a proper manner that will not be taunting."

"Dixie" became an issue in the state capital as well. Back in 1987, protests by black legislators (including Senator Patterson) had prompted Republican Governor-elect Carroll Campbell to remove the song from his inaugural program. During the run-up to Campbell's second inaugural, held in 1991, "Dixie" fans swamped the governor's office with calls demanding that the tune be reinserted into the ceremony. Patterson and others once again demanded that the song be kept out of the event. Citing the song's offensive character, Patterson said, "Who do you think picked all that cotton?"[21]

Meanwhile, at the other end of the state, a firefight had broken out over an Upstate high school's decision to ban clothing that bore the Confederate flag. The conflict, which erupted during the spring of 1991 (again, on the heels of Black History Month), came about after a number of students were suspended for refusing to adhere to the ban. Outraged parents, coming together to form a "Rebel support group," filed a lawsuit against the school district, claiming that the ban constituted a violation of their children's First Amendment rights. The state NAACP, meanwhile, wanted the district to force the school to drop its rebel mascot as well. The suit was eventually settled out of court when the school district agreed that the ban on Confederate paraphernalia would only continue through the end of the school year (which was, by then, nearly over anyway).[22]

In 1993, the pace of events swirling around the Confederate flag started to pick up. In neighboring Georgia, Democratic Governor Zell Miller, concerned that his state project a purely positive image during the approaching Olympic Games, proposed replacing the Georgia state flag with the pre-1956 pattern it had replaced—a pattern that itself contained elements of another Confederate flag: the First National, or Stars and Bars, flag. Meanwhile, up in Washington, D.C., the U.S. Senate, at the urging of Illinois's Senator Carol Moseley-Braun, voted not to extend the patent on the insignia used by the United Daughters of the Confederacy (UDC), which also incorporated the Confederate First National banner into its design.* And down in Alabama, the newly installed Democratic Governor Jim Folsom Jr. (son of "Big Jim") ordered the Confederate flag removed from the top of the state legislature (though he would later agree to return it, together with three other Confederate flags, to a site on the capitol grounds). That left South Carolina the only state still displaying the flag over its seat of government.

Back in South Carolina, meanwhile, the mayors of two of the state's largest cities, Joe Riley of Charleston and Bob Coble of Columbia, made public appeals

---

*It was following this vote that Senator Strom Thurmond, uttered the words that so flabbergasted Tom Turnipseed: "From all I have heard from my ancestors," South Carolina's senior senator said, "they treated their slaves well. When they had food, the slaves shared it. When they needed medicine, the slaves shared in it. When they needed a doctor, they got one." (See: "Thurmond Says Flag Was Symbol of Pride," *The State* (24 July 1993), p. 2B. For more of the U.S. Senate's thoughtful discussion of the UDC insignia and the history that surrounds it, see also: *The Congressional Record—Senate* (22 July 1993), pp. S9251–9270.

for a compromise they had crafted, aimed at bringing the flag down from the State House. And over in the state senate, two lawmakers—who hailed from the same part of the state (Charleston), but who sat on opposite sides of the political tracks—were working to come up with just such a compromise. Black Democrat Robert Ford and white Republican Glenn McConnell proposed replacing the current Southern Cross with the Confederate First National flag. "I don't think any black person in the country would oppose the Stars and Bars," Senator Ford said—a rather ironic claim given Moseley-Braun's opposition to this same flag within the UDC insignia.

With debate over the Georgia state flag heating up in the Peach State next door, Senator Kay Patterson again appealed to the state legislature to find some way of dealing with South Carolina's own Confederate flag problem. Patterson said that he would be looking for his colleagues to act in 1993. But he did not introduce any flag-related legislation himself, and had no plans to do so during the next legislative session. He made it clear that although he still considered the flag an important issue, he did not want to focus all his time and attention on it. "It is divisive, it is controversial," he said of the flag debate, "and it stirs up ill will. It sucks all of your energy from you. I don't want to spend all my energy fighting a flag. If I take a flag down today, what impact will that have on school systems that don't have any money to buy paper or supplies?" Perhaps Patterson was worried about political isolation. His campaign against the flag had clearly not made him any friends. On the contrary, he reaped bushels of hate mail for his effort. Some, Patterson remembers, "would start off, 'Dear N——.' Now that was a good letter when it started like that," he recalled jokingly. "That was a nice letter, clean. That was a liberal letter when it started like that." He'd gotten used to the attacks, he claimed. After a while they just rolled off, "like water on a duck's back." But one wonders.[23]

In the end, it did not matter all that much what Patterson chose to do himself. There were others ready and willing to take up the task of removing the flag. Senator Maggie Glover was one of several next-generation lawmakers who made the challenge part of her own legislative agenda. Even as a state representative, before entering the senate, Glover had introduced legislation calling for the flag to be taken down. The bill that she introduced in mid-1991 adopted an argument against the flag that gained currency for a time during the first few years of the new decade. Calling the display "compelled speech," the bill declared that "freedom of expression is not a collective right of states or public institutions, but rather an individual right of each citizen, protected by the First and Fourteenth Amendments to the Constitution of the United States." The resolution went on to say that "there are citizens of South Carolina who do not choose to participate in such expression and who find it contrary to their sincerely held religious and philosophical convictions and violative of their moral consciences to do so, but who are compelled to do so . . . through compulsory taxation."[24]

Although the bill was immediately buried in committee (a favorite means for disposing of unwelcome legislation), it nevertheless implicitly pointed to another argument advanced by some flag opponents: the so-called sovereignty argument. Glover's bill had said, in part, that the Confederate flag over the State House "is flown, not as an official representation of either [the United States or of South Carolina], but rather as a form of symbolic speech or expression" inappropriate to the site where the flag is displayed. Similarly, the sovereignty argument said that the pole atop the dome of the State House was reserved for "sovereign" flags that symbolized functioning national and state power. The Confederate flag, by contrast, symbolized a political regime that no longer existed; its display atop the State House was improper and illegitimate. This argument would gain momentum, peaking around mid-decade—though it, too, would not succeed in bringing down the banner.

It wasn't the only solution floating around, in any event. Another proposal suggested flying the Confederate flag only on certain predetermined days of the year. Interestingly, of the twenty-three dates proposed, five celebrated the birthdays of Confederate notables, but only two commemorated what might be termed "happy" events in the short life of the Confederacy (i.e., the signing of the South Carolina Ordinance of Secession on 20 November and the firing on Fort Sumter on 12 April). By contrast, a whopping ten of the total would have commemorated the darker turns of fate for the ill-starred Confederate States of America (e.g., Lee's surrender at Appomattox; the end of the battle at Gettysburg; the fall of Vicksburg; the surrender of the CSS *Alabama;* the burning of Columbia; and the surrender of the last of the Confederate forces on 26 May).[25] By celebrating defeat more often than victory, the measure reinforced the image of a South still very much enamored of the *loss* in the Lost Cause.

But it was the Democratic state attorney general, Travis Medlock, who stirred the waters most when he issued a legal opinion stating that the Confederate flag display atop the State House was not supported by law. "It is our opinion," Medlock wrote, "that the [concurrent] resolution [which had installed the flag on the dome in 1962] did not intend to permanently place the flag on the State House and did not originally intend to do anything other than pay tribute to the 100th anniversary of the Confederacy."[26] Medlock concluded that the flag could be ordered down by a simple majority vote of the State House Committee, a ten-member body within the General Assembly charged with overseeing the maintenance of the State House and determining which decorative items should be displayed there. The members of the committee in question, however, had no desire whatsoever to get out in front on the issue. Not only was their committee chairman a steadfast flag supporter, but several of its members openly expressed their reluctance to take any action without first getting the approval of the whole General Assembly (or the voters). The Republican candidate for state attorney general, Charlie Condon (who would replace Medlock after the 1994 elections), also came out against the Medlock opinion. Declaring that only the entire state legislature had authority to decide the issue, Condon said that he would take measures to see the flag re-raised should it be removed by a committee vote.

South Carolina's Confederate flag had become the proverbial political "hot potato," and no one wanted to be left holding it. The state's Republican governor seemed especially eager to avoid having the matter tossed into his hands. In spite of prompting and prodding from various factions, Campbell remained resolutely uninterested: "I will continue to focus my attentions on matters of substance, not symbolism," he said curtly.[27] The governor, who was rumored to be considering a run for the White House in 1996, had established his position in favor of the flag back in 1986, during his first campaign for the governor's office. Although his steadfast reluctance to get involved in the increasingly disruptive flag fracas may have served him well personally, his indifference allowed the issue to fester, further cementing the status quo. Instead of fostering compromise, Campbell sought to avoid being bloodied by the battles that raged over the issue during the remainder of his term.

Not that others were any more eager to step into the fray. The lowly state bureaucrats at the General Services Division of the Budget & Control Board— the state agency that had raised the flag in the first place and that replaced each worn banner with a fresh copy whenever needed—had no desire to be left holding the bag (or, in this case, the flag), either. Attorney General Medlock suggested they might conveniently choose not to replace one of the worn-out rebel banners —thereby solving the problem through inaction. But even some anti-flag folks thought the issue far too hot for a faceless administrator to decide. "He or she would lose their job yesterday," if they acted alone, Senator Patterson observed succinctly.[28]

At the state legislature, too, action on the flag seemed to be the thing to avoid. Though there was no lack of the means to reach a solution (in the form of the various compromise proposals already offered), there was little will to see any of them through. The Ford/McConnell idea—which had never even garnered endorsements from all the pro-flag senators, much less anyone else—folded when the Legislative Black Caucus refused to back it. Caucus members felt that some in the state, most importantly the state's business community, were starting to turn their way. This was no time, they believed, to settle for nothing more than a different Confederate flag over the dome, when chances were increasing that they might be able to rid the legislature of *all* its Confederate banners. "We don't want to be the only state left hanging out there like a sore thumb," one caucus member said.[29]

Along the widening battlefront over Confederate symbols, however, there was a noticeable stiffening of resistance and a general turning away from compromise. Down in Georgia, Governor Miller had backed away from his call for changing the state flag—out of a concern, he said, that debate over the issue might spark extremist reactions (though fear that his exposed position on the flag might prematurely end his political career surely must have played a role as well). In South Carolina, the opposing sides retreated into their respective corners and began rallying their troops. Anticipating a strong anti-flag push during the upcoming 1994 session, several pro-flag legislators worked to create a "save the flag" coalition between state lawmakers and various heritage groups—and raised money for an advertising campaign in support of keeping the flag flying.[30] Meanwhile, Senator Ford, guided as always by the belief that the state would never bring down its beloved Confederate flag, now floated the idea of adding a *fourth* flag to the other three already attached to the State House flagpole. Late in the year, Ford proposed adding either the red, black, and green Black Liberation flag to the display, or some newly designed flag that would combine elements of the Confederate flag with those of Black Liberation (something along the lines of NuSouth perhaps).[31]

In the fall of 1993, *The State* newspaper ran an editorial titled, "Most South Carolinians Weary of the Flag Issue."[32] Little did they know how much wearier the state would have to become before the matter would finally be resolved.

———•◦•••◦•———

South Carolina did not go mad in the 1990s, the way it had in the 1860s. But the 1860s, like the 1960s, and the decade-long debate over the flag, revealed the difficulty the state sometimes had in bringing its past into alignment with the present. And to that extent, Clyde Wilson may be correct: South Carolina does appear to possess a somewhat greater concern for continuity than do other parts of the country, a general feeling of obligation to see that the past is carried over in some form into the future.

Previous generations of South Carolinians had also struggled to find a way to join past with present. James McBride Dabbs attested to the difficulty of balancing present needs with a proper respect for tradition. Writing during the Civil Rights Era, Dabbs spoke of the "sacred patterns" of southern life and sought to explain why he thought the South's resistance to integration was a misguided effort:

> The fact that we are mistaken in defending, at this late date, status based upon race should not blind us to the fact that we are defending, however mistakenly,

a human value, the sense of place itself. All of us in the South, white and colored, have some place distinct from the racial, and are, however faintly, aware
of it: we are all Southerners, we live in communities, have kin-people, a past,
and, if we insist upon it, personalities. This sense of place, the product of our
past, is being rubbed out by our growing industrialism. Here is where the
danger lies. Here is where we should build our defenses.[33]

The defenses Dabbs wanted to see erected may have been as useless as the ones
he thought were misplaced. But at least the sentiments were more humane.

South Carolina in the late twentieth century was not a place seething with
nullification or burgeoning secessionism. It was not held captive by mobs of fire-
eating, wanna-be southern nationalists. It was not even nursing century-old
wounds. The state had long since hitched itself to the national gravy train. It was
far too concerned with the pursuit of its own sweet prosperity to indulge in
rebellion. On the contrary, the state was, generally speaking, quite levelheaded.

Those who bore the torches in 1860 and 1960 had aimed to set fires of a different kind. They were driven by their anxieties over the continued viability of
established racial hierarchies and their concerns about basic economic interests
—and also by a feverish attachment to a somewhat bloated sense of personal
honor. The torch-bearers (or flag-bearers, in this case) of the 1990s were motivated by an emotional concern with honor, too. But theirs was a reflected kind
of concern, not directly linked to immediate or concrete interests. It was a concern about upholding the honor and respecting the memory of their ancestors,
a concern about the judgments of history. It was driven by the passions of sentiment and not by any desire to maintain material advantage or a system of racial
oppression.

Except for those darker corners inhabited by the likes of the Council of Conservative Citizens and their Ku-Kluxing fellow travelers in the southern heritage
movement, most of South Carolina's flag defenders were not concerned with
broader pictures or grander schemes. They just wanted to keep their past intact
and the flag flying. And even if they were at times overzealous in their defense of
the flag and arrogantly insensitive to those who saw the flag differently, they were
nevertheless, on the whole, an upright lot. Most of them were quietly embarrassed
by the antics of their hotspur cohorts. The State House was not a seedbed for
hotheads—even though some of the rhetoric employed there came out rather
overbaked at times. There was no Robert Barnwell Rhett among the core of pro-
flag lawmakers—men like John Courson of Columbia, Verne Smith of Greenville, or Arthur Ravenel Jr. of Charleston, who did their best to see that the flag
stayed put. But they did consider themselves duty-bound as heirs of Confederate
heritage.

Although he demurs from the comparison, preferring to call himself "just one of a group," State Senator Glenn McConnell comes as close as anyone can to being the spiritual heir to John "Mr. Confederate" May. He may not strut around the senate chamber in Confederate garb, but his enthusiasm for Confederate heritage is at least as strong as May's was—and may be even more deeply rooted. A native Charlestonian attorney and businessman, McConnell became the preeminent spokesman for the pro-flag faction in the State House and a leading strategist in the legislative battle over the Confederate flag's fate. Fellow Republican and old legislative hand Ravenel has high praise for his senate colleague, calling him "brilliant and articulate, yet guileless and unbigoted." McConnell "pretty well runs the senate," Ravenel says.

Even though he may downplay his own part in the drama, McConnell clearly enjoyed the spotlight the flag fight cast on him. It is equally clear that both McConnell's dedication to the cause and his legislative ability—his handy use of sometimes arcane senate rules and his skill at legislative maneuver—were instrumental in keeping the flag's opponents at bay, preserving the flag's place atop the dome longer than otherwise might have been the case, and, later, ensuring that it did not disappear from the State House entirely.

McConnell's interest in the Civil War and the Confederacy runs deep and wide. It is both his vocation and his avocation. He is a member of the South Carolina Sons of Confederate Veterans (Secession Camp No. 4) and an avid Civil War reenactor—though he often ends up playing a federal soldier more often than a Confederate, because, as he explains, "they're always short on bluecoats down in this section of the country." His love of all things Confederate also placed him in charge of the effort to recover the sunken Confederate submarine, the *Hunley,* a holy relic of the South's late struggle.

In addition to his hobbies, his law practice, and his position in the state senate, McConnell is also part owner of CSA Galleries in North Charleston. The name of the store, which began life as a commercial art and framing company, stands for "Collectors' Selected Art" Gallery and not "Confederate States of America," as one might suspect. But "it's a good acronym," McConnell admits. "We picked it because it could play off the Civil War." McConnell invested in the venture on the condition that the store carry Civil War art—the kind of original paintings (of battle scenes, camp life, military leaders, etc.) that often adorn the covers of special interest magazines such as the *Civil War Times Illustrated* or *America's Civil War.* About half of the store is taken up with artwork—along with Civil War–era uniforms, books, pewter figures, statuettes, and other handicrafts.

The other half is a kind of upscale trinket shop dedicated to the Civil War theme. It offers for sale nearly everything and anything a Confederate heart might desire. Next to the rebel-flag t-shirts, the fake Confederate currency, and the CSA passports, you also can find a South Carolina–shaped door chime decorated in a battle-flag motif. Nearby is a wide assortment of collectors' plates and cups, most sporting either a Confederate flag or a portrait of one or another Confederate "immortal"—along with Confederate coffee mugs and bags of "Confederate coffee" (in various blends, including "Rebellion" and "Columbian Supremo"). For the famished, the shop offers Southern Comfort pancake syrup and a Mississippi Delta Fudge mix—as well as Maurice Bessinger's now-infamous brand of barbecue sauce. There are real Confederate flags, of course, in numerous patterns and sizes (most from the main source of Confederate flags, the Ruffin Flag Company of Crawfordville, Georgia). The shop also carries a veritable battery of flag-emblazoned bumper stickers, bearing such slogans as "It's a Southern Thing —You Wouldn't Understand" or "The most endangered Species" (meaning Southerners, of course), and "Lest We Forget: The Civil War, America's Holocaust." And then there are the novelty items, like the music box in miniature cotton-bale form, or a toilet-paper dispenser and bathroom melody-maker called "Dixie Toity Tunes" ("makes your toilet paper sing"). The store even sells an appropriate toilet paper, with images of General W. T. Sherman on each sheet, along with the words "Still wipin' up the South." For the higher-toned set, there are decorative pewter items, fine jewelry, and porcelain figurines (including one of a black ballerina and another of a small black boy playing marbles). Back in the rear of the store one can find photographs of Vivien Leigh as Scarlett O'Hara and other moonlight-and-magnolia motifs.

McConnell may be something of a southern romantic, but it is not the dreamy-eyed romanticism born of mushy nostalgia or vague sentimentality. His passion for the Confederacy is driven by his reading of history, which in turn helped shape his political philosophy (or vice versa, as the case may be). "I take the position, to the day I die," the state senator says, "that southerners were correct about their right to leave the Union. They had that right—and I've read enough to know. Their view of constitutional government was that a state was equivalent to a nation. That was their concept of our system of government—it was the original constitutional concept: that this country was not a unitary republic but rather a confederation of sovereign states. This was the question that was settled on the battlefields of America. And this country never operated again the way it had operated up through 1860."

McConnell may be a southern (even Confederate) apologist of sorts—and in that he differs not a whit from the neo-Confederates and heritage defenders in the southern solidarity movement. His take on the past and his positions on contemporary political affairs are both subsumed in a deep-going states' rights philosophy right out of southern tradition. But unlike neo-Confederates, he is a political practitioner who harbors no illusions about the nature of American politics and the need for political compromise. He has no interest in constructing the kind of southern castles in the air that so fascinate the neo-Cons, but he is consistent in his political views and forthright in his defense of the South's past.

"In 1861," he says, "if you had called up troops to fight over whether or not to free black slaves, you probably wouldn't have got a regiment. But Lincoln very craftily sold the war as a war to preserve the so-called Union. And so the great transformation of this country occurred, from a confederation of sovereign states to a unitary constitutional state, with the states becoming mere administrative units rather than sovereign entities. The South, though constitutionally right, held positions which were incompatible with the growth of a unitary republic. They lost on the battlefield what they could have won in the courts."

"Sure," McConnell continues, "I know that slavery was the catalyst for the war. But it was George Alfred Trenholm who put it best, I think. He was a shipping magnate, right here in Charleston, perhaps the richest man in the country at that time, the Onassis of his day. He was not a slaveholder, however—he didn't believe in slavery. But he put all his wealth and abilities at the disposal of the state in trying to free South Carolina from the Union—because he felt that, from an *economic* point of view, the two sections of the country were incompatible. It was Trenholm who summed it up best in 1860 when he said that John C. Calhoun warned us in 1850 that if we did not make the stand for states' rights on the question of tariffs, when the world's opinion was with us, we would be forced at a later time to make that stand for states' rights on the question of slavery, where the world's opinion will be against us."

McConnell's leap from past to present is direct and instantaneous: For him, the nature of the conflict is unchanged, though the character of the struggle may be different. "There are a lot of people who say, those people [the secessionists] were right," McConnell goes on. "Left unchallenged, the federal government would eventually get into every bit of your business. The main political thinking in this state is based on suspicion of government, that unbridled government wants to micromanage everything."

In terms of political philosophy, McConnell represents a direct link between the concept of government nurtured in the Confederacy (and in some parts of the early American Republic) and by a faction within contemporary mainline Republicanism. He sees himself as a keeper of the flame of the traditional constitutional order. "I'm a Goldwater-type Republican," he explains. "I believe in restraining the growth of government and keeping the government out of your private life. And sometimes I find myself not exactly in tune with all of my Republican colleagues on all issues. You've got Republicans who talk about being against big government, but then they turn around and try to give the governor as much power as they can—just because he's a Republican! They wanted to create a *strong* governor [under Campbell], and an all-powerful cabinet system.

I've gotten myself into quite a few squabbles with them over it. Or they're session-shorteners. They're all for weakening the powers of the legislature. It's just like on the federal level, where all these Republicans *flock* to the concept of term limits. I've never understood that. The federal courts are appointments for life, they're accountable to nobody. And yet, the one branch of government that we have that can stand up to unbridled federal court power is the legislative branch—and they wanna weaken that! Well, that is Lincoln Republicanism. That's what Republicanism used to be about in South Carolina—decreasing the impact of he legislative branch. But I'm not that kind of Republican—and I make no bones about it."

With McConnell it's all a seamless whole. Even the impetus that brought him into the conflict over Confederate heritage grew, in large part, from his understanding of the structure of American federalism, and in particular from the special bond between a state and its citizens.

"About 1984 or so," McConnell recalls, "the last remains of South Carolina's Confederate soldiers unearthed outside the state were found in a parking lot in a condominium complex in Virginia. The remains were returned to the state and the South Carolina Sons of Confederate Veterans, the UDC, and Civil War reenactors were going to re-inter them in the Confederate plots at Elmwood Cemetery in Columbia. They also asked permission for the remains to lie in state in the State House rotunda—the remains of the last unknown soldier comin' home from the war. Well, there was a lot of hand-wringing and tiptoeing around in Columbia, claiming they didn't know whether they could permit it or not. They tried to get around it by saying that the rotunda was under renovation and that it would not be safe. So the SCV folks called me up and told me how they were getting this put-off."

"So I went up to Columbia and took a look. Turns out they were doing some painting over in one corner of the rotunda. But more than 237 schoolchildren had been allowed to go through the rotunda that week. It was just incomprehensible to me that it was safe for schoolchildren, but unsafe for the remains of a soldier."

"This is what brought it all into focus for me: the concern about political correctness, about being criticized by the NAACP. That this state would turn its back on a person [who] had answered the call of the elected government, who had gone off to battle and made the supreme sacrifice; that we didn't have the guts to accept his remains and give him the respect he was due, because we were scared that we would be criticized by the NAACP or some other group. It was on this basis that I got into the issue. And the more reading I did, the more convinced I became that the right thing for us to do was to perpetuate the memory of those who had answered the call of their government. They were the soldiers of the state. The federal government does not preserve their memory. So it is to the state that this responsibility falls." And for McConnell, the Confederate flag was part of that commemoration. It was South Carolina's foremost war memorial to the soldiers and civilians who suffered and sacrificed for the Confederacy.

"My concern has been to protect the honor and the memory of those soldiers," he says. "You read history. I just don't know of a group that did more with less than those people did. I mean, when you consider: without a navy, without an army, [they] put a country together, put a currency together, put a court system together, put an economy together without an industrial base, carried on a war effort against a government that had all those things, and held it at bay for three good, solid years. And had it not been for those ridiculous blunders at Gettysburg, they could've, against incredible odds, beaten a vastly superior force in men and matériel."

And then there are the sufferings inflicted upon the women and children of the South. "The federal government did to this state what it's never done to a foreign power," McConnell continues. "It made war on an innocent civilian population—through naval bombardments of the city of Charleston. And, of course, when Sherman's men came through South Carolina, they did so with a vengeance. Killed people's pets! I mean, the stories are just awful. And yet, despite all that, when the war ended, South Carolinians put their animosity aside and went on to raise their children as loyal Americans, who have fought for this country and moved on. People don't want to go back and reestablish a Confederate States of America. But they do believe that a just and true history should be written of the cause for which these people stood—and that political correctness should not get in the way of that."

Southern heritage, McConnell believes, has to be defended against what he calls "cultural bullies"—folks "who throw their weight around and intimidate people. They toss the word 'racism' around like candy at a Christmas parade," he says. "That's what I find incomprehensible and regrettable about the NAACP. All the other groups in American history that have had wrongs done to them—women, Indians—have been able to move on. But [blacks] don't seem to be able to accomplish that. Instead, they pick out one emblem and ask people to sentence their ancestors to a reputation of shame. Their goal is to have southern Americans accept our heritage as a heritage of shame. And that," he defiantly declares, "we are not gonna do. We are not gonna turn our backs on our ancestors."

McConnell likes to refer to what he calls "the three hinges of South Carolina history: the struggle for liberty against the British; the struggle for states' rights; and the struggle for civil rights." All three lie along a historical continuum that grants to each equal value with the other two. And they are not only historically and politically coequals, deserving of equal attention and commemoration, they are also, McConnell believes, equals in terms of moral weight, so that each is equally deserving of its own kind of reverence—making them a kind of holy trinity of state history.

Blacks and other flag opponents practice what McConnell calls "selectavision" —picking and choosing the parts of history that support their arguments and point of view; engaging in a selective reading of the past that fuels their resentments and bolsters the righteousness of their grievance. (This of course obscures the fact that southern heritage defenders are at least equally guilty of the same offenses.) "They ignore historical facts," he says. "They forget that the U.S. Constitution protected slavery, even on the day the war began. The racism that existed in America wasn't confined to the South—it was in every state. Lincoln himself believed that blacks were inferior. It was not southerners who passed the 'Black Codes' in Illinois. It was not southerners who rioted in New York in 1863 and who lynched and beat up blacks."

For McConnell, and others like him, the pattern is clear. The list of anti-Confederate grievances is long—and growing longer. "I remind you of what Senator Moseley-Braun did [in opposing the copyright renewal for the Daughters of the Confederacy]," McConnell says. "Over in Tennessee they want General Nathan Bedford Forrest and his wife dug up, their remains exhumed and taken out of a state park and put somewhere else. They want the park renamed. There was a display of state flags someplace up in New York—and because the Georgia state flag had the Confederate flag in it, they had it removed from the display. And then there was all that hand-wringing over whether or not the Georgia state flag could be flown at the Olympics. They object to the playing of "Dixie" in parades. They objected when some lady wanted to do an ice-skating routine to the song. They object to anything related to it. So you see, if you take off the wrapper you'll see that the true goal is to wipe out southern heritage, to exterminate it. That's why I've used the term 'cultural genocide,' because their goal is a kind of genocide. The one thing that we've learned out of the struggle over the years is that no matter how far we've backed up on the memory of [our ancestors], no matter how much we've backed away from it, it doesn't satisfy the complainers. They want more."

Bitter words—words born during what might be called "The Campaign of '94."

1994 was the year that almost was—the year that brought real, serious negotiation on the flag issue and measurable progress toward a solution. After endless rounds of the dead-end haggling there suddenly seemed to be substantial movement toward settlement and talk of real compromise. But old habits of distrust and political one-upmanship eventually reasserted themselves, and it ended badly, hardening positions on both sides and creating the impasse that locked the state in political combat for anther five long years.

The path toward compromise that emerged during the first half of the year was not an inevitable development. There were still too many competing interests, conflicting plans, and diverging political agendas for anyone to see a clear path through to settlement. There was no obvious consensus about what to do about the flag—though an informal poll of state lawmakers and public opinion on the issue showed that the body of sentiment continued to mass around keeping the flag in place. Of the lawmakers who responded to the poll (147 out of the total 165 state senators and representatives), eighty-six opposed replacing the Southern Cross flag with the Stars and Bars (the main compromise plan at that time). Half were in favor of letting the voters determine the flag's fate in a statewide referendum. But the other half were opposed to any referenda. Among the general population, opponents of the Stars and Bars substitution proposal outnumbered those in favor by two-to-one, while support for a referendum ran three-to-one in favor. Some voters even wanted the state's elected representatives to ensure, by law, that the flag would continue to fly in perpetuity. Others wanted those same officials to summarily get rid of it. "The South lost the war," one flag opponent said, "so get over it."[34]

Governor Campbell, for one, was assiduously doing his part to get over the issue—mainly by trying to get around it. Campbell felt the flag controversy was "too divisive" and seemed to think that the trouble would go away if the state simply ignored it. He preferred to remain above the fray, focusing instead on the "big picture," on "macro-issues," as he called them. He did not want to become entangled in a parochial mud fight that could tarnish his image and ruin his chances for political advancement. There were more important things to worry about—"jobs solve about 95 percent of the problems" we have, he said. Some in the state (especially the governor's political opponents) faulted Campbell for failing to use the power of the bully pulpit to speak out on the flag issue. But in the house of mirrors that is state politics, it was often difficult to tell just how sincere the fault-finding really was, and how much it was merely a game of political hot potato, a way of forcing one side or the other into a situation where their opponents could shout "Gotcha!"

Politicians jockeyed for position in anticipation of the battles to come. Some mounted their favorite hobbyhorses and charged off on idiosyncratic political missions of their own making. Referenda seemed to be the flavor of the moment, but there were other proposals floating around the capitol as well. One called for the installation of a circle of flags on the State House grounds. The proposal, a further variation of the *State*/Bouknight idea, envisioned a display that would include both the Stars and Bars and the Southern Cross flag, along with the Union Jack, a Moultrie flag, the Betsy Ross flag, the Citadel's "Big Red," and two flags flown by units of federal colored troops stationed in South Carolina during the Civil War, as well as state and U.S. flags.[35]

Senator Robert Ford added a new version of his own idea to the rapidly growing pile of possible solutions. He proposed adding a fourth flag to the three already hanging on the dome flagpole, one that would serve as an "official recognition of the struggle for liberation and substantial contributions of [the state's black] citizens."[36] The red, black, and green Black Liberation flag, Ford believed, would afford symbolic recognition to almost all state residents (seeing as how the 1990 census showed that 99 percent of the state's population was either white or black.).[37] The Black Liberation flag, the senator's resolution pointed out, had "originated in the early part of th[e] century with Marcus Garvey and United Negro Improvement Association"; its colors "have been incorporated into the flags of various sovereign African nations," and it has been adopted by African Americans "to represent their struggle and unity."[38]

Unfortunately for Ford, however, the Legislative Black Caucus and other black leaders in the state were somewhat less than enthusiastic about his idea. In fact, the majority opposed it. One of Ford's fellow black senators called the proposal "simplistic," adding that it would "be a grave mistake to say that only two groups in South Carolina matter."[39] He speculated that the Indian tribes living in the state might want a flag of their own atop the State House as well. And then where would it all end?

Senator Maggie Glover was the only other black legislator to come out in favor of the Ford plan—though only for tactical reasons (and not because she shared in the growing comity between Ford and some of the pro-flag legislators, like Senator McConnell). "I said, if you can't beat them, then let's join them," Glover explains with a characteristic chuckle. She believed that the Confederate flag defenders "would take down the Confederate flag rather than give the same kind of respect and honor to the Liberation flag." By pushing for the Black Liberation flag, Glover hoped that the other side would see (or at least be caught in) the hypocrisy that revealed itself in the different attitudes toward the two flags. "If flying the Confederate flag represented heritage, then [the Confederate flag defenders] could not in good conscience say that the Liberation flag could not fly for the exact same reason. If you could not grant that same privilege to me and mine, then something is wrong. Everybody would see how bigoted and racist it was."

"Or," she continues, "let's say that by some great miracle, it passed" and the Black Liberation flag was unfurled over the State House. "Then African Americans would at least be able to say, yes, true, the Confederate flag still flies—*but,* out of respect for our heritage, so does the Liberation flag. We're flying them all! At least then it would create a win-win situation for us."

Reverend Joseph Darby, by contrast, was, like many of his fellow NAACP members, rather more skeptical of the idea. "Let me see how many reasons I could give for saying that the senator's idea could most charitably be called dubious," he said of the plan later. "The Garvey movement could be [thought of] as a separatist movement itself, because it was a movement of African people to scorn that which was America and return to Africa. Because of that, it has to it a separatist tinge, just like the Confederate flag. And I think that's reinforced by the fact that the [Black Liberation] flag did not regain its popularity until after the calls for Black Power, after the calls for black identity, and after the rise of the Black Panther Party. It was very militant, very separatist. I love the [Black Liberation] flag—but it does carry those kinds of connotations. To put that flag up alongside the Confederate flag would emphasize our separation—[it would] say, we have a white folks' flag and we have a black folks' flag, and that we enshrine and endorse separation. I think that's a *horrible* statement to make to the rest of the world."

Darby was also bothered by a nagging impression of second-class status associated with the proposed display of the Black Liberation flag. Speaking about a later variation of the Ford plan, Darby says, "I think his proposal would only put the flag up at certain times of the year [e.g., during Black History Month in February]. That would carry the implication that African American history is somehow less worthy than southern history. And if it does fly all the time, then the question becomes: which flag goes on top?!"

He was equally dubious about the support Ford's proposal enjoyed with pro-flag legislators. "I think they'd fly a rack of lamb up there if they thought it would enable them to leave the [Confederate flag] where it is. It's created a very interesting spectacle to see the senator together with Glenn McConnell on the same side of the fence, touching and agreeing, being chummy and spreading Kumbaya all over the place. I don't think [the Ford plan] would have solved anything. It would have caused more harm than good. I think it was disingenuous to have even suggested it. Senator Ford's idea, and the way he has attacked and demeaned people who disagree with his idea, does harm to the principles that he says are embodied in that flag."

Darby probably has in mind Ford's suggestion that black leaders harbored ulterior motives in failing to support his idea. Ford, who generally projects the image of convivial joviality, was somewhat less than charitable when he said of some black leaders: "There are people who don't want the flag brought down. They want something to run [i.e., campaign] on. Those are pimps."[40] Aside from the senator's uncomplimentary language, his suggestion that black leaders were using the flag controversy as a means of rallying political (and financial) support to themselves only reinforced the impression among many whites (fueled by similar suggestions coming from the pro-flag forces) that black leaders, and in particular the NAACP, were on the make. It was a criticism that stung.

It was undeniably true, though, that Ford's proposal enjoyed more support among pro-flag whites than among black flag opponents—even though much of that white support may have been perfunctory and tactical and not a whole-hearted embrace. Senator McConnell was one of the main backers of the Ford plan. For him, the Black Liberation flag would be a fitting symbolic expression of one of those three hinges of South Carolina history he is fond of talking about. (And besides that, it would also legitimize the equivalency between the Confederacy's struggle for states' rights and the black struggle for equal rights.) "It's gotta be give and take on both sides, if you're gonna build the center," McConnell says. "The future of the South—and of good race relations—is based on mutual respect, conciliation, and tolerance rather than on confrontation and exclusion. Because the reality is: Confederate heritage, the Confederate flag, and the Black Liberation movement—all those things are gonna be there no matter what. One should not be incompatible with the other. They should all be part of one great story," the senator says with a dramatic flourish.

But Ford's proposal might also be read as a pessimistic expression of a lack of faith in South Carolina's ability to change, of its unwillingness to agree to any compromise that would involve bringing down its beloved Confederate flag. In that sense, he was simply accommodating his position to South Carolina's intransigence. "If a vote was held to take down the flag," Ford said in early 1994, "we [the flag opponents] would get massacred." His own southern experience told him that it was unlikely the flag would ever come down, and that it was better to strive for the attainable rather than to grasp for the impossible. It was a position that many of his fellow black lawmakers would eventually come to share—even if they still disagreed with him on how to respond to that intransigence.

As his friend McConnell tells it, Ford's position on the Confederate flag came about through something akin to a conversion of faith. "Lemme tell you about Robert," McConnell begins. "We come from different political backgrounds. We have different philosophies. We once clashed on a radio show over the playing of 'Dixie' at the Citadel, as well as on the Confederate flag. But Robert and I were traveling to a public hearing together one time. I was sitting in the back reading. And he asked me, 'What you readin' back there?' And I said, 'I'm readin' about your ancestors.' He wanted to know more. So I told him, 'I'm reading about the black slave-owners from Charleston.' And he said, "Naw! Where'd you get something like that from?' And I told him, 'From the 1850 census.'"

"Well, we got to talking and he asked me why I liked what I liked. And I told him, 'Robert, why don't you come to one of our [SCV] events and see for yourself.'

And he did. And he told me [afterwards] that he saw emotion, he saw the tears—but he didn't see hate. What he saw in these peoples' faces was real love for their ancestors. He saw a perspective that he had never seen before. He said that his most lasting impression of the Confederate flag had come back in 1968, after being arrested while working on voter registration down in Mississippi. In the middle of the night about thirty Klansmen had gathered outside the jail where he was being held, dressed in white sheets and carrying a Confederate flag. It was a lynch mob, he told me."

"But going to this [SCV] event had opened his eyes. And although we had fought on different sides on the flag, when he looked back on the votes about other things—like helping blacks get elected to public positions, and programs that were important to blacks—he said that the folks who were defending the Confederate flag were, on the other hand, very supportive of things of importance to the economic advancement of the black community." Ford himself has written, "For 27 years I thought that anyone who loved the Confederacy was a bigot and a racist. However, spending time talking to many individuals that love the Confederacy reveals otherwise."[41] As with Kay Patterson, the fires of indignation that Ford had once felt over the flag had been tempered by the collegiality of the state senate. It was no accident that the first real moves toward resolving the flag conflict (as well as, eventually, the outlines of the plan that would settle the matter in 2000) would begin in the senate, and not in the House of Representatives.

———•◦×◦•———

In late March 1994, however—roughly two months before the end of the legislative session (to be followed by elections in the fall)—prospects for resolution of the flag matter seemed as dim as ever. The House of Representatives demonstrated its unwillingness to support measures of importance to the state's black community when it rejected efforts to have Martin Luther King Jr's birthday declared an official state holiday. The King holiday—linked together with Robert E. Lee's birthday as an "optional" rather than a "mandatory" holiday for state employees—would remain partially entangled in the flag debate for several years to come, until things finally began falling into place during the run-up to final resolution of the issue in 2000. A public referendum continued to lead the pack of proposals aimed at ending the flag impasse (reflecting a nationwide trend toward passing troublesome issues on to the general public for determination and resolution). McConnell was, by now, pushing his own referendum plan—though he said he also could back the Black Liberation flag proposal, if the Legislative Black Caucus would agree to endorse it (which, as he well knew, they refused to do).[42] Meanwhile, Governor Campbell had finally come down in favor of trading in the Southern Cross flag for the (lesser-known and, so he believed, "less divisive")

Stars and Bars flag. The governor's support arrived too late, however, since that idea had already been consigned to the reject pile.[43]

Consensus was a scarce commodity. Opinions and proposals about what to do with the flag went shooting off in different directions. Both Strom Thurmond and Congressman John Spratt stepped in line behind the governor's (Stars and Bars) proposal, but GOP Representative Floyd Spence and Republican State Senator Arthur Ravenel wanted to keep things as they were, while Congressman Bob Inglis (also a Republican) hoped to see the flag moved to the State House grounds. South Carolina's other U.S. senator, Fritz Hollings, along with the state's only black U.S. representative, Jim Clyburn (both Democrats), both wanted to see the flag removed from the grounds altogether.[44]

A special seven-member panel set up to deliberate over the matter (chaired by Senator McConnell) was itself unable to reach agreement. In April the panel dissolved without officially endorsing any specific plan. Some blamed Senator Ford for the panel's failure to reach consensus. He had tied his Black Liberation flag plan to a state referendum so that voters would have been forced to decide whether to fly both the red-black-green flag and the Confederate battle flag—or neither. By supporting a plan like that, McConnell complained, "I would be voting to put the [battle flag] in jeopardy," a risk he was clearly unprepared to take.

But McConnell was also concerned about the possible imperilment of the flag by the right wing within the pro-flag contingent itself, and in particular by groups such the Council of Conservative Citizens. The CCC was led by William Carter, a chiropractor from the small mid-Carolina town of Saluda who had headed up (former Klansman) David Duke's 1992 presidential bid in the state. Carter and the CCC were a ubiquitous presence in support of the flag, organizing pro-flag rallies at the State House on the first day of each legislative session throughout the 1990s. With its peripatetic rally squads, the CCC seemed ever vigilant, always ready to call its troops together for a pro-flag demonstration wherever and whenever circumstances called for one. While McConnell appreciated all the flag support he could get, the undeniably racist overtones in the council's appeal was not the kind of support McConnell sought. On the contrary: McConnell was eager to disassociate the flag as much as possible from any and all appeals couched in the language of racial animosity—a CCC trademark. The group embodied classic white resentment of perceived black advantage in the seemingly zero-sum game of American race relations. For the CCC, taking down the flag "would be one more sign that blacks are advancing at the expense of whites." Referring to whites as "second-class citizens in their own country," Carter wondered how blacks could "protest flying the flag when they have just about everything accorded to them already."[45]

Interestingly, though, groups such as the Council of Conservative Citizens could no longer make the kind of bald-faced appeal to race they once had. Aping the Civil Rights movement, they instead spoke in terms of "equal rights." They claimed they were not opposed to black advancement or black pride but were only out to uphold the idea of equity. It was fine for blacks to have "theirs," CCCers said, just so long as they did not try to take away "ours." "You wear your 'X' and I'll wear mine," the slogan went. Most pro-flag legislators kept their distance from the CCC—but one lawmaker who did attend a Council event was quoted as saying, "The only compromise is to move the bottom flag [the Confederate banner] to the top."[46]

Senator McConnell was anxious to erect a firewall between the Confederate flag and groups such as the CCC and the Klan. "My problem with Dr. Carter's group," he said, "[is] that they inject their political agenda into the flag effort. [That] does not get us one vote in the General Assembly."[47] He denied the racist groups any claim to the flag: "This is *not* their banner. It's a historical banner, belonging to the soldiers who carried it." But McConnell was treading a narrow path, because the line between the Confederate flag and racism was a difficult one to draw—and many questioned whether the line existed at all. After all, it had been televised pictures of a CCC-led pro-flag rally in Columbia in late 1993 that had prompted Governor Campbell to come off the fence and call for the flag's removal. But McConnell protested any implied association between the flag and racism and warned that bringing the flag down on account of the CCC would send the wrong signal; it would in effect be handing the flag over to the racist groups. Campbell's proposal, he said, "whets the appetite of flag opponents by suggesting that the flag has been appropriated by racist groups. They've *tried* to appropriate it, and if we take it down on [that] basis, then we've given it to them."[48] In a sense it came down to a question of exactly where to build the firewall. The governor wanted to save the state from the political embarrassment posed by the rebel flag, while the senator wanted to preserve the flag from any and all associations with race. For McConnell, it was a soldier's flag and nothing else.

In late April there was a significant sign of movement in McConnell's direction when a young black state senator, Darrell Jackson, joined with Columbia Mayor Bob Coble to unveil a new compromise idea. The new plan would have declared April "Confederate History Month" and would have limited the display of the Confederate flag over the dome to that month only. During the other eleven months of the year the flag would fly at some (yet undetermined) location on the State House grounds.[49] By allowing the Confederate flag to fly one month out of the year (and without calling for the addition of the Black Liberation flag), the proposal marked a significant concession on the part of the Legislative Black Caucus, which had for twenty years demanded the wholesale elimination of the flag. Moreover, the proposal, introduced by Jackson, took a rather more respectful tone toward the Confederacy, noting the large loss of southern life during the war and concluding that "the heritage of the Civil War deserves the attention and respect of all individuals in the state."[50] Senator Patterson backed the plan, too, and even went as far as to caution his fellow Legislative Black Caucus members "to respect flag supporters' feelings."[51]

Senator Jackson, a local pastor and president of a consulting firm in downtown Columbia, had quickly gained notoriety, following his election to the senate in 1993, as one of that new generation of black lawmakers ready to get out in front on the flag fight. Jackson would, in a sense, assume the mantle of leadership on the flag issue from his senior colleague Senator Patterson—while adopting a tone somewhat more moderate and conciliatory than his predecessor. Jackson's approach to the flag debate bespoke his coming of age in a South Carolina more racially integrated than the one Patterson had grown up in. No less important, it also reflected the fact that Jackson represented a district split 50/50 between white and black. He could not afford to continuously swing the sort of rhetorical halberds that his outspoken predecessor Patterson had enjoyed wielding. The respectful tone in Jackson's proposal helped calm the fears of some pro-flag legislators, perhaps helping to set the stage for the compromise to come. His proposal also refocused the Legislative Black Caucus's efforts on their primary goal: away from the Black Liberation flag and back to removing the Confederate flag from the dome (if only for eleven months of the year).

But this was not yet the plan that would break the deadlock. Although it gained the tentative approval of a slim majority of Legislative Black Caucus members, it failed to garner the support of the key players it needed to become more than just one more plan thrown onto a rapidly growing heap. Both Senators Ford and Glover rejected it, saying the plan failed to provide for proper recognition of the contributions blacks had made to the state's history. (In the section dealing with Confederate History Month, however, the bill did at least implicitly call on the State Board of Education to come up with a program plan that would include references not only to southern and Confederate luminaries such as John C. Calhoun, Jefferson Davis, and Robert E. Lee, but which should also include in it the study of black Reconstruction-era politicians such as Robert Smalls and Joseph Rainey and all-black military units such as the 33rd U.S. Colored Troops.) The bill also failed to gain the unqualified support of essential pro-flag legislators such as McConnell or Senator Verne Smith, an Upstate Democrat (now Republican) whose grandfather had walked home from a Union POW camp in Point Lookout, Maryland. "My goal is to not show any disrespect to our flag," the aging Senator Smith said. "If taking it down eleven months of the year is a sign we're ashamed of it, then I wouldn't agree to it."[52]

Blacks were clearly at a disadvantage in the flag fight. But they were not completely lacking in countermeasures. For one thing, black leadership held out the threat of an economic boycott against the state should things not work out to their liking in the legislature. Black lawmakers were not the originators of such a plan, however—nor were they among its strongest backers. Reverend Darby, AME Bishop John Hurst Adams, and other black church leaders were early advocates of a boycott, and the idea also garnered the support of the state chapter of the NAACP. Many black leaders sensed a rising support for their cause within the state's business community and hoped to make state businesses into full-fledged allies in the drive to remove the flag. Business groups had remained rather tentative on the issue thus far, reluctant to become openly involved in the fight, fearful of alienating white customers.[53] Some black leaders, including Reverend Darby, felt that pushing the boycott would force the business leaders out into the open, either for or against the flag. They believed that the state's business interests would quickly come on board rather than end up in the embarrassing position of supporting the continued display of the Confederate flag.

The simple fact of the matter was that South Carolina's flag defenders held the trump card: the Confederate flag was still over the dome. Those in favor of keeping it there only needed to play defense to see that it stayed put—they simply needed to "hold at the dome," as McConnell put it—and they spared no effort to see to it that that was exactly where it remained. McConnell, for example, quietly inserted an amendment into the bill funding the upcoming State House renovation work that ensured that any and all "ornaments and decorative items" that may be removed during the renovation would be returned to their original locations when the work was completed.[54] Although the amendment was cloaked in general terms, everyone knew that it was meant to prevent anyone from engaging in the kind of monkey business that had gone on down in Alabama. An 1895 state law prohibiting any other flags except for the state and national banners from being flown atop the Alabama state legislature had resulted in the 1993 decision by Governor Jim Folsom not to re-raise the Confederate flag there after it was removed during a general renovation of the building. As things turned out, however, the amendment was unnecessary. The Confederate flag flew proudly over the State House throughout the renovations.

By May, with the legislative clock rapidly running down and still no sign of a break in the political impasse over the flag, pressure began to mount for action. On Confederate Memorial Day, delegates assembled at the state Democratic Party's convention adopted a platform plank calling for the removal of the flag from the dome. It was the first time that the state party establishment had officially come out against the flag's display. Less than a week earlier, a group of four whites (including Brett Bursey) filed a federal lawsuit against the state, claiming that the flag was discriminatory and divisive and as such constituted a violation of basic constitutional rights. State Attorney General Travis Medlock said that, given his opinion of the previous year in effect agreeing with the grounds presented in the suit, he would not defend the state in court. Meanwhile, the state

NAACP was now seriously considering a multisided offensive against the flag, including filing lawsuits, calling for an economic boycott of the state, and organizing statewide protests. A high-profile public campaign, they believed, could prove especially effective in light of the spotlight shed on the region by the upcoming 1996 Olympic Games. A group of state business leaders, anxious to forestall potential protest actions, quietly began putting pressure on lawmakers to find some way to settle the matter (without, however, endorsing any particular compromise plan themselves).[55]

The senate—the scene of all the action thus far—appeared largely unfazed by all the clamor for a solution. It debated the flag question as part of its consideration of the state's general budget bill—and even took up yet another circle-of-flags idea, this one offered by Senator McKinley Washington (another of that group of black lawmakers who had first come to the State House back in the early 1970s). But holding up as important a piece of legislation as the state budget bill in order to consider such a comparatively trivial matter as the Confederate flag was a much too risky affair as far as most senators were concerned. Adding a flag proposal to the budget bill could spark a filibuster, tying the state in knots and preventing passage of an essential bill. Buckling under pressure, flag opponents decided not to press the issue at this time, opting instead for further negotiations. Pro-flag legislators could take additional comfort from the fact that sales of Confederate flags in the state had skyrocketed by as much as 50 percent over previous levels.* It seemed as if the flag might ride out the spring storm after all.[56]

But then lightning struck—or at least the closest thing you get to a lightning strike in South Carolina politics. In late May, one week before the end of the legislative session, a closed-door meeting took place that included most, if not all, of the major players in the ongoing flag fracas. Leading pro-flag senators McConnell, Courson, and Smith (all SCV members) met with seven of the eight sitting black state senators (including Patterson, Ford, Glover, and Jackson), along with the head of the Legislative Black Caucus, Representative Joe Brown. The result of the meeting was a brand-new compromise plan, to be called the Heritage Act of 1994. The new plan proposed removing the rectangular Southern Cross flag from the State House dome and instead placing a square Army of Northern Virginia (ANV) flag at the Confederate Soldiers Monument out front. It also called for the placement of a Confederate First National (Stars and Bars) flag at the Confederate Women's memorial on the opposite side of the building. And, in order to ensure that posterity not misinterpret the gesture, the proposal ordered that statements be placed in the legislative record saying that the flags

*The gift shop in the South Carolina State Museum was unable to profit from this flag boom, however. Citing curator disapproval, the shop did not offer the Confederate flag for sale.

were being flown solely for the purpose of honoring South Carolinians who had fought and sacrificed in the Civil War (and that no racial or segregationist sentiment of any kind should be inferred from the display). Lastly, the plan would have made the preservation of all Confederate monuments in the state a matter of state law. No monument could be removed—or even moved—without the consent of the state legislature. Those present at the meeting also agreed to work toward the creation of a monument designed to honor the achievements and contributions that African Americans had made to the state.[57]

Even though time was short, the new plan appeared at first to have a good chance of passing. Most of the key players were behind it. Although Chris Sullivan and the Sons of Confederate Veterans still opposed removing the flag from the dome, both the Daughters of the Confederacy and the state NAACP supported the scheme. "It would save South Carolina a lot of aggravation and negative press," Reverend Darby said at the time. "And it would go a long way toward . . . mending relationships in this state."[58] More importantly, state business leaders came out with a clear public statement calling on the General Assembly to "craft a final solution to the flag issue—one that would lower the flag but still pay tribute to the memory of the Confederacy." Corporate leaders were worried that the ongoing controversy "could harm business recruitment and trigger a boycott led by black ministers and the [NAACP]."[59] The business community's backing of the plan was important not only in general terms, but also as a means of pressuring Republican lawmakers—especially in the state House of Representatives—whose votes would be necessary to get the proposal enacted into law.

———◆•◆••◆———

The meeting that produced the new plan was, in part, the consequence of a new spirit of compromise engendered in the battle over state redistricting. Roughly two weeks before the meeting in which the Heritage Act of 1994 was crafted, black Democrats in the House of Representatives entered into a tentative pact with Republicans to force Democrats to redraw legislative districts in such a way that would increase the number of black legislators. The renegade black Democrats were supported by the U.S. Justice Department, which had rejected existing house districts on the grounds that they "protect white Democratic incumbents at the expense of black voters." Many white Democrats resisted the establishment of additional black districts, however, because it would mean "creating predominantly white ones nearby that tended to vote Republican."[60]

Some Democrats opposed the change for purely self-interested reasons: to protect their "safe seats" and avoid upsetting the comfort of the status quo. But others expressed a more principled objection. Former state Representative Harriet Keyserling, commenting on an earlier reapportionment debate, wrote,

I felt a plan that clustered all the blacks into one district would leave them with no political clout at all in the other districts. The coalition between moderate white Democrats and blacks would disappear, because moderate white Democrats would disappear. The Republicans were their friends only in reapportionment, under which they both gained. We would be resegregating ourselves. The districts surrounding the minority districts would become unnaturally white, with their representatives indifferent to the needs of the blacks to which they did not have to answer.[61]

Blacks, however (who still held only 18 of 124 house seats, in a state with a 27 percent black population), were impatient with the status quo and tired of being taken for granted by the Democratic Party. One black representative compared the situation to "slavery days, when we wanted to be free, and our benevolent masters said, 'Why do you want to be free?'"[62] Whites also chaired all eight of the major committees in the house and twelve out of thirteen in the senate—in a General Assembly, it should be noted, which was at that time still controlled by Democrats.

The Democrats were, in a sense, no longer masters of their own fate—and had even become something of their own worst enemies—because of their failure to respond to black concerns in a timely manner. The Confederate flag was just one example of that. All through the years of Democratic majority control, the state legislature had failed or refused to act on black calls for the flag's removal. Some, such as Senator Smith, opposed removing it on principle, believing that the flag should remain over the dome as a sign of respect for the Confederate dead. Others, though perhaps indifferent to the flag as such, were not indifferent to the cold electoral calculus that showed them losing white votes if they openly opposed its display. When they had a chance to act, they hadn't. Now it seemed too late. At a time when many representatives may have been increasingly blasé about (and even privately embarrassed by) the flag, the rise of an activist southern heritage movement (and its close association with conservative Republicanism) made it harder for Democrats to move away from the status quo without paying a political price at the ballot box. The same applied to other issues as well.

Black concerns were shunted onto a siding of Democratic politics out of a fear that the conservative trend nationwide could result in a defection of white votes to Republican candidates. In the process, Democrats had gone from status quo complacency to a me-too Demo-Republicanism.

Though the Democrats were themselves partly to blame for their fate, the result of redistricting was exactly what Democrats like Keyserling had feared: an "increasing balkanization and polarization in the state," as racially mixed districts (where the balancing of competing interests through political compromise was a necessary art form) gave way to more racially homogeneous ones (in which a similarity of interest mitigated against a willingness to compromise with competing interests elsewhere).[63] Moderate, mixed districts were replaced, on the one hand, by majority black, and on the other, by conservative white districts. Though they gained a few seats, blacks remained in the minority in the legislature. Republicans, meanwhile, were able to pick off vulnerable Democrats and gain control of the political agenda in the state—and eventually take over the legislature itself.

Some charged the Republicans with exploiting certain issues, such as the Confederate flag, as a means of splitting the Democratic vote and luring conservative voters over to Republican candidates. As Keyserling recollects in her memoirs about her years in state government:

> Issues were brought to the forefront, such as prayer in the schools, abortion, the Confederate flag, tax cuts, automobile insurance, and environmental regulations, and we Democrats knew that records of all votes, including procedural votes and double-edged amendments were going to be used against us in the next election if we voted the "wrong" way.[64]

This pressure made white Democrats into conspirators in their own decline, causing them to hunker down, to abandon any progressive notions they may have harbored in order to placate white conservatives while simultaneously alienating blacks (and the few liberal whites).

In Keyserling's opinion, "Republicans . . . played up the volatile issues of reapportionment, integration, and civil rights as a weapon to defeat Democrats and to become the majority party."[65] In the process, they contributed to a situation in which "[b]itter partisanship created an atmosphere of 'them against us': 'I'm right and you're wrong.'"[66] It was this atmosphere that would help fan the flames of passion over the Confederate flag during the coming years.

But for a short time in late May 1994, it appeared as if the momentary coincidence of interest between black Democrats and white Republicans might contribute to a new spirit of compromise that would usher the Heritage Act through the state legislature and bring the flag debate to a swift and amicable end.

The moment was brief and quick to pass—one thrill before it all fell apart.

Despite (unsuccessful) last-minute efforts on the part of some in the Legislative Black Caucus to include a provision adding the Black Liberation flag, the South Carolina senate successfully passed the Heritage Act—just one day before the end of the 1994 legislative session. It was the first vote on the flag ever taken in the senate—and only the second time (since those procedural votes over in the house eleven years earlier) that the issue had been voted on in either chamber of the legislature. Flag defenders such as McConnell and John Courson knew that the flag on the dome rested on shaky legal ground, that it was vulnerable to a direct legal challenge. They also knew that their support in the legislature was starting to fade. Better to compromise now, they thought, than possibly end up empty-handed later, with the symbol of their Confederate heritage swept away altogether. With tears in his eyes, Courson said that it would be better to agree to remove the flag now—under terms congenial to all—rather than possibly see it summarily removed by court order, with all the ill will that might engender. "If a judge orders that flag off the dome," the senator said, "we will never have the chance to protect our heritage . . . and I will resent that for the rest of my life."[67]

That was the Senate—the body that, as James Monroe said (in reference to the U.S. Senate), should cool the passions poured into it by the House of Representatives. In this instance, however, the legislation was headed the opposite way: from the comparatively cool climate of the South Carolina senate into the hot and tepid jungles of the state House of Representatives, to a place where infirm and fragile creatures should not go. It became immediately clear that the state representatives were not ready to dance to the senators' tune. All the action thus far, all the negotiation over the flag, had taken place in the senate. The house had not been consulted, and it did not take kindly to the senate dictating terms. House passions were still very much engaged on the flag matter, and many of its hotspur members were in no mood for compromise. "If I am able to get up . . . and I am not in the obituary column, if I am able to take nourishment and tie my shoes, I'll make sure [the plan doesn't pass]," said one pro-flag representative the day the senate sent its bill across the hall to the house. "They made a serious mistake in judgment,'" Charleston Representative Harry Hallman continued, "thinking they could force-feed that to us at the 11th hour. You can't have a compromise if you don't include everybody."[68]

The upcoming fall elections played a role as well. State representatives, closer to the passions of their constituents than their senate colleagues, would have been reluctant to vote for the Heritage Act in any event, fearing that the voters' passions might well up and sweep them from office. They could consider themselves lucky that the senate had reached agreement at such a late date. By doing so, the house could dodge the issue by simply invoking a procedure preventing the introduction of any new business that had not been on their desks for at least twenty-four hours. A single dissenting voice was all that was necessary to invoke the rule—and Representative Hallman was only too happy to provide that voice.

The clock had simply run out on the senate's Heritage Act, and it died a quick and ignominious death. Some put part of the blame on Governor Campbell for not getting involved in the negotiations sooner and more intensely, using his powers of persuasion as the state's chief executive officer to bring Republican representatives into line behind the senate compromise. But it was clear from the start that any flag proposal would have had difficulty getting through a House of Representatives in which flag defenders held the upper hand.[69]

Among disappointed and embittered flag opponents talk immediately turned to lawsuits and boycotts. But others counseled patience, fearing the damage such confrontational methods might cause to the new spirit of compromise. "[S]uch tactics are unnecessary," *The State* confidently editorialized. "By this time next year," it optimistically concluded,

> the flag will no longer be atop the dome. The senators who forged the compromise have vowed to prefile it for the 1995 session. By that time, flag opponents could have an ally in the Governor's Office. But even if they don't, the chances for passage look excellent.[70]

But others were rather less sanguine about the prospects for settlement. Senator McConnell, for one, rumbled ominously: "Now we're on a collision course."[71]

Within days, black leaders had already begun discussing their next moves against the flag. At a mid-June meeting of a task force set up at the behest of the state NAACP, seventy black activists, ministers, politicians, and business leaders drew up plans for a four-pronged attack, to include a boycott directed against the state's lucrative tourism industry and a series of protests and demonstrations to be held across the state, as well as a possible legal challenge and a voter-education campaign aimed in part at unseating pro-flag state lawmakers.[72]

In a new development—of the kind that worried pro-flag Senators Courson and McConnell most—Columbia Mayor Bob Coble joined together with a group of twenty-two lawyers, bankers, and business executives from around the state (almost all of them white) to spearhead a new court challenge aimed at bringing down the flag. This new suit (filed in state rather than in federal court) took a different tack from those previously filed. Rather than focus on the racial aspect of the controversy, on the allegedly discriminatory character of the symbol itself, the Coble suit instead challenged the legal authority of the 1962 resolution that had put the flag over the State House in the first place. The suit argued that a simple resolution did not have the same force and permanency of law that a bill would have. A joint resolution did not possess that kind of weight, the plaintiffs claimed. "If [the legislature] had intended it to be a permanent monument," Mayor Coble said, "they would have passed it by legislation, as opposed to a resolution."

By focusing their case on a technicality, Coble and his fellow plaintiffs sought to avoid the question of why the flag had gone up in the first place—whether or not it was meant as a statement of defiance against civil rights, as many of the flag's opponents claimed. By approaching the issue this way, they hoped to avoid rousing the ire of the flag defenders and thus promote compromise. "The lawsuit itself only addressed bringing [the flag] down. It didn't say what would happen to it after that," the mayor recalled later. As a means of bringing about the kind of compromise they were after, the lawyers in charge of the Coble case asked the state supreme court to appoint a mediator to help settle the issue outside of court.

Democratic Attorney General Travis Medlock stoked the legal pyre gradually gathering flame under the flag by issuing yet another opinion on the flag display, this one stating that the state could not prevail in pending court challenges and declaring that the State Budget and Control Board had the authority to remove the banner itself. But Governor Campbell, who chaired the board, pointed suspiciously at prior opinions issued by the attorney general's office, in particular at contradictions between the various rulings. He dismissed this latest opinion as a political maneuver designed to improve Medlock's prospects in the upcoming Democratic gubernatorial primary.[73]

The threat of a boycott against the state, meanwhile, had sputtered almost from the start. Precedent for such action had been set back in 1986, when a nationwide boycott was launched against the state of Arizona after that state's governor, Edwin Mecham, had refused to allow a state holiday celebrating the birthday of Martin Luther King. That boycott had lasted five years, ending successfully in 1992. In South Carolina, plans for a boycott were sponsored by a NAACP task force headed by AME Bishop John Hurst Adams and state NAACP leader Dr. William Gibson. Early efforts to put the idea into effect floundered when national black leaders failed to provide the plan with the kind of backing necessary to make such a large-scale undertaking successful. Controversy over alleged financial improprieties swirling around the national NAACP leadership, under Benjamin Chavis, further complicated matters, overshadowing the flag issue and undermining the coordination needed to put a boycott plan into operation. The boycott became an on-again, off-again thing—more off than on—as black leaders repeatedly threatened to unleash a boycott should prospects for a compromise settlement fail to materialize. But over time, many in the state ceased to take the threats seriously. Nevertheless, even though black leaders hesitated to follow through on the proposed tourism boycott throughout the rest of 1994, and for several years to come, the planning that began that year would eventually culminate in the declaration of a full-scale boycott of the state in 1999, an act that set the stage for the final grand battle over the Confederate flag's fate.

Though boycott plans faltered, the first large-scale anti-flag protest marches in the state occurred in 1994. The first of these took place at the end of July in South Carolina's premier tourist draw, Myrtle Beach. The second was held in early September further down the coast at the more upscale tourist center on

Hilton Head Island. Black demonstrators traveling to the events were urged not to spend any money in the state as a way of lending weight to their demands. Some chose to stay in nearby Atlantic Beach, a public beach reserved for blacks during the segregation era, where many businesses were still black-owned. Others stayed outside the state and brought along packed lunches for the day's events.

The State newspaper did not endorse the marches. It worried that confrontational tactics like these might "do much harm to the progress that black and white leaders [had] made . . . to depolarize the issue. These marches," the paper editorialized,

> come at a critical moment—when lawmakers are in a primary campaign, and considering whether to come back to consider the Senate plan [i.e., the Heritage Act]. Such demonstrations may force politicians to choose one pole or the other and cling to it. . . ."[74]

Some of South Carolina's black leaders, too, were critical of NAACP activism, preferring the kind of low-key approach that had seen the state through the Civil Rights Era. But the NAACP had traditions of its own—going back at least as far as the Montgomery bus boycott in the 1950s, which had launched the modern Civil Rights movement. It was the NAACP's style, Regional Director Nelson Rivers said, to prefer direct action.[75]

The other side had not folded its hands in its lap, though, either. The Council of Conservative Citizens, along with a related pro-flag organization called the Confederate States Preservation Society, organized counter-demonstrations in both Myrtle Beach and Hilton Head. The CCC's William Carter also claimed to have collected thirty thousand signatures on a "Save Our Heritage" petition and called for a counter-boycott against the businesses that supported the NAACP—such as AT&T (a co-plaintiff in the Coble case) and "The Snake" (Carter's derogatory term for *The State* newspaper).

Nor was the state GOP sitting idly by. Pro-flag Republicans successfully lobbied to have a referendum question added to the party's August primary ballot asking whether or not the Confederate flag should be removed from the State House (though, notably, without mentioning any alternative display, such as that proposed in the Heritage Act). Balloting in August showed that more than 75 percent of the Republican primary voters wanted to keep the flag flying. The result contrasted sharply with a recent statewide poll of all South Carolinians, which showed support for the flag falling from 55 percent to just 40 percent. The purpose and the consequence of the referendum were obvious: it reduced the chances for compromise by threatening wavering Republicans with electoral repercussions should they stray from the proscribed course. "This is a clear mandate to Republican leaders that they'd better support the Confederate flag," one flag-defending Republican pointed out following the primary vote. The tone of triumph and intimidation could scarcely be missed.[76]

Republican leaders (and others, too) got the message—and quickly signaled so. Contrary to expectations, the pro-flag backers of the 1994 Heritage Act did not resubmit the measure for consideration in the 1995 legislature, to convene in mid-January. After a meeting with members of the SCV and UDC in mid-September of the outgoing year, Senators Courson, McConnell, and Smith announced they were dropping their previous support for the Heritage Act compromise plan. They instead prefiled a bill (the first one for the upcoming session) that offered a new approach to the old referendum proposal. By acting to put something on the table early the pro-flag legislators hoped to forestall a harsh and summary judgment by the state supreme court in the Coble case. Rather than calling for a straight up-or-down vote on whether or not to keep the flag, this new referendum scheme would offer voters three choices instead of just two. They could vote to keep the flag where it was and protect that display for all time (option 1); they could have it removed without alternative (option 3); or they could vote for the second option on the list: the Heritage Act of 1996.

It is interesting to note that the authors of this new proposal did not find it necessary to explicitly define either the meaning of the flag or the purpose of the flag display in the event the voters opted to simply keep the flag over the dome. That was different if the voters decided for the Heritage Act, however. Those who voted for option 2 would automatically be signing off on a definition of the flag's meaning as laid out in the legislation. This statement said, in part, that

> The Confederacy fought for the American principle of self-government and in defense of their homes, families, and country. They served their state under great hardships, and won the admiration of the world by their courageous fight against an enemy overwhelming in numbers and resources. Despite their hardships and personal sacrifice, these men took consolation in the belief that they would not be forgotten by this state or people.
>
> . . . [the flag's] display affirms, as no mere words can, that those who answered their country's call to duty are indeed not forgotten. The Battle Flag also reminds all of us of the heritage of valor, patriotism, devotion to duty, and the spirit of self-sacrifice bequeathed to all of us by these Confederate ancestors—men and women, rich and poor, white and black. When we as a people no longer admire and pay tribute to these traditions, we will no longer remain a free and great nation.

The statement then went on to make clear that the "Confederate Battle Flag is displayed as a testimonial to our shared history and heritage as South Carolinians, Southerners, and Americans." The flag display "becomes a statement that we today understand its true meaning and refute those who would misuse this proud emblem for the wrong reasons." In this way, the statement concluded, the flag "becomes a sublime symbol, not only of our ancestors . . . but an affirmation of our identity as a people." In other words, if you wanted it moved to the monument, you also had to agree that the flag carried with it no negative meaning whatsoever.[77]

In addition, the bill linked the memorialization of black heritage in the state together with the Confederate flag and the Heritage Act's definition of that flag. The construction of an African American memorial was not part of either option 1 or 3; it was mentioned only as part of the Heritage Act in option 2.

What had caused this change in tactic—the sudden unwillingness to endorse the Heritage Act of the previous year? According to McConnell, it was the NAACP-sponsored protest marches and all the talk of a boycott that had erupted as soon as the previous legislative session had ended. These actions were symptomatic of a breach of faith, he said, a clear indication of an unwillingness to compromise, and a sign that the other side could not be trusted to end their attacks on the flag, no matter where or how it might be displayed. "I feel like I went out and tried to sell the Heritage Act to heritage groups and then got slapped in the face by the NAACP," McConnell said at the time.[78] "Rather than build support for the Heritage Act," McConnell recalled later, "the other side immediately began all that hot rhetoric about how they've got to get that red rag off the dome now—not Confederate battle flag, *red rag!* And it quickly appeared to us that there was no real intention to cease the attacks on heritage, that this was just a convenient maneuver to get the flag down."

"Then, in the fall," McConnell continued, "the Sons of Confederate Veterans in Newberry were having the centennial celebration of the founding of their veterans' camp up there. A hundred years earlier Confederate veterans had had their picture taken in front of the local courthouse, with the Confederate flag flying alongside. The SCV wanted to take a picture of those peoples' descendants at the same location, and fly the Confederate flag at the same place. The local NAACP objected to the picture—to flying the flag, even for that picture! The county council folded like a house of cards under the pressure; refused to permit them to fly the flag. Not one newspaper came to their aid. Not one public leader, that I can recall, stood up for their right to take that picture. How could I go to a group like that and say, let's take down the flag and move it to a monument as a gesture of goodwill? Things like that confirmed, to me, that I should not abandon the position of the flag at the dome until we get a final agreement from the other side, an agreement that they will cease the attacks on our heritage. Until we can do that, the best thing we can do is hold right at the dome."

"If there's one thing that we learned at Gettysburg," the senator says, almost as if he had been there himself, "it is not to abandon the high ground. From a strategic standpoint, if I aim to preserve the memory of those soldiers, the worse thing I can do is retreat from the fight at one spot and have to fight on many fronts, where we will not get public support because it's an inconvenience. So we're not backin' up another inch. If I thought that moving the flag to the monuments would solve everything and end everything, I would do that tomorrow. But I learned, when we proposed that in 1994, that it would be like passing a jigger of alcohol to an alcoholic and telling him, here, this should quench your thirst. It just whets the appetite for more. So we'll hold until we get a final settlement."

"And then, when we get a final settlement," McConnell added revealingly, "then it doesn't matter whether the flag flies at the dome or at the monument. Not as long as the honor of those people is preserved, so long as the emblem is protected from a reputation of shame, and the monuments, the graveyards, and the right to display one's heritage is guaranteed and protected. But if we took it off the dome without a final settlement, we just move the struggle to the State House grounds, and every monument in town squares across the state would be under siege. To let that flag go from the dome would be to desert my ancestors, and to desert all the people who respect our heritage, because they would be left to fend for themselves in small groups at Christmas parades and at athletic events and in public places everywhere. At the dome, we're together at one place. And we'll hold there until we get the final settlement. And I think that, eventually we'll force the NAACP to abandon their mean-spirited approach and get 'em to the table."

Such were the lessons drawn from the Spring Campaign of '94.

For a time, though, the forces of goodwill would have to step aside as a force stronger still swept over the state. The Republican tide that rolled across the country in the midterm elections of 1994 changed the face of South Carolina politics—and with it the character of the flag debate. The GOP took control of seven out of nine statewide offices, including the governorship (for only the second time since Reconstruction). They picked up several seats in the senate. And, following a party switch by a house Democrat, the House of Representatives went majority Republican for the first time in the state's history. With so many conservatives entering the State House, many of whom were sympathetic to neo-Confederate political views on the role of government and the need to preserve heritage, it was clear that those seeking to remove the Confederate flag from the capitol dome now had an even steeper uphill battle before them.

After the mid-November hearing on the Coble case before the state supreme court, Senator Courson warned the justices (all of whom were Democrats appointed to ten-year terms by the legislature) about the dangers inherent in bucking the tide of the recent election: "I would hope it sends a strong signal to them that the conservatives won big Tuesday in this state," he said. And in order to emphasize his point, Courson added: "Most of the people who vote conservative are generally very supportive of our heritage."[79]

With the controversy over the Confederate battle flag growing ever hotter, South Carolina's special tribute to Confederate heritage was itself becoming an increasingly marketable commodity. For years, the state had been selling flags flown from the roof of the State House as souvenirs. And because of the fight over the flag, the number of buyers had been steadily growing. Between 1992 and 1994, orders for flags flown over the State House had quadrupled. The overwhelming majority of those flags had not flown over the dome itself, however—waiting lists for actual dome flags were considerably longer. Instead, the bulk of the flags sold as part of this unique offer had been hoisted over the State House for perhaps ten seconds or less, raised one after the other in an assembly-line ceremony carried out once a month using a separate pole on the roof of the building. These flags sold for between $16 and $25 and came with a pedigree guaranteeing that they had indeed flown over the South Carolina State House. In 1992, Confederate flags had accounted for only 100 of the 324 flags sold. (Customers could also request the Palmetto and U.S. flags.) But by the end of 1993, orders for Confederate banners had swelled to 500. By 1998, the waiting period for a U.S. or state flag was roughly two to three years. The waiting period for a Confederate flag, by contrast, was ten to twelve years. Needless to say, most of the remaining orders would never be filled by the time the flag display was discontinued in 2000. In spite of the increase, however, the Confederate flag was still only the second-best selling item offered—behind Old Glory.[80]

Southern sympathies were still divided, it seemed. But the market for Confederate memorabilia was an expanding one, and chances looked better than ever that Dixie would not need to rise again—because many were more determined than ever to ensure that it never fall.

—◦•◦—

If 1994 had been the year of the senate, 1995 became the year of the house. And along with the shift from one front to the other, the year would also bring Confederate heritage defenders to the high-water mark in their campaign to protect the flag over the dome. The spirit of compromise that had lent part of the previous year a sense of purpose and prospect had all but vanished, replaced by renewed defiance. Hopes for a workable compromise appeared dimmer than ever.

The debate over the Confederate flag was now conducted in terms more black-and-white than before. Divisions deepened, and differences in perspective seemed starker than ever. But it was not only the character of the debate that had changed. The overtly racial element within the debate intensified, as the flag fight now became even more an issue of black *versus* white. As a result of the 1994 elections, white Democrats had become a rarer commodity in the state—and those who were left were often reluctant to speak out against the flag and similar hot-button issues because of the changed political atmosphere in the wake of the Republican tide. Of the twenty-two freshmen representatives arriving for the start of the new legislative session in January 1995, sixteen were newly elected Republicans. The other six were black Democrats. Moreover, only six of the twenty-six house lawmakers who had been elected in the 1992 general election were white Democrats—and three of those soon switched parties or became independents.[81]

In the mid-1990s, America once again returned to an age-old source of fascination and frustration: its long-running debate over race—and South Carolina was certainly no exception. With the breakdown of voting districts along racial lines, party affiliation and race became closely linked, with blacks still adhering to the Democratic Party while whites increasingly switched to the Republicans. As a consequence, racial overtones could be heard in an ever greater number of issues under consideration before the state legislature. Race popped up in debates over bills dealing with criminal justice, education, welfare reform, reapportionment, term limits, political appointments, and the state budget. It was clear that the debate over the Confederate flag had become a litmus test for the general state of race relations in the South and in the nation. But with those relations so unsettled, it seems unlikely that Carolina's flag fight could have been any less racially divisive than it was.

The change in the tone of political debate in the state—and in particular in the Confederate flag fight—was swift and thoroughgoing. Just how inflamed the conflict over the flag had become can be seen in the debate over concealed weapons in the state House of Representatives. One amendment to a bill on the subject would have forbid the possession of a concealed weapon "while wearing an article of clothing displaying the Confederate flag." The measure was defeated—though it is difficult to determine just how seriously it was meant to be taken, since it also prohibited the carrying of concealed weapons "into a person's former spouse's attorney's office" and "into an after Thanksgiving Day sale."[82] Talk of accommodation and negotiated compromise was replaced by a tougher line. The newly elected Republican attorney general, Charlie Condon, quickly announced that he was reversing the position his predecessor, Trevor Medlock, had taken on the flag. Condon felt there was ample evidence to show that the 1962 legislature had indeed intended the flag to stay on the dome indefinitely and that there were sufficient legal grounds for it to remain there. He said that only the state legislature should decide the fate of the flag and asked the state supreme court to either dismiss the Coble suit or else permit him to file a new brief reflecting the state's new pro-flag position.[83]

The new governor, too, favored keeping the flag in place—though, like his predecessor, David Beasley showed no desire to get out in front on the issue. He was prepared to support any compromise plan that the legislature might come up with, he said, but otherwise would leave the subject alone, at least for the time being.[84]

The pro-flag spring offensive was being waged over old ground. Lawmakers were once again debating various referenda schemes—though none of them had the support of the anti-flag side. Only the flag defense forces wholeheartedly favored referenda proposals—yet even some pro-flag Republicans were leery about holding a public vote on the flag. Public hearings held the previous year to discuss what should be done with the flag had often broken down into heated shouting matches as opposing camps lobbed verbal barrages at one another. Many representatives feared the prospect of having the same sort of thing happen in uncontrolled settings all across the state during the run-up to a high-profile referendum.[85] The problem of how to formulate a referendum question—the wording of it—contributed to the legislature's reluctance to embrace the idea. If they could agree on exactly how to word a question—itself an unlikely prospect—then they might just as easily put the same effort into reaching an agreement on the substance of the matter itself.

But the referenda proposals were really nothing more than sideshows. The real focus of attention was a measure introduced in the house by the Republican majority leader, Representative Rick Quinn, son of Republican strategist and political consultant Richard Quinn (of *Southern Partisan* fame). Unwilling to engage in flag negotiations while under the gun of the Coble suit, state representatives in late March 1995 added a passage into a bill on the pending State House renovations that required that "all portraits, flags, banners, monuments, statues, and plaques which may be removed from the State House during renovations be returned to their original location when the State House is reoccupied." Although the legislation made no specific mention of the Confederate flag as such, it was clear that the measure was aimed at protecting the flag.

That took care of any tricks that the anti-flag forces might try and pull during the two years scheduled to complete the State House reconstruction work. But the real clincher came at the end of this brief, unassuming piece of legislation, where it said:

> When all portraits, flags, banners, monuments, statues, and plaques are returned to their original location after the renovations are completed, the location of those items must not be changed unless approved by an act passed by the General Assembly.[86]

That plugged the last hole in the legal dike protecting the flag and it answered the challenge posed by the Coble suit. The measure lent the flag display the statutory underpinning which the Coble suit claimed it lacked while simultaneously giving the legislature sole power to decide the ultimate fate of the Confederate flags within and above the State House.

The House of Representatives approved the bill by a vote of 82 to 30. The senate soon followed, and Governor Beasley signed the bill into law in June 1995. Now only the state legislature had the legal authority to decide the flag's fate—a legislature still dominated by pro-flag sentiment. Flag opponents now appeared to be in full retreat across a wide front. Not only did the Coble group drop their suit against the state, the Legislative Black Caucus reaped a storm of protest from angry flag foes, disappointed with the caucus's failure to speak out against the Quinn measure. The bill instead passed without debate. Knowing they did not have the votes needed to block the bill, flag opponents seemed willing to get whatever they could—even if only very little. In exchange for their silence, Representative Quinn said that he would "let" the senate create a joint committee with the house to study possible flag compromises. But he also made it clear that he would not accept any compromise that did not leave a Confederate flag of some kind (ANV, First National, or whatever) over the dome.[87]

To the anti-flag forces, the South Carolina House of Representatives was clearly hostile territory, barren ground for nurturing the kind of compromise necessary to work out a solution to the flag problem. "We need to move to a place where reasoned discussion can occur," said Legislative Black Caucus member Joe Neal, "and that can only happen in the Democrat-controlled Senate instead of the Republican House, given the conservative political tenor in the state." Some caucus members said privately that it was best not to engage in an openly aggressive campaign against the flag, for fear of alienating those pro-flag lawmakers whose votes they might need on other issues.[88]

For the time being, however, the spirit of compromise appeared moribund in both the house and the senate. Flag-defending senators had stiffened their backs, soured, they said, over the lawsuits, protests, and boycott threats coming from the other side. As things stood, pro-flag lawmakers could afford to be unbending on the flag, because the political tide in the state appeared to be flowing in their favor. "You'd have to be a blind duck not to see there has been a sea change in politics in South Carolina," John Courson said. "If we get into a fight over the flag in the Senate, we're going to prevail," he added confidently. Appearing alongside Courson at a Confederate Memorial Day event on the State House grounds in early May, Charleston Senator Arthur Ravenel Jr. floated on a sea of optimism as he read from the legislation protecting the flag. Pointing to the banner over the dome, Ravenel exclaimed, "Hot dog, there she is up there!"[89]

———— ◦•◦═◦•◦ ————

The battle over Confederate symbols was reduced to occasional small-scale skirmishes for a time while state government took a break from the fight. Another legal scrap broke out in the ongoing tussle over t-shirts when a downstate middle-school—located in Barnwell County, home of the old "Barnwell Ring" and next-door neighbor to "Mr. Confederate" John A. May's Aiken—banned certain types of "disruptive" symbols and slogans and suspended several white students who violated the ban. Whites charged the school district with supporting a double standard, because it had failed to act when black students wore Malcolm X shirts and other items unsettling to whites. Several white families sued the district for their kids' right to don their own forms of personal body-expression (including a shirt showing the Confederate flag over the State House along with the words "I have a dream" and another bearing the slogan "Flying high, ain't coming down"). In an odd-couple legal alliance, both the left-leaning American Civil Liberties Union and the right-wing Council of Conservative Citizens offered legal counsel in defense of the teens' right to free speech. The school district eventually agreed to pay the suspended students $5,000 in an out-of-court settlement of a class-action suit brought by the Southern Legal Resource Center, a North Carolina–based law firm specializing in so-called southern heritage violations.[90]

Meanwhile, in a few locations around the state, yet another new flag joined the ones already flapping in the Carolina breeze. A small company calling itself Freedom Enterprises unfurled what it dubbed its "Anti-Confederate flag," a design that portrayed an upraised Black Power fist clutching a crumpled rebel flag. The banner, which originally had appeared back in the early 1970s (hand-drawn on a king-sized bedsheet) was meant to draw attention to South Carolina's flag controversy and pressure the state legislature to act. But the new ensign never caught on and so never had the effect intended. Just as well, some black leaders said, worried that such "in-your-face" gestures might spoil any chance of reaching an agreement with the pro-flag side.[91]

Having each taken its turn at bat, the senate and house now opted to take a break from the flag feud for a while. That left an opening for someone else to give it a try. Like Lincoln switching generals, the next to take command of the issue was the newly elected Republican governor, David Beasley, who began to engage the matter at the beginning of his second year in office. His approach was somewhat different from what had been tried so far, however. He chose not to go at the Confederate flag controversy head on—at least not at first. That would be too dangerous. Instead, he embedded the flag issue into a much broader approach, one that made the flag just one element in a range of issues and problems touching on race relations in South Carolina. Picking up on a recommendation put forward by the Columbia Urban League, Beasley established a Commission on Racial

Relations, composed of state business leaders and political officials. The commission would conduct a series of public meetings around the state and produce suggestions on how to deal with race-related problems in the areas of education, economic development, health care, crime, community relations—and the Confederate flag.

Some found the proposal dubious—just another example of "kumbaya" race relations, at best. Reverend Darby felt the commission was nothing more than a sop to the Urban League, a way of deflecting criticism from the governor's conservative political agenda. After all, Darby said, the commission had "no statutory authority, no power to do anything but interview, and would make recommendations that were not binding." "It offered nothing more than a symbolic gesture," he believed. "So most folks saw it as just a way to vent [their] frustrations. I went to one of those hearings, and that's what folks did—they vented. Everybody talked from their rock-hard positions. Nobody talked *to* each other, they talked *at* each other. And nothing really came of it."

The commission's final report was not issued until a year later than originally planned and, by many estimates, contained little if anything of any real substance or value.[92] Besides vague generalities and cheery self-praise (including a great deal about "tremendous strides" and "significant headway"), many found the report too much colored by the ideology of contemporary neo-conservative (not to say "neo-Confederate") Republicanism. "Government has limited power over the lives of individuals, which is exactly as it should be," the report stated boldly at the outset. It complained that the "media sometimes exacerbates" racial difficulties by "overplaying what are often isolated incidents of racial trouble." And it reckoned that "for every racial problem we face, there are a thousand good examples of the progress the state has made." It emphasized the limited role that government should play in improving race relations, saying that "government cannot change the hearts and minds of individual citizens," and it called for greater individual/private initiative to combat the problems that still exist.[93]

The section of the report dealing with the Confederate flag was the shortest of all—less than a page—despite the fact that the flag controversy dominated most of the public meetings. The report was very cautious in describing the debate over the flag. The battle flag over the State House, the report said, "has become a confusing symbol often misinterpreted and misused." "Yet," it quickly added, "it also remains a source of pride for many South Carolinians . . . who . . . reject that their support of its presence atop the State House dome represents any negative racial statement." That having been said, the commission did nevertheless find that "all races would find it much easier to engage in meaningful dialogue about race if the Confederate battle flag were moved to a place of honor on the State House grounds." It wasn't a very strong statement—but at least it was clear and unambiguous.[94]

The report didn't appear until late 1997, however, long after anyone had ceased to care what it had to say—and long after the firestorm unleashed by Beasley's forceful yet abortive flag compromise had subsided.

Back in early 1996, the governor was still tentative in his approach to the flag issue, still holding to the view that the flag "represents a heritage to celebrate—not racism," and apparently still in favor of keeping it on its perch over the dome. He wanted people to take a wider view of the problem of race in society and not focus on narrow issues like the Confederate flag. There were many who agreed with him—including many blacks, who felt that too much effort was being wasted on the flag, effort that could be better spent on problems of greater substance. But there were just as many, perhaps more, who believed that the settlement of the flag debate would have to precede progress on other race-related problems, that settlement might even serve as a door to greater cooperation between the races in the future. Some were suspicious of Beasley's motives, thinking he meant to merely draw attention away from the flag by talking about other aspects of racial conflict. But at least he was prepared to admit that the state of race relations in South Carolina were not where they should be. "Tensions are rising," Beasley conceded.[95]

Beasley (and his race commission) were right to remind us of how far the state had advanced toward becoming a more racially equitable society. A sign of the progress the state was making in dealing with its racial past came in July 1996, when the governor signed into law a bill calling for the construction of an African-American History Monument on the grounds of the State House—an undertaking near and dear to the hearts of all in the Legislative Black Caucus, and of special importance to those, such as Senator Darrell Jackson, who had pushed the issue hard since entering office. Several white house members, however, still resisted the idea of erecting a monument dedicated to a single ethnic group.* House Republican Dan Cooper worried it might open the gates for others demanding their own monuments. And as if to prove the point, Representative Jake Knotts, a self-described "strong-headed" Republican and staunch flag supporter, attempted to bottle up the bill authorizing the monument by offering thirty amendments calling for the construction of similar monuments for every minority group he could think of. But with the state's "Big Mules" finally hitched up in line in front of the plan (including Senator McConnell, who was made chair of the commission overseeing the project—a source of more black aggravation), the bill's passage was a foregone conclusion.[96]

The monument that resulted did seek to remind the state of the darker aspects of its race-burdened past. But, overall, the portrait it painted was of a state and

---

*When enacted, the monument would be the only memorial of its kind on the capital grounds in any of the fifty states.

a people moving forward toward what seemed an inevitably brighter future. Its panels depicted black progress in the state, from their arrival as slaves to the departure of the first black astronaut, a South Carolinian. Yes, the monument seemed to say, the past had existed, it was once as real as our own time. But those days had only been stepping stones along a path that we have long since passed over on our way to a more confident, sunnier present.

In 1996, however, the state—and its governor—were pulled back down to earth by reminders of a gloomier past not yet disappeared into the long dark night of history.

During the five years since 1991, thirteen black churches (along with eight white ones) had been set aflame by arsonists. An additional number of church burnings were of undetermined origin, but were considered "suspicious." Although it was a source of some debate whether or not the fires could be linked together into a pattern of anti-black racism (or even whether the number of fires was statistically outside the norm), it was clear that at least some of the black churches had indeed been the targets of racist attacks (as the Dees/Turnipseed case would show). Klan activity appeared to be on the rise again. In October 1996 two Klansmen were arrested for the drive-by shooting of three young blacks, after attending a pro-flag rally sponsored by the Council of Conservative Citizens. Events such as these sparked memories of the darker days of the Civil Rights Era in the nation's consciousness. And as images of church burnings, racist attacks, and the debate over the Confederate flag linked up in the public mind, it became clear that some sort of reply was becoming ever more urgent.[97]

After publicly stating that racial hatred had "struck the match" setting fire to black churches, it became apparent that Governor Beasley was looking for some way to signal that the state recognized and was responding to the threat. Appearing on ABC's *Nightline* in June 1996 to discuss the church fires, the governor hinted that he was looking at some kind of compromise to put an end to the Confederate flag controversy in the state. Other state politicians were at a loss to understand what he was talking about, since up to that point Beasley had not veered from his support for the flag or offered any plan aimed at dealing with the issue. Beasley was aware that he was treading a narrow path, since the primary voters who had helped him get the GOP nomination for governor were the same voters who had overwhelmingly voted on the primary referendum in favor of keeping the Confederate flag in place on the dome.[98]

"When I made the decision to go forward on this issue, I made the assumption that it would defeat me," Beasley recalled later. "I brought my staff into my office in the fall of 1996, when our poll numbers were great and re-election assured, and stated that I wanted to resolve the flag issue. I told them that I knew that it could jeopardize my political career as governor, and their jobs. I asked them to make the assumption that we would lose re-election as a result. I [can] proudly say that they all thought it worth it."[99]

It was clear that the Confederate flag had become a kind of third rail of South Carolina politics. When used well, it could propel a political agenda or a political career (as both pro- and anti-flag forces had demonstrated). But if handled improperly and carelessly, it might just as easily fling one's political prospects into the high grass growing along the tracks of state politics. Beasley was aware of the dangers involved. Georgia Governor Zell Miller's political fortunes had very nearly taken a tumble in a similar tussle over Confederate symbols in his state.

But Beasley was aware of the opportunities involved, too—of the political rewards waiting if the matter could be settled under his guidance. As a young man with higher political ambitions, he knew that if his initiative led to the successful resolution of the flag fight, under terms reasonable to all, then his image as a political dragon-slayer would be secured, his political prospects brighter than ever. The governor's fellow Republican, Senator Arthur Ravenel, recalled how party officials convinced Beasley that the fulfillment of his ambitions depended on sending the right signals to a national audience, including taking a stab at the Confederate flag. "They told him, man, David, you're doing so good, you'll end up on the ticket for vice-president!," Ravenel remembers. "You might not be able to get the flag down, but you got to at least try. And from that day, it was down hill."

From the governor's perspective, however, the timing seemed opportune. Not only were his poll numbers looking good, public opinion about the fate of the flag display appeared to be moving in his favor as well. Forty percent of the state's residents surveyed in early November 1996 were still for keeping the flag over the dome. But 49 percent now preferred that it be removed—by moving it to a location on the State House grounds (26 percent) or by eliminating it from the capitol grounds altogether (23 percent). Nine percent said they did not care one way or the other—although the true number may have been higher, given South Carolina's growing exasperation over the issue.[100] Perhaps as importantly, the state was under no immediate threat of a boycott—in part, Beasley later claimed, because he had privately warned the NAACP and other black leaders that he would oppose any effort to remove the flag if they followed through on such a threat (though it is just as likely that the NAACP's own internal problems at the time played at least as great a role).

After a year in which his administration had passed a number of conservative measures (many of which had met with broad criticism from the state's black leaders)—and in light of the increasingly negative publicity directed against the state in the wake of the church burnings, as well as the governor's own concern about the worsening racial climate—Beasley concluded that "it was an appropriate time to try to resolve the [flag] issue once and for all—for the good of the Republican Party [which was beginning to suffer because of it], and for the good of South Carolina" (which was already suffering on account of it). "South Carolina won't be viewed as a progressive state as long as the flag continues to fly," Beasley told a group of state business leaders.[101]

In a series of public comments and speeches, culminating with an eight-minute televised address to the state in late November, Beasley said that far from symbolizing pride in South Carolina's heritage, the Confederate flag had instead become "an unnecessary cause of division" in the state. "Any banner we choose to fly over the capitol," he continued, "should be one that everyone can claim as their own." Rather than serving to bring the state together, however, the debate over the Confederate flag was only contributing to an atmosphere of racial discord and conflict. "Do we want our children to be debating the Confederate flag in 10 years?," Beasley asked. "If we stay on the present course, such will be their fate. [The] debate will not subside, but intensify," and in the process undermine the good qualities that the flag should represent. If we instead work toward compromise and reconciliation to resolve the matter, Beasley continued, then "our children will be able to visit the State House, see the flags flying above the Confederate monuments and learn of their true meaning, which has nothing to do with racial hatred. I want them to respect the flag for all the right reasons," the governor said.[102]

Recent church burnings and other racially motivated crimes, Beasley went on, had cast a pall over the state's image—and its Confederate heritage. His aim was to protect the flag's true heritage, to protect it from being "defined by the two extremes"—by race-mongers in the Klan, on the one hand, and groups like the NAACP, on the other. Using what one observer described as a nuanced argument over semiotics (the study of symbols and their meanings), the governor said "the Confederate flag flying above the State House flies in a vacuum. Its meaning and purpose are not defined by law. Because of this, any group can give the flag any meaning it chooses. The Klan can misuse it as a racist tool, as it has, and others can misuse it solely as a symbol for racism, as they have."[103]

The governor, whose own ancestors had fought for the Confederacy and who felt that honoring Confederate heritage was fully fitting and proper, said he hoped to prevent the Confederate flag from being "torn asunder" by continued debate. He called on pro- and anti-flag groups to meet him halfway on a compromise settlement of the issue. Beasley's conciliatory tone on the flag was, in part, the result of the lesson he had taken from Governor Miller's experience in Georgia: Rather than confront the flag's friends with its elimination, he tried to assuage their fears by offering an alternative. To that end he proposed returning to the groundwork laid down in the Heritage Act of 1994, which had already passed the political test once before, having been supported by a good mix of Republicans and Democrats. As in the 1994 proposal, the governor endorsed taking the Southern Cross flag off the dome and moving it to the Confederate

Soldiers Monument, adding the First National Stars and Bars flag to the Women's Memorial and writing into law the protection and preservation of all the roughly 200 Confederate monuments and markers across South Carolina.[104]

Reaction to the governor's initiative ranged from strongly supportive, to tepid, to openly hostile. The state Chamber of Commerce and other business groups wholeheartedly endorsed the governor's efforts to relocate the flag to a "place of honor." All five of the state's living former governors—three Democrats and two Republicans (including Beasley's immediate predecessor, Carroll Campbell)—also rallied to the governor's call, as did Strom Thurmond and a number of other elected officials. One political analyst praised Beasley as "a son of the old South who spoke as a son of the new South."[105]

Elsewhere, the reaction was more guarded. Most state legislators kept their cards clutched close to their chests, lauding the governor for his courage but withholding their support until more details were available (i.e., until the political "weather report" came in). The Republican Speaker of the House of Representatives, David Wilkins, said that he did not want to see the flag issue get in the way of more-important legislative business. Noting the weak support for the governor's proposal in the legislature, Wilkins said that although he was keeping his door open to compromise, he was on record in favor of keeping the flag up.

More important, perhaps, was the Legislative Black Caucus's failure to immediately endorse the governor's plan. Some, like Senator Darrell Jackson, said they were reluctant to see the flag moved to such a prominent location at the front of the State House, where two of the city's busiest downtown thoroughfares intersected. By taking this position, however, the caucus opened itself up to the charge that they were unprepared to negotiate in good faith, and that their real intention was to eliminate the flag entirely. The state chapter of the NAACP was also less than enthusiastic, saying merely that it would reserve judgment for the time being. The Reverend Jesse Jackson chimed in as well. Saying "a half-truth is still a whole lie," Jackson also failed to lend his undiluted support to the idea.[106]

Most ominous, however, was the bleak and baneful reaction from within the governor's own party. Senator Ravenel, who had been Beasley's challenger in the GOP gubernatorial primary back in 1994, was mistrustful and skeptical of the governor's proposal. The flag opponents "won't be satisfied with moving the flag," he fretted. "The next thing we know they'll be screaming and hollering for removal of the monuments. They aren't interested in compromise. They want all vestiges of [the Confederate] era done away with." Senator McConnell said that he could not support an effort to remove the flag. "It's a cosmetic solution to the [real] problem we have, which is intolerance of other peoples' views."[107]

In an unusual move, several pro-flag lawmakers requested airtime to offer a rebuttal to the governor's address. Although Beasley was well aware of the resistance to his plan within his party, he was genuinely surprised when his fellow Republican, State Attorney General Charlie Condon, decided to offer the pro-flag response, to air immediately following the governor's comments.

Condon began his remarks by reminding the audience of Beasley's promise, as a candidate, not to seek to remove the flag. Now, Condon said, Beasley was giving in to the "drum beat of discontent" sounded by the media and others who were "driving a wedge of division" and creating an "atmosphere of malice" in the state. Condon professed surprise that the governor would make the Confederate flag the subject of his first statewide address: "It is a distraction from more important matters," he said. "I would rather hear the governor's proposals on education, on welfare reform, or on tax relief." But "if the question of whether the Confederate flag should continue flying atop the State House cannot be avoided," he continued, "then let the voters decide in a simple referendum. Let's measure the will of the majority and then move on." As for the substantive issues affecting race relations, Condon said he would rather place his priorities elsewhere: on fighting violent crime, for example, or on fighting church burnings and other hate crimes. Declaring the Confederate flag innocent of the crimes some had blamed on it, he then asked, "Would we rather take down the flag or take down the hate groups?"

Picking up on the semiotic struggle at the core of the flag debate, Condon said that the nub of the matter was a conflict over meaning.

> The root issue of the controversy is not where the Confederate flag flies. The issue is what the flag stands for. If that flag is a symbol of honor, as the governor and I agree that it is, then there should be no controversy. On the other hand, if it is a symbol of racism and hate, then it shouldn't be flying at all, at any place or any time.

After reminding South Carolinians of the sacrifices and suffering born by their ancestors and by their state during the Civil War (which he preferred to call "The War Between the States"), he then said that state residents should ask themselves this question:

> . . . what is the message of our past? Are we to regard our state's heritage as essentially good and decent? Or shall we agree with the extremist groups who define the flag as a symbol of hate?

For him, removing the flag would be exactly the wrong thing to do. "In my judgment," he said,

> moving the flag would be a victory for the extremist groups. They would immediately start planning their next crisis, their next outrage, their next demand. That's what they do. Controversy is their business. It is not possible to appease the merchants of hate. And it is a mistake to even try.

By "extremists," Condon did not mean the Klan but rather the NAACP and other elements of the so-called politically correct cultural left in America. To illustrate why it would be a mistake, he then described a series of precedents that demonstrated, he believed, "what happens when we, as a society, compromise our principles." The list was mainly neo-Conservative—and neo-Confederate. Those offended by expressions of religious belief in the classroom, he said, had eliminated our children's ability to pray in school. Those offended by the all-male tradition at the Citadel, he went on, had eliminated single-gender education across the country. By the same token, attempting to appease those who take offense at the display of the Confederate flag by removing it from the dome would not put a stop to the controversy. Quite the contrary:

> In no time at all, the same people who now criticize the Confederate flag on the dome will attack its location at the monument. And before long our history will be rewritten.

As a result,

> The children of South Carolina will be taught, in the name of political correctness, to be ashamed of their state's history.

So the conclusion was clear:

> It is never wise to sacrifice the truth in the name of political expediency.[108]

Condon drew a portrait of the opposition as an insatiable behemoth, which would be satisfied with nothing less than the eradication of all reminders of Confederate heritage in its drive to level society's historically derived distinctions and to erase cultural memory.

Senator McConnell, who joined Condon in counterattacking the Beasley offensive, picked up on the theme of appeasement and offered an even starker parallel from history:

> Our governor tonight has asked you to give all to those who will give you nothing. It reminds me of a man, Neville Chamberlain, who traveled . . . to Munich, Germany, with the best of intentions and made peace with militants. They told him the words he wanted to hear, and he surrendered a heritage, thinking he had guaranteed peace in his own time—only to find out that the eventual outcome was conflict on all fronts.

And as if that was not already sufficient to make his point, the senator went on to add his infamous suggestion that the governor's proposal was, in effect, part of a campaign of "cultural genocide" directed against southern heritage.[109]

Looking back on it several years later (but prior to the 2000 compromise settlement), McConnell stuck by his analogy. "I got some criticism for what I said about the governor, comparing him to Neville Chamberlain. He went to a conference and gave away everything and got nothin.' I mean, what *did* he get? He got *nothin'*! The NAACP did not give one inch. They weren't willing to settle for the flag being on the grounds. He got nothin.' And I talked to the governor before he announced his plan. And I warned him. I said, you biddin' against yourself. I've been down that road. And I told him: There's no lesson in the second kick of the mule. I got hit one time—and I'm not gonna get burned again."

"I was disappointed when all these public officials jumped on the bandwagon," McConnell went on, "because some of them *used* that flag to get elected—and then got out there and wanted to move it. But my greatest disappointment was that they said they wanted to give [the flag] definition—and that by moving it, they would give the flag definition. My response to them was: The flag has already been defined. It was defined by the people who carried it. It was defined by widows who sat beside the graves and buried their husbands and watched their children cry for their fathers. That flag was given definition *long* ago. It wasn't gonna be given definition by a group of politicians trying to make it appear they were doing something noble and good for the state. What the governor did hurt the Republican Party, because flag supporters don't trust those leaders anymore. They felt like he had lied to them and deserted them. And ultimately it led to David Beasley's defeat." McConnell himself would feel the same onus of distrust descend on him after he embraced the compromise that moved the flag from the dome in 2000.

McConnell aimed to forge a subtly crafted consensus using the hard-edged tools of political maneuver. "My strategy," he said, "is to build up the wall, to hold the line and make it clear that they cannot win, that it's not beneficial to the state for either side to achieve a political knockout, because that will not resolve the ongoing conflict. Moving the flag wouldn't have resolved anything, because ultimately what's gotta be resolved is not the presence of the flag at the dome, but the coexistence of the flag with modern society."

Whatever subtle coexistence McConnell may have sought to achieve, however, was drowned out in the political wrangling that ensued in the wake of the governor's address. Though Beasley, too, wanted to reach a compromise, for him that meant reaching a resolution while the atmosphere was still productive to settlement—while the state was under no immediate threat of boycott.

Beasley's initiative was as good as dead even before it was fully born. But it would be a while yet before its demise could be officially certified. Many state lawmakers had dropped down to periscope depth, cruising around as quietly as possible, popping up here and there like so many little *Hunleys* in Charleston Harbor. Some were on the prowl for political prey, but most were just lying low, waiting for the threat to pass while seeking out the nearest safe harbor.

Pro-flag ironclads in the House of Representatives fired off their warning salvo during an organizational meeting in early December, just a few days after the Beasley address. Pro-flag forces were especially eager to flush out wavering GOP lawmakers, because of the GOP's controlling majority in the house. Any member who voiced even the slightest willingness to consider the governor's compromise was immediately targeted. The losses incurred during this brief encounter included one candidate for a leadership post sunk, one damaged, and another badly frightened. But it wasn't only wavering Republicans who felt themselves under the gun. Democrats felt the pressure, too—especially those representing mainly rural or predominantly white districts. The threat of a primary or even general-election challenge made all the sitting members, regardless of party, think twice about openly endorsing the Beasley plan. Even though they possessed the advantage of incumbency, the additional campaign expense involved in fending off such potential challenges served to dissuade them from stepping too far out of line (or ahead of public opinion). According to the political cost-benefit analyses of electoral politics, the risk associated with taking a stand on such a relatively "minor" matter as the flag simply did not seem worth it.[110]

Most legislators would have preferred that the issue just go away—and eagerly sought to shift the burden of responsibility onto other shoulders. Republicans said it all depended on what the Legislative Black Caucus decided to do. The caucus said the Republicans had to get their folks behind the plan first. Others said that it was up to House Speaker David Wilkins, an Upstate Republican, that he needed to get out in front and work for the proposal. Wilkins, for his part, alighted atop the proverbial political fence, peered out at the Legislative Black Caucus on one side and at the Republican Caucus on the other, and proclaimed that he did not want to see the legislature get bogged down on a single issue like this. senate leaders, meanwhile, leaned back in their seats and said they felt something surely could be worked out—just so long as the house managed to get a plan through first, of course.

The prospects for the governor's proposal were not altogether gloomy, however. In fact, outside the halls of the state legislature, things were not looking all that bad. Business leaders in the state backed the plan. So, too, did many current and former state officials. And according to a new statewide poll, 48 percent of the state's voters also supported the Beasley plan, with 41 percent opposed—a near-even split of opinion in the state. The percentage of blacks who wanted to see the flag removed had gone up from 63 percent two years earlier to 79 percent in late 1996, while white support for the flag had dropped from 67 percent to 53 percent. More than half of those polled still saw the flag as a symbol of heritage, however—only a third felt it represented racism.[111]

The Beasley initiative also enjoyed broad support from the state's religious communities. Hundreds of pastors and other church leaders, representing both black and white congregations, proclaimed their support in resolutions and at conferences held across the state. They also helped organize events such as the "Circle of Love," when pastors from all parts of the state joined hands to form a ring around the State House early in the 1997 session. In a state as religiously conservative as South Carolina, having the backing of Christian groups—and, in particular, of conservative Christians—was exceedingly important, even for an openly religious, self-professed born-again Baptist like David Beasley. Gaining the endorsement of evangelical and fundamentalist churchmen was essential in order to pressure conservative Republicans (many from the intensely religious Upstate) into supporting the governor. Many conservative Christians did join the governor. But others remained silent, or were too divided over the issue to take a firm stand. And a few of the conservative cloth openly opposed the plan, while criticizing their fellow clergymen for approving the governor's scheme. Working in cooperation with *Southern Partisan* magazine, a group of fifteen pro-flag ministers issued a manifesto titled "A Moral Defense of the Confederate Flag." In it, they described the Confederate flag as "a Christian symbol" (because it incorporated the St. Andrew Cross) and praised the Christian character of many Confederate leaders. The Civil War was, for them, the culture war of the nineteenth century, pitting northern humanistic materialism and scientific modernism against a southern society based on faith and rooted in biblical truth. Similarly, contemporary "political correctness" represented for them "a path that leads to the betrayal of truth" because it asks us to deny our past, spurn our ancestors as "evil," and reverse the flag's true meaning. And since "truth is a supreme virtue derived from God," they went on, "any reconciliation based on conceding a lie [such as that embodied by the Beasley plan] is . . . sinful and immoral." Most clergymen, however, saw the flag as a hindrance to racial reconciliation and a jab at the southern tradition of good neighborliness.[112]

In late December, just in time for the holidays, the Legislative Black Caucus gave the governor a big Christmas present by declaring their support for his flag proposal. The caucus had remained lukewarm about the idea for almost a month. Many of its members were reluctant to see the flag moved to so prominent a location as the Confederate Soldiers Monument, preferring to see it retired to one of the display cases in the Confederate Relic Room instead.[113] Eliminating the flag from the State House grounds entirely was not something the heritage defenders were prepared to accept, however. And demands that it be eliminated or removed to a museum would have played into claims that blacks were out to erase Confederate heritage from public view. Besides, heritage enthusiasts pointed out, the flags displayed in the Relic Room were one-of-a-kind, authentic Civil

War battle banners, borne by Confederate soldiers in the field. By contrast, the flag over the dome was merely a mass-produced contemporary copy. There was nothing special about it that would warrant placing it in a museum. Its value was merely symbolic—and would be voided upon its removal from the dome.

Legislative Black Caucus support was one of the essentials; it brought the governor's plan closer to passage. But close only counts in horseshoes, as they say, and important elements were still missing from the mix—such as an endorsement by House Speaker Wilkins, for example. And even if all the essentials had been in place, it is by no means certain that they would have proven sufficient to see the plan through. So, without a consensus among state leaders, South Carolina did what it always does under such circumstances: it went on autopilot. The status quo prevailed, and the flag stayed up. The pro-flag forces were still successfully employing ol' Marse Robert's strategy of Confederate defense: wear your opponent down and hope he eventually gives up.

"Keep the Flag—Dump Beasley" was now the rallying cry on the lips of heritage defenders everywhere. The slogan cropped up on bumpers all over the state (and not just on pickup trucks), propagating like pokeweed. Groups such as the "Dixie Defenders," the "League of the South," the "Heritage Preservation Association," and the "South Carolina Heritage Coalition" sent out letters, sponsored ads, joined in on radio talk shows, and staged demonstrations for the flag around the state. Some called for legislation to lower the U.S. flag from the dome, while others wanted to see the battle flag incorporated into the state flag itself. In mid-January 1997, the Council of Conservative Citizens gathered in Columbia, just as they did every year, to greet state lawmakers returning for the opening of the new legislative session. This time the council had brought along their own special calling card. Hoisted on a crane hung what event organizers claimed was the world's largest Confederate flag, a monstrous fifty-by-eighty-foot statement of southern heritage. Large enough to have encased the State House in a Cristo-like Confederate caftan, the giant flag proved too unwieldy for its handlers, however. When cold winter winds caused it to drift into passing traffic, officials declared the flag a threat to public safety, and the behemoth was unceremoniously removed from the scene.[114]

Though returning state lawmakers ranked the Confederate flag issue far down the list of state priorities (twenty-sixth out of thirty-two items surveyed), one would have had a hard time proving it given the attention lavished on the matter during the first month of the new session. As the legislature set to work on the new year's business, including several matters possessing a clearly racial tinge, the flag referendum idea resurfaced in multiple variations in the ever-fractious house. Speaker Wilkins was said to be leaning in favor of a referendum himself. But the Beasley plan was nowhere to be found. The Heritage Act was an orphan left standing in a steady rain of referenda bills. No sponsor could be found to introduce the governor's proposal to the legislature. Not that it lacked verbal support. Straw polls showed that the Heritage Act had the backing of forty-two house members. But that was still considerably short of the sixty-three needed for passage.[115]

The math was clear. And as if to leave no doubt of their intentions to bury the Beasley plan, 72 of the 124 house members signed on as cosponsors to a bill calling for a binding referendum to decide the flag's fate. Many of these were dyed-in-the-wool flag backers, of course. Others, realizing the Heritage Act had no chance on its own, may have been hoping that the referendum bill could be amended later to incorporate some aspects of the act. They believed that, in an up-or-down referendum, voters would balk at the idea of removing the flag altogether and the state would then be right back where it started. Including an option such as the Heritage Act, some thought, would make the flag's removal from the dome easier to swallow. In any event, some observers of the mounting referendum frenzy could not help but note the irony of a legislature "passing the buck" to the voters after only just passing a bill (in 1995) granting themselves sole authority to remove the flag.[116]

The House of Representatives was hurtling down a track of its own, picking up momentum as it went. The same day that the house moved on the referendum bill, Governor Beasley made one last major effort to save the Heritage Act. Devoting the final fifth of his State of the State address to the issue, Beasley quoted Joseph Conrad's *Lord Jim*, the Bible, and even John C. Calhoun, before declaring the Heritage Act "a reasonable and honorable venture to protect our roots . . . while justly serving the good of all people." But it was no use. The house would have none of it. Beasley could stand by the side of the tracks and wave his little signal flag all he wanted, the House of Representatives charged ahead with its referendum plan in tow.[117]

The governor then switched tactics and began signaling that he was prepared to jump aboard—if the legislature would only add the provisions of the Heritage Act to its referendum bill. But the house did not need his support. They had all the votes they needed to pass their own plan and proved it by summarily rejecting a proposal to add the Heritage Act option to the proposed referendum (by a vote of 74 to 40). Then, in a vote of 85 to 32, they approved the referendum bill itself. Ironically, almost all the house Democrats voted to include the governor's proposal, but only three of the governor's fellow Republicans did. The referendum, according to the bill, would be held in a special election in the fall of the year, prompting fears of skewed results owning to its stand-alone character.[118] Most analysts believed that an off-year election would only bring out those most passionately devoted to a cause. And since the flag defenders were more passionate than the anti-flag lobby, many felt they would have the clear advantage in such a special-election referendum. In late January, the house authorized final passage of the bill, then sent it on to the senate for consideration.

As it left the house, the referendum plan seemed almost unstoppable. But like a ghost train, it simply rushed past, plunged into the fog, and was gone. It had not flown off the tracks. It had simply fulfilled its purpose—which was to derail the governor's initiative—and was no longer needed. The senate, for its part, was no more interested in passing a referendum bill than the house had been in passing the Heritage Act. Senate Majority Leader John Land declared his opposition to any referendum scheme—and that was the end of that. The house-passed bill was banished to committee to die of neglect.[119]

Beasley's decision to throw in the towel on the Heritage Act coincided with Charleston mayor (and declared flag opponent) Joe Riley's announcement that he would not be running for the Democratic nomination for governor—prompting some Beasley critics to conclude that the governor's initiative had merely been a ploy to help forestall a Riley challenge. Others criticized Beasley for failing to consult with state representatives before launching his bring-down-the-flag campaign and chided him for his attempt to pressure them through a political action committee rather than by direct persuasion. Some said his arguments had been badly formulated, that he should have avoided every implication that the flag was a racist symbol. Others said he had just failed to work hard enough to bring pro-flag lawmakers around to his point of view. Whatever the case, Beasley's lost cause hurt him politically, both within the Republican Party and with voters across the state. Although some credited him with courage in taking a stand, many criticized him for changing his position on the flag. The switch contributed to the perception that Beasley was as unfaithful a politician as any other and helped undermine his support among party regulars. Although the episode was not decisive in bringing about his defeat in the 1998 election (as pro-flag groups like to claim), it was nevertheless "a major contributing factor," as Beasley himself admits.[120]

Looking back on the episode later, Beasley could not see what McConnell had hoped to gain by holding out at the dome—and he is somewhat bitter about what happened with his own effort to resolve the flag debate in 1996. "Now Glenn *wants* the Heritage Act," Beasley observed in 2000 (shortly before passage of the final flag compromise). "What is he getting in return? *Nothin'*—'cept a couple years of embarrassment! Those people who stick their heads in the sand and think they're defending something, they're fooling themselves. Those who played politics with this issue [folks like McConnell and Condon, Beasley says] didn't think with enough depth and foresight to realize the consequences of not [removing the flag]. In fact, now our heritage is being tarnished, because we're not willing to be politically smart and sensitive about this issue. Whether the flag flies on the dome or on the grounds is a *foolish* argument. Saying that one protects heritage where the other does not—that's *silliness,* and anybody who thinks that way is *silly.*"

The battle flag thundercloud moved on without dropping even a trace of soothing rain on parched Carolina's political landscape. There were still a few distant rumblings to be heard; more talk about a circle of flags; and a brief flap over a Confederate memorial in a small Lowcountry town. Senator McConnell once again called on black leadership to end their attacks on Confederate heritage as a precondition for compromise negotiations. But state NAACP officials and black political leaders said it was absurd to ask blacks to change their opinion about the Confederate flag. It would be like blotting out history and pretending that slavery never existed, one said.[121]

The season's skirmishing over Confederate symbols petered out in a spat over car tags. The bruises and sore feelings left by the flag fight erupted briefly during discussion of a bill introduced by Representative Dan Cooper authorizing special vanity license plates for members of the Sons of Confederate Veterans (which would, of course, bear the rebel flag). One black lawmaker said the bill seemed aimed at rubbing their noses in their recent defeat and accused the bill's supporters of using the measure to try and settle the flag issue once and for all. A flag defender sprang to the podium and said that the matter had *already* been settled—and in order to eliminate any confusion about the outcome, added: "We *beat* your side!" Another pro-flag representative felt that resistance to the car-tag bill proved that flag opponents were out to destroy all vestiges of the Confederate past. Representative Becky Meacham reminded her black colleagues that the house had only recently commissioned new portraits of two of the state's black Reconstruction-era house speakers, and that it had also approved the construction of the African-American History Monument. "We have given and we have given," Meacham said. "Why can't you? When we want to honor our heritage, it's wrong. When you want to honor African-Americans, it's right." The flag-tag bill passed by a comfortable margin, 71 to 30.[122]

The ill-will created by the flag fight had caused tired old racial biases to ooze up to the surface once again. Back in late January, during debate over the house referendum bill, Representative John Graham Altman of Charleston set off a storm of protest when he told black representatives that they should "quit looking at symbols" and focus instead on things that mattered. "Get out and get a job," Altman insisted. "Quit shooting each other. Quit having illegitimate babies." Comments like Altman's enraged Reverend Darby. "I think there's a lot of shrill whining coming from the other side," Darby said. "Like when they tell us that we should worry about teen pregnancy and illiteracy. Those are not just *black* problems—

those are *societal* problems," and need to be dealt with as such. Moreover, he points out, dealing with one problem does not mean that we cannot also address others at the same time. "Those folks who think that black folk can't do but one thing at a time need to pull their heads out of their rear-ends and understand that we can fight the flag battle, pastor churches, go to work, raise families, address illiteracy, address violence, and do all these other things that need to be done, because we're just as ambidextrous as anybody else."

Passions calmed again somewhat once the car-tag legislation reached the senate. With talk of a compromise once again wafting through the sweltering halls of the legislature, black senate leaders agreed not to attack the vanity-tag bill, permitting it to pass without additional debate. Their acquiescence was meant as a show of good faith to wary flag supporters. But there were some, like Senator Kay Patterson, who were nevertheless disappointed to see the body act on an issue such as this, while failing to act on the broader question about what to do with the flag on the dome. "I ain't going to go along with you leaving me and the preacher standing at the altar," Patterson exclaimed, "and you run out of the church with your Confederate car tags! Don't do me like that! Let's get married!"[123]

Senator Darrell Jackson had been one of the driving forces behind the moderate tone taken in the senate. In remarks to his fellow senators, he tried to soothe frayed nerves by once again pointing out that it was not the Confederate flag as such that was the problem, but rather its presence over the dome of state government. Senator McConnell found Jackson's comments helpful. "Intolerance is what creates the . . . suspicion . . . that if you remove the flag, it will be attacked [elsewhere] in the future," McConnell said. Jackson's "comments may bring about a mutual understanding and respect that could open things up down the road."[124]

A sign of the kind of mutual respect the senator sought came just a few days later, when the senate passed two heritage-related bills. One protected all Confederate and civil-rights monuments and street names in the state, while the other made state holidays of Martin Luther King Jr.'s birthday and Confederate Memorial Day (deleting George Washington's birthday and Election Day in exchange). Although both measures quickly mired up in the quicksands of the House of Representatives and died at the end of the legislative session, both would become essential components in the overall compromise that finally ended the debate over two years later.[125]

A final solution to the state's Confederate flag quandary lay somewhere "down the road," McConnell had said—along a course set by mutual respect and tolerance. But old-time intolerance reared its ugly head again toward the end of the year when a black teenager was shot and wounded by a white flag supporter after the boy tried to tear down a "Keep the Flag—Dump Beasley" sign in the man's front yard.[126]

It could have been any number of reasons that sparked a shooting like this: a dispute over money, or a woman, or just plain drunken anger. The South was still a trigger-happy place. But in South Carolina in the latter half of the last decade of the twentieth century, a boy had been shot because of emotions inflamed by a flag—and by the mutually exclusive readings of history associated with that flag. If nothing else, the shooting revealed just how rough the road to reconciliation and resolution could be.

Six

OLD TIMES THERE ARE NOT FORGOTTEN

> *It matters little now, Lorena,*
> *The past is in the eternal past.*
> . . . .
> *There is a future, O Thank God!*
>
> *The Secession of the South will be almost as*
> *historical as the Revolution someday, maybe.*
>
> T. S. Stribling, The Forge *(1931)*

The past has a peculiar way of bonding with imagination, even (and perhaps especially) when it is no longer part of living memory. In a country such as America, impatiently pushing into the future, where history supposedly is of so little interest, the past somehow keeps a remarkable grip on our minds and emotions. The convergence of the past with contemporary affairs occasionally has made for a volatile political mix—the very thing most southerners were habituated to avoid. In late January 1997, amid the heat of battle swirling around the Confederate flag, one South Carolina teacher described her reluctance to deal with the history behind the flag: "[The Confederate flag] is such a hot current-events topic," she said, "that a teacher in the classroom would have to be very careful in how they deal with it, *because it's not history yet*" [emphasis added].[1]

Amazingly, even more than a 130 years after the Civil War ended, a symbol of that war was still thought too controversial to discuss in a public classroom. Rather than using the debate as a starting point for a general exploration of the conflict that gave birth to the flag—its causes and their persisting relevance as expressed through the controversies surrounding Confederate symbols today—most shied away from the subject. Instead of putting the debate to productive use as a means of sparking serious public discussion, most teachers and other academics steered a wide berth around it. The flag fight was dismissed as a waste of time, scoffed at as the sort of issue worthy only of yahoos and politicians. But while most folks professed a weariness with the whole affair—"flag fatigue," it was called—it was clear that South Carolina had largely neglected to properly cogitate the history behind the Confederate flag. It was not until late 1999—just prior to the final resolution of the flag dispute—that academics and news media finally began to give serious and just attention to some of the history that lay tucked away behind the flag flap. Until then, the state slumped sullenly in its seat, waiting with a kind of dull disdain for the next round of fighting to begin. The Civil War itself had only lasted *half* so long as this!, some no doubt thought.

By late 1997, the state's political leadership was sapped out. For Governor Beasley, the flag matter was a dead issue. "The flag is staying. It's not going any-where. The governor considers that the end of the story," his spokesman declared flatly.[2] But what appeared at first a rout was actually only a stalemate. The pro-flag forces still held the same ground they had before the battle began, but their adversaries had not been dispersed, let alone destroyed. The flag foes had merely withdrawn into their trenches to regroup, consult on tactics, and assemble their forces for the next assault. Both sides had suffered casualties, but the pro-flag contingent was suffering more from the attrition of battle than were their oppo-nents. Like Grant losing every battle but forging stubbornly ahead, the army of flag opponents simply refused to go away. And while their army continued to grow, as more and more new recruits joined up over the course of the protracted campaign, pro-flag support, though consistently loud and very active, was slowly dwindling and would continue to weaken over the following two years. The essentially defensive strategy that had successfully kept the flag in place was beginning to crumble. And it began to look as if the best course to take might be an orderly retreat.

For some of those leading the pro-flag operations—especially those in the legislature—the main effort now shifted away from keeping the flag over the dome at all costs toward seeing to it that its removal be done in such a way that would ensure the flag's continued presence on the grounds of the State House— and that its display there be given a "proper" interpretation (which the pro-flag contingent were more than willing to supply). In this semiotic battlefield, the location of the flag was loaded with meaning, distinct but not altogether sepa-rate from the meanings implied in the flag itself. McConnell, Condon, and the other soldiers of the semiotic liberation army sought to erect a syntactical defen-sive ring around the Confederate banner that would repel the sort of negative associations the flag's foes wished to attach to it. Flag defenders hoped that the meanings they associated with the flag would prevail once the anti-flag forces withdrew their siege and ended their campaign against the flag. Only then, they believed, could the flag survive the move from the dome with its "honor" (and meaning) intact.

Attempts to recalibrate the meanings applied to the Confederate flag have been wide-ranging and sometimes acrobatic. Thousands of Union soldiers had seen in it a symbol of perfidious and damnable treason. But for others, like

George Wallace, it came to represent nothing less than the purest American patriotism. Speaking in 1966, Wallace went at the matter head on:

> They tell you we're traitors. They tell you we're wrong to fly this flag. [But] whenever you see the Confederate flag flying, you will see people who will fight for their country with more zeal than anywhere else. [Where you] find this flag, you won't find college students taking up money for the Vietcong . . . or burning draft cards.[3]

Observing the flag fight in 1997, one letter-to-the-editor writer took a different tack, arguing that blacks should actually oppose the removal of the Confederate flag from public places. "Not only did the Confederate flag represent all of the free population," he wrote, "it also represented the struggle of the slaves . . . all the hard physical labor, beatings, bloodshed, torture, heartbreaks, separations, abuse, killings, hangings, and other mistreatments. . . ." Another writer agreed, adding: ". . . the Confederate flag not only represents the oppression of blacks. Because of black perseverance, it now represents their own progress through slavery and civil rights."[4] In short, because it was part of their history, too, blacks should embrace the Confederate flag rather than disdain it.

To a degree, both Wallace and these flag-friendly letter-writers were correct: The South did tend to be more patriotic; it did send more of its sons off to serve in the country's armed forces than other parts of the country. And yes, there were good reasons not to eliminate the symbols that remind us of our collective past, regardless of how we may choose to interpret them. On the other hand, post–Civil War southern patriotism could not obliterate the South's Civil War rebellion. Nor could the banner that served more than any other to represent the South's struggle to maintain a "way of life" based on slavery and racial segregation be transmogrified to serve as a symbol of the historical struggle of *all* southerners— both white and black. Certain historical divides cannot be bridged with such facility.

In any event, attacks on the flag and other Confederate icons continued. And though flag defenders appeared ready to hold out indefinitely, chances seemed slim that the siege of Fort Battleflag would be lifted any time soon. Skirmishing around the edges of the issue replaced open warfare for a time between 1997 and 1999 as both sides settled in for the long haul. Senator Ford was back again, searching for cosponsors on a bill to fly the Black Liberation flag over the dome and in both chambers of the State House.[5] Meanwhile, the other legislative proposal that refused to die—the referendum idea—resurfaced as well. The senate passed an amendment to the state budget bill (with the bulk of support coming from anti-Beasley Republicans as well as Democrats) that would have inserted a nonbinding referendum into the fall 1998 ballot asking voters whether or not the flag should continue to fly. Seeing the move as a blatantly political act by the Democratic-controlled senate aimed solely at embarrassing the governor, House Speaker Wilkins declared that the bill would "get the attention [it] deserves—which is zero."[6]

Battles on the cultural front continued unabated. The white principal of a high school in the Lowcountry town of Allendale was forced to resign after he suspended the black student body president for leading students in the black national anthem (the Baptist hymn, "Lift Every Voice and Sing") during an assembly held as part of Black History Month.[7] And in the Upstate, a high-school history teacher, Winston McCuen, sued his former employer, a private school associated with the Catholic Church, for wrongful termination resulting from his display of a small rebel flag. School officials had asked McCuen to remove the flag from his classroom after several parents voiced objections to the emblem. McCuen refused, saying that he used the flag as a teaching aid. When school administrators removed the flag themselves, McCuen responded by refusing to recite the Pledge of Allegiance during morning assembly and was fired. The school had offered to permit him to replace "one nation under God, indivisible" with "divisible," during the Pledge recitation, but McCuen rejected the offer. The judge hearing the McCuen case was somewhat taken aback that a teacher should be afforded any concessions at all: "If we start that," the judge asked incredulously, "what's the next step? Changing the words to the 'Star Spangled Banner,' changing the colors of the flag, or changing other things that represent our national image?" The case was later settled out of court.[8]

In the fall 1998 elections, Governor Beasley was defeated in his reelection bid by House Minority Leader Jim Hodges—returning a Democrat to the governor's mansion for the first time in twelve years and marking the first time an incumbent governor had been thrown out of office since 1886. The Confederate flag played only a subordinate role in Beasley's defeat—though the public's perception that he had invested a great deal of effort to so little effect may have hurt him at the polls. The question of whether or not to create a state lottery; of what to do about video poker; and concerns about public education aroused far greater interest among most South Carolina voters than did the Confederate flag. But Beasley's actions in the Heritage Act debate had revealed and deepened the discord that existed between the governor and parts of his own party, costing him Republican support. Above all it was the large turnout by black voters that ensured Hodges's narrow election victory. Despite the lack of a national race to draw voter interest, roughly 24 percent of those who went to the polls were black—about one hundred thousand more than had voted in the 1994 election. Ninety-two percent of them voted for Hodges. In spite of the change in state chief executive, however, the remainder of state government held to the status quo. Charlie Condon (in a contest with Tom Turnipseed) was reelected attorney general. The House of Representatives kept its Republican majority. And the Democrats held onto their narrow margin in the senate.[9]

In large measure, Hodges owed his victory to blacks—and black leadership was quick to underscore the point. In December, two hundred black church leaders, attending a conference of the Congress of National Black Churches being held in Columbia, marched to the State House to demand the removal of the Confederate flag. AME Bishop John Hurst Adams reminded the governor-elect, and everyone else in the state, that the "black community will not let the issue die."[10]

But in a state as fundamentally conservative and as increasingly Republican as South Carolina, the new governor also knew that he had to tread a fine line in order to keep his fragile electoral coalition from disintegrating. With regard to the Confederate flag, that meant pursuing a largely hands-off approach to the issue, avoiding as best as possible getting caught in the middle between the warring factions. Less than a month after his inaugural, it emerged that prior to the election Hodges had met privately with members of the Council of Conservative Citizens and the Sons of Confederate Veterans. He had ensured them that, if elected, he would not launch any campaigns to bring the flag down—but he also told them that he would approve any compromise plan that happened to work its way through the legislature.[11]

It quickly became apparent, however, that Hodges' hands-off strategy was not going to last. Black leaders in the state—and the state NAACP in particular— were not prepared to let him, or the state, rest easy for long. Facing an inactive, obstinate, and hamstrung legislature, stymied in the courts, and disappointed by both the governor's timid lack of interest and the public's generally lackadaisical attitude on the matter, some of the state's black leaders were ready to turn again to direct action. The idea of a boycott against the state's tourist trade, which had been sitting on a back burner since the abortive attempt in 1994, was now moved back up to the front.

"Green is the universal language," Reverend Joseph Darby observes pointedly. From his perspective, speaking in late 1999, the lessons of recent experience were clear. "The fact is, from 1994 until now, there has been zero movement on removing the flag. In South Carolina, if we took a purely political approach to trying to lower the flag, I don't think it could be done—because most of those who are in political control are conservative and Confederate. They live in districts where the electorate mirrors their thoughts, and so they don't have the political incentive to lower it. *But,* they do get contributions from folks who do business in South Carolina. And so, when you affect business, you affect [a politician's] . . . agreeability."

Senator Maggie Glover was in full agreement. "I believe that, in America, the only way to get [anyone's] attention is [through] money. That's the instrument that moves everything in America. The flag is no different. We were not getting anywhere," she recalled, "because the [other side] was not listening. For us to get something going statewide on the flag, we were going to have to aim at South Carolina's pocketbook. South Carolina needed to realize that she was losing money because of that flag. Then businesses—those white folks who were hit in their pocketbooks—would force the structures of this state to deal with the Confederate flag. Until we get that kind of pressure, we can talk until we're black and blue, but that flag will remain where it is."

Even so, blacks did not march together as one as they began their latest assault. Many were still skeptical that a boycott would work and reluctant to take the steps to initiate it. The mule hauling the carload of economic sanctions needed a swift smack on its hind parts to get things rolling. The folks holding the reins could bring things under control as it rolled along. History is often made spontaneously, without careful planning aforethought. And the NAACP resolution calling for sanctions against South Carolina came about as much by happenstance as by direction.

Glover recalls how it all came together. "It was not something we'd *planned out* ahead of time. In other words, unlike many other resolutions, this one had not come out of the state office, to be introduced and voted on at the national level. Prior to our trip to the [NAACP's] national convention [in July 1999], there had been no discussion at the state level about an economic boycott. So when the convention met, former Representative Enis Fant, from Greenville, wrote out [a resolution] in longhand, calling for a boycott. It was introduced from the floor—meaning, it hadn't gone through the resolution committee and all that. CNN carried the conference, as it always had done. And I honestly believe that if it had not been televised, there would have been a lot more debate among the different chapters and states about the Confederate flag and this boycott. But because it was televised, we simply could not allow America to see the National Association for the Advancement of Colored People waffle on the Confederate flag. So, without even any discussion, the resolution passed. And by passing it . . . well, like always, the media picked up on it and it was gone. Before the national organization ever had a chance to answer questions for itself, on what, when, where, and how, it was already out there. That's why you had some disorganization over the boycott at the beginning."

The resolution was issued in July and the NAACP's national board officially endorsed the action in October 1999. By then, the boycott had already taken on a life of its own. Black groups embraced the boycott with such enthusiasm that the national organization of the NAACP was, as Glover put it, "in awe." According to the resolution, sanctions were not supposed to take effect until 1 January 2000. But so many black organizations pulled their meetings and events out of South Carolina in late 1999 that the state had already suffered some $43 million in actual or prospective tourism losses by the time the boycott plan was officially approved.[12]

Church groups, lawyers' organizations, black academic institutions, cultural festivals, the Urban League, and the Southern Christian Leadership Council—all had withdrawn plans for events in South Carolina by late fall 1999. Sanctions were so popular that their scope began expanding even before they officially took effect. The original resolution had merely called on blacks planning family reunions in South Carolina (the host of many such events) to consider holding their gatherings elsewhere—and had asked black businesses, churches, and other organizations to conduct their meetings and conventions outside the state. But as soon as these sanctions were officially ratified, South Carolina's state NAACP chapter, under James Gallman, let it be known that it was considering plans for expanded sanctions, including targeting products manufactured by large corporations in the state (such as Michelin, BMW, and General Electric).

In the coming months, other prongs of attack would be added. Black athletes were urged not to attend South Carolina colleges and universities; out-of-state sponsors were asked to cancel their support of events scheduled in the state; and blacks in the state were encouraged to celebrate "spiritual holidays" by not purchasing gifts and other items on major holidays.[13] The NAACP also gathered financial information (available in the public record) on pro-flag state lawmakers, in particular their sources of corporate campaign contributions, implying they were ready to increase the pressure on lawmakers by attacking their sources of funding.[14] They also reminded legislators (lest it slip their minds) that they wanted to see the flags removed from inside the legislative chambers as well. Some black leaders announced plans to place anti-flag ads in black publications—as well as erect billboards (in Columbia and at state borders)—that portrayed a hooded Klansman standing in front of the State House, with Confederate flags in the background. Senator Darrell Jackson helped raise money for the ads and was unapologetic about the inflammatory effect they might have. "It's bad for South Carolina, because this is what the nation will see," he said.[15] By late fall, eighty-five groups and organizations had announced plans to cancel meetings and conventions originally scheduled to be held in the state.[16]

In actual dollar amounts, the economic impact of the NAACP's sanctions was comparatively minor, given South Carolina's multibillion-dollar tourism industry. The head of the state's Department of Parks and Tourism described it as a "kick in the shins," not a body blow.[17] More important than the campaign's direct effect, however, was the intensified media focus that accompanied the boycott campaign. The nation's attention focused on South Carolina to an almost unprecedented degree. And what the country saw left it alternately amused and dismayed. Entertainers such as Chris Rock and Jay Leno had a field day cracking jokes at the state's expense. Journalists from across the country, and around the world, came down South to see if they could find a reasonable explanation for all the brouhaha. They found only partial answers at best. Jackson was right, though: The impressions left in the country's mind were not good for the state's image. The question was: How much did South Carolina care?

The NAACP and South Carolina's black leadership had undertaken a risky strategy by unleashing an economic boycott. The state had proven more than once that it did not take criticism well and that it could turn awfully mulish when it felt threatened or put upon—especially when it felt like it was being told what to do by "outsiders." Even though the boycott was a thoroughly homegrown effort, planned and pushed through by the state chapter of the NAACP, it was portrayed by flag defenders as an attack on the state by an outside group: the *national* NAACP. The charge resonated strongly with the state's white residents. Using words that echoed the Civil Rights Era and other periods of Carolina cussedness, some spoke of "outside agitators" stirring up trouble in the state. The NAACP became the preferred whipping boy, just another "special interest group" inventing an issue to serve its parochial needs. Many in the state had grown weary of pro-flag pigheadedness. But now, with the NAACP boycott, there was a new target of disapproval. Many of those who were indifferent about the flag— and even some who might have preferred to see it taken down—were angered by the NAACP's action and reluctant to remove the flag under threat. Some cynically concluded that the organization was simply out to raise its sagging profile— and fill its coffers with fresh contributions—by going after a secondary concern like the flag, while ignoring problems like crime, poverty, and drug abuse.

Reverend Darby said that a major reason why the boycott came off in 1999, after failing in 1994, lay in the fact that the state had several well-placed members in national offices within the NAACP that it had not had back in the earlier part of the decade—men such as Nelson Rivers III, a native Charlestonian, who had been NAACP executive director in South Carolina before moving up to become the NAACP's director of national field operations. Rivers was familiar with the groundwork being laid by the state NAACP chapter, and it was his involvement that proved key in persuading the national leadership to support the boycott campaign. Rivers reportedly became convinced that the time for action was right after attending the unveiling of a new monument dedicated to the memory of slaves who had arrived in the New World on Sullivan's Island, near Charleston. Just as importantly, the new head of the state NAACP chapter, Jim Gallman, had been elected to the post promising to pursue the flag issue with renewed vigor.[18]

"The NAACP is nothing more than a few individuals trying to build a political and economic power base from which to advance their own personal agendas," one opinion-page letter-writer said. "The NAACP . . . seek[s] to intimidate and control by protest and boycott," wrote another. "As I see it," said still another, "the NAACP is part of the system that keeps black Americans where they are today. Their in-your-face dialogue does nothing but promote racism on both sides of the fence." Speaking for many, no doubt, one letter-writer called for the flag's relocation "to a place of honor," in order to "make the NAACP find another way to cause trouble." "The second 'A' in NAACP represents the word 'advancement,'" he continued. "But the removal of the flag and a boycott do not create advancement for anyone other than the arrogant NAACP leaders. If the NAACP leaders are true Christians, they will read their Bibles, pray and seek peaceful negotiations for removal of the flag."

Others found harsher biblical injunctions against the group. Calling the NAACP a "terrorist" organization, one letter-writer said it "was time to cast these dispensers of hate [he meant the NAACP, not the Klan] into the biblical bottomless pit." Another expressed a willingness to remove the flag, but still resented the NAACP's campaign. "I feel the flag needs a place in our history," he wrote, "but not above our state dome. Groups such as the KKK and NAACP, that have clearly shown their 'racist' demands . . . have no right to interfere . . . in the state of South Carolina." Even some blacks believed the boycott campaign to be a waste of precious time. "Once again the NAACP is out wasting time and energy on the wrong issues," wrote one self-described "40–year-old black male."[19]

It was opinions such as these that led flag defenders such as Senator Arthur Ravenel to cheerfully conclude that "the flag is a lot stronger now with the boycott a-goin' on than it was before. You don't really think the General Assembly of South Carolina is gonna knuckle under to the N-A-A-C-P, headquartered in . . . wherever the hell they are—where is it, New York?" With droll cockiness, the senator declared the boycott "wonderful" especially in terms of its positive effect on the state's tourist traffic: "There are too many people in Charleston anyhow," Ravenel declared. "If you can cut 'em down by a few thousand a year, it'd be just great! And I'm serious about that," he added half jokingly.

To an old political hound like Ravenel, the NAACP-induced hoopla over the flag was just something to be endured with patience and amused poise. "This'll all pass," he said with relaxed confidence. "It's a stage we're going through." He chalked up most of the anti-flag agitation to political correctness and opportunism. "Lemme tell ya about the N-A-A-C-P," Ravenel explains. "They have realized all their major goals. Everything's been settled in the civil rights struggle. And of course they've had trouble with the national organization, because of all the corruption. A lot of the large corporations quit contributing because of the financial irregularities and all. So they have to have a cause. They have to be beatin' up on something, somethin' to march around about, and hoop and holler and yell about—and to get people to contribute to. Moving the flag from the top of the State House of little ol' South Carolina is their current cause celebre. We realize this, of course," he says with a wink.

"You know the old song, 'I'm an old hippie and I don't know what to do'?" Ravenel asks. "Well, the last thing them old hippies have left to do now," he says with a chuckle, "is to attack the flag—because there are no other perceived dragons out there."

A majority of Ravenel's fellow legislators agreed with him—and dug in their heels as the boycott took effect. An early August 1999 poll of Columbia's lawmakers showed that 58 percent of the state's senators and 53 percent of its representatives believed the flag should be left where it was.[20] Senator McConnell was still holding out at the dome, still demanding "full and final settlement" of all conflicting viewpoints (what came to be known as "finality") before he would consider the idea of taking down the flag. Most of the other leaders also thought the time was not yet ripe for settlement. Senate Democratic Majority Leader John Land felt that "the ill-will that's created [by the boycott threat] may be counter-productive." He believed "behind-the-scenes negotiating" would be "the best way to bring the flag down."[21]

Behind-the-scenes negotiation was certainly the method of choice in the senate. But to many blacks, it seemed like the same old runaround. Some called to mind Martin Luther King's letter from a Birmingham jail and asked, "If not now, when?" Nelson Rivers III said, "We've done it every way they've asked us. We've been nice about it; we've been quiet about it; we've been invisible about it. Every time they tell us, 'Not now, we're in the middle of an election,' or 'Not now, we're doing the budget.' The bottom line is, we've been waiting too long, and the time has come for us to make a decision about this."[22]

Senator Robert Ford could not help but disagree. He felt there were more important things to be concerned about—things of real value to the black community—that would require the support of white, pro-flag legislators if they were to pass. Moreover, he doubted whether the black community would be willing to make the sacrifices necessary to make the boycott a success (especially since the bulk of those employed in the tourism industry, those who would be hardest hit by a tourism boycott, were themselves African American). And more importantly, he feared the backlash a boycott would unleash among whites. "If a vote on this issue is forced during the next session of the General Assembly," Ford wrote, "the Republicans will gain control of the South Carolina Senate, win the . . . House by a larger margin, and Democrats will lose control of the governor's office for a long time to come."[23]

Ford's worries appeared borne out by the sales of souvenir State House flags (those Confederate flags hoisted for a few seconds over the roof of the state capitol and sold to the general public). If sales figures were any indicator, folks seemed to be rallying around the flag in ever-increasing numbers. In the year since the State House reopened following renovations, 487 Confederate flags had been sold, beating out both state (438 copies) and U.S. (379) flags.[24] Then again, increased demand for Confederate flags may have been nothing more than a case of "panic buying"—get one now before they're all gone! New statewide opinion polls, taken in September, indicated most South Carolina residents were ready to see the flag come down. Although nearly 40 percent still wanted to keep the flag flying on the dome, 46 percent now thought it should be removed (with 17 percent calling for it to be removed altogether and 28 percent asking that it be moved to a location on the capitol grounds). Support for the flag was strongest in the Upstate and weakest in the Midlands (the swath across the center of the state where many blacks live). Most surprisingly, though, the results also showed Republican voters about equally split on the issue: 39 percent for removal and 44 percent against. The poll also revealed a weakening of the pro-flag front within the State House itself. Only 43 percent of house members and a mere 42 percent of senators now felt the flag should stay up.[25]

With the legislature out on recess until the following year, Governor Hodges became the next target of opportunity. Pressure quickly mounted on him to take action, or at least to be more directly involved in finding a solution. Although he had no power to remove the flag himself, his participation in helping to form a consensus was considered essential. But Hodges continued to lay low, cognizant, no doubt, of what had happened to his predecessor after he got out in front on the issue. "If you know the dog's gonna bite ya, you don't put your hand in his mouth," Senator Ravenel observed wryly, adding, "Hodges is not gonna fool with that flag. That flag'll bite ya!"

The governor did begin holding meetings with legislators, businessmen, and others to talk about the matter. But he clung as much as possible to neutrality, offering neither a proposal of his own nor endorsing any of the ones already on the table. When the chairman of the state Democratic Party suggested that Democratic legislators who favored keeping the Confederate flag flying should be targeted for defeat in the 2000 primaries, Hodges responded quickly, saying that "kind of political hyperbole doesn't get us anywhere near a compromise" on the flag. He knew he was treading on thin political ice: On the one hand, he had to avoid alienating blacks, who had assured his victory at the polls; but on the other hand, he also needed to avoid alienating those pro-flag lawmakers (both Democratic and Republican) whose votes he would need to pass legislation.[26]

House Speaker David Wilkins faced similar pressure—from both sides. He needed to please business interests, increasingly concerned about the boycott's impact on the state's image and economy. But he also had to be wary of the strong pro-flag sentiment in the Upstate (his home base) and the pro-flag pressures on many of his house colleagues, whose support he would need to remain Speaker.

Though acknowledging that he had the power to remove the Confederate flag hanging in the house chamber, Wilkins said he would not exercise that authority without a majority of the legislature voting to back the move. But he believed such majority support was unlikely unless the NAACP first called off its boycott or the governor offered a proposal for them to vote on. All in all, it looked like the state was in for another round of political hot potato.[27]

Tired of waiting (and with the now officially ratified sanctions beginning to take hold), South Carolina's NAACP head, Jim Gallman, erupted in a stinging attack on Hodges. Speaking before an annual convention of the state NAACP (being held for the first time outside of the state), Gallman said of the governor: "He can't be trusted, folks. He's just like the other one," comparing Hodges to his predecessor, David Beasley. "On November 3, we took care of that situation—at least we thought we took care of that situation." But now things suddenly looked altogether different. "We've been hoodwinked," Gallman continued, "we've been bamboozled, we've been deceived into thinking our governor would do the right thing." Hodges, Gallman complained, "refuses to take the lead in standing up for removal of the flag and won't come out of hiding and say what he believes." Speaking in his own defense, the governor simply reminded everyone that he had never promised to take a leading role on the issue.[28]

But then, with pressure mounting, Hodges went ahead and took the bait—or at least he gave it a good hard nibble.

In a speech to the Columbia Urban League in early November, Hodges offered a deal: If the NAACP would suspend its tourism boycott for a time, he would work with House Speaker Wilkins to push through a bill to make Martin Luther King Jr.'s birthday an official state holiday. Acts of mutual respect and good faith such as these, the governor believed, might create an atmosphere that would allow pro- and anti-flag forces to come together to negotiate a settlement to the flag impasse. Pointing to the negative examples offered by Georgia's Governor Miller and former Governor Beasley, Hodges said that "the lesson of history" is, direct opposition will fail. And, he added, "if I follow their example, so will I."[29]

The governor might just as well have spared himself the bother. His proposal was rejected almost as soon as it passed his lips. And far from nurturing an atmosphere of goodwill, the NAACP's Gallman described the proposal "an insult" to African Americans. He said the King holiday was a separate issue from the flag and should be handled on its own merits—not bartered against the flag in a shabby political trade-off. The NAACP emphasized that it had turned to economic sanctions only after all other routes had been taken. "Suspension or removal of the call for economic action," it went on, "would leave the door open for those who have refused to bend in the past to again do so." Nelson Rivers said the short answer to the governor's plan was "No"—and the long answer was "Hell no."[30]

Once again the state's political leadership seemed to be slipping back into familiar patterns of charge and countercharge—a political exercise deriving much of its energy from the combustion resulting when the remaining undercurrents of racial suspicion combined with the naked pursuit of political advantage. The past kept intruding into the present, providing the essential substance necessary to keep the issue aflame. Even though some disagreed with the NAACP's tactics, many blacks saw in the governor's overture just another instance of racial paternalism, just another way of "putting blacks in their place."[31] Whites, on the other hand (and heritage defenders in particular), saw the NAACP as nothing more than a "special interest" pleading for yet another exceptional dispensation based on a political correctness most of them could not abide. Whites felt they had done nothing they need regret, nothing that called for special gestures of atonement. They resented the suggestion that nothing had really changed in the South—even though their own actions sometimes appeared to reinforce the impression they sought to deny. No one likes having his dirty laundry aired. But he likes it even less when somebody leads others to the laundry line and points out the stains. So it was with the flag and southern heritage. No one felt the need to dredge up the ugly past—especially when most folks (at least most white folks) believed that the past was over and done with.

There were any number of paths leading out of the morass—just about everybody had a plan about what to do with the flag. The mayoral team of Coble and Riley were back again with a revamped version on an old suggestion. Their latest proposal called for the erection of a Confederate memorial on the grounds of the State House. The structure would include a wall (similar to the Vietnam Veterans' Memorial in Washington) bearing the names of the more than twenty thousand soldiers from South Carolina who had died during the Civil War—surrounded by five different Confederate banners.[32] The idea flew like a lead flag. Black lawmakers such as Senator Glover were appalled at the thought of that many Confederate flags planted in front of the capitol building. Trading in one flag for five (flying at "eye level") was hardly the kind of deal she was after. "A wall that size would practically *surround* the State House," Glover exclaimed. What she could not understand, however, was why the flag defenders had not embraced the plan. "If they think about it long enough," she said, "they'll see that, hey, this isn't a bad idea. And I hope we can get rid of the idea before they realize what a great opportunity [it is]!" The heritage folks were dug in much too deeply to move now, though. And besides, they could hardly stomach the thought of allying themselves with a couple of "scalawags" like Coble and Riley.

Even more grandiose was the plan put forward late in the year by a diverse group from the Upstate, headed by Greenville Senator David Thomas. This proposal envisioned the construction of a rather sizeable "heritage/history park" on the State House grounds—a kind of multifaceted, multipurpose, multicultural monument set to a Civil War theme. The design of the "shrine"—an odd cross between museum, memorial, and sculpture garden—would incorporate "all facets of the Civil War, including [facts about] Confederate and Union armies, black and white South Carolinians, [and a description] of events leading to [the] Civil War," as well as "reunification" afterwards. Some were intrigued with the idea—but most were skeptical. A project this vast would take a great deal of planning and a lot of the legislature's time—time it did not have to spare, especially in light of the NAACP's boycott. Some blacks worried that the cost of realizing such a plan (up to $10 million) would act as a financial black hole, sucking up contributions that might otherwise go to the African American memorial and setting off "a monument arms race" between the competing plans. The search for an appropriate "context" for the flag was proving just as elusive as the struggle over a flag compromise—and threatened to become downright expensive besides.[33]

But while the problem of determining exactly where to put the flag kept state government tied up in knots, public consensus appeared to be coalescing around the realization that it was time to remove the flag from the dome. A mid-October 1999 opinion poll (taken after the official endorsement of the NAACP's boycott plan) showed that a slim majority (51 percent) of South Carolinians were now in favor of removing the flag—by placing it in a museum, at some location "of honor" on the capitol grounds, or by eliminating it altogether. Forty-one percent —still a sizeable minority—wanted to keep it on the dome. And for the first time, public attention began focusing on the issue in a serious way. Despite their weariness with the seemingly endless wrangling and speechifying over the issue, 63 percent of those polled declared the flag affair either a "somewhat" or "very important" matter for the state to settle.[34]

With the state's central governing elites still in temporary limbo, "outside" players continued to enter the fray. City governments and county councils around the state passed resolutions in favor of compromise. So, too, did various institutions of higher learning. Business groups, increasingly concerned about the boycott's effect on the business climate, continued to apply pressure in a quiet, though forceful way. The state Chamber of Commerce, in particular, took a leading role in pushing for compromise. Chamber representatives subtly suggested that a lawmaker's stance on the flag would "go into the equation" of determining how much financial support a candidate might receive during the upcoming elections.[35]

Churches and religious organizations, large and small, black and white—including the influential S.C. Southern Baptist Convention—also continued to call for resolution of the conflict. Many of them referred to the biblical injunction against offending one's neighbor in order to underpin their argument against the flag's display. Even conservative religious leaders such as Bob Jones III (president of the pietistic and fundamentalist—and occasionally controversial—

Bob Jones University, located in the Carolina Upstate) joined the call for the flag to come down. Though he disagreed with the anti-flag interpretation of the banner (which Jones still considered "a proud symbol of states' rights"), and after excoriating the NAACP for its boycott campaign, Jones, too, cited the Bible's admonition to avoid "unnecessary offense" as his reason for supporting the flag's removal from the dome. Contemplating the mounting pressure against the flag display, senate Democratic leader John Land wondered how long Republican flag stalwarts could to hold out. "Their natural constituencies—business and Baptists—are at odds with them on the flag," Land observed wryly.[36]

And the pressure continued to mount. In early December, fifty-one of the sixty-seven surviving members of the 1962 South Carolina General Assembly, along with two former governors—Robert McNair (1965–1971) and John West (1971–1975)—made a public appearance to present a petition asking that the Confederate flag be removed from the dome. In their statement, the former legislators said that the flag had been placed atop the dome during a phase of "pride and euphoria throughout [the] state . . . as part of the Civil War commemorative activities." "No member of the General Assembly," the statement went on to say, "consciously intended for the Confederate flag to fly over the State House for all time." It had been their intention, the legislators said, that the flag come down at the conclusion of the centennial in 1965. Unfortunately, the resolution creating the display had "failed to provide for the timely removal of the flag." It had been a mere oversight on their part, the aging former lawmakers said, and asked the current legislature to "correct our omission by removing the flag to a place of honor on the State House grounds." In conclusion they expressed their hope that "if a compromise is reached . . . it will end the divisive opinions on the Confederacy."[37]

Former Representative Charlie Boineau, who in 1961 had become the first Republican elected to the state legislature since Reconstruction, added that he "was not proud of the present Republican members of the legislature who are saying 'over my dead body.' That really bothers me." But one of those pro-flag stalwarts, Rick Quinn, called it "the ultimate hypocrisy to say, 'Oops, we forgot.' That's real easy to do when you're not burdened with representing every citizen of South Carolina," Quinn protested.[38]

But some of those same citizens Quinn claimed to represent had begun organizing "bring-down-the-flag" campaigns of their own—an unusual development, one academic pointed out, in a "state [that] has been governed by elites most of its history."[39] A biracial, grass-roots organization calling itself "United 2000," formed during 1999, drew together a diverse group of community organizers, church leaders, business people, lawyers, and just plain folks in an attempt to coordinate efforts to bring the flag debate to a satisfying conclusion. The group's members agreed to put aside their differing opinions about the Confederacy, about the meaning of the flag, about the southern past, and about contemporary politics in order to push for a final resolution of the flag issue. The one thing they all agreed on was the need to remove the Confederate flag from the pole on top of the State House. Their rallying point was the old sovereignty argument. They said that only the state and national flags should be permitted to fly over the state legislature—as symbols of existing political authority—and urged the state's leaders to make that happen. Exactly how this feat was to be accomplished was left for the legislators to determine—though it was precisely that part of South Carolina's peculiar Gordian Knot that was proving to be the most difficult one to unravel.[40]

While South Carolinians at large were slowly coming together around a consensus that the flag's time was up, the state legislature, by contrast, seemed almost ready to fly apart. Senator Jackson, often seen as one of the more moderate voices within the Legislative Black Caucus, surprised everyone late in the year by calling on Senator McConnell to step down as chairman of the African-American Monument Commission. Jackson pointedly demanded that McConnell justify how he could legitimately serve on the commission, "when you are critical of the NAACP—not only critical, but insulting to the NAACP?'" Adding fuel to the fire, Jackson also announced his intention to introduce a bill calling for the complete elimination of the Confederate flag from the State House. "I've come to the conclusion," Jackson said, "that if the flag is offensive, then it will be just as offensive flying in the yard as it would flying on a flag pole." He now thought it best if the flag were placed in the Confederate Relic Room. That idea was a nonstarter with flag defenders, of course, as Jackson must have realized (leading some observers to conclude that he was merely using the issue to advance his prospects in the approaching elections). The pro-flag forces in the legislature responded by declaring that they would allow no action to be taken on the flag until the NAACP removed its boycott and agreed not to seek the obliteration of South Carolina's Confederate history.[41]

Jackson surprised everyone again in late December, when he declared that if McConnell remained as head of the African-American Monument Commission, he would not attend either the groundbreaking or the dedication ceremonies for the memorial—and that he would "lead an effort to keep [other] blacks away as well." Jackson felt the whole climate of the debate over the flag had changed for the worse. "We've entered a warlike atmosphere," he said. "And once you enter a war, people who were once friends and allies [like he and McConnell] find themselves on opposite sides." Even some of Jackson's black colleagues were taken aback by the senator's more strident tone. "It shocks the hell out of me," said Senator Kay Patterson, himself no stranger to controversial remarks. "How the hell can anyone jump that far in his thinking overnight," Patterson wondered. Jackson refused to back down, though, despite criticism—and a "trip to the woodshed" with senate president pro tempore, John Drummond (for what amounted to "conduct unbecoming a senator"). "I do what I think is right," Jackson said later. "Yes, I'm frustrated. I'm angry. And I get more angry as things persist. If we don't settle this flag dispute, it's going to get worse before it gets better. If it's not resolved this session, next summer will be worse."[42]

In light of this new round of division and dissension, prospects of finding a resolution seemed dimmer than ever. Several of the old hands at the State House were worried about the direction things appeared to be taking. "I'm really depressed about it," Senator Verne Smith admitted. His colleague, John Drummond, broke into tears as he pleaded with his fellow legislators to "think about the state before igniting a racial debate. . . ." And Senator John Courson fretted "that the state stood on the brink of a racial 'abyss' over the flag."[43]

The conflict seemed to grow ever more absurd—and yet necessary if the state were to move ahead. As the world left the twentieth century behind and moved into the third millennium, South Carolina was still addressing the present in terms of its Civil War past. Images and references to that long-ago conflict still swelled the hearts and peppered the tongues of the state's elected and unelected leaders—though it remained unclear just how much of it was real and how much mere rhetorical overkill. "As the state burned in 1865, it may burn again," Senator Jackson observed ominously.

"Figuratively speaking," he quickly added.[44]

The new century got off with a bang in South Carolina—several bangs, actually. Just beyond the glare of the fireworks celebrating the start of a new millennium, there was, first of all, the official beginning of the NAACP boycott, which, by 1 January 2000, already had prompted eighty-six groups to cancel planned meetings in the state.[45] The new year also marked the beginning of a new marching season for many in South Carolina—and all routes led to Columbia, to the State House, to the center of the storm where the Confederate flag waved in a crisp winter breeze, oblivious to all the fuss below it, just as it had for the previous thirty-nine seasons.

The flag defense forces were the first to take to the streets. For them, these were gloomy and increasingly desperate times. "This is our summer of '64," said Danny Verdin, head of the state division of the Sons of Confederate Veterans. Verdin's reference to General Grant's unwavering drive toward the Confederate capital made for a rather dramatic analogy. But heritage folks are fond of drama—and besides, the description was fitting. Their only hope now was to try and hold their ground, to interpose what resources they had left between the flag and its detractors—just as Lee had against Grant in their deadly foxtrot through

Virginia near the end of the Civil War. For Verdin and his cohort, the conflict was much the same in 2000 as it had been in 1864, only shrunken down in size to fit on a field of red bearing a star-studded cross of St. Andrew. It was a miniaturized Civil War, a battle over symbols and memory, fought in defense of ancestral honor and aimed at vindicating the Confederate era's "struggle to maintain a Christian civilization in this state." The flag defenders believed they were marching in the footsteps of their forebears, revivifying a blood kinship by reenacting a conflict over a hundred years lost. "If our side, if our cause, prevails for six months," Verdin declared grimly, "we will win this war." [46] It was a battle against time—against both the legislative clock and the shifting perceptions of a new epoch.

The heritage defenders assembled in the state capital in early January under a sea of Confederate flags, of all kinds and sizes. The world's largest battle flag was back again. This time it lay draped over the State House steps like an enormous welcome mat or a gigantic billboard proclaiming the day to interstellar space. The flag-bearing troops, many of them clad in the gray and butternut of their ancestors, moved down Main Street like the massed color guards of all the Confederate armies that ever were. They had even brought along their own little mascot: a black dachshund decked out in his own diminutive rebel-flag sweatshirt. Along the way, a black man joined in with the nearly all-white throng, wrapping himself in a Confederate banner—a symbol of his heritage, too, he said. And as the believers gathered at the capitol steps, the last living Confederate widow, ninety-three-year-old Alberta Martin, was rolled out on her wheelchair to lend a special link of authenticity to the affair.

The event, billed as "Heritage Celebration 2000," had begun the day before with a recitation of the 18,600 names of South Carolina's Confederate war dead that continued through the night. Among those reading the names was a black man, H. K. Edgerton, former head of the Asheville, North Carolina chapter of the NAACP and current board member of the Southern Legal Resource Center. Edgerton said of the boycott: "If the NAACP is successful, all it will have done is alienated white people, who have been very tolerant." Ceremonies on the day of the march opened with a memorial service held in the Civil War section of Elmwood Cemetery—which had been decked out with rows of bright new battle flags for the occasion. The graveside ceremony served as a rededication; it was another way of linking with the past, of reminding all those assembled what the fight was all about. A military brass band played devotional tunes as musket volleys rang out in a salute to the ancestors. Then the heritage-defense force, some six thousand strong, marched through town to the capitol building for the culmination of their pro-flag parade. [47]

It was a day of much high-flying—and some low-flying—rhetoric. Besides the lofty though sometimes archaic-sounding incantations to duty, honor, sacrifice, and, of course, heritage, there were any number of verbal volleys discharged at the NAACP. Senator Ravenel, one of seven state lawmakers attending the day's events, set the tone when he called the civil-rights organization "corrupt," and dubbed it the "National Association of Retarded People"—a much-reported comment that would reap the senator from Charleston a harvest of criticism in the weeks to come. (Despite angry disapproval over the comment, however, the outspoken Ravenel never retracted it or apologized—except to the "retarded people of the world for unfairly lumping them together with the NAACP.") Speaking from the floor of the state senate a few days later, Ravenel did hold out the offer of an apology—but only if Senator Jackson would first submit his own apology for helping sponsor the Klansman ad campaign. Jackson, who said that Ravenel's comment had insulted Rosa Parks, Thurgood Marshall, and Jackson's own father, refused to take him up on the offer. Fellow Charleston Republican, Representative John Graham Altman, followed Ravenel's lead when he said, "If they keep trying to bring it down, they're going to find out why they call it a *battle* flag." At that the crowd broke into a chant: "Never bring it down," prompting another state lawmaker, Representative Charlie Sharpe (a Republican from Aiken), to shout, "Let's move it—from the bottom of the pole to the top!"[48]

Unfortunately for Sharpe, however, a brand-new opinion poll showed that fewer South Carolinians than ever shared his enthusiasm for the flag. Rather than move it to the top, 59 percent now preferred that it be moved off the State House flagpole. Only about a third (32 percent) wanted to see the flag continue flying there. Though most said the NAACP's boycott had no effect on their opinion, a clear majority believed it was important to reach a settlement on the matter.

As a consequence of shifting public opinion, the tectonic plates in the state legislature began to move, however slowly—and the first contours of a compromise began to emerge. While House Majority Leader Rick Quinn continued to remind every one of the fifty or so lawmakers still holding out in defense of the flag, House Speaker Wilkins spoke of a "shift in the dialogue, from up or down to what are some possible compromises." Senator Courson and others began taking another look at the 1994 Heritage Act as a possible way out of the tangle. Courson felt a compromise could be reached on that basis—if the boycott were called off first. But with the boycott now in full bloom, the possibility that it would be called off seemed remote.[49]

The state legislature returned to work in mid-January 2000—and the battle resumed as the opposing sides lobbed legislative bills into the political no-man's-land that separated them. The Ravenel flap continued to rattle around for a time. The head of the state Republican Party refused to ask Ravenel to apologize and blamed the NAACP for inflaming the debate—which Jackson said was "like blaming Rosa Parks for making the buses run late." Against this backdrop, Courson declared that there could be no forward movement on the matter until it was clear that flag opponents were prepared to settle the dispute on the basis of "finality and honor." Senator Thomas, a Republican from Greenville, said that "as agitated as both sides seem to be about this, it could be that [resolution] is not going to happen this year." And senate chief Drummond worried about all the incendiary rhetoric flying about. "I've actually had people say to me, 'Let's have a race war,'" the senator reported.[50] Some also worried that the flag fracas might spill over into the legislature's selection of a state supreme court justice, which pitted one black candidate against two white candidates in a race opened up by the retirement of the state's first black chief justice since Reconstruction.

Flag talks continued over at the governor's office, with no sign that the two sides were moving closer together. Even though the general trend appeared to be in its favor, the NAACP remained coy on the question of what should be done with the flag once it came down, saying only that the flag should be moved "to a place of historical context." Did that mean the Soldiers Monument? Or anyplace on the grounds *other* than the monument? Or did it mean the flag should be removed from the grounds altogether? Seeking to bring some clarity, the Legislative Black Caucus (despite internal divisions) announced in mid-January that it would stand with the NAACP and oppose moving the flag to the Confederate Soldiers Monument in front of the State House. This was probably nothing more than a negotiating ploy, but it was a somewhat precarious position to take, nevertheless, since everyone knew the pro-flag forces would never accept it. By taking such a stance, the Legislative Black Caucus risked being labeled "extremists" with whom one could not seriously negotiate.[51]

As their leaders debated, the people marched once more. This time it was the turn of the flag opponents, whose rally served as a counter-demonstration to the heritage march two weeks earlier. Billed as "King Day at the Dome," the Martin Luther King Birthday protest march, organized by the NAACP, turned out to be one of the largest mass demonstrations in the state's history, rivaling or exceeding those of the Civil Rights Era itself. Originally expected to draw between ten thousand and twenty thousand participants, the event instead brought an estimated forty-six thousand people to town.

The day was filled with echoes of a side of the southern past very different from the one celebrated by the pro-flag groups. Protestors sang "The flag is coming down" to the old tune "We Shall Overcome." Others let go with a forceful rendition of "Ain't gonna let Arthur Ravenel turn us 'round / Ain't gonna let Gov. Hodges turn us 'round." Martin Luther King III, son of the civil-rights leader, was there to begin the day's activities at a prayer breakfast held at the University of South Carolina. As with the rededication ceremony at Elmwood Cemetery two weeks earlier, King's presence served to link past and present, to represent continuity across the generations. Those who had lived under segregation marched alongside those born long after the demise of Jim Crow.[52]

There was one other notable difference between the heritage celebration and the King Day march. The latter demonstration was not buried under a canopy of flags, the way its Confederate heritage counterpart had been. Except for a few U.S. and state flags (along with the occasional Black Liberation banner) scattered around the crowd, there were few flags to be seen. Instead of flags there were t-shirts, many of them bearing the slogan, "Your heritage is my slavery." Others read simply, "All God's Children," offering witness to the religious overtones of the gathering. The parade of demonstrators flowed down Main Street, flooding the grounds and streets around the State House and almost inundating the Confederate Soldiers Monument and the statue of "Pitchfork" Ben Tillman nearby.

Addressing the crowd, state NAACP head James Gallman said, "We're not here to build walls of division, but to build bridges of unity. We're here to let it be known that not everyone in South Carolina is still living in the 1860s. Let it clearly be understood that we deny no person's opportunity to celebrate his or her heritage, but we will not tolerate or accept the forced celebration of any one heritage by rule of law." As Governor Hodges watched the gathering from inside his State House office, keynote speaker Kweisi Mfume, president of the NAACP, mounted to the podium and declared, "We stand here now . . . under the symbol of hatred and bigotry and Klan activity, to proclaim that we will not be moved. We stand under this symbol of bigotry and say that Jim Crow Sr. is dead, but Jim Crow Jr. is alive and well." To roaring cheers, Mfume reaffirmed that "We will continue to march and continue to boycott until [the flag] flies no more."[53]

Only a smattering of flag defenders came to the anti-flag demonstration. Just a few openly declared their allegiances. One said he could understand why the marchers had come and why they felt the way they did—but he still thought they were ill-informed about the flag. "The flag is about bravery, not slavery," he said simply. He had to admit, however, as he stood among the massed body of anti-flag sentiment, that the day's protest might be the event that finally turned the tide against the flag. Resigning himself to what seemed like the inevitable, he said, "With this kind of political pressure, the politicians have got to buckle."[54]

Governor Hodges—who had not appeared at either rally—now stepped out into the spotlight once again. In his State of the State address before a joint session of the General Assembly delivered just two days after the King Day rally, the governor said that the flag needed to be moved. But backing down from his previous position, Hodges no longer demanded that the NAACP suspend its boycott as a precondition to removing the flag. "Sanctions can no longer keep us from doing what is right," the governor said. He believed that, "in its current position on the dome, the Confederate flag claims an inappropriate position of sovereignty." And, in terms that closely paralleled those used by the NAACP, Hodges said that the flag should be removed from the dome "to a place of historical significance on the State House grounds." He did not suggest a specific location, only that there were "four or five places that would work," adding that there was "still no consensus on where it should go." Significantly, the governor did say, however, in separate comments following the speech, that he believed placing the battle flag at the Soldiers Monument was an idea that was probably "not going to fly."[55]

Flag supporters were at their battle stations, on full alert. In the Republican response to Governor Hodges's speech, House Majority Leader Quinn said the governor's proposal had broken no new ground. He again blamed the impasse on the NAACP, saying the group had rejected "all reasonable compromise," and demanded that it lift its boycott and work to end the controversy. Yet, earlier that day, in a move toward the NAACP's position, Senator McConnell had said he believed a plan that included the Soldiers Monument and protections for other monuments and memorials around the state "could probably be sold" to heritage groups and flag defenders. Quinn seconded the idea, saying such a proposal could pass "in thirty seconds." Barring that, however, McConnell felt "there was nothing left to negotiate." In any event, it appeared to him unlikely that "anything is going to happen this year."[56]

McConnell was discouraged not only by black opposition to the Soldiers Monument. He and others were also frustrated by the division within the Legislative Black Caucus (and between that group and the NAACP) that had resulted in inconsistencies in their public statements concerning the flag's location. Having only just declared their opposition to moving the flag to the Soldiers Monument, for example, several members of the caucus ended the week of rallies and speeches by appearing to pull back from a flat-out rejection of the monument proposal. They now said there was no agreement on what position the group should take and fell back on the general suggestion that the flag be placed in a "place of historical context." "We're open to discussion about where we go from here," said one black house member. "We have not taken a position on where the flag will be relocated after . . . it's removed."[57]

Senator Patterson, by contrast, declared that "black lawmakers could never accept moving the flag to the [Confederate] monument." Jackson vowed that he would "filibuster, holler, scream, and do whatever I can to prevent that." And he added, "Right now, I think it should go where it was prior to 1962 . . . in somebody's closet or in a museum somewhere." Meanwhile, the state NAACP leadership, which had only days before demurred on taking a clear stance on the question, now indicated that it was the NAACP's "official position" that the "battle flag should not be placed on the grounds." The Confederate flag "needs to be in a museum," James Gallman said. In light of all this, an exasperated Senator McConnell complained, "The closer you get to them, the further they move away from you."[58]

McConnell was not the only one annoyed by the way things were going (or not going). His senate colleague, Majority Leader John Land, was so fed up that he threatened to introduce legislation that would simply strike the flag from the dome (without moving it anywhere), if lawmakers failed to find a compromise soon. With just a two-seat majority, though, the Democratic leader must have realized that his threat was an empty one (though not without resonance, given his senior position in the senate). But in order to try and break up the logjam, Land decided to throw a few rocks at it. He pitched several "new" ideas into the stagnant legislative waters, hoping to stir things up and perhaps get things moving forward again. As if putting together a mix-and-match ensemble, the senator suggested that the Stars and Bars flag could be placed at the Soldiers Monument and the square (ANV) flag might go to the Wade Hampton statue on the opposite side of the capitol. Or, alternatively, the ANV flag could go to the Hampton statue and the Stars and Bars could be added to the Confederate Women's Memorial nearby. Or, the flag on the dome might simply be placed on display in a glass case in the State House foyer. By now, just about anything seemed worth a try.[59]

Flag-removal proposals were soon popping up like mushrooms on a muggy southern morning. The legislators embarked on an Alice-in-Wonderland romp through a Never-Never-land of notions, enjoying many adventures as they allowed their imaginations to run free. Senator Land was himself a most prolific generator of proposals, with several flag plans to his credit (even if none of them could be counted among the most innovative solutions offered). Besides the ideas offered earlier, he now suggested another variation on the old "mall (or avenue) of flags" proposal (jumping off from the circle of flags plan of several years back). Land's plan would have placed a number of "historically significant" flags in two rows to either side of the Confederate Soldiers Monument. University of South Carolina history professor Walter Edgar was given the task of compiling a list of flags that had flown over or were in some way associated with South Carolina during its history, from colonial times to the present. Edgar came up with a catalogue of more than a dozen flags to choose from, including Christopher Columbus's Lions and Castles flag; the Fleur-de-lis banner of fifteenth-century France; the red colonial ensign of the British Empire; the Gadsden "Don't Tread on Me" flag; the "Betsy Ross" flag; three Confederate-era flags (though not the rectangular design above the dome)—and, to make the idea more palatable to the state's black residents, a thirty-seven-star U.S. flag used during the Reconstruction era. It was a truly valiant attempt to provide "context" and "definition" to the state's different historical personae.[60]

In a noble gesture of their own, the dynamic mayoral duo of Joe Riley and Bob Coble returned to the stage one more time to offer an expanded version of their proposal from the previous year. They now envisioned a semicircular memorial complex on the eastern side of the State House grounds. It would still include a wall of names and five Confederate flags, as before, but now they had embroidered it with a reflecting pool—for effect. Not to be outdone, Greenville's Senator Thomas and his band of Upstate memorialists had set their own creative juices flowing and were back with a revamped version of the "Heritage/History Park," which they proposed be erected on the western side of the capitol, at the site of the old wooden State House (burned during Sherman's travels through the state in 1865). The memorial would include five Confederate flags (including the one over the dome); a list of the state's Civil War dead; information panels covering events in the pre-war, wartime, and postwar periods of state history; as well as an audiovisual component and a "water/fire feature" with the Emancipation Proclamation as its centerpiece.[61]

It all seemed rather overwhelming—especially all those flags. "I wouldn't want to see Confederate flags *ringing* the entire State House," Reverend Darby interjected with alarm. And his friends over in the Legislative Black Caucus agreed. "It's a problem to have too many of those flags out there," croaked Senator Patterson. Interestingly, his "good friend," Senator McConnell, was not too keen about any of these proposals, either. And it wasn't just the cost involved in realizing these schemes that made the senator pause. The State House grounds were already cluttered with enough statues and monuments as it was, he thought. Adding anything else would just contribute to the muddle. It nevertheless marked a significant shift on McConnell's part. Now that the Legislative Black Caucus opposed moving the flag to the Confederate Soldiers Monument, he could safely come out in favor of the idea. McConnell had gone from holding out at the dome to holding out at the monument. "Certainly," he said, "[given their] supreme sacrifice, [the state's Confederate dead] would warrant a battle flag at their monument." "I am not going to surrender that flag to shame," McConnell declared once again.[62]

Undeterred by the flag-*plan* fatigue that was threatening to replace the flag fatigue everyone already felt, Governor Hodges finally stepped forth with his own (rather more modest) flag proposal in mid-February. The governor's plan would have removed the flag from the dome (and the two legislative chambers) and replaced it with a square ANV flag at the Wade Hampton Monument (erected in 1906). His proposal also incorporated those parts of the 1994 Heritage Act protecting Confederate monuments and street names around the state—and made Confederate Memorial Day and Martin Luther King Jr.'s birthday state holidays.

Hodges's offer received a great deal of friendly attention—but few were actually interested in buying the pooch. Hodges was aiming for a low-profile display, as low as possible while still fulfilling the flag folks' demands that the flag remain somewhere on the grounds. Since the Wade Hampton Monument was set off to one side and toward the back of the State House, sandwiched between the State House building itself and nearby legislative offices, away from downtown thoroughfares and screened off from view by several tall trees, it seemed to be the perfect hiding spot. But the location was too remote for Senators McConnell and Courson and the other pro-flag legislators. McConnell called the governor's proposed site "down in the gully." Opposition to the governor's plan wasn't merely a question of aesthetic judgment, either. The search for political advantage played its role, too. No Republican wanted to see a Democratic governor get the credit for solving a sticky problem like the flag.[63]

If that was not enough to kill the governor's idea (and presumably it was), then the mixed (and rather tepid) reactions the plan elicited from the black legislative leadership doubtless were. A few members of the Legislative Black Caucus had nice things to say about the governor's proposal, but many dismissed it outright. "Dead on arrival," Senator Jackson declared—and the NAACP agreed. Both wanted to see the flag tucked away someplace less conspicuous, either in the Confederate Relic Room or in a glass case somewhere in the State House (with accompanying inscriptions stating both pro- and anti-flag viewpoints, if possible). McConnell brushed aside the suggestion. "That'll fly like a lead balloon," he said flatly. McConnell knew he still had enough votes in his pocket to shoot down any kind of balloon, lead or not. The legislative blunderbuss, the filibuster, was like a thermonuclear warhead: the mere threat to use it deterred the other side from acting. Any plan that had less than twenty-nine senators backing it was not filibuster-proof. More importantly, for any plan to stand a chance in the rougher seas over on the house side, it would have to emerge from the senate with a full head of steam, backed by a clear majority of Senators, both black and white. Only then would there be enough momentum to carry it through to the governor's desk. The senate, with its emphasis on good-ol'-boy consensus building was the most likely launching point for a real flag compromise. By contrast, the house, where close votes were more commonplace, was far too contentious to craft a workable compromise. The senate could dodge its fate no longer. It would have to take up the mantle and lead the way, if any solution was going to be found.[64]

The flag-plan frenzy continued, with no sign of abating, as the state slipped into spring. In spite of his concern about all the granite and bronze bric-a-brac already cluttering the capitol grounds, McConnell decided to jump onto the bandwagon with his own notion about how to settle the flag wrangle. He proposed constructing what he called a "healing pool" between the Confederate Soldiers Monument and the front steps of the State House. It would incorporate a statuary ensemble that portrayed black and white Civil War soldiers reaching out to one another in a gesture of reconciliation. It also would include both the Confederate flag and a Union flag pattern carried by black troops stationed in the state during the war. But even McConnell seemed less than optimistic about his proposal's chances. "If it doesn't work, it doesn't work," he said somewhat indifferently. "I tried. It's all I can do."[65]

A novel (though impractical) idea about what to do with the flag came from one of South Carolina's citizens. In a letter to *The State* newspaper in the spring of 2000, this fair-minded soul suggested an on-again, off-again solution to the flag battle. Noting that the Thirteenth Amendment to the U.S. Constitution (outlawing slavery) had been ratified on 5 May 1865, he proposed the date be celebrated once every other year in a ceremony at the State House, during which the Confederate flag would be removed from the dome. The dome would then remain free of the flag until 12 April (the day of the Fort Sumter bombardment) of the following year, when it would be hoisted over the dome once again, where it would remain during the twenty-three days until 5 May, then be lowered again for another year. This perpetual commemoration machine would supposedly give each side its due. But it also would have lent eternal life to the division over the meaning of the flag. Enshrining that division in an annual public ceremony was perhaps not the best way of dealing with the problem. And besides, flag defenders no doubt would reject the suggestion that their side enjoy anything less than equal treatment.[66]

Others had tried splitting the difference, too—each in his own way. Senators Jackson (flag critic) and Courson (flag defender) teamed up to announce their own solution to the flag tangle in a proposal that mixed and matched demands made by both heritage groups and the NAACP. According to this plan, *authentic* Civil War–era flags would be placed on display in glass cases at three locations around the capitol grounds: an Army of Northern Virginia (ANV) flag at the Confederate Soldiers Monument; a First National (Stars and Bars) flag at the Confederate Women's Memorial; and a flag of the First South Carolina Volunteer Infantry Regiment, a black federal unit, at a yet undetermined site (though not at the future African-American History Monument). Although the proposal appeared to square the circle of discord by placing a Confederate flag at the Soldiers Monument while also respecting the NAACP's wish that it not *fly* there, the idea got hung up on concerns about cost and the problems associated with protecting such rare and fragile historical artifacts from vandalism and the elements. Despite the backing of his fellow Republican (and SCV member) John Courson, Senator McConnell thought little of the idea. "Encasement represents entombment," McConnell grumbled disparagingly, proclaiming that he "would have no part in symbolically burying the Confederate banner."[67]

While lawmakers in Columbia were bandying flag plans back and forth, the NAACP's tourism boycott was being felt across the state. By the middle of January, the state capital had already suffered around $2.6 million in canceled business, or about 15 percent of the city's yearly tourist trade. Charleston had lost roughly

$2 million, with Myrtle Beach and Hilton Head reporting about $1 million each in losses. And that only accounted for announced cancellations. There was no way to know how many individuals or groups had simply decided to avoid the state from the start. By spring, the estimated losses had risen to $4 million for Columbia and over $3 million in Charleston. Those losses were still small compared to the state's $7-billion tourist industry (and some of the losses were recouped by new business the state was able to drum up), but the implications for the future were not good. Some groups were only just now beginning to plan events, so that the losses over time could only be expected to grow. "If this persists for another two or three years," one business analyst said, "we'll be in big trouble."[68]

More important than any dollar amount the state may have lost was the negative publicity associated with the growing wave of cancellations and boycott announcements. Big names, such as the American Bar Association and the New York Knicks, let it be known that they would avoid the state as long as the boycott was in effect. In addition, several performing groups announced their intention not to appear at the Spoleto Festival in Charleston, the state's premier arts (and social) event of the year. It was beginning to look as if South Carolina would have to choose between worshiping its ancestors and saving face.

Worries about potential losses in corporate investments soon joined with the growing concern over losses in tourist trade. A few years earlier a rumor circulated that Mercedes-Benz had chosen Alabama over South Carolina as the site for a new assembly plant partly out of concern over the flag debate. (The company denied the reports.). Now, however, the difficulties involved in selling South Carolina to outside investors became ever more concrete. Firms and businesses concerned about their public image took a second look before committing to settle in the state. Just as bad (and, for some, worse): the flag fight also threatened the NCAA's Southeastern Conference basketball championship games, scheduled to be held in the state in 2001. In a state as sports crazy as South Carolina, that was serious business, the kind no public official could ignore.[69]

As the legislative session trundled on, with no sign that a flag compromise was about to emerge, Governor Hodges appealed to the state Chamber of Commerce and businesses around the state to redouble their efforts at persuading lawmakers to work toward a solution. Business responded by underwriting a public-relations effort (at a reported cost in the six figures) that included a phone-lobbying campaign. South Carolina voters were contacted by phone and asked whether or not they wished to see the Confederate flag removed from the State House dome. Those who responded positively would then be connected to their respective representative or senator in Columbia to make their opinion known. Business leaders also formed "Courage to Compromise," an impromptu lobby group and informational clearinghouse aimed at persuading lawmakers to support removing the flag. But pressure from the business lobby brought out heritage preservationists, too. Ron Wilson of the SCV complained about the power of corporate interest. "It bothers me," he said, "when multinational corporations like BMW, Michelin and others come into this state and wring us out for millions of dollars in tax breaks. Heritage wasn't a problem for them then. But now that they have . . . their hooks into us, they are trying to tell us what to do. That galls me and it galls the average South Carolinian too." It certainly galled Chris Sullivan, who complained that big companies just wanted to "turn South Carolina into one big shopping mall."[70]

The combined pressure coming from the NAACP, business interests, and diverse political groups soon began showing results. Even Republican voters were now ready to admit that the flag was not worth all the fuss. The same folks who, in the 1994 party referendum, had voted overwhelmingly to keep the flag flying now were ready to see it come down (or at least fifty-plus percent of them were, polls showed). Those same voters also reported that their decision about whether or not to support a Republican candidate would not be determined by his stand on the Confederate flag. It was a signal to Republican lawmakers that it was now politically safe for them to come out in favor of removing the flag from the dome.

GOP voters seemed anxious to save their party from its own self-destructive inclinations. "Democrats are beating Republicans at the public relations game," a longtime observer of state politics Lee Bandy commented. The "Democrats are seen as the party that cares about education and provides for the elderly," he said, while "the GOP is viewed as the Confederate flag-waving party that resists efforts to establish a Martin Luther King holiday." Concerns like these—along with worries about the power of the ultra-right wing in state-party affairs—prompted two GOP state representatives to switch parties, leaving the Republicans with just a seven-seat majority in the state House of Representatives. The flag was becoming a political albatross hung around the collective neck of the state Republican Party. But even so, worries about possible primary challenges by pro-flag stalwarts made wavering Republicans (along with some potentially threatened Democrats) wary about speaking out too clearly or too soon in favor of hauling the flag down. Most chose to keep their own council—at least until 31 March, which was the last day for filing to run in the state's primary campaigns. In other words, all the chatter about alternative plans and all the fretful hemming and hawing over the flag's fate was due, at least in part, to considerations of political self-interest that lapsed at the end of March. The talk had been a way of killing time until then. After 31 March, things suddenly seemed possible that only a short time before were anything but. You could almost hear the sound of scales falling from eyes.[71]

But it was not merely the cold calculus of political tactics or the pressures of economic competition, or for that matter even a concern about saving face, that made folks change their minds about the Confederate flag. There was also a fresh reconsideration of history as well. The state suddenly began getting the history lesson that it had been lacking—or at least bits and pieces of one. Articles dealing with the state's past began appearing in South Carolina newspapers with greater frequency, with stories about the flag, the Civil War, and slavery—along with commentaries discussing our understanding of the past and the meanings that the past still holds for us today.[72]

Even South Carolina's academics—who, up to now, had remained wallflowers in the debate on the flag—finally began to raise their voices. In early April (and only days before the full senate was to take up the flag issue in floor debate), over ninety of the state's historians (representing more than twenty state institutions) issued a statement declaring that "the cause of the present controversy is not in the flag itself but in the conflicting interpretations of the meaning of the Civil War." The historians sought to set the record straight by reminding us of the prominent, indeed central, role that slavery had played in South Carolina's secession convention of 1860 and its place in the "Declaration of the Causes of Secession." They recalled the words of Jefferson Davis and Alexander Stephens, as well as those of native South Carolinians, like Governor Francis Pickens and his close associate Edward Bryan, who had declared, during the election campaign of 1860: "Give us slavery or give us death!" All the evidence made it clear, the historians' statement went on to say, "that their new nation was created for the specific purpose of perpetuating slavery." States' rights had been a revisionist interpretation of events added "after the war had been lost," when "the Lost Cause was in need of justification." "The historical record," their statement concluded "clearly shows that the cause for which the South seceded and fought a devastating war was slavery."[73]

The statement was a red flag waving in the faces of heritage-minded academicians across the country—who promptly responded by issuing a statement of their own. In their lengthy response (signed by thirty-six academics and scholars, mostly from the South, including Clyde Wilson of the University of South Carolina), they offered their interpretation of southern history and a defense of South Carolina's Confederate flag display. Ironically, they took an oddly postmodern approach to the issue. They declared that "there are no immutable truths in secular history. History . . . may be viewed always from many different perspectives. The primary . . . value of the study of history," the pro-flag statement continued, "is developing the ability to see different sides of a question." By insisting on the "truth" that slavery was the cause of the war, the authors of the previous statement had demonstrated both intellectual arrogance and paternalistic elitism.

Their statement had said that "the people of South Carolina are suffering from ignorance and delusions about their history," delusions that "must be corrected by superior wisdom." The previous statement was not only intellectually self-righteous, the pro-flag scholars complained, it was also an insult to South Carolina's noble heritage. The anti-flag statement, they said, required "the people of South Carolina to accept the judgment that their heritage is shameful and should be erased."[74]

Though they admitted that "differing opinions in regard to the longstanding institution of domestic slavery were involved in the conflict," this small band of pro-flag academic activists insisted that slavery had been only one of many factors leading to secession. Slavery, they insisted, "did not cause the war." "Southerners left the Union because they saw [in it] an inveterate hostility toward their society, culture, political heritage, and economic interests." The Civil War had "no one single simple explanation or cause," the statement read—but the "invasion and conquest of the Southern States" was the primary impetus for war. Worse than military defeat, however, had been the subsequent domination of the South by the victorious North—a state of affairs, these scholars believed, that continued to this day, as evidenced by the attacks on the flag and other aspects of the southern past. "If there is any lesson to be drawn," they said, referring to the battles over Confederate symbols, "it is not that our flag is shameful but that our institutions are in a sadly colonial condition."[75]

Not only the past was being drawn into the black hole that had opened up in the maelstrom swirling around the Confederate flag. Contemporary political decisions were being sucked in, as well. Aside from the racial overtones connected with replacing the state's only black supreme court justice, there was also the irksome struggle that had broken out over the Martin Luther King holiday. Although King's birthday had been recognized in state law and had even been made a legal state holiday in 1983, state employees did not necessarily get the day off. Unlike mandatory holidays, the King birthday was one of four "optional holidays" (together with Jefferson Davis's birthday, Confederate Memorial Day, and R. E. Lee's birthday) from which the state's public servants could choose. The dispute over whether or not to make King's birthday a mandatory state holiday (giving it equal status with other major holidays and bringing the state into line with the rest of the Union) lent the issue a thematic similarity to the flag controversy, causing the two debates to become partially entangled with one another (at least in the minds of some state lawmakers).[76]

The senate had passed legislation a year earlier making King Day a mandatory state holiday—in a bill initiated by Senator Robert Ford that also made 10 May, Confederate Memorial Day, a permanent holiday. Now it was up to the contentious house to decide whether or not South Carolina would join together with the rest of the country to celebrate this black son of the South. Several representatives vehemently opposed the idea. During subcommittee deliberations on the bill, Representative John Graham Altman of Charleston, no stranger to inflammatory remarks, accused King of plagiarism and reminded the body of the civil-rights leader's promiscuity. Representative Jake Knotts from the Midlands called King an "enthusiastic serial adulterer" and recommended the holiday be renamed "Civil Rights Day," to eliminate any explicit veneration of King. The episode soon passed, but the wrangling continued. When the bill was brought to the house floor for debate in early March, blacks and other Democrats balked because of the Confederate Memorial Day component it contained. House Republicans counterattacked by attaching an amendment to the bill that included a statement stipulating that the Confederate flag should be considered a symbol of heritage, and not "a racist banner per se." Rather than swallow this pro-flag amendment, Democrats agreed with house leaders to send the measure back to committee for repair. Emerging bruised and battered from the brawl over the King holiday bill, state lawmakers wondered how much worse it would be when debate turned to the question of the Confederate flag.[77]

Before those debates could begin, however, South Carolina would be the scene of one last grand flag march. In the wake of the King Day debacle in the state legislature, Charleston Mayor Joe Riley (with support from his friend, Mayor Bob Coble of Columbia) organized a march from his city by the sea across the state and up to the steps of the State House, some 120 miles away. Riley (who is white, but who has been referred to on occasion as "Little Black Joe," or "LBJ," by some of his detractors) said that the event was meant to counter the national impression that the struggle over the Confederate flag in South Carolina was a conflict between the NAACP and the rest of the state. The march aimed to demonstrate that it was not simply a matter of black versus white, that there were many others in the state who were just as eager as the NAACP to see the flag come down. Dubbed "Get In Step" (an appeal to the state legislature to "get in step" with the majority of South Carolinians), the march would be led by Riley, who would be joined at various stations along the way by other state leaders and dignitaries. "Celebrity" participants ranged from former Governor John West and novelist Pat Conroy to race-car driver Cale Yarborough. On the final leg into downtown Columbia, former Governor David Beasley joined in as a surprise guest. On the walk into town, Beasley joked that he was "the last living casualty of the Civil War."[78]

In an echo of the Civil Rights Era, a crowd of roughly two thousand marchers headed out of Charleston under the state's palmetto banner in early April, while a plane circled overhead trailing a sign that read, "Keep the Flag, Dump Riley." As is often the case in heirloom-laden Charleston, past and present had a way of bumping into each other in unexpected moments. On their way out of town, the Riley-led cortege happened past a group of antebellum-clad concertgoers, off to hear selections from the Civil War film *The Hunley.* Each group eyed the other with cool curiosity for a moment, then went their respective ways.

During its trek across the Carolina outback, the parade dwindled to sixty marchers or fewer. But its numbers swelled again (to several thousand) by the time it reached the state capitol. Heckled by small bands of roving flag supporters along the way, the "Get In Step" campaign would also face a pro-flag counter-demonstration when it reached the State House. The capitol grounds were sufficiently large enough to accommodate all comers, however, as the pros took up position on one side of the building and the antis on the other. (And as chance would have it, the flag supporters ended up on the *northern* side and the antis on the *southern* side. It was like a world turned upside down.)

This time Governor Hodges decided to join in the festivities. He was presented with the South Carolina state flag that the seven-term Charleston mayor had carried up from the coast. Speaking from the capitol steps, Riley repeated his call for lawmakers to get in step with the people of the state. "In our state," he said, "every religious denomination, every business organization, every civil rights organization, college boards-of-trustees and presidents, athletic directors, community leaders and average citizens, have said, remove the Confederate battle flag." In his remarks to the crowd, Hodges said simply, "I don't know about you, but, frankly, I'm tired of the debate." The message was clear: Let's get this thing out of the way and move on.[79]

Most South Carolinians were in full agreement with their governor. They were as tired of the debate as he was. Whatever entertainment value the flag story once may have had had long since dried up and blown away. But many in the state laid equal blame on both the flag stalwarts *and* the NAACP for stoking the fires that kept the dispute boiling. One state resident suggested flying the flag around Senator McConnell's neck, while another offered a succinctly elegant proposal: "Burn the flag. Spread the ashes around the NAACP headquarters. Get back to work."[80]

True, the State House's Confederate flag sales had shot through the roof—with 3,252 copies sold during the previous nine months—far outstripping orders for either state (582) or U.S. (256) flags. But the buying boom was due as much, no doubt, to the increased awareness of the sales brought about by the flag debate, and to speculation over the value of such flags once the display was discontinued (which it appeared it soon would be), as it was to any devotion to Confederate heritage. Cancellations accruing to the NAACP boycott were on the rise, as well. By early April, at least 122 meetings and conventions had been called off statewide, with estimated losses to the state economy totaling around $10 million.[81]

Time was running out on finding a solution. By the time the "Get In Step" marchers reached the State House steps in early April, there were only a little more than twenty working days left in the legislative session—with elections to come in the fall. If the senate were to begin work on a bill, it would need to debate and pass the measure on to the house before 1 May, or else face the two-thirds rule for introducing new business—the same hurdle that had tripped up the Heritage Act six years earlier.

There had been talk for some time of "negotiations" going on between Senators McConnell and Jackson, who were reportedly working on a proposal based on the Heritage Act framework. Senator Courson had publicly endorsed the idea in February—though on condition that the NAACP first stop its boycott campaign. Boycott or no boycott, however, the senate now appeared ready to take up the matter in full floor debate. What was needed was a "vehicle"—a bill—that the body could chew on. The specific content of the bill did not matter very much, since any bill could be altered by amendment (so that even its own author would no longer recognize it). The first attempt, using Senator Thomas's Heritage Park proposal as a platform, failed when Thomas rejected his own plan, out of concern that it would be gutted and refashioned beyond recognition.[82]

The legislative "vehicle" that the senate leadership finally settled on (in a decision taken by the body's committee chairmen, at the insistence of Senate President John Drummond) was a bill, No. 1266, originally introduced by Senator Ford. The final product bore only remote resemblance to the bill Ford had originally submitted. His bill was meant merely to serve as a container, to be filled with whatever content the senate leaders chose.[83]

Drummond, the 80-year-old senate president pro tem, was pushing hard to find a way through all the wrangling. But he very nearly set off a tangle of his own when he was quoted in a newspaper interview calling the Confederate flag "a racist symbol." His pro-flag colleagues jumped at the offense. Senator Ravenel demanded that Drummond apologize for the remark, and Drummond backpedaled. "It's not a racist symbol to me. It's a racist symbol to all those people over there," Drummond said, pointing to a group of black lawmakers. Senator McConnell rose to reiterate his demand that the flag must be moved to the Soldiers Monument, or not at all. Senator Patterson responded by refusing to support the move to the monument, "come hell or high water."[84]

In mid-April, a week after the "Get In Step" march had reached the State House—and, by a remarkable coincidence, exactly 139 years to the day after the first shots were fired on Fort Sumter, the South Carolina senate was ready to debate once again the question of what to do about the Confederate flag. But the night before the big debate (which would be televised live), there was still no clear plan about what to do with the flag. A swelter of different ideas and proposals were still floating around. And though many of them looked promising, none had enough votes to pass. Some eleventh-hour discussion centered on the Courson/Jackson flag-encasement idea. The state NAACP had made positive signals about the plan—though they had also said that its chances could be improved if a site could be found for a black regimental banner as well.[85]

Late in the evening, a group of senate leaders, including Drummond, Courson, Majority leader John Land, John Matthews (head of the Legislative Black Caucus), and Tom Moore of Aiken, walked from their offices over to the State House to scout for possible locations for a black banner. Standing in the lobby, looking out of the window past the large columns and across to the Confederate Soldiers Monument out front, Drummond vented his frustration at all the wearisome debate over the Confederate flag and the dizzying array of proposals about what to do with it. "I'm tired of all these new flags," he said to the others. "We're talking about putting flags here and putting flags there. What we're really trying to do is eliminate a flag." At bottom, it came down to getting rid of one flag, Drummond insisted. All the rest was just evasion.

Earlier in the day, McConnell had indicated his willingness to go along with a stripped-down version of the 1994 Heritage Act—one that would simply switch the flag from the dome to the monument and enact legal protections for all Confederate (and civil-rights) memorials in the state. Courson agreed that this might be the best route to take, since it would probably be the only plan that could gain a majority consensus in the senate. Matthews said he would take the proposal to the NAACP.

The following morning, all seven black senators gathered in John Land's office. It was now clear that the Heritage Act was the only plan with a chance of passing. White lawmakers Drummond and Land made their own support for the plan contingent on their black colleagues' approval. It was important to black senators that the flag to be placed at the monument not be the same one that flew over the dome—the rectangular design so closely associated with the Klan. And in agreeing to this change, pro-flag legislators were tacitly acknowledging the taint that adhered to the banner over the dome. Senator Jackson went to talk to the NAACP, telling them that it was a choice between "fighting a bloody battle that might not end this year, and bringing an end to an issue that has torn the state apart." The NAACP still refused to endorse the move and declared that sanctions against the state would not be lifted. For his part, however, Senator Patterson had concluded, with a measure of resignation, that "In this business, after being down here for 26 years dealing with this issue, you have to know when to hold 'em and when to fold 'em. This," he said, "is folding time."

By the time the senate convened later that day, 12 April, the compromise that would bring the Confederate flag down from the dome had already been worked out. There was really very little left to discuss.

Even so, the senators didn't hesitate to spend some time at the podium "'spressin' themselves," as Senator Patterson had once put it. The proceedings were, for the most part, serious, even somber at times, occasionally broken up by the kind of light banter typical of the good-ol'-boys club known as the South Carolina senate. For the pro-flag remnant, the day had about it the air of a wake, filled with sometimes stumbling efforts at eloquence and pathos. The tone of the senate debate was more respectful than contentious. But there was still a palpable undercurrent of rancor and resentment. Underneath the sporadic, mostly good-natured verbal sparring one could still catch glimpses of bruised feelings and lingering hair-trigger mistrust. But they all knew the country—and the world—were watching. So they were careful about what they said and how they said it.

In his opening remarks, Drummond appealed to the senate's spirit of camaraderie, petitioning his fellow senators to adhere to a proper decorum. "Let's be civil about all of this," he said. "Let's put aside pride of authorship. Let us not worry about our images and our egos for a while. This ought not be about winning and losing today. This ought not be about finding the perfect solution. Let's find a good imperfect settlement." Then, linking the state's past and its present, he added: "Almost forty years ago, two great South Carolinians, Senator Edgar Brown and Bob Edwards, President of Clemson [University], challenged this Senate to do the right thing by desegregating Clemson. We did, and history has recorded the greatness of that moment. Let's challenge each other to do the right thing again."[86]

The State House lobby and the balcony in the senate chamber were filled with devotees of southern heritage. Some flag supporters arrived decked out in uniforms of Confederate gray. Most wore or bore some kind of flag-decorated accouterment—and one stood in the lobby wrapped in a full-sized Confederate battle flag. At one point, flag defenders broke into a spirited rendition of "Dixie" and had to be shushed by capitol guards.[87] Despite all the heritage hoopla, however, the debate in the chamber remained orderly and sedate. The most delicate topic still to be determined was the height of the pole on which the new flag would be flown. The pro-flag faction wanted to make sure it was not too short, while the anti-flag forces were determined to see that it not be too tall. Like Goldilocks looking for "just right," the senators eventually settled on a twenty-foot pole (later changed to thirty by the house). Several amendments were offered to the bill. One senator proposed that the Confederate flag be lowered to half-mast on Confederate Memorial Day. He also asked approval of an amendment that would allow the Confederate naval jack to be run up the flagpole over the dome every day at lunchtime (and then be immediately lowered again). Both ideas were swiftly rejected.

The proceedings in the senate did not really qualify as a debate—at least not in the sense that we usually understand such things. It hardly even qualified as a deliberation, since there was very little left to deliberate. More than anything, it was a time for explaining—for revisiting the reasons each had taken the position he had. Black senators had to explain to black citizens (and to the NAACP) why they had reversed themselves and decided to go along with the compromise moving the flag to the monument—and that it remained a thorn in their side, despite the settlement. Pro-flag senators had to explain to their backers in the southern heritage movement why they were giving up on the dome. It was a debate only in that it reflected the underlying differences in opinion over history. It became, for those watching, a kind of conversation, an exchange of perspectives—even though many of the perspectives exchanged did not so much conjoin as drift past one another. If nothing else, it reflected well the ongoing disputes and differences of opinion, both in the state and in the country at large, over southern history and the country's past. In the end, the lawmakers reflected divergent public perceptions and so proved themselves the people's representatives.

A large chunk of the senate's time was occupied by a rambling, stream-of-consciousness soliloquy delivered by Senator Bill Branton, a flag defender from Dorchester County, near Charleston. He wondered at the speed at which the compromise had come together—and asked how it was possible. "Our leader sent out a fax," Branton noted. "He said, 'bring more clothes [to the flag session],' and I did—because I thought it was gonna be an extended debate. But all of a sudden, we've all come together in glory land! There is a rush to get it through tonight, just as quick as I sit down. The senator from Mt. Pleasant [Ravenel] said, he wants to feed his guineas and ride his horse by six o'clock."

Speculating as to the cause of this sudden onset of legislative consensus, Branton asked, "Where did the pressure come from? Did it come from the mayor of Charleston, who marched up here demanding that [the flag] come down? Was there pressure from [the governor's office] downstairs? Did it come from within the Senate? Did it come from Mr. Darby of the NAACP? Is it politics? Is it concern about which party is gonna control the Senate after the next election?"

"I'd like to think," Branton continued, "that it was the effort of a lot of people that brought this thing together. But it looks to me like pressure has come from somebody to settle this issue, and settle it now!" Branton indirectly accused his fellow senators of abdicating their responsibilities by giving in to the coercive tactics of the NAACP. "We've let a group . . . beat our people up in South Carolina for almost four months! All over the national news—for four months! And what have we done? Just sit around and allowed 'em to beat our people up."

Branton held the podium—and the stage—so long that it was impossible to stifle the impression that he was filibustering. To Branton, though, it was just a matter of bringing a little balance to the picture. "We've been beat up on TV so bad about the flag—what's wrong with saying a few good things about keepin' the flag flying? And if anybody thinks I'm filibustering," he wanted to assure them, "I'm just talkin.'"

A filibuster was pointless now anyway, as the senator surely knew. There were more than enough votes to cut him off—just as there were enough votes to pass the flag-compromise bill. But if they could not filibuster, flag defenders could at least bluster yet a little while longer. "If I really thought taking that flag down would foster goodwill and help build bridges among our people in South Carolina," Branton went on, "I would gladly vote to do that. But if you think that passing this little bill tonight is gonna bring finality to race relations in this state—it's not gonna happen. If anything, it's gonna make things worse."

Branton's Upstate colleague, Senator Harvey Peeler of Cherokee County, saw the matter in a similar light. To Peeler, race relations in South Carolina remained commodious so long as both sides sought goodwill, so long as no one stirred things up by attempting to set one side against the other. He recalled his own youth, during the 1950s and 1960s, as a time when the races "lived in harmony, with respect and mutual admiration of each other. My brothers and I," the senator remembered, "played and worked with people of other races, and we got along fine." He recalled the integration of the local high school as a time of peaceful coexistence, goodwill, and even eager anticipation, as locals speculated on the athletic power that would be unleashed by combining the skills of black and white football teams.

Others would remember those times differently than Senator Peeler, of course. Some remembered the Klan bombing of the home of a Cherokee County white couple, in 1957, after the pair openly endorsed the idea of racial desegregation. An all-white jury acquitted the bombers in 1958. Their court defense had been provided by attorney and state senator John D. Long, legislative patron of the state's Confederate flag displays. Others recalled a sign, posted in a local grocery-store window, that read "Niggers and Dogs Not Allowed." The sign remained in place into the 1960s. And still others recalled a boycott, led by black high-school students, protesting the hiring practices of Peeler Dairy, Peeler's family business.[88] Some memories remained neatly segregated—even long after legal segregation had vanished.

In Peeler's memory, the 1950s and 1960s had been a time of harmony and mutual respect. "Football was our priority then," he said, "and we went through the '60s without much controversy. We got along pretty well." More importantly, Peeler said as he pointed to the three flags hanging behind the rostrum, "we made it through those times . . . under those three flags." He recited the racial progress accomplished in the state "under those three flags," including the election of the first black senator (since Reconstruction); the appointment of a black state supreme court chief justice; the seating of the first female supreme court justice; and the selection of the first black to head the state's Employment Security Commission. All of that, Peeler repeated, had come about "under those three flags."

"I'm proud of that flag," the senator said. It was a pride derived not only from a love of heritage, but from a desire to stand apart—even in the face of world opinion. For some, Peeler said, "the flag is a symbol of freedom and justice . . . a symbol of people who do not like to be told what to do," who cherish their personal liberty. To them, "it's called the *rebel* flag," the senator declared. The rebels are "a group of people who love this state," he went on, "who love their independence, who love their freedom—and they DON'T WANT TO BE TOLD WHAT TO DO BY ANYBODY!—especially if we think we're right."

"So," the senator concluded, "if you take that flag down tonight, in the morning South Carolinians will greet each other differently than they did yesterday, if they greet each other at all. If you take that flag down tonight, ten thousand flags will be hoisted around the state of South Carolina that look just like it—in the yards, in the houses, on the vehicles, all around this state in the morning, if you take that flag down tonight. If you take that flag down tonight," Peeler warned dramatically, "in the morning, the rebels will yell. Race relations will not be the same in this state in my lifetime, if you take that flag down."

In attempting to explain their love for the Confederate banner, pro-flag senators, both stalwarts and compromisers, repeatedly spoke of family, of place, and of history. Senator Thomas asked, "Why is this such an emotional issue for South Carolinians?" Then he offered an answer: "We who have been brought up in South Carolina, on the knees of grandfathers and grandmothers and uncles, [we have heard them] tell the stories of war, [stories which] bring home the emotions of those great-grandparents, and great-great-grandparents, who fought in that horrible conflict. And that emotion is as galvanizing in our minds as if we had gone through that ourselves."

To many others, the pain of past suffering still seemed almost as near as yesterday. For Senator Scott Richardson of coastal Beaufort County, it was the weight of history itself that touched the sentiments. "This war was fought *in the South*," he said sharply. "Nobody burned New York! Nobody burned Boston! When you drive through the South," the senator said, his voice hesitating with emotion, "you can't go ten miles without seeing a marker—or a graveyard. And I think that's why we're so serious about this."

Speaking in a drawl as slow and thick as pure cane molasses, Senator Verne Smith talked about his own family's links with the past—and about his concern over the way his feelings, and the feelings that others have, for that past have been portrayed. "This is something that's deep, deep in my heart," Smith said. "People outside of this state—and a lot of 'em *in* this state—don't understand what's in our hearts. They think we're a bunch of rednecks and a bunch of racists. But the truth of the matter is, I'm just tryin' to protect the dignity of my grandmother and my granddaddy and my great-granddaddy."

"Now I'm not tryin' to say that the cause was right," Smith went on. "I'm not tryin' to say, honor slavery. I'm not tryin' to say, honor the old southern conventions. I'm sayin', honor our people, who went through so much affliction, who went through so much horror, terror, and held their families together. . . . This is a soldier's flag at a soldier's monument," he said, trying to draw the all-important distinction. "It's not the flag that's been misused by the Kew-Klux Klan or the Skintheads. My great-granddaddy walked under it. My granddaddy marched under it."

"But we've wore out all those old stories," he admitted, "we've told 'em so many times. Told about the mistreatment of our black citizens. . . . We're gonna outgrow that now—we wanna get above that now," Smith insisted. "I've said many times . . . I'd never vote to take that flag off the top of the State House. But there's not a doubt in my mind that we've come to the point where it serves the public interest" to take it down. As he spoke, a group of senators worked to refine the language in the flag bill. From the rostrum Smith urged them to "get the wording just right, so that both sides understand it, and make absolutely sure nobody's tryin' to play a trick on anybody. And if they do [try something]," the senior senator warned, "I think all of us oughta jump on 'em and whoop 'em."

"I believe we're comin' together now," Smith said hopefully, "and it'll be a blessing for our state."

Some senators were still bothered by the way the state had been portrayed in the national media and sought to present alternative images of a state in which racial harmony, not conflict, was the norm. Senator Richardson declared emphatically, "We're not some backwoods southern state," and then described the state's racial progress during the preceding decades. Senator Addison Wilson recalled his own participation in the harmonious and uneventful desegregation of his high school, back in the early 1960s. Senator Thomas Alexander, from the far northwestern corner of the state, described the biracial cooperation that went into rebuilding the Shiloh Baptist Church after Klansmen burned it to the ground. And Senator Ernest Passailaigue of Charleston called the flag relocation "part of the biblical healing experience for South Carolina."

There was a bit too much "Kumbaya" in all this, as far as some black senators were concerned. The heritage perspective, and the eager hustling to reach a kind of contrived reconciliation, needed to be balanced by a glimpse into the black view of the past.

"Did you know that I grew up in a different period?," Ralph Anderson, a black senator from the Upstate, asked his white colleague Verne Smith. For Anderson the southern past meant, not glory and honor but "segregation, discrimination, rape, back-of-the-bus, no job opportunities. Do you know," Anderson went on, "when I look at the flag . . . it suggests all the bad things than can happen? If you notice, when we do the pledge in the morning, I turn my head the other way, because I cannot look at that Confederate flag, because when I see it, I see my grandmother and all the suffering that she had, and that my parents had. If this capitol belonged to you, it would be different," Anderson reminded his pro-flag colleagues. "But the capitol belongs to all of us."

Several pro-flag lawmakers were troubled by the NAACP's rejection of the senate's plan. They worried that, with the boycott continuing, the state might ultimately be forced "to go through this again, six months or a year from now," Senator Thomas said. For flag stalwart Larry Grooms, another Lowcountry senator, the NAACP's rebuff of the compromise offer was reason enough for him to reject the bill. "I believe the NAACP's decision . . . is the beginning of a crusade to ban . . . all things southern and all things related to the Confederacy," Grooms said. "We sent the flag on a journey from the dome to a pole outside. And I don't believe that's where the journey will end. I believe that the journey will eventually lead to the removal of the flag from the State House grounds. And then it'll only be a memory, for those who *care* to remember."

But while some felt that NAACP approval was essential for the compromise to work, others, ironically enough, only endorsed the plan *because* of the NAACP's failure to back it. "This does not meet their demands," said Senator Larry Martin of Pickens, in the Upstate, "and I have no intention of voting for something that does." When Thomas fretted that the NAACP's rejection might mean having to revisit the issue in the near future, Martin shot back, "I would think this would be the last time we will discuss this issue for the next *100 years!*" NAACP approval of the compromise plan would taint the effort, he believed. And any flag defender who voted in favor of an NAACP-backed agreement would be guilty of capitulation. "If . . . the outside groups came in and said, we're gonna bless this thing, you know what I'd do?," Martin asked Thomas. "I'd vote against it!" Then he added, in a tone of embittered defiance, "If we pass this bill, I hope they continue to boycott. It doesn't matter to me. We're done. This is it!"

Senator Ford agreed that it was time to put the matter to rest—and appealed to the NAACP to drop its opposition to the compromise. Stepping up to the podium with a buoyancy that bordered on jubilance, Ford declared that "South Carolina has made tremendous progress in the last twenty-four hours." He recalled King's "I Have a Dream" speech—and "in particular the time that he had spoken of 'when the sons of former slaves'—that's me—'and the sons of former slaveowners'—that's some of you," Ford said with a chuckle, "would get together as brothers and try to work out our differences, so that we could respect each other." King "had a lot of love for the Southland," Ford added, transforming King into something of a heritage defender himself. "He never denied his southern history or heritage."

Ford said he knew how hard it was for flag defenders such as McConnell, Smith, and Courson to support the compromise and praised them for showing "the Confederate side of South Carolina the way." Without their leadership, he said, "it could have been all hell [breaking loose] in South Carolina today, just like Senator Peeler said." He also praised the "strong leadership of colleagues in the African American community." He said he understood how some might want to take the campaign a step further and demand more. But he believed that once one's demands had been met, the cause should not be pressed. "The goals that I set for myself on this issue in 1967," Ford declared, "have been met." And he appealed to the NAACP to join with him in celebration. "I'm begging the NAACP to declare victory. They won! Now it's time to bring [people] together and make Dr. King's dream a reality."

When he rose to speak, the other old veteran of the flag wars, Senator Patterson, sounded like the weary warrior who chooses to fight no more—or like someone forced to cry uncle. The compromise plan was not entirely to his liking, but he would hold his nose and vote for it, he said. "I been preachin' since 1974 to take the flag down," Patterson reminisced. "I used to get into some heated debates. I used to love to get up and rant and rave, cuss, and raise hell. And so, it's kind of hard for me to buy this so-called compromise—because you're putting it at Main and Gervais [Streets]. And I told you that I didn't want it at Main and Gervais. But as you get older, you learn things, and you mellow down, and you get some sense. I'll probably vote for it, because South Carolina has been through a lot, I mean a *whole* lot, about this flag. And really, my God, when you been on something for *26 years!*—well, that's long enough to be on anything"

"I know the NAACP is not gonna accept it," he acknowledged. "But I got a feeling that this is the best we can do, under the circumstances. So if we can come together and resolve it, today or tonight, then I think we oughta come together and resolve it. And when we leave here," he implored, "let's leave here as brothers and sisters. Don't leave with your lips juggin' out and your jaws full of wind, mad about which side won and which side lost. If we can resolve this, I think South Carolina will win."

For Senator Jackson, it was a day of mixed emotions. He could not share in Ford's jaunty exuberance. But anger or sadness seemed just as inappropriate. Relief and sober resignation was probably a better approximation of his feelings at the time. Even more than Patterson, Jackson felt a need to explain his vote. It was true that he had cosponsored the 1994 Heritage Act that formed the basis of the current compromise. But the very public stance he had taken against placing the flag at the Soldiers Monument left him with a lot of ground to cover. And in clarifying his reasons for supporting the compromise, Jackson also sought to illustrate how one's view of history breaks down along fissures formed by the tectonic displacements of historical experience.

"I think it's necessary," Jackson said, "to show you how difficult it was for those of us 'on the other side,' as Senator [Branton] referred to us, to come to where we are now. To some of us, believe it or not, Sherman was a hero. I can trace my ancestry back to a great-great uncle who marched behind Sherman's army when he invaded the city of Columbia. He later told his family, that was the greatest day of his life. For that young black boy on Taylor's Plantation (which probably included the area we're standing on right now), that invading army was coming to liberate him. And so he ran, marched, skipped, and danced behind that army, because that army, to him, represented freedom and liberty."

Jackson then went on to address another, equally burning concern. "I also came up here to say that I think that we owe the NAACP a debt of gratitude, because I'm convinced that, if it had not been for the NAACP, we wouldn't be here now, and it would be another generation who would be fighting this fight. There are some of us who feel as passionately about the NAACP as others of you feel about the Sons and Daughters of the Confederate Veterans. It was a very difficult thing to look them in the eyes, people who are close friends of mine, and say to them that I am going to have to vote for this resolution. They looked back with tears in their eyes and felt as if I had just betrayed them. That is a very difficult thing to do."

"As I woke up this morning," he went on, "and heard on the news that this was the day on which the first shots were fired on Fort Sumter, I said to myself, 'Wouldn't it be wonderful if on the same day the war began, the war would end?' My son said to me then, 'Well, daddy, that's up to you and your colleagues.' And he's right. It is up to us. And I think we are doing the right thing, even though it's a hard thing to do. Because, as much as I love the NAACP, I love South Carolina even more." Then, turning to answer Senator Branton's question, "What has pressured us to come to this position?," Jackson said simply, "the right thing has pressured us, and that is the great sovereign state of South Carolina."

Talk of "great sovereign states" was no doubt music to the ears of Senator McConnell. But this was not a day for hot and swollen talk of states' rights. For his part, McConnell sought a higher plane and a more soothing tone, full of appeals to reconciliation and concord, to peace with honor—for both sides. "To my friends who are opponents on this," McConnell said, "I understand your commitment against the flag. There's not one of you that doesn't have the guts to get up here and fight over it. It's the same on both sides. There's courage, there's determination, there's a willingness to fight for your position on this."

McConnell's speech was steeped in overtones of the past. The parallels he drew to the Civil War made it seem as if this day were a second encounter at Appomattox, a meeting of old veterans, of fellow soldiers, drawn together in mutual respect and brotherly feeling after a long and bitter campaign. Recalling the special significance of the date, McConnell spoke not only of the 12 April "when the war began." He spoke also of another 12 April, four years later, "when General [John B.] Gordon brought the Confederate troops in and laid those flags and arms down before the Army of the Potomac." He quoted Union General

Joshua Chamberlain's quietly respectful words about the Confederate surrender at Appomattox and appealed for the same sense of amity and equitable generosity in ending the debate over the Confederate flag. It should be a conclusion without victory or defeat, he insisted, a meeting of equals.

"I can only hope that the goodwill generated in this Senate extends now beyond these doors out across South Carolina," McConnell said. Then, turning to those who spoke of capitulation and sellouts, he said, "None of us are acting because of speeches. None of us are acting because of demands. None of us are acting because of ultimatums. I think we're acting because we all know the reality of where we are, pretty much like General Lee when he was confronted with Appomattox."

"It is very difficult," McConnell continued, "extremely difficult, for us on our side to vote to move that flag. It has to be equally difficult for my brethren on the other side to vote with us to move it to the monument. It has to be just as difficult, just as challenging to defend." Only then can it be fair and equitable.

McConnell extolled the heritage-defending virtues of those on his side, of Senators Courson, Ravenel, and Smith, "a person," he said, "whose blood runs warm for the memory of those soldiers." He praised Senators Patterson, Jackson, and Glover as well, singling out his friend Senator Ford in particular. He said that it was Ford "who pointed the way for us on this" by extending "enough courtesy to want to know more about me," to get past "the wall of disagreement" so that I might "do the same and understand his history as well."

Mixed in with his appeal for understanding and mutual respect, McConnell nevertheless felt it necessary to admonish the other side to cease its attacks on the Confederate legacy and let the conflict end. Here, too, he drew on history—on his own reading of Reconstruction—for lessons on avoiding the errors of excess. "We're pretty much at the crossroads of history," McConnell said, "like they were that day at Appomattox. And I hope that we leave this day not making the same mistake that was made after that war. Because, as Lee would say, looking back on the way Reconstruction went, 'Had I known that we would be treated this way, I would not have surrendered at Appomattox.' Each and every one of us has had to give. Those of us on our side—if we expect to be treated with respect, we have to extend that [same] respect [to the other side]." He was counting on the other side to do the same.

"I can tell you that it's very difficult for me to say goodbye to that flag on the dome. I love it up there, as a war memorial. I enjoy seeing it at night—looking out the windows at it. But it's going to fly at the soldier's monument, where it probably should have gone in the first place—then maybe we wouldn't have been at this place at this time," McConnell admitted. "But if sadness comes, at least there's optimism and hope for the people of South Carolina. South Carolina has come from within and said we have the strength to pull ourselves through this and to take a significant step toward trying to bring our people, black and white, together, so that it's not necessary that people embrace what other people believe, but that we simply have respect for one another within the ambiance of those beliefs."

"I am voting," he concluded, "with the optimism that we are taking the flag to a position of honor and finality, [out of concern for the feelings of] South Carolinians who are offended by it on the dome. The hour has come, as it came with General Lee and the Army of Northern Virginia. We have fought this thing and fought this thing, and now the olive branch is out on both sides—to extend a hand to try to move forward and not make the mistakes that were made after Appomattox, and instead use this opportunity to bring this state together, to close this issue, and to hope that we build on it for our future and not let it be something that divides us further."

Amid the applause that followed, John Drummond rose to invoke the past once more. Praising McConnell's address as "the greatest togetherness speech that I have ever heard in this Senate," the senior leader offered the highest of compliments when he said, "I think everyone will agree: We still have a John C. Calhoun."

With all the speech-making done, there was nothing left to do but vote. As the roll call came around to Senator Glover, there was a moment of hesitation. In tears and unable to bring herself to vote in favor of the bill, she was instead recorded simply as "not voting." It was the only abstention among the seven black members of the senate. With their support, the measure passed 36 to 7. And even though they all knew their support was essential to achieving this partial victory, Glover was certainly not the only one of her colleagues who had hoped to accomplish more. In a perfect world, more might have been possible.

Jackson left the senate that day in a pensive mood. He drove around town for an hour afterwards before finally heading home. He realized the vote was necessary, in order that the "healing may begin," but it was at best a partial victory, shaped by the peculiarities of South Carolina history and the realities of its politics. For Jackson, as for many others, this was not the day of jubilo.

<hr />

The Heritage Act of 2000 had taken one hurdle. But the greater one still had to be cleared. A viable solution to the flag deadlock had gotten this far once before, back in 1994, only to be picked off by sharpshooting flag partisans in the House of Representatives. The unpredictable volatility of that body, its more pronounced factionalism and its shorter electoral fuse, combined with the Republican majority and the strength of the conservative (neo-Confederate) wing, made passage of the senate bill anything but certain. The old Carolina cussedness—that old digging-in-at-the-heels aversion to being told what to do—was fired up and humming. More than the senate, the South Carolina House of Representatives is a bazaar of political barter, where a rough-and-tumble competition for advantage produces a kind of egalitarian free agency among its assorted polit-mongers. Whereas the senate functions as a kind of Sotheby's of Carolina politics, the house more closely resembles the New York Stock Exchange on a hot trading day.

But this time there were factors pushing toward compromise that had not been in play before. In contrast to 1994, conservatism was no longer the power it once was. Instead of a rising tide relentlessly sweeping all before it, it now had become part of the established order, concerned with maintaining its position and averse to risking future electoral success over matters of merely symbolic significance. Flag fatigue was having its effect, too. Lawmakers, who always enjoyed talking, were "talked out" on the issue, tired of the endless wrangling. And unlike 1994, the senate bill arrived on the house side of the legislature with plenty of time to spare, leaving lawmakers with several weeks to mull it over, thrash it out, and build a consensus behind it.

The NAACP's boycott and its rejection of the senate plan also played a role, in both a negative and a positive sense As Jackson had said, without the NAACP-led campaign, the legislature probably would have remained just as inactive and evasive as ever. But the boycott—and in particular the NAACP's opposition to the senate compromise—had reframed the debate and helped pro-flag lawmakers reposition themselves. They now could both stand with the flag *and* agree to move it. By moving the flag, the flag defenders could claim that they were actually protecting it from those who would like to see it removed altogether. The NAACP's position became, in effect, one extreme in the spectrum of options facing the flag—with the "fire-eating" flag fanatics, heritage groups, and southern diehards at the other end. With the NAACP now drawing the bulk of pro-flag fire, pro- and anti-flag representatives could come together on a resolution with less concern about heritage retribution. Flag-defending state legislators claimed that they were forced to rescue the state from the destructive effects brought on by extremists on either side.

A sign that the house was ready to come together and put the matter behind it once and for all came the same day that the senate passed its flag plan. That day the House of Representatives finally passed a bill making Martin Luther King Jr.'s birthday an official (and mandatory) state holiday. The legislation establishing the holiday was still a difficult thing for some to swallow, however, because in addition to the King holiday it also made 10 May, Confederate Memorial Day, a state holiday in its own right. It was clear that the southern heritage defenders were not ready to give up just yet—certainly not without getting something in return.[89]

Speculation grew that black state representatives might balk at the senate flag compromise, coming as it did right on the heels of their acquiescence to the Confederate Memorial Day holiday. Several black lawmakers had voted against the King holiday bill because of the "equal opportunity" it granted the Confederacy. And now there appeared to be an unlikely alliance forming between Confederate flag supporters and black house members in opposition to the senate flag bill. "I'd rather it stay where it is than to bring it where they're talking about putting it," one black representative said. "It should be impossible to convince anyone sensitive to the historical and present day struggles of African-Americans to support flying such a divisive symbol, especially at the most public of all approaches to the State House," wrote James Gallman. To many black lawmakers, moving the flag to one end of "South Carolina's Main Street" seemed less a victory than a cynical and backhanded slap-in-the-face.[90]

The state NAACP and its core of black church leaders held fast to economic sanctions. They sought to buttress support for the campaign by calling on black state residents to forgo major purchases and avoid dining out during the upcoming Easter holiday. Churches organized potluck get-togethers as an alternative to the traditional Easter Sunday restaurant outings. Some feast-goers showed up in t-shirts bearing the slogan "We're not shopping until the flag starts dropping." The campaign prompted one minister to declare, "We can pinch this economy so much that Arthur Ravenel will go up on top of that dome and take the flag down himself."[91]

It was an overly optimistic assessment of the situation, to say the least. The public-relations pressure brought about by the attention focused on the state through the boycott was out of all proportion to its economic effect. The NAACP-led boycott had been effective in rousing attention, but it could not direct the specific course taken to deal with the flag at the center of that attention. State business leaders all were lined up in favor of the senate compromise plan. Without their support—and in particular that of the state Chamber of Commerce—the NAACP's ongoing economic sanctions would be largely ignored. The boycott would be effective only so long as the state refused to take any action. Once it began to make an effort to resolve the flag matter, pressure dwindled precipitously. By early spring, the boycott had already passed the point of maximum potency. For most people (even for many blacks), it only mattered that the flag was coming down from the dome—not where it went once it was removed.[92]

State leaders still hoped that the compromise plan might eventually garner enough biracial support in the house to imbue it with a sufficient measure of political legitimacy. But with so many black representatives coming out against it, even its passage now appeared imperiled. Opponents of the senate bill sought, for example, to force lengthy debate on all bills still on the legislative calendar. Their aim was to try and run out the clock on the current session before the flag bill could reach the floor for consideration. Speculation about black anti-flag and white pro-flag lawmakers coming together in the house to defeat the senate plan led some to believe that the only way to keep the whole flag effort from coming apart at the last minute would be by trying another approach to the problem. In hopes of avoiding a debacle, house Democrats introduced yet one more alternative flag plan. They hoped it would receive the kind of broad-based, biracial support everyone claimed to be after.[93]

The newest idea was first broached by two former state judges, Ernest A. Finney Jr. and Alex Sanders, one of whom, Finney, had only recently retired as chief justice of the South Carolina Supreme Court. Their proposal would have taken the flag from the dome, cast it in bronze (the way baby shoes sometimes are), and mounted it on a slab of South Carolina granite placed near the Confederate Soldiers Monument. And in order to insure that both those living and those yet to come understood the reasons for the move, the marker would be engraved with the following inscription:

> The Confederate battle flag was relocated from the dome of the State House and cast in bronze to unite the people of South Carolina at long last and as a permanent memorial to the Confederate soldiers who died in the performance of their duties.

The idea met with an immediate and unconditional thumbs-down from key Republican leaders. Speaker Wilkins said it made "no sense for us to pass a plan that's going to be met by a Senate filibuster." Others compared the bronzed flag to a tombstone and announced that they would have nothing to do with a symbolic burial of Confederate heritage. The proposal surfaced later as an amendment offered to the senate bill and occupied a sizeable segment of house floor debate but was eventually rejected by a comfortable margin, despite support by a majority of Democrats.[94]

Room for agreement was narrow and shaky. Republicans such as Rick Quinn claimed that Democrats were not acting in good faith and countered with a proposal of their own meant to appeal to flag stalwarts. In it, Republicans offered to fly the flag over the dome three times a year, on Confederate Memorial Day, Lee's birthday, and Jefferson Davis's birthday. Democrats considered the offer a bluff, an attempt by Republicans to pressure Democrats into supporting the senate plan. In reaction, Democrats crafted a resolution aimed at black lawmakers, offering to place five flags not from the Civil War–era alongside the Confederate banner in front of the State House—each to serve as a memorial to a military operation in which South Carolinians had been engaged (e.g., World War I and the Gulf War). This idea had the advantage of providing a clearly military context to the Confederate flag. And it also served to "dilute" the Confederate flag's visual affect. But the plan also called for flying the Confederate banner over the

State House one day a year, on Confederate Memorial Day (in an appeal to flag supporters)—an element that undermined any support the proposal may have had among black legislators. Black leaders felt they had worked too long and hard on this issue to allow the flag to return to the dome for even one day a year.[95]

◆◆◆◆◆

The first day of house debate began, as it had in the senate, with a prayer appropriate to the occasion. "Keep us from impatience, irritability, and tempers too quick," the house chaplain implored. "Save us from eyes focused on the faults of others and tongues turned to criticism. And when evening is come, may we rest in that peace which inevitably comes [when] we have kept the Golden Rule: 'Do unto others as you would have others do unto you.'"[96] When evening came, however, the house would still be just as far from agreement as it had been when morning dawned—and the Golden Rule had somehow gotten lost in the shuffle, replaced with the rules of competitive advantage. Outside, at the foot of the Confederate Soldiers Monument, civil-rights activists set flame to Confederate and Nazi flags—both of them symbols, they said, of the same brand of racial hatred. Other protestors had spattered the monument with red paint. The house responded angrily to the vandalism by increasing the penalty for defacing monuments on the State House grounds, making it a crime punishable by a five-year prison sentence (placing it on a par with involuntary manslaughter).[97]

The final legislative altercation in the long struggle over the Confederate flag lasted just a little over two days. But it was not a stormy session. There were no noisy eruptions of hostility, no heated crossfire between opposing camps, and little fiery rhetoric. Though the seams that held the body together were showing signs of wear and the scars of debates past were there for all to detect, the members watched their p's and q's and, for the most part, stuck to the matter at hand. In contrast to the senate and its sometimes sputtering efforts at high-flying rhetoric, the language of the house was prosaic and workmanly, colloquial and often rather homely. (This was, after all, the body that housed the voice of the people.) Consensus was not so much a product of agreement as it was of exhaustion and simple mathematics: whichever plan obtained the majority of votes would be the one to pass. All democratic government comes down to this in the end. But in South Carolina's flag debate, it became the essence of political settlement.

When the house went to work on the flag in earnest, it faced a pile of 100 proposed amendments to the senate bill. Each had to be addressed individually and dealt with by voice or roll-call vote. Some of the amendments were only symbolic in nature, meant mainly to send comforting signals to voters back home. Others were trial balloons, meant to elicit test votes to check the legislative temperature on various ideas and proposals and determine what kind of coalitions might be possible. Many amendments were rejected summarily by voice vote in a matter of minutes. Others were withdrawn without discussion. But some became the subjects of hours-long explications and discussion, followed by procedural tallies and more roll-call votes. Democracy is often a slow and laborious process. It all took time—lots of time.

A multitude of ideas—old and new—resurfaced, were revivified, revamped, refashioned, then rewritten, rejected again, revived, reconsidered, and rejected once more. One by one, all the alternative plans and proposals made one last encore appearance, parading by like ghosts from Confederate debates past. Here was the referendum plan, there the circle-of-flags plan, then came the bronze-flag plan, the Stars and Bars option, the heritage-park proposal—and numerous other variations and sub-variations besides. The overwhelming majority of them were rejected quickly and resoundingly. The only amendments that gained majority approval made only minor alterations to the senate plan: the illumination of the flag at night; the placement of the last dome flag in the State Museum; an increase in the height of the new flagpole (to make it a better "aesthetic match" with the Soldiers Monument, its proponents claimed).

Flag backers in the house knew they were fighting a losing battle. Their only hope lay in delaying the final vote in hopes of adding a measure, any measure, that would make the bill unpalatable to a majority of representatives. With almost all the black legislators opposed to the senate plan, passage already seemed rather precarious—possibly only a matter of three or four votes. Every amendment posed a potential danger to the shaky support behind the Heritage Act. One proposition that resurfaced time and again over the course of the debate was a proposal to fly the flag over the dome one day in the year, on Confederate Memorial Day. Even Speaker Wilkins favored the idea and voted for it. Each time the proposal came up, it failed by only a slim margin—once by only a single vote. Had it passed, it likely would have alienated the last of the black lawmakers still supporting the senate plan. And even if it had prompted some pro-flag legislators to come on board in support of the compromise measure, its inclusion likely would have undermined the measure's chances during conference committee talks with the senate over the final shape of the legislation.

Two of the representatives charged with deciding the fate of the Confederate flag that day had a distinctive perspective on the issue. Out of the 123 members of the House of Representatives they were the only ones who had been members of the body thirty-nine years earlier, when it voted to raise the flag over the dome. One of them rose to add his voice to those calling for the flag to come down. He spoke for many when he said that, during his long years of service in the legislature, "I have never seen another debate as emotional as this one." The reason for the emotion was clear. Unlike most of the legislature's daily business, this issue was not about money, or regulations, or districting, or any of the routine matters of law and politics. This was instead about the intangibles of history, about convictions, and about perception.

One lawmaker said that dealing with the flag was really no different than any other issue the legislature had to confront. All of the issues they faced reflected a difference of opinion, he observed. But the differences of opinion over the flag were of a different quality altogether. They spilled out from the crevasse opened up by slavery, civil war, and many long years of racial discrimination. One black lawmaker said to his white colleagues: "I just can't understand why we see this flag so differently." A white flag defender might have asked the same question— but had the opposite thing in mind as he said it. There is power in perspective, a power as real as anything we might touch or see. It has at least as great an influence on the way we deal with human affairs (which is all politics really is) as any concrete matter we can examine with our five senses. As one black representative put it: "In many ways, your heritage is my regret." Perspective is abstract, yet it can be as solid in the mind as any phenomenon of nature.

The battle over the flag was a battle over meaning, the search for clearer definition and for redefinition. What was needed, one black representative said, was "a vehicle whereby that flag may fly, but with a different connotation," as a "celebration of our common humanity." That was probably asking too much. Such an attempt would have robbed the flag of all substance, forever untying it from its historical moorings. And besides, flag defenders would have opposed it. They did not want to see any new meanings attached to the flag. For them, avoiding alterations (especially at the insistence and under the direction of the flag's critics) was what the struggle was all about. To them, the Confederate flag was a "stainless banner"—untainted by moral culpability or historical guilt—and they meant for it to remain that way.

When something as clearly held as personal perspective combines with politics, emotion is not the only thing released. The resulting chemical reaction also generates pressure. Several representatives, from both sides of the aisle, noted the prodigious political pressure that was being applied during the flag deliberations. "This debate has brought out some of the most horrendous arm-twisting that I have ever seen," one member commented as he offered his fellow legislators a dose of ointment for their aching muscles. "For those of you . . . in the brotherhood of twisted arms; for those of you . . . in the fraternity of broken bones—I offer you some Ben-Gay."

Even Wilkins felt the pressure and the emotion. "This has not been an easy two months for any of us," he said.

I've been threatened. My wife's been threatened. I've been told my speakership's over with. I've been told the Republican majority's over with. I've been told that I [will be] the ruination of the Republican Party in South Carolina.

My office's been picketed. I've seen bumper-stickers sayin' "Dump Wilkins." I've seen signs that say "Dump Wilkins." And I heard radio ads that ran all over the state last week calling Rick Quinn and myself cowards. But I'm not gonna be bullied any more by anyone.

The flag fight was "hurting our state," he insisted. It was time to deal with this thing once and for all. This would be the last opportunity for the legislature to do something about it this year, he warned.

By late in the second day of debate, the exasperation and exhaustion were obvious. Amendments were starting to sound alike, proposals repeated themselves. The members were tired of it. The flag issue was like an old TV rerun that no one wanted to see anymore, having seen it so many times already. "All I wanna do is get to that Senate bill," one self-described "voice from the middle" declared. "I'm tired of dealing with avenues of flags, flags in the corner, crosses of flags, circles of flags, healing pools, cesspools, celebrity hot tubs—I'm sick of it! We need to vote now!"

In the end, it came down to a simple process of elimination. After the house waded through all the alternative schemes and notions, after it had debated and discarded each of them, then there was only one thing left that it could do: vote on the senate bill. And once it came to that, Wilkins believed, the house would step into line and pass the measure—rather than see the fight drag on any longer and take the blame for prolonging it. "What's going to happen if this bill fails?," he asked his fellow legislators in remarks from the podium just prior to the final vote. "We cannot *afford* to let this bill fail."

The flag defenders had always depended on flag fatigue to save their cause, because, up to now, it had always been easier for the majority to do nothing rather than find a way to remove the flag and end the debate. Like the Confederacy itself, flag partisans had sought to wear down their opponents and make them give up the fight. All they needed to do was hold out long enough until the flag's foes and their allies began to drift away. Once that happened, the siege would crumble, and the threat would pass. But the strategy could not work indefinitely. The issue was not going away this time. Ignoring it was no longer an option. The point had come when it finally became clear to a majority of legislators that the only way to effectively rid themselves of this bothersome matter was by ridding the dome of the Confederate flag. This time the tactical advantage lay with the flag's opponents. This time, voting to remove the flag became the path of least resistance.

And so they voted. And by another ironic twist of history—of the kind that Senator McConnell liked so much—the vote came on 10 May, Confederate Memorial Day. One-hundred-and-thirty-five years to the day after the final ignominious demise of the Confederacy, the legislature of the State of South Carolina, the cradle of that Confederacy, voted to lower the most familiar symbol of that long-ago lost cause and end the state's long civil war over the Confederate flag. Another irony lay in the flag chosen to fly at the monument. The authors of the senate bill made every effort to ensure that the flag be historically "authentic"—in the sense that it be a flag design specifically associated with South Carolina's Confederate soldiers; a pattern that they had actually carried in battle—in part, to distinguish the new flag from the one over the dome. And for that purpose they specified that the flag would be the "South Carolina Infantry Battle Flag of the Confederate States of America, the South Carolina, Georgia, Florida Department version," describing its dimensions as "fifty-two inches on each side." Unfortunately, no record exists that there was ever an official flag of this pattern made in those dimensions. "Authenticity," it seems, was a difficult thing to achieve, even terms as mundane as this.

The vote was close: 63 to 56 in favor of the senate plan. Only three black representatives, 3 out of 26, chose to vote for the plan. The rest joined with hardcore flag defenders in opposing the measure. It was perhaps the crowning irony of the entire episode that the all-white vote of 1962, which had placed the Confederate flag over the dome, was voided and replaced by an *almost* all-white vote to remove it. In that vote one could see, at one and the same moment, both how far we had come *and* how little some things had changed.

"This debate is over," Governor Hodges declared with obvious relief after he signed the flag bill into law.[98] And it certainly seemed as if the finality that everyone had been seeking had at last been attained. But history is a fluid thing. The past is not forever as unchanging and unalterable as we think. Even the fly captured in amber is only a token of the insect that once flew in primeval forests. Since time before memory, men have sought to lock into place the "authentic," to protect it from the ravages of time and to preserve it for generations yet to come. They have contrived to project themselves into the future whole and unchanging—to have eternity see them as they wished to be seen. But they have always failed—even when their memory has been guarded and cultivated by watchful descendants. Our recollections are continuously shifting—even within a single lifetime. How much more will they be altered by passing centuries? Our memories of the past cannot be fixed in place for all time. They can neither be safeguarded from the weathering of forgetfulness and the mutilations of falsification, nor should they be given sanctuary from the alterations and amendment that a more enlightened examination may bring. In that sense, then, the debate never ends.

The Confederate flag was going to the Confederate Soldiers Monument, "where it probably should have gone in the first place," Senator McConnell had said. Those who had erected that monument had understood the fleeting nature of memory, perhaps better than their descendants almost a hundred years later.

They appreciated the corrosive effects of time and changing circumstances. In the inscription they chose for the monument they seemed to have anticipated the struggle to come, the struggle to preserve the past as they saw it and as they wished it should forever remain:

> Let the stranger, who may in future times read this inscription, recognize that these were men whom power could not corrupt, whom death could not terrify, whom defeat could not dishonor. . . .

The debate over the Confederate flag atop the State House was at an end. But the debate over the winds of history on which the flag flew continues still.

POSTLUDE

It was supposed to be the day when dispute ended and healing began. But that first day of July 2000, the day the Confederate flag came down from the State House dome, was instead a day on which persisting divisions in South Carolina were spread out in bright colors across the grounds of the state capitol. Neither a single day nor a single event could seal the ruptures rent deep in history by slavery, war, and memory. The past still intruded into the present.

"This is an historic day in South Carolina," historian Walter Edgar remarked as he watched the gathering at the State House. But it was history written in small, not bold letters. No great war was ending. No groundbreaking scientific discovery had been made. No far-reaching political accord was about to be brokered. Man was not preparing to set foot on some uncharted celestial body. What was happening that summer Saturday in South Carolina was more a simulacrum of history, a reflected image of the original, not the raw and authentic thing itself. The flag's removal marked a turning point of sorts, but not a watershed. It was a gesture, nothing more, a slight course correction along our journey from history past to history future. The flag ceremony in Columbia might not have reflected the way we all think about our shared history, but it did reveal how far we still are from a truly integrated view of our collective past.

Early in the day, the NAACP marched in silence to the front of the State House, its members dressed in white—to symbolize unity, they said. Along the way they were barraged by catcalls, howls, and rebel yells coming from heritage defenders formed up behind a wall of state police. "What's next?" one flag enthusiast yelled as the marchers passed. "Are you gonna dig up every dead Confederate?!" The procession moved on undeterred to the cadence of African drums. Once they reached the capitol grounds, the marchers turned their backs to the State House, its dome still sporting the rebel flag, in protest against the compromise solution. They paused for a few moments of silent prayer, then moved on.[1]

The opposing factions set up their respective base camps at various locations around the State House. The Council of Conservative Citizens had staked out a perimeter around the James F. Byrnes Monument. Members of the Confederate States of America Heritage Preservation Association gathered on the northern side of the capitol, forming a defensive ring around the Confederate Soldiers

Monument, while the Association of African American leaders assembled its anti-flag followers on the southern side of the State House building. And over at the Ben Tillman Monument stood a bevy of bogus "southern belles" who called themselves the "Step-Daughters of the Confederacy." The group, organized by the South Carolina Progressive Network (headed up by Brett Bursey), consisted of both men and women, all of whom were decked out in antebellum attire. With wigs awry, this spoof of Old South society proclaimed as its motto: "Working to keep South Carolina bass-ackward since 1860." Several in the group held up signs that read "Hate is not a family value" and "Ignorance is bliss." The State House had seldom played host to a more motley cast of characters.[2]

Several thousand spectators had gathered to watch the day's events. It was a racially integrated crowd—brought together by a fundamental disagreement over a flag. Some were there to watch the old flag come down—while others had come to see a new one go up. Each side could find something to applaud in the day's ceremonies—but each also would find something to deplore, as well. Words flew—sometimes hot and angry words, fired off in nose-to-nose confrontations. Fists were balled in passion, but none flew in anger. Tensions were high. But for the most part, folks held onto their tempers—or were held apart by state police—and exhausted their frustrations and resentments in loud verbal combat.

The pro-flag faction came decked out in the latest rebel wear: caps, capes, vests, shirts—their flag-bedecked attire matched to the Confederate flags they waved above the crowd. Many of the antis had armed themselves with simple yellow signs bearing the single word "Shame." Blacks held up placards that read: "Remember our heritage, too." And of course t-shirts were still blazing—with logos that shouted out their wearers' convictions and allegiances. "Kiss My Rebel Ass," read some. "I'm dreaming of a *white* Christmas," sneered another, its rebel banner held aloft by a hooded Klansman. One portrayed a slave in chains, set to the words, "Southern Discomfort." The clash of opinion rang out in song and chant, as well. Strains of "The Black National Anthem" and "We Shall Overcome" clashed with "Dixie" and cries of "Off the dome and in your face!," "Go back to Africa," and "NAACP—the Klan with the tan."[3]

It was quieter inside the State House. There, the noisy tumult from the grounds outside was reduced to a gentle hum, barely ruffling the staid atmosphere of almost funereal anticipation. Senator Branton, the loquacious Lowcountry legislator, was back, still grumbling about the compromise and declaring that Dixie's flag would someday rise again. Senators McConnell, Courson, and Ravenel were there, too, huddled in prayer with a group of Confederate reenactors—the Palmetto Battalion—who had been assigned the honor of hoisting the new Confederate flag at the Soldiers Monument. In an improvised sacramental rite, the assembled lawmakers and reenactors placed a tiny fragment from an authentic

Civil War–era Confederate banner into an eyelet on the new ANV flag. The senators signed their names to the flag's white border. Then the reenactors took position.

The simultaneous flag lowering/raising ceremonies began at noon, as the recently passed Heritage Act required. Within the cupola high over the dome of the State House, two Citadel cadets—one white, one black, and both decked out in full dress uniforms, complete with ruby sashes, swords, and plumed caps—stood at the ready while the Confederate flag was lowered through a trapdoor above. As the flag began dropping, the noise from the crowd below swelled to an awesome din. Cheers, whistles, yelps, boos, and hollers of all kinds mounted up as the Confederate flag came down. A loud, anguished "Noooo!" mixed with shouts of "Dixie forever!" and "Don't give up the fight!" From the other side came the call-and-response chant: "Take the flag down!—Burn it!" In a matter of minutes, the Confederate flag was gone.

The moment it disappeared into the dome, a drum cadence rang out from the grounds below as the troop of Confederate reenactors stepped off toward the Confederate Soldiers Monument. Dressed in woolen gray and butternut, the color guard bore U.S. and state flags at one end of the front rank, with a sword-bearing commander to its front. At the other end, a white-gloved soldier carried a folded Confederate flag clasped to his breast with both hands.

While the color-bearers marched over a patch of green to the new flagpole at the monument, the cadets in the dome above ceremoniously folded the old flag into a neat square (triangles being reserved for U.S. flags) and then began their long, circuitous descent through the upper innards of the State House attic. Whether by choice or chance, the distinction of conveying the flag on its last trip down had been given to the black cadet. He held it clutched to his chest in much the same fashion as his Confederate-era counterpart on the grounds below.

As the cadets descended, the troop outside moved into position at the monument. The flag bearers gave a crisp salute and their commander brought the tip of his sword to his shoulder while the new flag was slowly run up the pole. As it rose, the noise from the crowd mounted again. This time it was the heritage defenders who rejoiced, raising their voices in a rippling wave of screeching rebel yells. Elsewhere, someone cut up a certified State House Confederate flag and handed out the small scraps as souvenirs.

Inside the capitol foyer, Governor Hodges waited expectantly as the Citadel cadets emerged onto the balcony above. The pair completed the last leg of their long trek, then saluted briskly as they presented the governor with the recently retired dome flag. The governor immediately turned and without comment passed the flag off to two representatives—one white, one black—from the State Museum. The participants then departed silently through their respective exits—

and the deed was done. Outside, the new Confederate banner hung limply in the breezeless July heat, indifferent to the blustery ululation swirling around it.

Some time later, long after the roaring crowds had gone and the fevered hoopla had faded away, passers-by noticed that the banner's bold red had bled into the white border surrounding it. The once bold stars and stainless trim had now turned a sickly shade of pink. Time and the elements were already exacting their toll.

A half-year after the Confederate flag was moved, a new monument joined the others already nesting in the State House's historical sculpture garden. The granite and bronze African-American History Monument, dedicated in February 2001, took its rightful place in the state's pantheon of cultural memory. The panels to either side of its semicircular form reach out to the approaching visitor, embracing him and inviting him into the story it seeks to tell. It is a long and involved story, probably more than any single monument could ever hope to convey.

The grander tale is only hinted at. But the careful observer may infer a deeper meaning from the arrangement of nearby monuments—their proximity suggesting an impromptu ensemble. Mounted on his horse not far away, and visible just overtop one of the new memorial's arching panels, rides Wade Hampton, Confederate general and "redeemer" of the state's postwar order. Across the other way, over the outstretched panel to the right, stands the Confederate Soldiers Monument, with its new flag. Together, the three monuments form a kind of triptych to the state's past. The African-American History Monument stands as the centerpiece, set in a frame formed of the other two—apart, but forever locked in a chilly Confederate embrace.

The three belong together as one—but do not rest easily in each other's company. Neither Confederate general nor rebel soldier acknowledges its black counterpart. Each stares intently into space, eyes stubbornly fixed on other vistas. The three stand in stony tribute to the state's divided past, separate-but-equal memorials to contending memories and identities. They are an unhappy reminder of our still-segregated sensibilities.

And yet, perhaps this is the best we can do—at least for the time being. Coming together, seeking reconciliation, is well and good. But it can only go as far as existing circumstances and prevailing sentiments permit. The things that divide us were born in history, in a history that was itself segregated into black and white through the hierarchies of race, the experience of slavery, and the structures of Jim Crow. Reconciliation is a worthy goal. But we should not expect too much of it, nor press it too far. Nor should we pursue it to the exclusion of all else. After all, complete reconciliation would be a denial of history, a denial of the very identities born in historical experience. By smoothing out the rougher edges of our collective past, we may be blurring the subtler contours of lived history, substituting a picture-book morality for the richly detailed drama of human affairs.

My own childhood memories are marked by desegregation. I have no active recollection of the overt forms of segregation practiced in the South into which I was born. As a white child, discrimination simply did not exist for me in the way it did for black children growing up at the same time. There are no separate waiting rooms and no segregated drinking fountains in the memories from my youth —only dim recollections about places and neighborhoods where white folks didn't go and memories of an unknowing childhood anxiety riding behind locked car doors though a black part of town.

But there are other, later memories, too, memories of a young adult's encounter with a remnant of the past, an echo of a time before desegregation, of a time in the South when discrimination was practiced openly and without remorse.

During a brief stop at the municipal offices in my hometown, I happened past a whitewashed restroom door. Something about it caught my eye, so I turned to take a closer look. Still clearly visible beneath the thin, cosmetic veneer were five block letters that spelled out the word "W-H-I-T-E." Had I made the effort to look further, it's likely that somewhere else in that same building, in the basement perhaps, there may have been another door, one that bore the letters "C-O-L-O-R-E-D," also washed-out and pale under a transparent layer of whitewash. Then again, perhaps the other door no longer existed. Rendered obsolete by the demise of legal segregation, that second door may have been discarded as an unnecessary redundancy in the dawning age of equal rights—an embarrassing reminder of a past best consigned to oblivion.

But we should not fool ourselves into believing that by erasing the reminders of our unflattering past we can eliminate the power that the past still has over us. We should not attempt to whitewash over our undeniable differences. History has etched them into our collective identities, made them part of our unabridged heritage. Every aspect of our past is not due equal commemoration—let alone veneration or celebration—but they are at least deserving of being remembered, both the good and the bad in them. "It is a common delusion," writes historian and heritage scholar David Lowenthal, "that to retain any memory of past iniquity serves to justify it."[4] It would be as much of a mistake to purge the southern landscape of its Confederate memorials as it would be to eliminate all vestiges of its slaveholding days and all reminders of its Jim Crow past. They are all part of us, part of the history that made us. They should be woven together to make our story whole, complete, and strong.

Did South Carolina's struggle over the Confederate flag bring us any closer to this goal? Did it help us to see our history whole? Many are skeptical. The last surviving member of the state Confederate War Centennial Commission, retired University of South Carolina historian Daniel Hollis, believes little was gained from the ten-year flag fight. It brought no improvement in racial understanding and did not increase our appreciation of our collective past, he says. Dr. Hollis speaks for many South Carolinians. For most, the debate was "all negative, with no beneficial effects (or side effects)." Many would probably prefer that the episode be quickly forgotten.

But as with many things in life, a lot depends on what we choose to make of this chapter of state history. The lowering of the Confederate flag was certainly a last (and late) step in the process of desegregation. But it could also have been (and may yet still become) a first step on the road to a more integrated view of our past. The new integrationism we should seek will mean coming to terms with *all* of history, with the grand narrative of our collective historical experience. Efforts toward true integration should not be directed at creating a society in which differences no longer matter, but one in which we come to understand both our mutualities and our divergences. It means finding unity in diversity. It will involve reaching a point where we finally embrace the "unenforceable obligations" of true neighbors, so that we may finally realize King's dream of a fully integrated society.[5] It means coming to appreciate that the things that divide us are not inborn, but are instead the creations of history. That does not make them any less real. But it does offer us hope—the hope implied by our power to choose how we use the past.

In his novel, *Cold Mountain,* set in the aftermath of the Civil War, author Charles Frazier describes a South in the throes of defeat. One of his main characters offers the following on the options open to the vanquished:

> It's often believed by preachers and old women that being beaten breeds compassion. And they're right. It can. But it also breeds hardness. There's to some degree a choice.[6]

The South still has that choice. It cannot alter its past. But it can lay the foundation for a better future—a future in which a compassionate reading of our history shapes our understanding of our true heritage. Then perhaps we can at last move beyond the mere physical proximity of desegregation and toward the spiritual affinity of true integration. That would surely be the greatest monument we could erect to southern heritage.

NOTES

Prelude

1. Willie Morris, *North toward Home* (Oxford, Miss., 1930; reprint, Jackson: University Press of Mississippi, 1999), p. 230.

2. "Deliberation on Flag Is Key to 'More Important' Issues," *The State*, 19 February 1997, p. A7.

3. Allen Tate, *The Fathers* (Athens, Ga., 1990), p. 22.

One—Dixie's Conquered Banners

1. From the introduction to Ken Burn's PBS documentary *The Civil War.*

2. Ibid.

3. Walt Whitman, "Song of the Banner at Daybreak," *Leaves of Grass* (New York: Carlton House, n.d.), p. 249.

4. Information on the military and historical role of flags taken from informal conversations with Benjamin Franklin Cooling, head of military studies at the National Defense University, Washington, D.C., and perusal of general information on flags at www.britannica.com. Musings on the reasons men fight gleaned from Chapter 1 of James McPherson's *For Cause and Comrades: Why Men Fought in the Civil War* (New York: Oxford University Press, 1997) and Bell Irvin Wiley's *The Life of Johnny Reb: The Common Soldier of the Confederacy* (1943; reprint, Baton Rouge: Louisiana State University Press, 1978). Thoughts on the mutability of symbols were spurred by Sanford Levinson's *Written in Stone: Public Monuments in Changing Societies* (Durham, N.C.: Duke University Press, 1998), pp. 3–26.

5. For the history of the South Carolina state flag, see Wylma A. Wates, *A Flag Worthy of Your State and People: The History of the South Carolina State Flag* (Columbia: South Carolina Department of Archives and History, 1996).

6. Taken from *The Charleston Mercury*, 16 and 17 November 1861, as quoted at "The Civil War in South Carolina" (www.researchonline.net/gacw/conflag3.htm).

7. Wates, pp. 14–15.

8. Based on email correspondence with S.C. state archivist Bryan McKown (dated 19 July 2000) and on Wates, *A Flag Worthy of Your State and People.*

9. Richard Rollins, *"The Damned Red Flags of the Rebellion": The Struggle over the Confederate Battle Flag at Gettysburg* (Redondo Beach, Cal.: Rank and File, 1997), p. 55.

10. Alan Tate, *The Fathers* (New York: Putnam, 1938), p. 155.

11. On the local character of the Confederate army and its relationship to the flag, see Rollins, pp. 1–2 and 11–19.

12. Ibid., p. 55.

13. Ibid., p. 62.

14. Gregg Briggs, "The Flags of the Confederacy," at www.confederateflags.org.

15. Charles Frazier, *Cold Mountain* (New York: Atlantic Monthly Press, 1997), p. 346.

16. John Bentley Mays, *Power in the Blood: Land, Memory, and a Southern Family* (New York: HarperCollins, 1997), p. 200.

17. Charles Reagan Wilson, *Baptized in Blood: The Religion of the Lost Cause, 1865–1920* (Athens: University of Georgia Press, 1980), p. 36.

18. Irwin Silber, ed. *Songs of the Civil War* (New York: Dover, 1995) pp. 356–57.

19. users.erols.com/kfraser/confederate/postwar/banner.html

20. users.erols.com/kfraser/confederate/postwar/reply.html

21. Gaines M. Foster, *Ghosts of the Confederacy: Defeat, the Lost Cause, and the Emergence of the New South, 1865–1913* (New York: Oxford University Press, 1987), p. 40–41.

22. Ibid., p. 89.

23. James McBride Dabbs, *The Southern Heritage* (New York: Knopf, 1958), p. 4.

Two—A Land Primed for Fatality

1. Joseph S. Stroud, "State Gets Pulled into Flag Battle," *The State*, 30 January 2000.

2. Cindy Ross Scoppe, "Monument Wasn't Always in Current Prominent Location," *The State*, 2 July 2000.

3. Quoted in Wylma A. Wates, *A Flag Worthy of Your State and People: The History of the South Carolina State Flag* (Columbia: South Carolina Department of Archives and History, 1996), p. 15.

4. Ibid.

5. Bryant Simon, *A Fabric of Defeat: The Politics of South Carolina Millhands, 1910–1948* (Chapel Hill: University of North Carolina Press, 1998), p. 17.

6. Quoted in Simon, p. 32.

7. Ibid., p. 31.

8. *Time* (7 August 1944), as quoted in Simon, pp. 189.

9. Ibid., pp. 194–195.

10. Quoted in Harry Ashmore, *An Epitaph for Dixie* (New York: Norton, 1958), pp. 100–101.

11. Quoted in Simon, p. 195.

12. Francis Butler Simkins, *A History of the South* (New York: Knopf, 1963), p. 561.

13. Walter B. Edgar, *South Carolina in the Modern Age* (Columbia: University of South Carolina Press, 1992), p. 79.

14. See Edgar, *South Carolina: A History* (Columbia: University of South Carolina Press, 1998), pp. 509–510; Simon, p. 195; Edgar, *South Carolina in the Modern Age,* p. 79; and "Majority Leader Keeps Senators Busy Saturday," *The State,* 9 January 1938, p. 1.

15. "Southerners Win on Principle," *The State,* 3 February 1938, p. 4.

16. *Journal of the House of Representatives of the 82nd General Assembly of the State of South Carolina Being the Regular Session, Beginning Tuesday, January 11, 1938,* vol. 1 (March 2, 1938), p. 784.

17. Quoted in Simon, p. 228.

18. Ibid.

19. See Edgar, *South Carolina: A History,* pp. 515–520, 523–525.

20. Ibid., pp. 520–528.

21. Edgar, *South Carolina: A History,* p. 528, and R. E. Grier, "Around the State House," *The State,* 11 April 1956, p. 12B.

22. Printed in *Journal of the Senate of the Second Session of the 91st General Assembly of the State of South Carolina,* pp. 1184–1185.

23. Dan Hoover, "Flag's Ally Fought 'Black War,'" *Greenville News,* 27 January 2000, p. 1A.

24. *Journal of the Senate of the Second Session of the 91st General Assembly of the State of South Carolina* (22 January 1957), pp. 133–136.

25. Quoted in Edgar, *South Carolina: A History,* p. 538.

26. Correspondence, South Carolina State Confederate War Centennial Commission, National Archives.

27. John Temple Graves, *The Fighting South* (1943; reprint, University: University of Alabama Press, 1985), pp. 235–236.

28. S.685, *A Joint Resolution to Establish a Commission,* 5 March 1958, records of the South Carolina Confederate War Centennial Commission, National Archives.

29. Ibid.

30. Letter, dated 14 August 1959, from Senator Strom Thurmond to General Ulysses S. Grant III and letter, dated 24 August 1959, from Grant to Thurmond, South Carolina Confederate War Centennial Commission, National Archives.

31. "'South Won Centennial,' May Sums Up Centennial," *The State,* 10 July 1965, p. 18; letter, dated 25 August 1961, from John A. May to Karl S. Betts (Executive Director, U.S. Civil War Centennial Commission), South Carolina Confederate War Centennial Commission, National Archives; photographs, *The State,* 7 April 1961, p. 1C.

32. "Sen. Long Is Praised," *The State,* 7 April 1961, p. 6A.

33. Hoover, "Flag's Ally Fought 'Black War.'"

34. Letter, dated 25 June 1959, from Karl S. Betts to Daniel W. Hollis (University of South Carolina Department of History and member, S.C. Confederate War Centennial Commission), South Carolina Confederate War Centennial Commission, National Archives.

35. Correspondence re: the centennial observance of the firing on the *Star of the West* (March 1960), from Lieutenant Colonel C. L. Anger (Chairman, Confederate Centennial Committee, The Citadel) to General Mark W. Clark (President, The Citadel); and letter, dated 11 May 1960, from Julian Metz (Executive Director, Charleston Chamber of Commerce) to Senator Olin D. Johnston, South Carolina Confederate War Centennial Commission, National Archives.

36. Neil Gilbride, "Gen. Grant Says Dixie Still Proud," *The State*, 2 April 1961, p. 1A.

37. Ibid.

38. Letter, dated 7 October 1959, from John A. May to Karl S. Betts, South Carolina Confederate War Centennial Commission, National Archives.

39. *South Carolina Commemorates the Confederate War Centennial, 1961–1965: A Manual for Observance in the Counties and Cities of the State of South Carolina* (Columbia: South Carolina Confederate War Centennial Commission), p. 17.

40. *South Carolina Commemorates the Confederate War Centennial, 1961–1965*, p. 8.

41. Beaufort County (S.C.) Civil War Centennial Commission, "Fort Royal Commemoration—November 7, 1961," dated 20 October 1961, South Carolina Confederate War Centennial Commission, National Archives.

42. "Spirit of Centennial," *The State*, 10 April 1961, p. 4A.

43. *South Carolina Commemorates the Confederate War Centennial*, pp. 1–3, 9.

44. Billy Wilkins, "Port City Praised for Dual Event at Fort Sumter," *The State*, 11 April 1961, p. 1A.

45. "The Stars and Bars Fly Again," *The State*, 8 April 1961.

46. Joe Barnett, "State House Flagpole under Fire," *The State*, 2 April 1961, p. 2E; "No Confederate Flag Graced Capitol Dome," *The State*, 12 April 1961, p.5A.

47. "Nazism Termed Defunct," *The State*, 11 April 1961, p. 1A.

48. Arthur Everett, "'Village' Seethes in Race Mixing," *The State*, 11 April 1961, p. 1A.

49. "US Job Equality Is Pushed," *The State*, 12 April 1961, p. 1A.

50. See "Statue Painted Blue; Southerners See Red," *The State*, 12 April 1961, p. 2B.

51. "Address of Hon. James F. Byrnes at the Charleston Confederate Centennial" (11 April 1961), in *South Carolina Speaks* (Columbia: South Carolina Confederate War Centennial Commission, 1961), pp. 5–12; "Byrnes Doubtful about Centennial," *The State*, 12 April 1961, p. 1A.

52. "An Address by Senator Strom Thurmond before the Banquet of the South Carolina Confederate War Centennial Commission, April 11, 1961, 'To Ensure Domestic Tranquility . . . and . . . Liberty,'" in *South Carolina Speaks*, pp. 39–43; "Thurmond Criticizes 'Sameness,'" *The State*, 12 April 1961, p. 1A.

53. Monty Morton, "N.J. Asks for Removal of Centennial Head," *The State*, 12 April 1961, p. 1A; Billy Williams, "Centennial Called 'Capitulation of Free Speech,'" *The State*, 14 April 1961, p.1A.

54. "A Worse War," *The State*, 13 April 1961, p. 4A.

55. See letter, dated 3 September 1963, from John A. May to James I. Robertson; and letter, dated 6 September 1963, from Robertson to May, South Carolina Confederate War Centennial Commission, National Archives.

56. "An Address by Hon. John A. May, Chairman of the South Carolina Confederate War Centennial Commission, 'South Carolina and the Confederate Centennial'" and "An Address by Hon. John A. May before Various Chapters of the United Daughters of the Confederacy," in *South Carolina Speaks,* pp. 17–30.

57. *Journal of the Senate of the State of South Carolina, Regular Session Beginning Tuesday, January 10, 1961* (10 May 1961), pp. 1474–1479.

58. Ibid.

59. Letter, dated 13 December 1961, from John A. May to Allan Nevins (Civil War Centennial Commission); letter, dated 18 December 1961, from Edward C. Gass (Acting Executive Director, Civil War Centennial Commission) to May; letter, dated 26 December 1961, from Nevins to May; letter, dated 5 February 1962, from James I. Robertson to John May; letter, dated 10 February 1962, from May to Robertson; and letter, dated 14 February 1962, from Robertson to May, South Carolina Confederate War Centennial Commission, National Archives.

60. "The Potentials of 1962," *The State,* 1 January 1962, p. 4A.

61. "Civil Rights Proposals Made Again," *The State,* 12 January 1962, p. 5A.

62. See "President's Civil Rights Bill Comes under Southern Guns," *The State,* 27 January 1962, p. 1A; "A Glowing Opportunity," *The State,* 23 January 1962, p. 4A; "Voting Qualifications," *The State,* 27 January 1962, p. 4A; "An Election Year Device," *The State,* 31 January 1962, p. 4A; "Court's Ruling Received Calmly," *The State,* 27 February 1962, p. 3A; and "Losing Liberties for Rights," *The State,* 24 February 1962, p. 4A.

63. Letter, dated 22 June 1964, from Nathan G. Baker (Director, U.S. National Park Service), to John A. May, South Carolina Confederate War Centennial Commission, National Archives.

64. "'South Won Centennial,' May Sums Up Centennial"; and email correspondence with Michelle Baker, Chief Registrar, South Carolina State Museum, 13 March 2000.

Three—Standing Guard at the Gates of Southern History

1. Edmund Wilson, *Patriotic Gore: Studies in the Literature of the American Civil War* (New York: Oxford University Press, 1962), p. 339. Even this older "Old South" hearkened back to a pattern that predated it and served as its model: the baronial estates of Mother England.

2. James McBride Dabbs, *The Southern Heritage* (New York: Knopf, 1958), p. 182.

3. See Paul M. Gaston, *The New South Creed: A Study in Southern Mythmaking* (New York: Knopf, 1970).

4. Joseph S. Stroud, "Flag Advocate Says Fight Isn't Over," *The State,* 29 June 2000.

5. All quotes, unless otherwise noted, are taken from the author's interviews, conducted during the fall of 1999 and spring of 2000.

6. *Southern Partisan,* 23 (Second Quarter 1999): 1.

7. Tommy M. Stringer, "The Friendliest Tour of the South," *Southern Partisan,* 23 (Second Quarter 1999), pp. 40–41.

8. *Southern Partisan* 23 (Second Quarter 1999): 9.

9. Gaines M. Foster, *Ghosts of the Confederacy: Defeat, the Lost Cause, and the Emergence of the New South, 1861 to 1913* (New York: Oxford University Press, 1987), p. 73.

10. See Wilson, pp. 395–396.

11. Monte Paulsen, "Suburban Rebels Find Assemblage in 90s-Style Trenches," *The State,* 28 September 1997).

12. All quotes are from the "Declaration of Southern Cultural Independence," as published in the official publication of the South Carolina League of the South, the *South Carolina Patriot* (Summer 2000).

13. "Essential Clyde Wilson," *Southern Partisan,* 23 (Second Quarter 1999), p. 47.

14. From "A Proposed Cultural Mandate for South Carolina," *South Carolina Patriot* (Summer 2000), pp. 40–43.

15. "Essential Clyde Wilson," p. 50.

16. See FAQ on the League of the South web site, at www.dixienet.org/faqs/ls-faq.html

17. "'No Votes for Turncoats' Press Release," *South Carolina Patriot* (Summer 2000), p. 7.

18. All quotes taken from "Why Are We Defending the Flag?," South Carolina Heritage Coalition, at www.kudzumedia.com/schc.html

19. Quoted in Charles Reagan Wilson, *Baptized in Blood: The Religion of the Lost Cause, 1865–1920* (Athens: University of Georgia Press, 1980), p. 86.

20. Quoted in Margaret L. Coit, *John C. Calhoun: American Portrait* (Boston: Houghton Mifflin, 1950), p. 146.

21. William Lee Miller, *Arguing about Slavery: The Great Battle in the United States Congress* (New York: Knopf, 1996), p. 126.

22. Ibid., p. 124.

23. Ibid., p. 126.

24. Quoted in Miller, p. 127.

25. Ibid., p. 116.

26. Calhoun, "Resolutions on Abolition and the Union, December 27, 1837," in *The Essential Calhoun,* edited by Clyde Wilson (New Brunswick, N.J.: Transaction, 1992), p. 373. South Carolina religious luminaries also engaged in pro-slavery argument; see Dr. Richard Furman's *Exposition of the Views of the Baptists, Relative to the Coloured Population in the United States, in a Communication to the Governor of South Carolina,* second edition (Charleston: Printed by A. E. Miller, 1833).

27. Calhoun, "Speech on the Slavery Question, 19 February 1847," in *The Essential Calhoun,* pp. 388–389.

28. Calhoun, "From the Speech on the Compromise, Senate, 4 March 1850," in *The Essential Calhoun,* p. 392.

29. Ibid.

30. Calhoun, from his *Works,* volume 6, edited by Richard K. Crallé (New York: Appleton, 1855), p. 309.

31. U.S. Civil War Center virtual exhibit "Beyond Face Value" at www.cwc.lsu.edu/cwc/BeyondFaceValue/beyondfacevalue.htm

32. Lewis P. Jones, *South Carolina: A Synoptic History for Laymen* (Columbia: Sandlapper, 1971), p. 127.

33. Ibid.

34. "Declaration of the Immediate Causes Which Induce and Justify the Secession of South Carolina from the Federal Union, as Adopted December 24, 1860," in J. A. May and J. R. Faunt, *South Carolina Secedes* (Columbia: University of South Carolina Press, 1960), pp. 76–81; online: http://sunsite.utk.edu/civil-war/reasons#South%20 Carolina

35. Quoted in Jones, p. 161.

36. Quoted in Walter B. Edgar, *South Carolina: A History* (Columbia: University of South Carolina Press, 1998), p. 347.

37. Quoted in Jones, p. 167.

38. Edgar, p. 347. Some of the Brooks trophies and other memorabilia are now housed on display at the South Carolina State Museum and the McKissick Museum, both in Columbia.

39. Ibid., p. 352.

40. See William W. Freehling and Craig M. Simpson, eds., *Secession Debated: Georgia's Showdown in 1860* (New York: Oxford University Press, 1992), p. 93.

41. Alexander Stephens, "Cornerstone Speech, as Delivered on March 21, 1861" (as printed in the *Savannah Republican,* 22 March 1861), in Jon L. Wakelyn, ed., *Southern Pamphlets on Secession, November 1860–April 1861* (Chapel Hill: University of North Carolina Press, 1996); excerpt available at www.templeofdemocracy/alexstephens.htm

42. Declaration of the Immediate Causes which Induce and Justify the Secession of the State of Mississippi from the Federal Union," available at http://sunsite.utk.edu/civil-war/reasons#Mississippi

43. From Ernest William Winkler, ed., *Journal of the Secession Convention of Texas, 1861* (Austin: Austin Printing Company, 1912), p. 65, at Texas Electronic Archive (www.tsl.state.tx.us/ref/abouttx/secession/2feb1861.html).

44. Edward A. Pollard, *The Lost Cause Regained* (New York: Books for Libraries Press, 1970), pp. 13–14.

45. Robert Penn Warren, *The Legacy of the Civil War* (1961; reprint, Harvard University Press, 1983), p. 47.

46. Gary Wills, *Lincoln at Gettysburg: The Words That Remade America* (New York: Simon & Schuster, 1992), p. 39.

47. James McPherson, *For Cause and Comrades: Why Men Fought in the Civil War* (New York: Oxford University Press, 1997), p. 118.

48. Ibid., p. 120.

49. Ibid., p. 106.

50. Ibid., p. 12–13.

51. For more on the role of "honor" as a motivating factor behind southern action, see, among others, Bertram Wyatt-Brown, *Honor and Violence in the Old South* (New York: Oxford University Press, 1986), and Kenneth Greenberg, *Honor and Slavery* (Princeton, N.J.: Princeton University Press, 1996).

52. Bell Irvin Wiley, *The Life of Johnny Reb: The Common Soldier of the Confederacy* (1943; reprint, Baton Rouge: Louisiana State University Press, 1978), p. 309.

53. David Lowenthal, *The Heritage Crusade and the Spoils of History* (Cambridge, U.K. and New York: Cambridge University Press, 1998), p. 250.

54. Ibid., p. 106.

55. Ibid., p. 112.

56. Ibid., p. 115.

57. Ibid., p. 119.

58. Ibid., p. 107.

59. Ibid., p. *xv.*

60. Coit, p. 228.

61. Tamar Jacoby, "Whatever Became of Intergration?," *Washington Post*, 29 June 1998, p. 2C.

62. Michael Hill and Thomas Fleming, "The New Dixie Manifesto: States' Rights Will Rise Again," at the League of the South web site (www.dixienet.org/dn-gazette/newdixiemanifesto.html).

63. Wilson, *Baptized in Blood*, p. 119.

64. Lowenthal, p. 231.

Four—The Other South Carolina

1. Walker Percy, *Lancelot* (New York: Farrar, Straus and Giroux, 1977), p. 236.

2. Wendy Brinker, "Jury Hits Klan with $38 Million Verdict," *South Carolina Black News*, 28 July 1998, available at www.seedshow.com

3. Ralph Ellison, *Invisible Man* (New York: Random House, 1952), p. 499.

4. Tamar Jacoby, "Whatever Became of Integration?," *Washington Post*, 28 June 1998, p. 2C. See also her book, *Someone Else's House: America's Unfinished Struggle for Integration* (New York: Free Press, 1998).

5. Ibid.

6. Ibid.

7. Ralph Ellison, *Invisible Man* (New York: Random House, 1952), p. 440.

8. See the table at www.law.umkc.edu/Faculty/projects/trials/shipp/lynchingsstate.html

9. "South Carolina—Fossil No More," in Neal R. Peirce and Jerry Hagstrom, *The Book of America: Inside Fifty States Today* (New York: Norton, 1983), p. 423.

10. Joseph B. Cummings Jr., as quoted in Peirce and Hagstrom, p. 423.

11. Ibid.

12. Dan T. Carter, *The Politics of Rage: George Wallace, the Origins of the New Conservatism, and the Transformation of American Politics* (New York: Simon & Schuster, 1995), p. 113.

13. Walter B. Edgar, *South Carolina in the Modern Age* (Columbia: University of South Carolina Press, 1992), p. 106.

14. *From Will the Circle Be Unbroken? A Personal History of the Civil Rights Movement in Five Southern Communities*, episode 2: "The Road to Litigation," produced by the Southern Regional Council, written by Steve Suitts and George King, with Vertamae Grosvenor, available at www.unbrokencircle.org/scripts02.htm

15. Ibid.

16. From *Will the Circle Be Unbroken? A Personal History of the Civil Rights Movement in Five Southern Communities*, episode 3: "Under Color of Law," written by George with Grosvenor, available at www.unbrokencircle.org/scripts03.htm

17. Quoted by Billie Fleming in *Will the Ciricle Be Unbroken?*, episode 3.

18. Ibid.

19. Edgar, p. 99.

20. David K. Shipler, *A Country of Strangers: Blacks and Whites in America* (New York: Knopf, 1997), pp. 187–188.

21. "School Answers Suit over Confederate Flag Ban," *The State*, 19 April 1991, p. 3B.

22. This brief history of the Redneck Shop is drawn from Monte Paulsen, "Ex-Klansman Changes His Ways," *The State*, 24 May 1997, pp. A1, A8.

23. For an interesting exploration of this aspect of the southern self-image, see Midge Dexter, "Southern Comforts," *Commentary* 106 (July 1998): 26–33.

24. Shipler, p. 5.

25. Ibid., p. 7.

26. Ibid., p. 8.

27. Quoted in "Disruptive Symbols?," *The State*, 5 March 1994, p. 3B.

28. Ibid.

29. Ibid.

30. Lois D. Roberts, "New South Flag Merges Symbols," *The State*, 13 February 1994, p. 16A.

31. Shipler, p. 149.

32. Sanford Levinson, *Written in Stone: Public Monuments in Changing Societies* (Durham, N.C.: Duke University Press, 1998), pp. 96–97.

33. Ellison, pp. 501–502.

34. Martin Luther King Jr., "The Ethical Demands for Integration" (speech delivered in Nashville, Tennessee, 27 December 1962), in *A Testament of Hope: The Essential Writings and Speeches of Martin Luther King, Jr.*, edited by James M. Washington (San Francisco: HarperSanFrancisco, 1991), p. 124.

Five—Taking Their Stands

1. See: S.C. Code of Laws, Section 16–17–220, "Desecration or Mutilation of Flags," at www.lpitr.state.sc.us/code/t16c017.doc

2. From Robert Ford, "Racial Tolerance Means Respecting Both Heritages" (Speech to the South Carolina State Senate, 16 February 1999); and press release, office of Senator Robert Ford, August 1999.

3. Quoted in Clark Surrat, "Lessons Learned—Kay Patterson Says He's Matured While in Office," *The State,* 9 December 1988, p. 1C.

4. See HR.2912, *Journal of the House of Representatives of the Second Session of the 103rd General Assembly of the State of South Carolina,* volume 1 (16 January 1980), p. 280.

5. Ibid.

6. Ibid., pp. 281–285.

7. Ibid., p. 286.

8. *Journal of the House of Representatives of the First Session of the 105th General Assembly of the State of South Carolina,* volume 2 (4 May 1983), pp. 2544–2545.

9. See David Beasley, "Vote to Debate Does Not Represent Position" (letter to the editor), *The State,* 27 June 1993, p. 6A; see also "Flag Supporter Beasley Voted Otherwise in '83," *The State,* 17 June 1994, p. 4B.

10. Harriet Keyserling, *Against the Tide: One Woman's Struggle* (Columbia: University of South Carolina Press, 1998), pp. 105–106.

11. Ibid., p. 109.

12. Walter Edgar, *South Carolina: A History* (Columbia: University of South Carolina Press, 1998), p. 549.

13. Keyserling, pp. 67–68. On the persistence of the seniority system, see also Cindi Ross Scoppe, "Oh My! Senate in a Partisan Tie. What Does It Mean? Not Much," *The State,* 10 November 2000.

14. James McBride Dabbs, *The Southern Heritage* (New York: Knopf, 1958), p. 123.

15. Resolution reprinted in John M. Cosky, "The Confederate Battle Flag in American History and Culture" (photo essay), *Southern Culture* (Winter 1996), p. 226.

16. Quoted in Surrat, "Lessons Learned."

17. Hunter James, "S.C. Backs Farm Aid, Poll Shows," *The State,* 31 January 1988, p. 12A.

18. Bill Higgins, "Minister Challenges Civic Clubs," *The State,* 20 December 1988, p. 1A; and "Place for Stars and Bars" (editorial), *The State,* 10 April 1989, p. 6A.

19. Higgins, "Methodist Bishop Favors Removing Confederate Flag from State House," *The State,* 6 June 1989.

20. "Citadel Should Retire 'Dixie' Flag, Panel Says," *The State,* 6 March 1992, p. 1B.

21. See Jeff Miller, "Don't Look Away from 'Dixie,' 155 Callers Told Governor's Staff," *The State,* 15 November 1990, p. 1A.

22. See "'Rebels' Protest School's Flag Policy," *The State,* 8 March 1991; Mark Wood, "Parents to Sue for Students' Right to Wear Flag," *The State,* 14 March 1991, p. 1B; "NAACP in Rebellion against School's Rebel," *The State,* 20 March 1991; Mark Wood, "Suit Seeks Right to Wave Confederate Flag at School," *The State,* 21 March

1991, p. 3B; "School Answers Suit over Confederate Flag Ban," *The State*, 19 April 1991, p. 3B; "Flags to Rise Again on Byrnes' Students," *The State*, 23 April 1991; "Rebel Mascot Decision Delayed," *The State*, 14 June 1991.

23. Nina Brook, "Kay Patterson Passes on Rebel Flag Fight," *The State*, 16 December 1992, p. 1B; Kenneth A. Harris, "Patterson's Tenacity Finally Pays off Today," *The State*, 1 July 2000.

24. Bill no. 3989, *A Concurrent Resolution to Declare That the Confederate Flag Should Be Removed from atop the State House*, introduced 9 May 1991, available at www.lpitr.state.sc.us.

25. Bill no. 4225, *Confederate war memorial—Confederate flag*, introduced 20 May 1993, available at www.lpitr.state.sc.us.

26. Quoted in Brook, "Medlock: Panel Can Take down Rebel Flag," *The State*, 19 October 1993, p. 1A.

27. Brook, "Campbell Pushed to Take Stand on Confederate Flag," *The State*, 20 May 1993, p. 3B.

28. Brook, "The Controversy Nobody Noticed," *The State*, 20 October 1993, p. 1B.

29. Brook, "Black Caucus Won't Bend on Battle Flag," *The State*, 30 October 1993, p. 1B.

30. Brook, "2 Senators Lead Pro-flag Ad Charge," *The State*, 12 November 1993, p. 1B.

31. Brook, "New Flag Proposed for State House," *The State*, 18 November 1993, p. 5B.

32. *The State*, 20 October 1993, p. 8A.

33. Dabbs, p. 120.

34. "New Districts, Rebel Flag Crowd Agenda," *The State*, 9 January 1994, p. 6D.

35. See Bill no. 1401, *Circle of Historic Flags on State House Grounds*, introduced 4 May 1994, at www.lpitr.state.sc.us.

36. Bill no. 1009, *Black Liberation Flag*, introduced 11 January 1994, at www.lpitr.state.sc.us.

37. Brook, "Fly a Flag for Blacks, Senator Says," *The State*, 10 March 1994, p. 6B.

38. Bill No. 1009.

39. Brook, "Fly a Flag," op cit.

40. Brook, "Senator: Those Who Won't Compromise on Flag Are Pimps," *The State*, 11 March 1994, p. 1B.

41. From informational material issued by the office of Senator Robert Ford, August 1999.

42. Brook, "Lawmakers Map out Strategy for Flag Battle," *The State*, 24 March 1994, p. 1B.

43. Scoppe, "Campbell: Time to Furl Battle Flag," *The State*, 30 March 1994, p. 1A.

44. Brook, "Campbell: Flag Isn't My Fight," *The State*, 31 March 1994, p. 1B.

45. Brook, "Flag Supporters: 'Keep It Flying,'" *The State*, 10 April 1994, p. 1B.

46. Ibid.

47. Brook, "Confederate Flag Friends Warn March May Backfire," *The State*, 8 April 1994, p. 3B.

48. Scoppe, "Campbell: Time to Furl Battle Flag."

49. See Bill no. 1367, *Confederate History Month*, introduced 19 April 1994, available at www.lpitr.sc.state.us.

50. Ibid. It is interesting to note the choice of language contained in the bill. It uses objectively historical terms, such as "Civil War" and "Reconstruction," and avoids reference to the Confederacy, referring, for example, to "Civil War heritage" rather than "Confederate" heritage. Language like this was problematic for McConnell and others in the heritage defense forces (who still preferred terms such as "War Between the States"), and it contributed to their rejection of the proposal.

51. Brook, "Flag Plan Gains Ground," *The State*, 20 April 1994, p. 1A.

52. Brook, "New Plan Would Fly Battle Flag Once a Year," *The State*, 19 April 1994, p. 1A.

53. Brook, "Black Ministers Might Push Boycott over Flag," *The State*, 17 April 1994, p. 1A.

54. Scoppe, "McConnell Tightens Flag's Foothold," *The State*, 22 April 1994, p. 6A.

55. Brook, "Democrats Say Furl the Flag," *The State*, 8 May 1994, p. 1A; Brook, "White Voices Join Chorus to Remove Confederate Flag," *The State*, 3 May 1994, p. 1B; Lee Bandy, "Medlock Won't Defend the Flag," *The State*, 7 May 1994, p. 1A; Brook, "A Clear View to a Controversy," *The State*, 20 May 1994, p. 1B; Brook and Fred Monk, "Business Leaders Pursuing Battle Flag Compromise," *The State*, 27 May 1994, p. 1B.

56. Brook, "Budget Now Battlefield in Fight to Furl Flag," *The State*, 12 May 1994, p. 5B; Brook, "Senators Opt for Continued Negotiations on Flag," *The State*, 13 May 1994, p. 1B; Dewanna Lofton, "Flag Sales Rise as Debate Rages," *The State*, 27 April 1994, p. 6A.

57. Brook, "New Flag Plan Might Furl Flag This Year," *The State*, 28 May 1994, p. 1A.

58. Lisa Greene, "Flag Foes Rally around Lawmakers' Compromise," *The State*, 29 May 1994, p. 1A.

59. Paul Tosto, "Lower Battle Flag, Business Leaders Say," *The State*, 28 May 1994, p. 6A.

60. Scoppe, "A House Divided Sweats out Remap," *The State*, 12 May 1994, p. 1A.

61. Keyserling, p. 99.

62. Scoppe, "A House Divided Sweats out Remap." House voting records showed that only about twenty white representatives could be consistently counted on to vote with the Legislative Black Caucus (see Brook and Scoppe, "Black Caucus Coming of Age," *The State*, 13 June 1994, p. 1A). See also Joseph S. Stroud, "Legislative Districts' Fragmented Politics Help Keep Flag Flying," *The State*, 5 March 2000; Brad Warthen, "Legislature More Racially Polarized than Public—by Design," *The State*, 23 January 2000; Scoppe, "A Cautionary Tale about Coalitions of Convenience," *The State*, 2 May 2000.

63. Keyserling, p. 127.

64. Ibid., p. 312.

65. Ibid., p. 127.

66. Ibid., p. 278.

67. Brook, "Flag Compromise Coming Apart," *The State*, 1 June 1994, p. 1A; Brook, "Furl Battle Flag, Senate Says," *The State*, 2 June 1994, p. 1A; Bandy, "Praise, Scorn Greet Flag Compromise," *The State*, 2 June 1994, p. 5A; Brook and Scoppe, "Compromise Simply Couldn't Beat the Clock," *The State*, 5 June 1994, p. 1A.

68. Brook, "Furl Battle Flag," op cit.; Brook, Bandy, and Scoppe, "Lawmakers Leave, Battle Flag Stays," *The State*, 3 June 1994, p. 1A.

69. Brook, Bandy, and Scoppe, "Lawmakers Leave, Battle Flag Stays."

70. "Flag Failure Disappoints, but Progress Encouraging" (editorial), *The State*, 4 June 1994, p. 8A.

71. Brook, Bandy, and Scoppe, "Lawmakers Leave, Battle Flag Stays."

72. Warren Bolton, "Foes Draw Battle Plan against Flag," *The State*, 12 June 1994, p. 1A.

73. Bandy, "Medlock: Flag Shouldn't Fly," *The State*, 17 June 1994, p. 1B; Charles Pope, "Uncertain Budget Board Wants Legal Advice on Flag," *The State*, 18 June 1994, p. 4B.

74. "Marching against Solutions" (editorial), *The State*, 23 July 1994, p. 12A.

75. Brook, "Anti-flag Groups See Value in March," *The State*, 3 September 1994, p. 1B.

76. "Republican Referendum Makes Confederate Flag Decision Harder," *The State*, 11 August 1994, p. 4B; Brook, "New Poll Shows Flag Issue Waning," *The State*, 12 July 1994, p. 1A.

77. See Bill no. 1, *Heritage Act of 1996*, introduced 10 January 1995, at www.lpitr. state.sc.us.

78. "State Senators Resurrect Measure That Would Lower Confederate Flag," *Greenville News*, 11 January 1995, p. 4A.

79. Brook, "Flag Flap Unfurling in Court," *The State*, 13 November 1994, p. 1A.

80. Robert Tanner, "Confederate Flag Sales Soar above State House Dispute," *The State*, 8 July 1994, p. 3B.

81. Warren Bolton, "Are South Carolina Politics Fueled by 2 Races or 2 Parties?," *The State*, 12 February 1995, p. 1A.

82. See: *Journal of the House of Representatives of the First Session of the 111th General Assembly of the State of South Carolina* (Tuesday, 16 May 1995), printed page 3511, available at http://www.lpitr.state.sc.us/sess111_1995-1996/hj95/351.htm

83. Brook, "Attorney General Backs Battle Flag," *The State*, 18 February 1995, p. 1B.

84. Ibid.

85. Brook, "Flag Compromise Flies Again," *The State*, 17 March 1995, p. 1B.

86. Bill no. 3816, *State House Renovations, Return of Objects*, introduced 16 March 1995, available at www.lpitr.state.sc.us.

87. Brook, "House Makes Room for Flag Vote," *The State*, 23 March 1995, p. 1B; Brook, "Battle Flag Wins House Protection," *The State*, 31 March 1995, p. 1A; Brook, "Mayor Offers to Withdraw Flag Suit," *The State*, 8 April 1995, p. 1B.

88. "Battle Flag Wins in House," *Greenville News*, 30 March 1995, p. 1A; Brook, "A War of Words," *The State*, 28 May 1995, p. 1D.

89. Brook, "Both Sides Dig in Deeper after Vote to Protect Flag," *The State*, 5 April 1995, p. 1B; Pete Iacobelli, "Flags Unfurled, 1,000 Honor the Confederacy," *The State*, 7 May 1995, p. 4B.

90. Lisa Greene, "Students Sue to Wear Confederate Flag T-shirts," *The State*, 19 April 1995, p. 1B; Carol Farrington, "'It Doesn't Have Anything to Do with Race,'" *The State*, 21 April 1995, p. 8A; Bill Robinson, "School District Settles over Confederate Flag Shirts," *The State*, 27 January 1996, p. 3B.

91. Wendy Warren, "Banner's Foes Rally around 'Anti-flag,'" *The State*, 24 June 1995, p. 3B; Christine Crumbo, "Anti-flag Goal: 'Inflame' Sensible Debate," *The State*, 25 June 1995, p. 1B.

92. Crumbo, "Race Commission Hears Same Song," *The State*, 4 August 1996, p. 1B.

93. *The Commission on Racial Relations Report*, issued 5 December 1997, by the Office of the Governor of South Carolina, p. 6.

94. Ibid., p. 50.

95. Cliff LeBlanc, "Beasley Urges Races to Find Common Path," *The State*, 6 January 1996, p. 1A.

96. Scoppe, "African-Americans' Monument on Hold," *The State*, 10 May 1996, p. 3B; Michael Sponhour, "Knotts Untied: No Battle Too Hot," *The State*, 5 July 1996, p. 1A. The monument commission, comprised of five blacks and four whites (including Representative Cooper, who had voted against the bill authorizing the monument), was also given the responsibility of studying the possible development of a state African American history museum.

97. Greene, "Group Disavows Shootings," *The State*, 30 October 1996, p. 1B.

98. Greene, Douglas Pardue, and Monte Paulsen, "In Fires, Beasley Sees Racism," *The State*, 2 October 1996, p. 1A; Gary Karr, "Officials Choose Words Carefully in Confederate Flag Controversy," *The State*, 16 June 1996, p. 3B. Those same Republican voters did not take kindly to Beasley's call to remove the Confederate flag. Donations to the party declined precipitously after the governor announced his flag plan. See Bandy, "GOP Donors Close Ranks, Close Wallets," *The State*, 29 January 1997, p. 1B.

99. "South Carolina and the Confederate Flag—an Online Discussion with Former Governor David Beasley" (14 February 2000), at www.washingtonpost.com

100. "The South Carolina Poll—the Flag Issue," *The State*, 13 November 1996, p. 7A.

101. "Beasley: Flag Flap Harmful," *The State*, 23 November 1996, p. 1B.

102. Bandy and Pat Butler, "Baptists on Flag: Furl It," *The State*, 13 November 1996, p. 1A; Sponhour, "'Let's End This Debate,'" *The State*, 27 November 1996, p. 1A.

103. Bandy and Butler, "Baptists on Flag"; Jack Hitt, "Confederate Semiotics," *The Nation* (28 April 1997), p. 11.

104. Dan Hoover, "Flag Defiled by Hate in Air, Beasley Says," *Greenville News*, 27 November 1996, p. 1A; Sponhour, "'Let's End This Debate.'" The Beasley proposal did not mention the flags inside the legislative chambers. These were considered a separate issue, to be dealt with later.

105. Sponhour, "'Let's End This Debate.'"

106. Bandy and Butler, "Baptists on Flag"; Hoover and James T. Hammond, "Upstate Lawmakers Split along Race, Party on Plan," *Greenville News*, 27 November 1996, p. 1A; "Jackson: Flag Proposal Sustains a 'Half-truth,'" *The State*, 29 November 1996, p. 2B.

107. Bandy, "Flag Decision Puts Beasley on the Spot," *The State*, 16 November 1996, p. 1A; "Beasley: Flag Flap Harmful."

108. Charles Condon, "Guarding Our Future by Preserving Our Past—Rebuttal by Attorney General Charles M. Condon to Governor David M. Beasley's Proposal to Remove South Carolina's Confederate Battle Flag," at the Heritage Preservation Association web site (www.hpa.org).

109. Quoted in Hoover, "Flag Defiled by Hate in Air, Beasley Says."

110. Scoppe and Sponhour, "Banner Divides House," *The State*, 4 December 1996, p. 1A; Bandy, "Flag's Past, Future Collide in Rural S.C.," *The State*, 8 December 1996, p. 1A.

111. Bandy, "Poll: Voters Shifting against Flag," *The State*, 21 December 1996, p. 1A.

112. Tom Inman, "Beasley's Bold Move Has Bolder Meaning," *Greenville News*, 1 December 1996, p. 6A; Bandy, "Flag Still Flies but Winds Are Shifting," *The State*, 8 December 1996, p. 4D; Robert Tanner, "Flag Debate Rewriting State's Political Landscape," *Greenville News*, 15 December 1996, p. 3B; Carolyn Click, "Flag's Day Is Over, 60 Pastors Say," *The State*, 20 December 1996, p. 1A; Allison Atkins, "Silent Vigil to Speak Volumes on Flag," *The State*, 21 January 1997, p. 7A; "The Moral Defense of the Confederate Flag: A Special Message for South Carolina Christians," by a collaboration of Fifteen South Carolina Minsters and the Staff of *Southern Partisan* magazine, *Southern Partisan* (Winter 1996), p. 16.

113. Allison Atkins and Chuck Carroll, "Flag Move Gets Caucus Support," *The State*, 24 December 1996, p. 1A.

114. Scoppe, "GOP Voters Voice Support for Flag," *The State*, 31 December 1996, p. 1B; Paulsen, "Supporters of Confederate Flag Shiver, Shout at State House," *The State*, 12 January 1997, p. 8B; Sponhour and Scoppe, "As Gavels Fall, Flags Rise," *The State*, 15 January 1997, p. 1A.

115. See "Results of the 1997 House membership survey of priority issues," at www.lpitr.state.sc.us/reports/97survey.htm. Scoppe and Sponhour, "Legislature Set to Grapple with Several Racial Issues," *The State*, 14 January 1997, p. 1A; Scoppe, "23 in House May Face New Elections," *The State*, 15 January 1997, p. 1A; Scoppe and Sponhour, "Beasley Losing His Flag Fight," *The State*, 19 January 1997, p. 1A.

116. Scoppe and Sponhour, "Flag's Fate Unfurling in House," *The State*, 22 January 1997, p. 1A; Sid Gaulden, "House Calls for Flag Vote," *Charleston Post and Courier*, 22 January 1997, p. 1A.

117. Bandy, "Beasley Sees Roads past Flag," *The State*, 23 January 1997, p. 1A; Scoppe, "Sparks Fly as House Forges Flag Plan," *The State*, 23 January 1997, p. 1A; "State of the State Address" (22 January 1997), *Journal of the Senate of the State of South Carolina*, at www.lpitr.state.sc.us/session112_1997-1998/sj97/19970122.htm

118. Scoppe, "Sparks Fly as House Forges Flag Plan"; Scoppe, "'Let the public decide,'" *The State*, 24 January 1997, p. 1A; Hammond and Tim Smith, "House Refuses to Pass Beasley Flag Plan," *Greenville News*, 24 January 1997, p. 1A; Scoppe, "Timing May Seal Flag's Fate," *The State*, 27 January 1997, p. 1A

119. Hammond and Smith, "House Refuses to Pass Beasley Flag Plan." The governor might have had enough votes to get his plan through the senate, but not enough to stifle a filibuster. And even if it had passed, the house had already clearly stated its unwillingness to ever consider the idea.

120. Scoppe and Bandy, "Beasley's Lost Cause," *The State*, 13 July 1997, p. 1D.

121. Bruce Smith, "Confederate Marker Battle Sparks Monumental Debate," *The State*, 3 February 1997, p. 2B; Bandy, "'Circle of Flags' Catches Beasley's Eye," *The State*, 19 February 1997, p. 1B; Hoover, "Both Sides at Rebel Flag Hearing Unleash Volleys of Well-Tested Arguments," *The State*, 12 March 1997, p. 1A; Scoppe, "Flag Compromise Rejected," *The State*, 22 March 1997, p. 1B.

122. Scoppe, "House Unravels on Flag," *The State*, 4 April 1997, p. 1A.

123. Scoppe, "Sparks Fly as House Forges Flag Plan."

124. Scoppe, "Senators Lift Hopes for Flag Solution," *The State*, 30 April 1997, p. 1B.

125. Scoppe, "Confederacy and MLK Both Win in Senate Vote," *The State*, 1 May 1997, p. 1B.

126. "Teen Shot in Flag Dispute," *The State*, 24 December 1997, p. 1B; "Mother Defends Son in Shooting of Black Teen over Flag," *The State*, 25 December 1997, p. 5B.

Six—Old Times There Are Not Forgotten

1. Paul Tosto, "The History We Don't Teach," *The State*, 26 January 1997, p. 1A.

2. Michael Sponhour, "Senators Shackling Governor to 2 Issues," *The State*, 6 May 1998, p. 1A.

3. Quoted in Dan T. Carter, *The Politics of Rage: George Wallace, the Origins of the New Conservatism, and the Transformation of American Politics* (New York: Simon & Schuster, 1995), pp. 283–284.

4. "Letters from Readers," *Greenville News*, 24 January 1997 and 14 November 1999.

5. See Bill no. 980, *Black Liberation Flag*, introduced 3 February 1998, at www.lpitr. state.sc.us. The bill would have flown the Black Liberation flag during the week of Martin Luther King's birthday, during Black History Month in February, during "Juneteenth," and during "Kwanzaa."

6. Sponhour, "Let S.C. Vote on Flag, Lottery, Senate Says," *The State,* 6 May 1998, p. 1A.

7. Lisa Greene and Douglas Pardue, "Black Anthem Flap Forces Principal Out," *The State,* 3 March 1998, p. 1A.

8. Andrea Weigl, "Confederate Flag Lawsuit Allowed to Go Forward," *Greenville News,* 2 October 1999, p. 1B. McCuen was represented in court by the Southern Legal Resource Center, the neo-Confederate law firm.

9. Sponhour and Joseph S. Stroud, "Big Turnout, Lottery Fever Forge an 'Historic' Upset," *The State,* 4 November 1998; Rick Brundrett, "Condon Wins Attorney General Contest," *The State,* 4 November 1998.

10. Carol Weir, "Church Leaders Protest Confederate Flag," *The State,* 10 December 1998; Dave Morantz, "Black Ministers March to Protest Statehouse Flag," *Greenville News,* 10 December 1998.

11. "Hodges Met with Ex-chief of CCC," *Charleston Post and Courier,* 12 February 1999, p. 12B.

12. Michelle R. Davis, "NAACP Ratifies Flag Boycott," *The State,* 17 October 1999. The final resolution also added a new clause to the original July version calling on the U.S. Department of Justice to investigate whether the flag display constituted a civil rights violation by creating "a hostile work environment for all South Carolinians" and asking the department to take steps to remove Confederate flags from all public properties.

13. Dan Hoover, "NAACP Set to Boycott State Products," *Greenville News,* 19 October 1999, p. 1A; Tim Smith, "NAACP Set to Expand Boycott," *Greenville News,* 24 October 1999, p. 1A; "NAACP Encourages Athletes to Stay Away," *The State,* 2 November 1999.

14. Leigh Strope, "NAACP Trolling for Ammunition in Flag Controversy," *Greenville News,* 5 August 1999, p. 7B.

15. Christine Schweikert, "More Voices Joining Chorus against Flag," *The State,* 19 November 1999. Strope, "Hooded Klansman Featured in Anti-confederate Flag Ads, " *The State,* 20 November 1999.

16. "NAACP's Boycott over Confederate Flag Sends Money, Conventions North," *Greenville News,* 18 December 1999.

17. Ibid.

18. See also Stroud, "How It Happened: Timing Key on Flag," *The State,* 25 June 2000.

19. "Letters from Readers," *Greenville News,* 29 July, 14 August, 15 November, and 19 November 1999.

20. "Most Legislators Want to Keep Flag Flying," *Greenville News,* 2 August 1999. It should be noted, however, that only about two-thirds of the members of each chamber responded to the poll, leaving a sizeable margin for error.

21. Stroud, "NAACP's Call for Boycott against S.C. May Backfire," *The State,* 18 July 1999.

22. Ibid.

23. From public-relations material provided by the office of Senator Robert Ford. The senator was only partially correct. The GOP did pick up several seats in both chambers as a result of the 2000 elections. But they did not take over the senate immediately. Instead, the election left the senate evenly split between the two parties.

24. Strope, "Rebel Flag Outsells State, U.S. Flags at Statehouse," *Greenville News*, 6 August 1999.

25. Hoover, "Most Want to See Flag Removed, Poll Finds," *Greenville News*, 27 September 1999, p. 1A; Stroud, "Flag Losing Favor with S.C. Voters," *The State*, 27 September 1999.

26. Stroud, "Hodges Aims for 'Solution' on Rebel Flag," *The State*, 5 August 1999; Henry Eichel, "Pressure Mounts on Hodges to Act on Confederate Flag," *The State*, 7 August 1999; Bandy, "Chairman: Democrats Must Target Flag's Allies," *The State*, 19 August 1999.

27. Tim Smith, "NAACP: Hodges Can't Be Trusted," *Greenville News*, 23 October 1999, p. 1A; Hoover, "Wilkins Walking Fine Line on Flag, Peers Say," *Greenville News*, 5 November 1999, p. 1A.

28. Stroud, "NAACP Chief: Hodges 'Can't Be Trusted,'" *The State*, 22 October 1999.

29. Chuck Carroll, "Governor Offers Deal to NAACP on Flag Issue," *The State*, 18 November 1999; "Governor Jim Hodges Urban League Speech," *The State*, 10 November 1999.

30. Hammond, "NAACP: Hodges' Offer an 'Insult,'" *Greenville News*, 12 November 1999, p. 1A; Bandy, Carroll, and Kenneth A. Harris, "Critics Shred Governor's Flag Proposal," *The State*, 12 November 1999; "Statement from NAACP," *The State*, 12 November 1999; Strope, "Hodges Presses for Flag Vote, Lifting of Boycott," *The State*, 19 November 1999.

31. Stroud and Carroll, "Black Leaders Haven't Given up on Hodges Yet," *The State*, 22 November 1999.

32. Strope, "Mayors Say Take Confederate Flag down from Statehouse," *Greenville News*, 4 September 1999, p. 1B.

33. Hammond, "Upstate Leaders Join Effort to Remove Flag from Statehouse," *Greenville News*, 10 December 1999, p. 1A; Tim Smith, "Reviews Mixed on Park for Flag," *Greenville News*, 14 December 1999, p. 1A.

34. Bandy, "51 Percent Favor Removing Flag, Poll Says," *The State*, 23 October 1999.

35. Hammond and Rudolph Bell, "Businesses Work Quietly to Resolve Capitol Flag Issue," *Greenville News*, 20 October 1999, p. 1A; "Business Leaders Finding Roles in Flag Debate," *The State*, 25 October 1999; "Tallying Round the Flag," *The State*, 14 November 1999; Dave L'Heureux, "The Flag: New Pressures Are Pushing for Resolution," *The State*, 14 November 1999; Crumbo, "S.C. Colleges Might Enlist in Flag Fight," *The State*, 17 November 1999; "Confederate Flag Harming School Reputation,

USC Faculty Senate Says," *The State*, 17 November 1999; Schweikert, "More Voices Joining Chorus against Flag"; "Business Leaders, GOP Air Differences over Flag," *The State*, 3 December 1999; "Election Cash, Flag Deal Linked," *Greenville News*, 8 December 1999, p. 1A.

36. Hammond, "Churches Want Flag Down, but Past Efforts Failed," *The State*, 27 October 1999, p. 1A; Cara Bonnett, "Bob Jones Calls for Removal of Flag," *Greenville News*, 29 October 1999, p. 1A; "BJU President: Time to Furl Confederate Flag" (letter to the editor), *Greenville News*, 29 October 1999; Debra Lester, "Remove Flag, Baptists Urge Lawmakers," *Spartanburg Herald-Journal*, 10 November 1999; Bonnett, "State Baptist Convention Backs Lowering of Flag," *Greenville News*, 10 November 1999; Cindy Landrum, "Pastors: Take down the Flag," *Greenville News*, 19 November 1999.

37. Hammond, "Ex-legislators Want 'Mistake' Fixed," *Greenville News*, 8 December 1999, p. 1A; "Resolution Calls for Flag Removal," *The State*, 10 December 1999.

38. Stroud, "Fix 'Oversight' by Furling Flag, '62 Legislators Say," *The State*, 8 December 1999.

39. L'Heureux, "The Flag."

40. Carroll, "Umbrella Organization to Focus Flag Foes' Efforts," *The State*, 11 December 1999; April Simun, "Why a Mom Fights the Flag," *The State*, 17 December 1999.

41. "Sen. Jackson Says Flag Supporter Shouldn't Lead Black Monument Effort," *The State*, 10 December 1999; "Confederate Flag Should Move from the Statehouse Grounds, NAACP Leaders Say," *The State*, 9 December 1999; Carroll, "Legislators Say NAACP Must Yield," *The State*, 12 December 1999.

42. Bandy, "Sick of Talking, Jackson Goes to 'War' against Flag," *The State*, 26 December 1999.

43. Tim Smith, "Reviews Mixed"; Tim Smith, "Flag Debate Disrupts Monument Meeting," *Greenville News*, 15 December 1999, p. 1A.

44. Bandy, "Sick of Talking."

45. "South Carolina Starts Millennium under NAACP Boycott," *Greenville News*, 1 January 2000.

46. Hammond, "Supporters March on Statehouse," *Greenville News*, 9 January 2000, p. 1A.

47. Jim Davenport, "Flag Supporters Arrive as Bell Tolls for Civil War Dead," *Greenville News*, 9 January 2000, p. 5B; Stroud, "6,000 Rally Peacefully for Flag," *The State*, 9 January 2000.

48. Stroud, "As Legislators Return, S.C. Senator's 'Insult' Hardens," *The State*, 11 January 2000.

49. Hammond, "Poll Points to Taking Down Flag," *Greenville News*, 10 January 2000, p. 1A; Tim Smith, "Flag Talks Shift toward Compromise," *Greenville News*, 11 January 2000, p. 1A.

50. Tim Smith, "Senators: Flag Too Hot for Quick End," *Greenville News*, 11 January 2000, p. 1A; Tim Smith, "GOP Chairman Refuses to Seek Ravenel Apology,"

Greenville News, 13 January 2000, p. 1B; Mark Pratt; "Flag Controversy Could Affect Pick for Supreme Court," *Greenville News*, 15 January 2000, p. 1B.

51. Harris and Stroud, "New Site for Flag Is Next Question for Banner's Foes," *The State*, 13 January 2000; Hammond and Tim Smith, "New Flag Home Focus of Talks," *Greenville News*, 14 January 2000, p. 1A; Stroud and Harris, "Answers Elude Flag Summit," *The State*, 14 January 2000.

52. Allison Askins and Jeff Wilkinson, "King March Expected to Draw 2,000," *The State*, 16 January 2000.

53. Davenport, "Protestors Urge Removal of Confederate Flag from Statehouse," *The State*, 17 January 2000; "Thousands March to Celebrate MLK, Protest Flag," *The State*, 17 January 2000; Stroud, "46,000 Attend King Day Rally," *The State*, 18 January 2000; Hammond and Tim Smith, "Largest Protest in Capitol's History Draws National Attention," *Greenville News*, 18 January 2000, p. 1A; Claudia Smith Brinson, "King Day at the State House Lifted 46,000 Peaceful Voices," *The State*, 21 January 2000; James Gallman, "We Gathered for What Is Right," *The State*, 23 January 2000.

54. "Thousands March to Celebrate MLK, Protest Flag."

55. Stroud and Carroll, "Now, Hodges Faces the Flag," *The State*, 19 January 2000; Hammond and Tim Smith, "Hodges: Remove Flag Now," *Greenville News*, 20 January 2000, p. 1A; Hammond, "In Address to Legislature, Governor Says Boycott Doesn't Justify Delay," *Greenville News*, 20 January 2000, p. 1A; Stroud, "'We Must Move the Flag,'" *The State*, 20 January 2000.

56. Rick Quinn, "Republican Response to the State of the State," *The State*, 20 January 2000; Hammond and Tim Smith, "Hodges: Remove Flag Now."

57. Tim Smith, "Senator: Flag Compromise in Peril," *Greenville News*, 21 January 2000, p. 1A; Harris and Carroll, "Flag's Foes Soften Position, Flag's Armies Maneuver," *The State*, 21 January 2000.

58. Smith, "Senator: Flag Compromise in Peril"; Harris and Carroll, "Flag's Foes Soften Position."

59. Stroud, "Senator Drafting Three Options for Confederate Flag's Fate," *The State*, 22 January 2000; Tim Smith, "Senate Leader Ready to Strike Flag," *Greenville News*, 26 January 2000, p. 1A.

60. Hammond, "Leaders Look for Symbols That Unify in Flag Debate," *Greenville News*, 31 January 2000, p. 1A.

61. Tim Smith, "Rival Senators Hear Flag Monument Ideas," *Greenville News*, 2 February 2000, p. 1B; Stroud, "Senators Review 2 Proposals for Confederate Memorials," *The State*, 2 February 2000; Stroud, "'Avenue of Flags' Proposed," *The State*, 5 February 2000; April E. Moorefield, "New Proposal for Flag Called 'Starting Point,'" *Greenville News*, 9 February 2000, p. 1A.

62. Stroud, "'Avenue of flags'"; Moorefield, "New Proposal for Flag."

63. Katherine Winiarsky, "Hodges' Plan Garners Critics, Fans," *The State*, 13 February 2000; John Monk, "Flag Plan an Effort to Flank McConnell," *The State*, 13 February 2000; Hammond, "Hodges Offers New Flag Plan," *Greenville News*, 13 February

2000, p. 1A; Stroud, "Governor Lays out Flag Plan," *The State*, 15 February 2000; Monk, "Playing Ball over the Confederate Flag," *The State*, 15 February 2000; Stroud, "Senators Slow to Salute Hodges' Flag Proposal," *The State*, 16 February 2000.

64. Stroud, "NAACP Fighting Hodges' Flag Plan, Senator Says," *The State*, 18 February 2000; Hammond, "NAACP, Top Blacks Split on Flag Plan," *Greenville News*, 18 February 2000; Stroud, "Move Flag to Glass Case, Museum, NAACP Says," *The State*, 3 February 2000.

65. Stroud, "McConnell to Propose 'Healing Pool,'" *The State*, 31 March 2000.

66. "Two Celebrations Would Honor Important Dates" (letter to the editor), *The State*, 10 April 2000.

67. Hammond, "Senators Unfurl New Flag Plan," *The State*, 24 March 2000, p. 1A; Harris, "Senators Seek to Display Historic Flags," *The State*, 23 March 2000.

68. "S.C. Tourist Meccas Feeling Pinch of Boycott," *Greenville News*, 23 January 2000, p. 1B; "Boycott's Effects Being Felt Statewide," *Greenville News*, 24 January 2000, p. 3B; L'Heureux, "Boycott Does No Damage to Heritage," *The State*, 10 April 2000.

69. Ann Green, "Socon, NAACP Make Deal," *Greenville News*, 22 January 2000; Rudolph Bell, "Flag Controversy May Cost Greenville a New Insurance Headquarters," *Greenville News*, 25 January 2000, p. 1A; Bruce Smith, "Confederate Flag Boycott Impacting S.C.—in the Wallet," *The State*, 28 February 2000.

70. Harris, "Governor Asks Business Leaders to Push for Flag Resolution," *Greenville News*, 21 March 2000; Hammond, "Chamber Urged to Act on Flag," *Greenville News*, 21 March 2000, p. 1A; Hammond, "Confederate Flag Signs Sprout along Midlands Roads Overnight," *Greenville News*, 22 March 2000; Stroud, "How It Happened," *The State*, 25 April 2000.

71. "GOP Voters Want Flag Down," *The State*, 1 February 2000; Brent Nelson and James Garth, "Debating the Flag Will Ultimately Weaken GOP Position," *The State*, 16 February 2000; Bandy, "Democrats Dancing as GOP Bleeds," *The State*, 2 April 2000; Stroud, "Legislative Districts' Fragmented Politics Help Keep Flag Flying," *The State*, 5 March 2000; Bandy, "S.C Republicans No Longer Driven by Far Right," *The State*, 6 January 2000.

72. See especially Brad Warthen, "We're Supposed to Learn from History, Not Repeat Its Mistakes," *The State*, 9 January 2000; Hoover, "Strutting Lawmaker in Confederate Uniform Helped Plant Flag Feud," *Greenville News*, 24 January 2000, p. 1A; Tim Smith, "Flag's Ally Fought 'Black War,'" *Greenville News*, 27 January 2000, p. 1A; Stroud, "Statue Gets Pulled into Flag Debate," *The State*, 30 January 2000; Hoover, "State Forefathers Pointed to Slavery as Cause for Secession," *Greenville News*, 4 February 2000, p. 1A; Warren Bolton, "Flag Extremists Seek to Manipulate Whites to Justify Flying Banner," *The State*, 8 February 2000; Stroud, "Accounts of Black Legislators Forgotten," *The State*, 29 February 2000; Rickey Hill, "Bring down the Flag and Bring an End to Bad History," *The State*, 5 April 2000; Monk, "Robert E. Lee Would Say: Bring down the Flag," *The State*, 9 April 2000; Michelle R. Davis, "Coming to Grips with the Costs—and Profits—of Slavery," *The State*, 9 April 2000; Bob Deans, "Lee

Saw South as Region of Healing," *The State*, 9 April 2000; Belinda Gergel and Richard Gergel, "An Appeal to the Noble Heritage of South Carolina," *The State*, 12 April 2000; William W. Starr, "Southern History: Myth and Memory," *The State*, 18 April 2000; Monk, "Funny How South's Good Old Days Don't Stir Same Memories in Everyone," *The State*, 23 April 2000; "Excerpts of McCain's Comments to the South Carolina Policy Council," *The State*, 23 April 2000.

73. Bandy, "Historians Contend War about Slavery," *The State*, 1 April 2000; "The Civil War Was Fought over Slavery, Not States' Rights," *The State*, 1 April 2000.

74. "Statement of College and University Professors in Support of the Confederate Battle Flag atop the South Carolina Statehouse," available at LewRockwell.com (www.lewrockwell.com/orig/profs.html).

75. Ibid.

76. Mark Pratt, "Flag Controversy Might Affect S.C. Supreme Court Election," *Greenville News*, 15 January 2000, p. 1B; Cindi Ross Scoppe, "MLK Holiday Debate Less about Respect Than about Employee Benefits," *The State*, 19 January 2000.

77. "Legislators Moving toward Approving Martin Luther King Holiday," *The State*, 20 January 2000; Stroud, "House Panel to Consider Proposal for King Holiday," *The State*, 2 February 2000; Harris, "King's Character Questioned as Panel Backs MLK Holiday," *The State*, 9 February 2000; Stroud, "Vote Expected Today on S.C. King Holiday," *The State*, 2 March 2000; "Flag Fight Entangles King Day," *The State*, 3 March 2000; Strope, "Ford Says He'll Play Legislative Games to Get King Bill through the House," *The State*, 8 March 2000.

78. Jeff Stensland, "Flag Supporters, Marchers Will Rally at State House," *The State*, 1 April 2000; "Riley March from Sea to Capitol Worthwhile," *The State*, 1 April 2000; Warthen, "March Is about Helping Legislators Get in Step with the Rest of Us," *The State*, 2 April 2000; David Broder, "South Carolina Deserves a Better Reputation," *The State*, 27 March 2000.

79. Stroud, "Marchers Begin Trek to Columbia," *The State*, 3 April 2000; Bandy, "Flag Supporters Demonstrate," *The State*, 4 April 2000; Stroud, "Governor to Meet with Riley, Accept S.C. Flag," *The State*, 5 April 2000; Davenport, "Confederate Flag Opponents, Supporters Both Rally at S.C. Statehouse," *The State*, 6 April 2000; Harris, "Flag Journey to Reach End at State House," *The State*, 6 April 2000; Monk, "Riley Marches on Long-held Convictions," *The State*, 6 April 2000; Harris, "Protestors Call on History to Defend Flag," *The State*, 7 April 2000; Stroud, "Charleston Mayor Challenges Legislature to Take down Flag," *The State*, 7 April 2000; Monk, "Beasley Returns to State House to Get Flag Down," *The State*, 8 April 2000.

80. Letters to the editor, *The State*, 12 March and 26 February 2000.

81. Strope, "How Much Is That Confederate Flag on the Capitol?," *The State*, 15 April 2000; Davenport, "Confederate Flag Opponents."

82. Davenport, "Hodges to Offer Plan," *The State*, 12 February 2000; Harris, "Senate Sets up a Floor Fight on Flag," *The State*, 17 March 2000; Stroud, "Senate Plan Gaining Ground in Flag Debate," *The State*, 29 March 2000; Stroud and Chuck Carroll,

"Flag Could Continue to Fly if Senate Misses Deadline," *The State,* 5 April 2000; Stroud, "Senate Steps into a Storm," *The State,* 9 February 2000.

83. Stroud, "Lawmakers to Debate Flag Plans," *The State,* 12 April 2000.

84. Stroud, "Lawmakers Agree Debate Needed," *The State,* 6 April 2000.

85. The following segment drawn from Stroud, "'It's Not but One Flag,'" *The State,* 16 April 2000; and Bandy, "Jackson Dug in Heels, Then Spun on Them," *The State,* 30 April 2000.

86. *Journal of the South Carolina Senate,* 12/13 April 2000, at www.lpitr.state.sc.us/session113_1999-2000/sj00/20000412 and /20000413. All subsequent quotes from the debate on the senate floor are taken from *Senate Journal* transcripts or from the author's recordings of the televised debate.

87. Stroud, "Compromise Bill Wins Support of Both Parties," *The State,* 13 April 2000; Chuck Crumbo, "Witnesses Glimpse History," *The State,* 13 April 2000.

88. Monk, "Funny How South's Good Old Days."

89. Harris, "S.C. House Vote Creates a Confederate and MLK Holiday," *The State,* 13 April 2000.

90. Harris, "Opposition to Flag Plan Surfaces in House," *The State,* 14 April 2000; Wilkinson, "Columbians Unhappy with Prospect of Flag at South End of Main Street," *The State,* 14 April 2000.

91. Askins, "Rally Stirs Opposition to Flag Compromise," *The State,* 17 April 2000.

92. Eichel, "NAACP Would Keep Boycott if Bill Passes, but with What Support?," *The State,* 7 May 2000.

93. Hoover, "Flag Bill Divides Black Senators, House Members," *Greenville News,* 15 April 2000, p. 1A; Stroud, "Flag Plan Divides Democrats," *The State,* 19 April 2000; Jamie Jones, "Unlikely Allies May Fight Flag Compromise," *Greenville News,* 19 April 2000, p. 1A; "Lawmakers Try to Stall Flag Bill," *Greenville News,* 27 April 2000, p. 1A.

94. Ernest A. Finney Jr. and Alex Sanders, "A Flag Cast in Bronze Would End Civil War," *The State,* 26 April 2000; Stroud, "Democrats Back Plan for Marker, Memorial," *The State,* 3 May 2000.

95. Jones, "Flag Opponents Maneuver for Vote Leverage," *Greenville News,* 5 May 2000; Stroud, "House Is Set to Begin Debating Flag Tuesday," *The State,* 4 May 2000.

96. From *Journal of the South Carolina House of Representatives, Tuesday, May 9, 2000,* at www.lpitr.state.sc.us. All quotes that follow are taken from the author's recordings of the televised house proceedings.

97. See "Protesters Burn Flags at Statehouse," and Tim Smith and Jamie Jones, "Protesters Face off Outside Statehouse," *Greenville News,* 11 May 2000, p. 1A.

98. From the author's recording of Governor Hodges's bill-signing comments, broadcast statewide on 22 May 2000.

Postlude

1. Lynn Riddle, "Tempers Fly as Flag Brought Down," *Greenville News,* 2 July 2000; also from television, radio, and web coverage by SCETV, National Public Radio, and South Carolina Public Radio.

2. Rachel Graves, Brian Hicks, "Emotions Run High as Flag Comes Down," *Charleston Post and Courier,* 2 July 2000; Joseph S. Stroud and Kenneth A. Harris, "Flag Comes Down from Dome," *The State,* 2 July 2000; Lee Bandy and Roddie Burns, "Emotions Run High on Both Sides," *The State,* 2 July 2000.

3. Jamie Jones, "Heritage or Hate? Both Factions Proud, Passionate," *Greenville News,* 2 July 2000.

4. David Lowenthal, *The Heritage Crusade and the Spoils of History* (Cambridge, U.K. and New York: Cambridge University Press, 1998), p. 159.

5. See Martin Luther King Jr., "The Ethical Demands for Integration," in *A Testament of Hope: The Essential Writings and Speeches of Martin Luther King, Jr.,* edited by James M. Washington (San Francisco: HarperSanFrancisco, 1991), pp. 117–125.

6. Charles Frazier, *Cold Mountain* (New York: Atlantic Monthly Press, 1997), p. 346.

SELECTED SOURCES

Interviews

Prof. Clyde Wilson, Columbia, S.C., 20 September 1999
Sen. Glenn McConnell, Charleston, S.C., 21 September 1999
Rev. Joe Darby, Charleston, S.C., 21 September 1999
Tom Turnipseed, Columbia, S.C., 22 September 1999
Sen. Maggie Glover, Florence, S.C., 22 September 1999
Sherman Evans and Angel Quintero, Charleston, S.C., 23 September 1999
Chris Sullivan, Columbia, S.C., 4 October 1999
Sen. Arthur Ravenel Jr. (telephone), 5 October 1999
Mayor Bob Coble, Columbia, S.C., 6 October 1999
Gov. David Beasley (telephone), 5 May 2000
Prof. Daniel Hollis (telephone), 7 May 2000

Newspapers and Magazines

The State (Columbia, S.C.)
The Greenville News (Greenville, S.C.)
The Washington Post

Books and Articles

Applebome, Peter. *Dixie Rising: How the South Is Shaping American Values, Politics and Culture.* New York: Times Press, 1996.
Ash, Stephen V. *When the Yankees Came: Conflict and Chaos in the Occupied South, 1861–1865.* Chapel Hill: University of North Carolina Press, 1995.
Ashmore, Harry S. *An Epitaph for Dixie.* New York: Norton, 1958.
Bass, Jack, and Jack Nelson, *The Orangeburg Massacre.* New York: World, 1970
Bates, Eric. "Look Away." *Southern Exposure* 18 (Spring 1990): 35–37.
Billson, Marky. "The Confederate Flag in Hazzard." *The* [Oxford, Mississippi] *Eagle,* 18 May 2000.
Blount, Roy, Jr. "The Confederate Flag." *Southern Magazine* (June 1987): 44–45.
Britt, Brian. "Neo-Confederate Culture." *Z Magazine* 9 (Dec. 1996): 26–30. Online at www.orderofwhitetrash.com/cFish/britt.htm or zenz.secureForum.com/Znet/Zmag/dec96Britt.htm
Calhoun, John C. *The Essential Calhoun: Selections from Writings, Speeches, and Letters.* Edited by Clyde N. Wilson. New Brunswick, N.J.: Transaction, 1992.

Carter, Dan T. *The Politics of Rage: George Wallace, the Origins of the New Conservatism, and the Transformation of American Politics.* Baton Rouge: Louisiana State University Press, 1996.

Cash, W. J. *The Mind of the South.* 1941. Reprint, New York: Vintage, 1969.

Cobb, James C. *Redefining Southern Culture: Mind and Identity in the Modern South.* Athens: University of Georgia Press, 1999.

Cohodas, Nadine. *Strom Thurmond and the Politics of Southern Change.* New York: Simon and Schuster, 1993.

Coit, Margaret L. *John C. Calhoun: American Portrait.* Boston: Houghton Mifflin, 1950.

Dabbs, James McBride. *The Southern Heritage.* New York: Knopf, 1958.

"Debating the Confederate Flag." *Talk of the Nation* (NPR radio broadcast), 31 January 1994.

"Debating the Flag." *The Newshour with Jim Lehrer,* 29 May 2000, www.pbs.org/newshour/newshour_index.html.

Decter, Midge. "Southern Comforts." *Commentary* 106 (July 1998): 26–33.

DuBois, W. E. B. *The Souls of Black Folk.* 1903. Reprint, New York: Gramercy Books, 1994.

Edgar, Walter B. *South Carolina: A History.* Columbia: University of South Carolina Press, 1998.

Edgar. *South Carolina in the Modern Age.* Columbia: University of South Carolina Press, 1992.

Egerton, John. *Speak Now against the Day: The Generation before the Civil Rights Movement in the South.* New York: Knopf, 1994.

Ellison, Ralph. *Invisible Man.* New York: Random House, 1952.

Faulkner, William. *The Unvanquished.* New York: Vintage International Edition, 1991.

Fifteen Southerners. *Why the South Will Survive.* Athens: University of Georgia Press, 1981.

Foster, Gaines M. *Ghosts of the Confederacy: Defeat, the Lost Cause, and the Emergence of the New South, 1865 to 1913.* New York: Oxford University Press, 1987.

Frazier, Charles. *Cold Mountain.* New York: Atlantic Monthly Press, 1997.

Freehling, William W., and Craig M. Simpson, eds. *Secession Debated: Georgia's Showdown in 1860.* New York: Oxford University Press, 1992.

Gaston, Paul M. *The New South Creed: A Study in Southern Mythmaking.* New York: Knopf, 1970.

Genovese, Eugene D. *The Southern Tradition: The Achievement and Limitations of an American Conservatism.* Cambridge: Harvard University Press, 1994.

Graham, Michael. "The Luckiest Politician in America?" *National Review* (24 May 2000).

Graves, John Temple. *The Fighting South.* 1943. Reprint, University: University of Alabama Press, 1985.

Greenberg, Kenneth. *Honor and Slavery.* Princeton, N.J.: Princeton University Press, 1996.

Hitt, Jack. "Confederate Semiotics." *Nation* (28 April 1997): 11–18.

Hoagland, Jim. "A Little Homer at the Beach." *Washington Post,* 26 July 1998, p. 7C.

Hobson, Fred. *But Now I See: The White Southern Racial Conversion Narrative.* Baton Rouge: Louisiana State University Press, 1999.

Horwitz, Tony. *Confederates in the Attic: Dispatches from the Unfinished Civil War.* New York: Pantheon, 1998.

Hutchinson, Earl Ofari. "NAACP Misses the Point with Rebel Flag." *Mother Jones* (12 April 2000).

Jacoby, Tamar. *Someone Else's House: America's Unfinished Struggle for Integration.* New York: Free Press, 1998.

Jones, Lewis P. *South Carolina: A Synoptic History for Laymen.* Orangeburg: Sandlapper, 1971.

Keyserling, Harriet. *Against the Tide: A Woman's Political Struggle.* Columbia: University of South Carolina Press, 1998.

King, Marin Luther, Jr. *A Testament of Hope: The Essential Writings and Speeches of Martin Luther King, Jr.* Edited by James M. Washington. San Francisco: HarperSanFrancisco, 1991.

Levinson, Sanford. *Written in Stone: Public Monuments in Changing Societies.* Durham, N.C.: Duke University Press, 1998.

Lichtenstein, Alex. "Right Chuch, Wrong Pew: Eugene Genovese and Southern Conservatism." *New Politics* 6 (Summer 1997): 59–69.

Lowenthal, David. "Fabricating Heritage." *History and Memory* 10 (Spring 1998): 5–23.

Lowenthal. *The Heritage Crusade and the Spoils of History.* Cambridge, U.K. and New York: Cambridge University Press, 1998.

Mays, John Bentley. *Power in the Blood: Land, Memory, and a Southern Family.* New York: HarperCollins, 1997.

McPherson, James M. *For Cause and Comrades: Why Men Fought in the Civil War.* New York: Oxford University Press, 1997.

Miller, William Lee. *Arguing about Slavery: The Great Battle in the United States Congress.* New York: Knopf, 1996.

Peirce, Neal R., and Jerry Hagstrom. "South Carolina: Fossil No More," in their *The Book of America: Inside Fifty States Today.* New York: Norton, 1983.

Percy, Walker. *Lancelot.* New York: Farrar, Straus and Giroux, 1977.

Raspberry, William. "South Carolinians Should Run This up their Flagpole." *Seattle Times,* 8 February 2000.

"Re-assessing Civic Symbols." *The Newshour with Jim Lehrer,* 25 November 1997 (www.pbs.org/newshour/newshour_index.html).

Robbins, Becci. "Governor's Task Force Opens to Mixed Reviews." *The* (Columbia, S.C.) *Point* (12 February 1995).

Roberts, Diane. "The American South and the Rise of the New Right Wing." *Amerika Studien* (Spring 1997): 197–206.

Roberts, D. K. "League Brings Old South Rhetoric to Academia," *Florida Flambeau* 14 February 1997 (www.fsunews.com).

Rollins, Richard. "*The Damned Red Flags of the Rebellion": The Struggle over the Confederate Battle Flag at Gettysburg.* Redondo Beach, Cal.: Rank and File, 1997.

Shipler, David K. *A Country of Strangers: Blacks and Whites in America.* New York: Knopf, 1997.

Simkins, Francis Butler. *A History of the South.* New York: Knopf, 1963.

Simon, Bryant. *The Fabric of Defeat: The Politics of South Carolina Millhands, 1910–1948.* Chapel Hill: University of North Carolina Press, 1998.

Smith, Thomas W., Jr. "The Segregationist Who Saw the Light." *U.S. News and World Report* (6 December 1999).

South Carolina Commemorates the Confederate War Centennial, 1961–1965: A Manual for Observance in the Counties and Cities of the State of South Carolina. Columbia: South Carolina Confederate War Centennial Commission.

South Carolina Speaks. Columbia: South Carolina Confederate War Centennial Commission, 1961.

Springer, Chris. "The Troubled Resurgence of the Confederate Flag." *History Today* 43 (June 1993): 7–9.

"Stars and Bars." *The Newshour with Jim Lehrer,* 17 January 2000 (www.pbs.org/newshour/newshour_index.html).

Stribling. T. S. *The Forge: An Epic Novel of the War-Torn South.* 1931. Reprint, University: University of Alabama Press, 1985.

Sword, Wiley. *Southern Invincibility: A History of the Confederate Heart.* New York: St. Martin's Press, 1999.

Tate, Allen. *The Fathers.* New York: Putnam, 1938.

Taylor, John M. "Grover Cleveland and the Rebel Banners." *Civil War Times Illustrated* (September/October 1993): 22–24.

Thornton, Kevin Pierce. "Symbolism at Ole Miss and the Crisis of Southern Identity." *South Atlantic Quarterly* 86 (Summer 1987): 254–268.

Twelve Southerners. *I'll Take My Stand: The South and the Agrarian Tradition.* 1930. Reprint, Baton Rouge: Louisiana State University Press, 1982.

Underwood, Thomas A. *Allen Tate: Orphan of the South.* Princeton: Princeton University Press, 2000.

Warren, Robert Penn. *The Legacy of the Civil War.* 1961. Reprint, Cambridge: Harvard University Press, 1983.

Wates, Wylma A. *A Flag Worthy of Your State and People: The History of the South Carolina State Flag.* Columbia: South Carolina Department of Archives and History, 1996.

Whitman, Walt. *Leaves of Grass.* Brooklyn, N.Y.: Fowler and Wells, 1855.

Wiley, Bell Irvin. *The Life of Johnny Reb: The Common Soldier of the Confederacy.* 1943. Reprint, Baton Rouge: Louisiana State University Press, 1978.

Wills, Gary. *Lincoln at Gettysburg: The Words That Remade America.* New York: Simon and Schuster, 1992.

Wilson, Charles Reagan. *Baptized in Blood: The Religion of the Lost Cause, 1865–1920.* Athens: University of Georgia Press, 1980.

Wilson, Edmund. *Patriotic Gore: Studies in the Literature of the American Civil War.* New York: Oxford University Press, 1962.

Woodward, C. Vann. *The Burden of Southern History.* Baton Rouge: Louisiana State University Press, 1968.

Woodward. *The Strange Career of Jim Crow.* New York: Oxford University Press, 1974.

Wyatt-Brown, Bertram. *Honor and Violence in the Old South.* New York: Oxford University Press, 1986.

Yoder, Edwin M., Jr. "The Battle over the Battle Flag." *Washington Post,* 3 June 2000, p. A17.

INDEX

BERKELEY COUNTY LIBRARY

3 9852 00289 1512

WITHDRAWN

DEMCO